In this book Gareth Winrow provides the first comprehensive account in English of East German foreign policy towards Africa since the early 1950s. He challenges the conventional view of the GDR's role in Africa as solely that of a proxy for the Soviet Union. Instead, as he convincingly argues, East German foreign policy in general, and in Africa in particular, should be understood as a strategy both for closer ties with the Soviet Union and for international recognition and legitimacy.

Gareth Winrow explores the development of GDR relations with Africa and shows how they remain of particular significance as a means of discrediting the West German presence and supporting Soviet interests. He discusses military involvement in the continent, trading relationships and the extent of GDR development assistance. He also compares the new Soviet political thinking on Africa – accommodation rather than confrontation – with GDR policies and in a concluding section raises questions on the GDR's future role.

The foreign policy of the GDR in Africa is based on an extensive use of official East German texts and statistics. It will be of interest to specialists and students of Soviet and East European studies, with special reference to the GDR, North–South relationships, superpower competition and the politics of development.

T0372745

THE FOREIGN POLICY OF THE GDR IN AFRICA

Soviet and East European Studies

79 MICHAEL D. KENNEDY
Professionals, power and Solidarity in Poland
A critical sociology of Soviet-type society

78 GARETH M. WINROW
The foreign policy of the GDR in Africa

77 JOZEF M. VAN BRABANT
The planned economies and international economic organizations

76 WILLIAM MOSKOFF
The bread of affliction: the food supply in the USSR during World War II

75 YAACOV RO'I
The struggle for Soviet Jewish emigration 1948–1967

74 GRAEME GILL
The origins of the Stalinist political system

73 SANTOSH K. MEHROTRA
India and the Soviet Union: trade and technology transfer

72 ILYA PRIZEL
Latin America through Soviet eyes
The evolution of Soviet perceptions during the Brezhnev era 1964–1982

71 ROBERT G. PATMAN
The Soviet Union in the Horn of Africa
The diplomacy of intervention and disengagement

70 IVAN T. BEREND
The Hungarian economic reforms 1953–1988

69 CHRIS WARD
Russia's cotton workers and the New Economic Policy
Shop-floor culture and state policy 1921–1929

68 LÁSZLÓ CSABA
Eastern Europe in the world economy

67 MICHAEL E. URBAN
An algebra of Soviet power
Elite circulation in the Belorussian Republic 1966–1986

66 JANE L. CURRY
Poland's journalists: professionalism and politics

65 MARTIN MYANT
The Czechoslovak economy 1948–1988
The battle for economic reform

64 XAVIER RICHET
The Hungarian model: markets and planning in a socialist economy

Series list continues on p. 288

THE FOREIGN POLICY
OF THE GDR
IN AFRICA

GARETH M. WINROW

Boğaziçi University, Istanbul

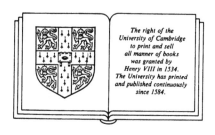

The right of the
University of Cambridge
to print and sell
all manner of books
was granted by
Henry VIII in 1534.
The University has printed
and published continuously
since 1584.

CAMBRIDGE UNIVERSITY PRESS

Cambridge
New York   Port Chester
Melbourne   Sydney

CAMBRIDGE UNIVERSITY PRESS
Cambridge, New York, Melbourne, Madrid, Cape Town, Singapore,
São Paulo, Delhi, Dubai, Tokyo

Cambridge University Press
The Edinburgh Building, Cambridge CB2 8RU, UK

Published in the United States of America by Cambridge University Press, New York

www.cambridge.org
Information on this title: www.cambridge.org/9780521122597

First published 1990
This digitally printed version 2009

A catalogue record for this publication is available from the British Library

Library of Congress Cataloguing in Publication data
Winrow, Gareth M.
The foreign policy of the GDR in Africa/Gareth M. Winrow.
   p.   cm. – (Soviet and East European studies: 78)
Includes bibliographical references.
ISBN 0 521 38038 3
1. Germany (East) – Foreign relations – Africa.
2. Africa – Foreign relations – Germany (East)
I. Title.   II. Series.
JX1549.Z7A2   1990
327.43106 – dc20   89-71281 CIP

ISBN 978-0-521-38038-6 Hardback
ISBN 978-0-521-12259-7 Paperback

To Nazan

Contents

List of tables	page xi
Preface	xiii
Abbreviations	xv

1 Introduction 1
Preliminary remarks 1
Surrogates and proxies 6
The GDR as an affiliate 9
Affiliation and the development of East German foreign
policy in general 15

**2 The development of GDR relations with Africa in the
pre-recognition period** 33
Introduction 33
The Hallstein Doctrine 37
Attempts to secure recognition 47
Diplomatic breakthrough 72

3 The GDR in Africa in the 1970s 85
Introduction 85
The increased East German role in Africa 90
Continued inter-German rivalry 104
The importance of 1979 113

4 East German military/security involvement in Africa 121
Introduction 121
The importance of the military/security role of the GDR in
Africa 124
The employment of NVA combatants in Africa 134

The work of East German military/security advisers and
    technicians   139
Arms exports and other forms of military cooperation   144
Conclusion   150

5   **East German economic relations with Africa**   152
    Introduction   152
    General characteristics of East German economic
        involvement in Africa   156
    The importance of Africa as a source of raw materials   160
    East German development assistance and the New
        International Economic Order   173
    Conclusion   184

6   **The GDR in Africa in the 1980s**   187
    Introduction   187
    Problems of the early 1980s   189
    East Berlin's rivalry with Beijing and Bonn   195
    The GDR's continued prominent profile in Africa   200
    The impact of Gorbachev on the GDR's *Afrikapolitik*   207

7   **Conclusion**   217
    The importance of Africa for the GDR   217
    The GDR and Africa in the future   225

    Notes   228
    Select bibliography   266
    Index   277

Tables

1 Percentage of trade with developing states in the total trade of East European states, 1960–1987 *page* 44–5
2 East German imports, exports and trade turnover with African states and selected oil exporting states, 1960–1987 57–8
3 Diplomatic recognition of the GDR by African states, 1964–1984 73
4 Visits by leading African officials to the GDR, 1973–May 1989 91–2
5 Visits to Africa by SED Politbüro members and Foreign Minister Fischer, 1973–May 1989 94–6
6 GDR–Africa, visits by military/security delegations, 1967–1988 126–8
7 Numbers of Soviet, Cuban and East German troops and military advisers in Africa, 1978–1988 133
8 Trade balance of the GDR and other East European states with the Third World, 1975–1987 154
9 Sources of East German oil imports, 1960–1987 162–4
10 Official development aid of the FRG and the GDR, 1970–1987 179

Preface

The problem with examining contemporary international politics is that work when published is already out of date. This will be particularly so when attempting to investigate current developments in Eastern Europe and in southern Africa and the Horn. Indeed, since the preparation of the typescript, dramatic events have occurred in the GDR. Erich Honecker was forced to 'retire' from the SED Politbüro and Egon Krenz became new party leader on 18 October 1989. The change of leadership resulted in sweeping personnel changes in the government and Politbüro and led to the introduction of a number of political and economic reforms. The opening of the borders between the two Germanies has made the Berlin Wall to all intents and purposes redundant. And then, on 3 December 1989 it was dramatically announced that Krenz and the top party leadership had resigned due to popular pressure.

As yet, these internal developments have not seriously affected the nature of the GDR's involvement in Africa. However, for practical purposes, I have decided to keep in the text the original names and titles of key East German officials although many of these individuals no longer hold office. Hence, throughout the text, Honecker is still referred to as SED General Secretary.

Despite recent events this work remains, to the best of my knowledge, the first full account in the English language of GDR foreign policy in Africa. Originally written as a Ph.D. thesis, and although considerably revised, I have maintained for the benefit of the specialised reader a certain amount of detail along with footnotes. However, I hope that this work will also attract the general reader interested in the GDR.

I am grateful to the Universities of Manchester and Leicester for providing the necessary finance to enable me to prepare the original thesis when certain national award-making bodies refused to offer financial support. I would also like to thank the University of Leicester Research Board and the British Council for financing my research trips to the FRG and the GDR.

I am greatly indebted to my original Ph.D. supervisor in the Department of Government at the University of Manchester, Mr Christopher Binns, for his guidance and advice. Also my thanks go to Herr Horst Brasch, Honorary Vice-President of the 'Liga für Völkerfreundschaft' of the GDR, and member of the Central Committee of the SED, for his helpful comments and personal views. Dr Johannes Kuppe of the Bonn Branch of the Gesamtdeutsches Institut – Bundesanstalt für Gesamtdeutsche Aufgaben, and Dr Christopher Coker of the London School of Economics, also offered helpful advice. I am grateful to Mrs Gillian Austen for typing the original manuscript. Finally, a special acknowledgement to my wife, Nazan, for her invaluable support, interest and tireless encouragement.

Abbreviations

ACDA	Arms Control and Disarmament Agency (US)
ACP	African Caribbean, Pacific
ADN	Allgemeiner Deutscher Nachrichtendienst
ANC	African National Congress
ASU	Arab Socialist Union (Egypt, Libya)
CAR	Central African Republic
CDU	Christlich–Demokratische Union (Christian Democratic Union)
CMEA	Council for Mutual Economic Assistance
COPWE	Commission for Organising the Party of the Working People of Ethiopia
COREMO	Comité Revolucionário de Moçambique (Revolutionary Committee of Mozambique)
CPP	Convention People's Party (Ghana)
CPSU	Communist Party of the Soviet Union
DBD	Demokratische Bauernpartei Deutschlands (Democratic Farmers' Party of Germany)
DISA	Department of Information and Security of Angola
DM	Deutschmark
EDF	European Development Fund
EEC	European Economic Community
ELF	Eritrean Liberation Front
ELF–RC	Eritrean Liberation Front – Revolutionary Council
EPLF	Eritrean People's Liberation Front
FDGB	Freier Deutsche Gewerkschaftsbund (Free German Trade Union Federation)
FDJ	Freie Deutsche Jugend (Free German Youth)
FLN	Front National de la Libération (National Liberation Front, Algeria)

FLNA	Frente Nacional de Libertação de Angola (National Liberation Front of Angola)
FLNC	Front de la Libération Nationale Congolaise (National Congolese Liberation Front)
FRELIMO	Frente de Libertação de Moçambique (Liberation Front of Mozambique)
FRG	Federal Republic of Germany
GATT	General Agreement on Tariffs and Trade
GDR	German Democratic Republic
ICFTU	International Confederation of Free Trade Unions
IUS	International Union of Students
LDC	Least Developed Country
MLSTP	Movimento de Libertação de São Tomé e Príncipe (Movement for the Liberation of São Tomé and Príncipe)
MPLA	Movimento Popular de Libertação de Angola (Popular Movement for the Liberation of Angola)
MPLA–PT	MPLA–Partido de Trabalho (MPLA–Party of Workers)
NATO	North Atlantic Treaty Organisation
NIEO	New International Economic Order
NMP	Net Material Product
NVA	Nationale Volksarmee (National People's Army)
OAU	Organisation of African Unity
ODA	Overseas Development Assistance
OECD	Organisation for Economic Co-operation and Development
OPEC	Organisation for Petroleum Exporting Countries
PAC	Pan Africanist Congress (of South Africa)
PAIGC	Partido Africano de Independência da Guiné e do Cabo Verde (African Party of Independence for Guinea and Cape Verde)
PLO	Palestine Liberation Organisation
PMAC	Provisional Military Administrative Council (Ethiopia)
POLISARIO	Popular Front for the Liberation of Saguia el Hamra and Rio do Oro
SADCC	Southern African Development Coordination Council
SADR	Saharan Arab Democratic Republic

SED	Sozialistische Einheitspartei Deutschlands (Socialist Unity Party of Germany)
SIPRI	Stockholm International Peace Research Institute
SWAPO	South West African People's Organisation
TR	Transferable rouble
UNCTAD	United Nations Conference on Trade and Development
UNIP	United National Independence Party (Zambia)
UNITA	União Nacional para a Independência Total de Angola (National Union for the Total Independence of Angola)
VDJ	Verband der Deutschen Journalisten (German Journalists' Union)
VM	Valuta mark
WFDY	World Federation of Democratic Youth
WFTU	World Federation of Trade Unions
WPE	Ethiopian Workers' Party
WTO	Warsaw Treaty Organisation
ZANU	Zimbabwe African National Union
ZAPU	Zimbabwe African People's Union

1 Introduction

Preliminary remarks

The traditional view prevalent in the West is that on account of ostensible total subordination to the Union of Soviet Socialist Republics (USSR) an analysis of the foreign policy of the German Democratic Republic (GDR) is of little intrinsic value or interest. It is the contention of this book that there is an East German foreign policy in Africa worthy of serious analysis, and which is not merely an appendage of Soviet activities on that continent. An examination of the GDR's involvement in Africa enables one to comprehend the development of East German foreign policy in general, in which rivalry with the Federal Republic of Germany (FRG) has been an important factor. Indeed, through investigating its *Afrikapolitik*, one is offered an insight into the advancement of the GDR as an independent state entity.

West German analysts naturally have assumed an interest in the activities of their fellow-German 'socialist brothers' in the Third World. Indeed, until recently, the works of these analysts were the only serious Western publications which examined East German relations with African states.[1] Through these analyses it became apparent that the GDR's *Afrikapolitik* was not solely a replica in miniature of Soviet policy. Lately, a number of articles and case studies have been published by English and American scholars which have contributed to the examination of East German involvement in Africa. Thus, David Albright's assertion in 1980 that Eastern European interest in Africa was 'sufficiently minor or ancillary to the inputs of other actors (i.e., the USSR in particular)' to warrant exclusion from separate discussion has been increasingly challenged with regard to the GDR at least.[2] Nevertheless, no detailed study exists, in the English language, of East German foreign policy in Africa. The

1

popular conception of the GDR as a Soviet satellite has proved difficult to surmount.

The GDR was a victim of non-recognition both in the international political system and in the Western academic world throughout the 1950s and 1960s. The so-called 'Soviet Zone' was perceived as neither German, nor democratic and definitely not a republic.[3] Writing in the mid-1960s the American political affairs expert, Zbigniew Brzezinski, interpreted East German dependence on the USSR as complete and advocated that Western policy should be aimed at the liquidation of the GDR which was 'doomed to remain a Soviet puppet'.[4] Only from the late 1960s, with the evolutionary development of the East German polity, its economic growth, the dynamics of inter-German relations and final diplomatic recognition were Western analysts prepared to examine the GDR more seriously.

However, those wishing to continue to sponsor the notion of total East German dependence on the USSR could refer to the text of the third constitution of the GDR in 1974. Article 6, section 2 read: 'The GDR is for ever and irrevocably allied with the Union of Soviet Socialist Republics.'[5] A year later Article 1 of the Treaty of Friendship, Mutual Assistance and Cooperation between the GDR and the USSR stated that the two states 'will continue to strengthen the relations of eternal and indestructible friendship and fraternal mutual assistance in all fields'.[6]

According to the American political scientist, James Rosenau, writing in the mid-1960s, the GDR's dependence on the USSR was depicted as an example *par excellence* of a so-called 'penetrated system': 'One in which the non-members of a national society participate directly and authoritatively through actions taken jointly with the society's members, in either the allocation of its values or the mobilisation of support on behalf of its goals.'[7]

Rosenau regarded the GDR as almost a permanently penetrated system. Here, the implication was that the GDR's subordination to the USSR was virtually complete.

Writing a decade later, Edwina Moreton's conceptualisation was of a penetrated system, more dynamic and subject to change: 'Its relative permanence is determined by the persistence of the capability shortages which fostered it initially and also by the nature of the issue area on which this capability shortage is based.'[8]

Despite a gradual enhancement of the GDR's economic and political stature, undoubtedly the East German government has remained obliged to follow the USSR's policy on those issues which Moscow perceived important, especially in Europe. Thus, Moreton's revision of Rosenau's analysis of a penetrated system is of some relevance in explaining the GDR–USSR relationship. However, it does not adequately account for how exactly these changes in the relationship have occurred which have provided the East German authorities with more freedom of manoeuvre.

In practice, after an initial period under Josef Stalin when East German dependence on the USSR was complete, the relationship between East Berlin and Moscow has become more interdependent, although clearly the GDR remains more dependent on the USSR. Asymmetric dependence should not necessarily be equated with such attributes as lack of influence over the predominant partner, or a supposed inability to manoeuvre relatively freely. The GDR has manipulated the bargaining power of the weak *vis-à-vis* the USSR as the latter has valued the strategic, economic and political significance of the East German state. The East German authorities have played consciously on the USSR's traditional fear of the particular vulnerability of the GDR as an outpost of the Soviet bloc flanked by the capitalist West German state.[9]

Asymmetric dependence with scope for bargaining is a feature of patron–client relations. Clientelism in the context of inter-state relations involves an exchange between unequals in which the patron (i.e., the protector state) provides rewards for services performed by the client state. The American political scientist, Melvin Croan, has drawn attention to what he perceived as the clientelist nature of the GDR–USSR relationship.[10] However, in a genuine patron–client relationship clients are able to escape domination from their current patron by exercising bargaining power in threatening to change, or indeed, actually changing their protector-state. One such example was the Soviet–Egyptian relationship in the 1970s when Anwar as-Sadat eventually transferred allegiance to an American patron.[11] Hitherto, on account of the USSR's obvious stake in the GDR, the East German authorities could scarcely have emulated the Egyptian example even if they wished to seek a new patron. Because of this major constraint on the GDR's freedom of manoeuvre the GDR–USSR relationship is not an example of a genuine patron–client interaction.

It will be demonstrated that the GDR is rather an 'affiliate' of the USSR. As an affiliate the GDR would not enjoy the extent of freedom accorded to a client state. On the other hand, in contrast to the almost total subordination of Rosenau's penetrated system example, through affiliation a relationship based on interdependence is formed. The development of East German foreign policy in general, and in Africa in particular, may be understood through an analysis of the GDR's conscious and willing pursuit of an affiliation strategy with the USSR.

The first detailed West German studies of East German activities in Africa and throughout the Third World were prepared in the early 1970s under the auspices of the Forschungsinstitut der Deutschen Gesellschaft für Auswärtige Politik.[12] These works indicated that the GDR pursued a particular policy objective in Africa separate from that of the USSR, i.e., the goal of diplomatic recognition. However, they did not examine in detail certain factors beyond the African environment which conditioned the success or failure of the GDR's quest for diplomatic recognition in Africa.

Throughout the 1970s – after the GDR had secured international diplomatic recognition – the number of West German studies of East German foreign policy in Africa or in the Third World in general proliferated.[13] It was now acknowledged by West German academics that the perceived intensification of East German involvement on the African continent warranted close analysis. These analyses concentrated on specific ideological and economic factors that dictated GDR behaviour. The importance of East German military/security activities on the continent was also raised. However, these analyses did not incorporate any detailed discussion of factors external to Africa which influenced the GDR's relations with the USSR and the FRG in both Europe and Africa.

Only in recent years have English-speaking scholars such as Michael Sodaro, Christopher Coker, Edwina Moreton and Melvin Croan made important contributions to an expanding Western literature (no longer exclusively West German) on the GDR in Africa, as the East Germans have appeared to maintain an active involvement there. Interestingly, while avoiding a detailed examination of East German activities in Africa, these and other writers have presented conflicting assessments of the role of the GDR's *Afrikapolitik*. A controversy has emerged with regard to whether the GDR has been operating as a 'surrogate', 'proxy' or 'partner' of the USSR in Africa. This debate will be considered shortly.

The foreign policy priorities of the GDR have remained focused on Europe, and especially on relations with the USSR and the FRG, as the East German authorities have endeavoured to boost their legitimacy. Nevertheless, in the Third World, the African continent in particular has become an important field of activity for the GDR. Indeed, involvement in Africa has been connected to East German concerns much nearer to home – including the crucial issue of legitimacy – within the affiliation strategy.

It will be demonstrated that as early as the 1950s it was the African continent as a whole – regardless of religious, political and economic dissimilarities between north and sub-Saharan Africa – that was specifically targeted by the East German government in its attempt to secure international recognition. It was in Africa that the largest wave of decolonisation eventually occurred. In effect, the GDR, itself a new state seeking international recognition and legitimacy, was attracted towards the emerging new African states. The East German authorities could also exploit African hostility to the Western colonial powers to secure propaganda points over the West Germans through the FRG's direct links with these Western states in the North Atlantic Treaty Organisation (NATO). Moreover, one may presume that the GDR's interest in Africa was also influenced in part by past German involvement there prior to World War I. The East German authorities have, however, attempted to distance themselves from earlier German colonialism (see chapter 2).

This book will also show how Africa continued to have particular significance in East German foreign policy after international recognition was obtained. Declaring their support for national and social liberation and condemning neo-colonialism and apartheid, the East Germans have simultaneously sought to continue to discredit the West German presence in Africa and support the USSR's interests there.

The analysis is in part historical and in part thematic. Less stress has been put on an analysis of the ideological components that may be seen to motivate or influence the GDR's *Afrikapolitik*. West German scholars have already explored in great detail East German ideological pronouncements on the nature and state of progress of the African social and political 'revolution'. Here, the emphasis is rather on a study of actual events, although, of course, a background discussion of East German views of national liberation and socio-economic development in Africa is presented where necessary to assist in the analysis of these events.

One should underline again that the purpose of this book is to understand the development of the GDR and its foreign policy through a close examination of its involvement in Africa. Consequently, although certain details concerning the African environment are included wherever required in order to comprehend East German policy objectives, successes and failures, this analysis is not intended to represent an Africanist approach. Nor is it proposed to discuss East German relations with each African state. Attention is naturally focused on those African states in which the GDR was actively involved.

Surrogates and proxies

As indicated earlier, English and American scholars have opened up a debate with regard to the nature of the GDR's role in Africa and in the Third World generally. American analysts, in particular, have referred to the GDR acting as a surrogate and/or proxy of the USSR in Africa. According to this school of thought, the East Germans are compelled or at least obliged to perform certain tasks and functions in Africa in the interests of the USSR. As a result, the Soviets' ambitions on the continent have benefited from the tapping of East German expertise in such fields as military/security training and operations, party organisation, and experience in trade unionism, journalism and youth work. Through these activities African regimes sympathetic to Moscow were consolidated. The Soviets were also saved the expense of despatching greater numbers of their own advisers and officials thereby possibly avoiding a serious deterioration in relations with the United States.

In contrast, while not challenging the importance for the USSR of the GDR's role in Africa, English commentators have tended to question the assumption that the East Germans were forced by Moscow to become involved on the continent. Suggesting that the East German leadership was eager to volunteer its services abroad, and that the interests of the GDR and the USSR in Africa usually corresponded, Coker and Moreton have become critical of this surrogate/proxy approach. However, a common failure to define accurately and apply properly the terms 'surrogate' and 'proxy' has not facilitated the task of assessing the GDR's role in Africa.

The terms 'surrogate' and 'proxy' in the context discussed here began to be employed more extensively after the substantial Cuban military involvement in the Angolan War of Independence in 1975 and in the Ethiopia–Somalia conflict in 1977–8. A debate ensued on whether Cuba was operating independently or as a surrogate/proxy of the USSR in Africa. However, it has now become fashionable to present an alternative view which emphasises the interdependent nature of the Soviet–Cuban relationship in Africa. This interdependence was most obvious in the 'cooperative intervention' with the Soviet airlift of Cuban expeditionary forces to Angola and Ethiopia in the 1970s. Moscow's dependence on the successful deployment of substantial Cuban troop contingents in Africa enabled Fidel Castro to acquire an amount of leverage and autonomy in his African dealings. Castro's desire to strengthen his regime's legitimacy by enhancing Cuba's prestige as perceived in the Third World and in the non-aligned movement through consciously escalating Cuban involvement in Africa was also noted.[14]

In the light of these developments commentators have become more circumspect in their use of the terms 'surrogate' and 'proxy' with reference to Cuban involvement in Africa. But the GDR could scarcely appeal to an Afro-Caribbean heritage to account for its active profile in Africa. Hence, it has proved considerably more difficult to dispense with the prevailing orthodoxy that the GDR's role in Africa was simply that of a surrogate/proxy for the USSR.

Other terms have been applied with reference to the GDR's involvement in Africa which denote extreme forms of dependence and subservience. For example, in a statement issued in 1982 the American Senator, Jeremiah Denton, labelled the GDR and Cuba as 'puppets' of the USSR with respect to their operations in Africa.[15] More recently, the American political scientist Andrzej Korbonski has depicted the GDR in particular as an 'obedient vassal' of the USSR.[16] Similarly, the East German state has been depicted as the example *par excellence* of a Soviet 'satellite'.[17]

Surrogacy has also been employed to emphasise the subordination of one state to a superior. Brian Crozier has used the terms 'surrogate' and 'satellite' interchangeably in his account of Cuban and East European programmes of assistance in support of Soviet ambitions in the Third World.[18] Sodaro lays particular stress on the GDR's role as a surrogate of the USSR in Africa noting the importance of East German support for Soviet policies in the Third World. The emphasis is on Soviet and not East German interests, although Sodaro acknowledges that the GDR may also pursue its own ambitions in Africa.[19] Subordination is not total. Likewise, another American, John Starrels, insists that although the East Germans conduct their African affairs 'as an appendage of Soviet foreign policy . . .', a surrogate like the GDR may still pursue specific goals of its own in Africa.[20]

Hence, two different constructions of surrogacy have emerged which, indeed, the Americans Stephen Hosmer and Thomas Wolfe appear to have noted. By one construction a surrogate or proxy in the 'strictest sense' (Hosmer and Wolfe unfortunately use the terms interchangeably) acts on the authority of the principal state and in the interests of the principal only. A second, broader formulation employs these terms for states 'that serve Soviet purposes while sparing the USSR direct involvement in some particular Third World activity'.[21] The latter construction emphasises the value of the surrogate's role as a substitute for the principal or dominant state while not necessarily excluding the possibility that the surrogate may also be able to pursue interests of its own.

Bertil Dunér and Gordon McCormick have made further important observations. McCormick argues that a surrogate or proxy (again using the terms interchangeably without qualification) may pursue its particular ambitions within the broader framework of Soviet policies, although he emphasises that the question of interest is less important ultimately than the issue of control or coercion.[22] Dunér's distinction between a proxy (employed like McCormick's surrogate/proxy) and a partner demonstrates more clearly the importance of this coercive element. Although a proxy and a principal state may share a 'compatibility of interests', a proxy is referred to as such because it has been compelled by the principal through either 'negative sanctions' (threats) or positive sanctions (rewards) to act in the interests of the latter. States which have not been forced to intervene in the interests of the principal are partners and not proxies. According to Dunér, the major difficulty with this distinction is that it is impossible to prove where compulsion rather than voluntary behaviour is responsible for a state's actions.[23] Western observers have traditionally assumed that the GDR was compelled by the USSR to conduct an active *Afrikapolitik*.

The term 'proxy' by dictionary definition indicates that one state has been *authorised* by another (it is presumed a more influential state) to act *solely* in the interests of the authorising state. A 'surrogate' by dictionary definition is merely a 'substitute', again implying that a state thus characterised is acting solely in the interests of a state which has authorised, or, indeed, *required* the less influential state to act in its interests. Hence, the terms 'surrogate' and 'proxy' are closely related in meaning but not necessarily synonymous. Therefore, by strict definition, a proxy could scarcely be compelled to act in the interests of another state – it is only *authorised* to do so. Dunér's important criterion of compulsion is actually only applicable in practice in contrasting surrogate states with 'partners'.

As noted earlier, Coker and Moreton have questioned earlier assumptions about surrogate or proxy states with reference to East German activities in Africa. Moreton has properly emphasised that although the GDR's policies in Africa are sponsored by the USSR and under overall Soviet command, a certain autonomy is accorded by the USSR to East German activities on the continent. More importantly, the GDR authorities were not compelled by the USSR to initiate or upgrade their involvement in Africa.[24] Interestingly, Coker suggests that the GDR performs the roles both of proxy and partner, while also emphasising that the East Germans have pursued their own policies in Africa which were occasionally at variance with Soviet objectives. Indeed, Coker wonders if the role of proxy and partner may not be identical.[25] Obviously, these notions of a dual or simultaneous role can not be accommodated within Dunér's classification.

Avoiding the above problems, the GDR may rather be referred to as an 'affiliate' of the USSR, both in general, and in relation to Africa specifically. As an affiliate the GDR enjoys advantages akin to those Cuba enjoys in its interdependent relationship with the USSR. Castro was able to maximise Cuba's close links with the Third World and the non-aligned movement. On the other hand, the East German leadership has consistently stressed close and loyal ties with the USSR as embodied within the strategy of affiliation, in order to secure their interests and obtain a measure of autonomy.

The GDR as an affiliate

By the conscious pursuit of a strategy of affiliation – i.e., a policy demonstrating the GDR's value as that of a faithful ally of the USSR – East Berlin has succeeded in securing a measure of freedom of manoeuvre, and enhanced its leverage *vis-à-vis* Moscow.

In the words of K. J. Holsti, the role of a faithful ally is 'one in which the policy-makers declare that they will support, with all means possible, their fraternal allies. They are not so much concerned with receiving aid as with giving the appearance of committing aid to others.'[26]

Holsti lists the GDR and Britain as examples of faithful allies who often stressed their alliance commitments. The above definition excludes the likelihood that faithful allies would wish to receive rewards for their policy of affiliation. Holsti has also omitted reference to the possibility that faithful allies might employ an affiliation strategy to increase their bargaining capabilities and thereby enlarge their perceived stature.[27] On the other hand, Astri Suhrke has correctly observed that within an alliance the bargaining powers of a smaller state may be enhanced by stressing its role as a 'loyal' and 'contributing' ally in order to obtain rewards for compliance and support from the dominant alliance leader.[28]

In practice, the GDR voluntarily and consciously pursued a strategy of affiliation in which Soviet interests were assiduously supported in order to receive rewards and secure backing for East German initiatives when superpower concerns were of less consequence. In any clash on an issue of significance to both the GDR and the USSR, the Soviet will would prevail. The strategy of affiliation could succeed though because interests rarely conflicted on major issue areas. Invariably, interests ran parallel or mutual accommodation was obtained on less crucial issues after compromise or bargaining.

The gradual transformation of the GDR's status from that of a Soviet satellite to that of a junior partner or junior ally highlighted the effectiveness of the affiliation strategy. The term 'junior ally', with reference to relations between the USSR and East European states, was first employed by Brzezinski. It was used to describe the changing nature of Soviet–East European relations in the 1960s as the latter were able to secure an increasing freedom of manoeuvre in the conduct of their policies. However, although no longer demanding the 'liquidation' of the GDR, Brzezinski remained reluctant in his book, *The Soviet Bloc – Unity and Conflict*, to bracket the GDR together with other East European states in the category of junior allies.[29]

By the late 1970s the GDR was entitled to regard itself as the most important junior ally or junior partner of the USSR through the successful pursuit of an affiliation strategy. Although, traditionally, other East European states to a greater or lesser extent have been eager to support the policies of the USSR, none had so consistently nor so enthusiastically backed Moscow than the GDR. Until recently, through an almost paranoid concern with their legitimacy the East German leadership alone has determinedly charted a course of almost constant and purposeful affiliation with the USSR.

The successful pursuit of affiliation, which is then connected with the GDR's gradually elevated status within the Soviet bloc, is also of particular importance in an analysis of the GDR's *Afrikapolitik*. In line with its foreign policy in general, the GDR consciously adopted a strategy of affiliation with the USSR in Africa.

After the GDR had secured international recognition, in another demonstration of affiliation with the USSR the East German leadership willingly embarked on an enhanced political and military involvement in Africa. The East German authorities volunteered to undertake certain tasks and perform specific roles in Africa that were intended to benefit the interests of both the GDR and the USSR. Here, East Berlin was eager to differentiate its foreign policy from that of Bonn and to acquire the status of Moscow's most dependable junior partner. Through this enlarged *Afrikapolitik*, it will be argued, the East German leadership wished to continue to secure preferential economic treatment from the USSR, as well as Soviet support for East German interests in Europe with reference to the German question.

Furthermore, I suggest, in contrast to the surrogate/proxy hypothesis, that the Soviet leadership, increasingly perceiving the GDR as an important junior partner through successful affiliation, was willing to accord it increasing autonomy in the conduct of its policies in Africa.

But in order to comprehend more clearly why the GDR opted to pursue consciously a policy of affiliation with the USSR, certain preliminary observations on the East–West German relationship must be noted and the question of the legitimacy of the GDR raised.

Certainly, the issue of inter-German rivalry in Africa has been little explored because the attention of Western scholars has been on the dynamics of East–West German interaction in Europe. However, up to the present day a continuing inter-German competition in Africa dating from the early 1950s has to a large extent dictated the evolution and nature of the GDR's *Afrikapolitik*. Prior to 1972 it was the West German concern to prevent international recognition of the GDR, embodied in the Hallstein Doctrine, which hindered the development of East German relations in Africa. After 1972 rivalry was maintained as part of the GDR's policy of *Abgrenzung* (delimitation) from the West German state. For example, the controversy over the status of Berlin was employed by the East German authorities to score certain propaganda victories over the FRG in Africa.

Created artificially as a state entity after a division of the German nation following the Second World War, the GDR has had to contend with the increasing economic expansion and international recognition of West Germany. Enshrined in the FRG's Basic Law, a provisional constitution in effect, was the demand for German reunification which would entail the dismantling of the East German state structure.

According to the Preamble of the Basic Law, acting 'on behalf of those Germans to whom participation was denied . . .' (i.e., those in the then 'Soviet Zone of occupation', later, the GDR), 'the entire German people are called upon to achieve in free self-determination the unity and freedom of Germany'.[30]

On account of the West German government's refusal to recognise the legitimacy of the GDR as an independent state after 1949 in accordance with the terms of the Basic Law, an active foreign policy to secure international recognition of the East German state was deemed essential by the leadership in East Berlin. In these circumstances, the only option for the East German government was to pursue consciously a policy of affiliation with the USSR. As William Zimmerman stated: 'Regimes which have not sought to achieve a sense of legitimacy in the eyes of key social groups by engendering in those groups a sense of participation in the political system are most likely to seek national security, i.e., perpetuation of the regime, by a policy of competing to demonstrate their fidelity to the regional Superpower.'[31]

In basic agreement with Max Weber's classic exposition, legitimacy is depicted here as concerned with the popular acceptance of a perceived lawfully and rightfully constituted ruler or ruling body within a given state. Through this popular acceptance (active or passive) the ruling body within the state in question is vested with authority.[32] Authority, by definition, implies a command–obedience relationship not based on coercion alone. In practice, the acceptance of this authority is acquired through the successful policies of a stable decision-making elite body. In the example of the GDR, the elite is represented by prominent officials of the ruling Socialist Unity Party of Germany (Sozialistische Einheitspartei Deutschlands – SED).

However, the above working definition only involves what may be termed 'internal legitimacy', i.e., the acceptance of a certain recognised authority by the public within that state in which the authority exercises command. This definition does not take into account the importance for the elite in question of the recognition of their authority by other external publics and governments, i.e., the elite's concern for their 'external legitimacy'. I would suggest that the interaction between what might be termed the pursuit of 'internal' and 'external' legitimacy is of fundamental importance. In order to illustrate this more clearly a discussion of how legitimacy (internal and external) may be generated is necessary.

Legitimacy in general possesses an 'incremental' quality that may be either 'amplified' or 'squandered',[33] i.e., legitimacy *per se* is neither constant nor guaranteed. Legitimacy needs to be generated. It also needs to be protected from possible challenges.

One Western analysis has drawn attention to the fact that any unit undergoing political development may be confronted with a challenge to its legitimacy which if not resolved may result in a legitimacy crisis. According to this analysis, the obvious 'institutional solution' to this challenge involves 'Any effort to create loyalty to and confidence in the established structure of political institutions in the given system and to ensure regular conformity to rules and regulations issued by the agencies authorised within the system.'[34]

With specific reference to the states of Eastern Europe, it has been argued that the policies of a stable elite necessary to generate legitimacy (and also protect it) include a prosperous economy, social security, social mobility, regime longevity, success in the sciences, arts and sports, and the identification of the elite and the general public with a sense of nationhood.[35]

However, unlike in other East European states, the East German elite's attempts to inculcate a sense of nationhood in the GDR have encountered continued difficulties on account of the failure to eliminate an alternative German state – the FRG. The FRG has posed a constant challenge to the GDR's legitimacy since the foundation of the East German state. In order to prevent this challenge becoming a legitimacy crisis the SED authorities, as a part of their 'institutional solution', have had to employ another legitimising tool in addition to those policies pursued by other East European states. As previously noted, this additional legitimising tool used by the SED authorities has been the pursuit of an active foreign policy to secure global recognition of the GDR as an independent state.

According to one commentator, for 'the leaders of a regime striving for legitimacy, diplomatic recognition may be interpreted as recognition and "proof" of its proffered claims for legitimacy which they then broadcast to their underlying population in their attempt to justify themselves'.[36]

Here, the differentiation of the internal and external components of legitimacy and their interaction is of importance. A successful foreign policy aimed at securing international recognition of the GDR, and also distinguishing the external activities of the two Germanies to create a favourable impression of the non-capitalist German state, would facilitate the SED ruling elite's task of generating internal legitimacy by convincing the East German population of the reality and permanence of the GDR. Conversely, consolidating internal stability and economic growth would assist in fostering external recognition of the East German state – i.e., the acceptance of the SED's authority within a defined territory by world public opinion – given that the GDR possessed those prerequisites of statehood in customary international law by which states could be recognised diplomatically (i.e., territory, population, economic base, functioning government).

Through this interaction, it is argued, the East German strategy of affiliation with the USSR facilitated the generating of legitimacy by promoting the differentiation of the foreign policies of the two Germanies, while also providing the GDR with a certain freedom of manoeuvre. Concerned with the vulnerability of the East German regime, post-Stalin governments in the USSR perceived it in their interests to accord the GDR a more autonomous conduct of foreign policy that was visible to the international community beyond Eastern Europe. Hence, in the pre-recognition period especially (i.e., before the GDR secured world-wide diplomatic recognition in 1972–3), the SED elite were required to demonstrate publicly that a measure of autonomy was in evidence within this affiliation strategy in order to avoid the charge that East German foreign policy was merely a duplicate of Soviet external activity. A failure to exhibit autonomy would deepen the problem of generating external legitimacy already made difficult by the FRG's international stature.

If East German foreign policy is divided chronologically into pre-recognition and post-recognition periods, the interaction between the pursuit of internal and external legitimacy can be demonstrated in both phases. Hence, prior to 1972, the primary purpose of the strategy of affiliation with the USSR was to obtain global diplomatic recognition of the GDR as an independent state entity. In a desperate attempt to gain international recognition the SED authorities targeted the African continent. In return, for services rendered within the strategy of affiliation, the USSR supported the GDR's attempts to generate legitimacy through preferential economic treatment (intensified in the post-recognition period for several years), and also promoted East German endeavours to gain diplomatic recognition in Africa, and indeed elsewhere, within the constraints of Soviet influence in the Third World. Although the USSR did not exercise sufficient leverage over African governments to compel (rather than to persuade) them to recognise the GDR diplomatically, the Soviet acceptance of an increasingly visible autonomous East German foreign policy in Africa (particularly with reference to inter-German rivalry on the African continent) assisted the GDR's quest for recognition.

In the post-recognition period the affiliation strategy with the USSR was maintained and expanded upon to enforce the GDR's policy of *Abgrenzung* with the FRG. Fearful of continued legitimacy shortcomings in the face of West German attempts, commencing in the 1970s, to establish increased linkages with the East German population in a period of détente, the SED leadership endeavoured to generate further legitimacy by various stratagems. These included

Abgrenzung with the FRG and even closer linkages (i.e. *Annäherung*) with the neighbouring socialist states of Eastern Europe. As noted earlier, in this heightened pursuit of affiliation with the USSR the SED authorities were eager to upgrade East German involvement in Africa in order to stress further the separate policies of the two Germanies and secure the status of the USSR's most important junior partner. However, in most recent years, with an improvement in inter-German relations in Europe, and with the accession to power of Mikhail Gorbachev, certain questions concerning the future of the GDR's *Afrikapolitik* need to be raised.

Before examining more closely the importance of the GDR's *Afrikapolitik*, a background knowledge of this historical development of the GDR's foreign policy in general is necessary in order to illustrate more clearly the application of affiliation in practice.

Affiliation and the development of East German foreign policy in general

Even before the founding of the GDR in October 1949, local communists in the Soviet Zone of occupation were concerned that Stalin might accede to a plan for German reunification before the prospects of a reunited 'socialist' Germany were real. Hence leaders of the SED (already formed in April 1946 from a merger between German communists and social democrats) were eager to demonstrate their allegiance to the USSR. Stalin's expulsion of Yugoslavia from the Cominform in 1948 was endorsed, and the SED authorities also dissociated themselves from their previous espousal of a 'Titoist' German road to socialism.

The announcement of the formation of the FRG on 23 May 1949 forced the USSR to approve the founding of the GDR on 7 October 1949. Thereafter, until the FRG's admission into NATO in May 1955, all public Soviet initiatives linked with the possibility of German reunification were primarily connected with the attempts of Stalin and his successors to prevent the remilitarisation of the West German state. However, at that time certain governments and publics (including leading SED officials it seems),[37] could have concluded that the USSR might be prepared to jettison the GDR in the interests of a neutral, reunified Germany.

Walter Ulbricht, who had established control within the GDR after becoming SED General Secretary in 1950, never renounced his 'ultimate' goal of German reunification on socialist terms. But, once the

West German state was founded and recognised in the West, the more immediate and important goal for Ulbricht and the SED authorities was the securing of international recognition for the new state. External recognition beyond the Soviet bloc would boost considerably the legitimacy of the SED regime as perceived within the GDR.

In the pre-recognition period internal problems within the GDR did not boost the credibility of the East German regime as perceived externally. Following continued political repression, the popular uprisings in East Berlin and other cities in the GDR on 17 June 1953 triggered by Ulbricht's decision to increase the work norms to raise the productivity of a sagging East German economy highlighted the SED's continued lack of domestic support. Continuing economic problems, together with forced agricultural collectivisation and the suppression of intellectual freedom resulted in over 2.7 million East German refugees fleeing to the West between 1949 and August 1961.[38] Confronted with this mass exodus, construction of the Berlin Wall commenced on 13 August 1961. This prompted one Western expert, convinced of the bankruptcy of the East German state, to brand the GDR as that 'detested Ulbricht regime'.[39]

Ironically, although the Berlin Wall appeared to have caused irreparable damage to the GDR's external image, the position of the SED authorities was bolstered internally. For once, negative external perceptions of the GDR did not work to the disadvantage of the SED's attempts to generate legitimacy. Indeed, the reverse occurred. Within the GDR, any disappointment resulting from the events of August 1961 soon turned to disillusionment and anger at the inability of the West and the FRG to prevent the construction of the Wall. As one Western account noted, the East German populace, their option of fleeing to the West effectively checked, increasingly demanded: 'Recognise us and be done with it.'[40] And according to another analyst, the Wall's construction provided the SED leadership with the 'first opportunity to establish their authority on a lasting basis . . .'[41] Moreover, in the following years the East German economy dramatically improved as substantial numbers of the labour force were no longer able to abandon the GDR.

In the Stalinist period the GDR had remained almost totally subordinate to the USSR. The East German state remained a zone of Soviet occupation. The total costs of the Soviet dismantling of East German industries, forced occupation payments and production from enterprises 'jointly' owned by the GDR and the USSR amounted to DM (Deutsche mark) 40–60,000 million.[42] These 'reparations' were only alleviated by the USSR after January 1954. This Soviet economic exploitation of the GDR had contributed to the destabilisation of the East German government in June 1953. Only after 1956 did Moscow commence to allocate credits and grant East Berlin implicit trade subsidies (e.g., charging the GDR less for imported Soviet oil, wheat and other raw materials) to encourage the growth of the East German economy. This change of policy by Moscow helped stabilise the GDR internally and contributed to the development of the Council of Mutual Economic Assistance (CMEA), the organisation of economic cooperation for states of the 'Socialist Community'.[43]

East German efforts to secure international recognition were not assisted by the USSR's failure to accord the GDR sovereignty in internal and external affairs until a treaty between the two states was signed in September 1955; although the USSR, like the three Western occupying powers, Britain, France and the US, retained certain ill-defined responsibilities over Berlin and Germany as a whole. This treaty was signed six years after the founding of the GDR, and, even more significantly, one week after the official commencement of diplomatic relations between the FRG and the USSR.

Furthermore, only in June 1964 did the USSR finally conclude its first Treaty of Friendship, Mutual Assistance and Cooperation with the GDR in which each contracting party agreed to come to the assistance of the other in the event of external aggression (Article 5). This treaty was clearly an upgrading of the 1955 GDR–USSR treaty which had not referred to mutual assistance (the GDR technically had not possessed an army at that time).[44] By contrast, as early as 1948 the USSR had concluded mutual assistance treaties with all other East European states.

Within the Soviet bloc, the GDR was accorded inferior status for several years after its official founding. Prior to 1953 those few states which recognised the GDR – the USSR, Bulgaria, Poland, Czechoslovakia, Hungary, Romania, the People's Republic of China, North Korea, Albania, Mongolia and the 'Socialist Republic of Vietnam' – only established diplomatic missions and not embassies in East Berlin.[45] Entitled a 'Democratic Republic' and not a 'People's Republic', the East German state only secured admission to the CMEA in September 1950, almost one year after the GDR's founding.[46] Continued Polish and Czechoslovak suspicion of the East German regime resulted in the GDR's admission into the Warsaw Treaty Organisation (WTO) in January 1956 on the unprecedented condition that the East German armed forces would come under direct Warsaw

Pact control.[47] Furthermore, Moreton has noted that in contrast to similar agreements concluded by the USSR with East European states, in the GDR–USSR agreement of 12 March 1957 on the 'temporary' presence of Soviet troops in East German territory, the two governments agreed only to 'consult' with one another on the movement of these troops. Hence, in theory, the USSR could conduct manoeuvres and declare martial law without East German consent.[48] As late as 1988 over 350,000 Soviet troops remained stationed on East German soil.

With the exception of Yugoslavia (1957), Cuba (1963), Zanzibar (1964), and perhaps Guinea temporarily (1960) – no other state recognised the GDR diplomatically prior to 1969. This was on account of the refusal of the West German authorities to recognise the legitimacy of the East German state.

Addressing the Bundestag on 21 October 1949, Chancellor Konrad Adenauer contrasted the freedom, sovereign rights and democratic nature of the FRG with the repressive political system in the Soviet satellite state in the Eastern Zone of Germany. In accordance with the Basic Law, Adenauer claimed *Alleinvertretungsanspruch* (sole right of representation) when he declared that: 'The Federal Republic of Germany is alone entitled to speak for the German people.'[49] The three occupying Western Powers endorsed Adenauer's claim.

Undoubtedly, the *Alleinvertretungsanspruch* seriously damaged the credibility of the SED regime as perceived both externally and internally. It clashed with Article 1, section 3 of the GDR constitution of 1949 which stated that the East German government represented the interests of all Germans.[50] In December 1955 the *Alleinvertretungsanspruch* was reinforced by the FRG's adoption of the Hallstein Doctrine which intended to check the USSR's attempt to encourage international recognition of both German states after Moscow had established diplomatic relations with Bonn in August 1955 – the USSR thereby becoming the first state to recognise diplomatically both the FRG and the GDR. By the Hallstein Doctrine (examined in detail in chapter 2), Bonn threatened to take reprisals in the event of any state recognising the GDR. Hence, when Yugoslavia and Cuba recognised the GDR diplomatically, FRG retaliation against these states included the severing of diplomatic relations.

The Hallstein Doctrine successfully checked the GDR's attempts to secure international recognition. The FRG also succeeded in gathering support to bar East German entry into the United Nations. Even East German attempts to obtain observer status in UN specialised organisations were obstructed, although by 1960 the FRG had secured entry to all UN specialised bodies (without officially joining the UN). Moreover, while East German contacts outside the USSR's closest allies were, in general, restricted to official and informal commercial agreements, the FRG had few problems in establishing diplomatic relations with states beyond the Soviet bloc.

Through a strategy of affiliation with the USSR the SED authorities hoped to secure Soviet support to overcome the *Alleinvertretungsanspruch* and the Hallstein Doctrine and obtain international recognition of the GDR. Together with efforts to encourage other states to recognise the GDR diplomatically, more favourable economic and political treatment accorded by the USSR would boost the GDR's perceived status within the Soviet bloc, raise morale within the East German state, and thereby also increase the possibility that other states might recognise the GDR.

Certainly, until 1969–70, Ulbricht pursued the strategy of affiliation with the USSR in Europe with considerable acumen. The SED leader assumed the role of 'socialist inquisitor' within the Soviet bloc in the 1960s.[51] Hence, with the Sino-Soviet rift, unlike other East European states, and in particular Romania, the GDR did not exploit events to enlarge its bargaining capabilities *vis-à-vis* the USSR by appearing to threaten to withhold complete support for Moscow. On the contrary, the GDR's bargaining capabilities were enhanced by Ulbricht's offer to mediate in the Sino-Soviet dispute through a genuine desire to maintain socialist solidarity and prevent the formation of a Beijing–Bonn axis, which never actually materialised.[52]

The invasion of Czechoslovakia in August 1968 was wholeheartedly supported by Ulbricht in order to prevent the spread of 'liberal' contagion which issued from Prague.[53] East German troops participated with other forces of the WTO (excluding Romania) to crush the Prague Spring.

Under Ulbricht, until 1969, the GDR most loyally and diligently supported Soviet policies. In return, Moscow eventually concluded the mutual assistance treaty of 1964 with the GDR, and continued to allow East Berlin to import Soviet raw materials at discount prices as the East German economy became the most modern and industrialised within the CMEA. The GDR's economic and political stature within Eastern Europe had risen dramatically within a decade.

However, it was a breakdown in affiliation with the USSR which resulted in Ulbricht's enforced retirement as SED leader on 3 May 1971. Ulbricht's removal was evidence of continued Soviet ultimate control over East German policy.

The SED leader failed to adapt to a reassessment of West German policy in an era of emerging détente. In his inaugural speech on 28 October 1969, and in his Report on the State of the Nation on 14 January 1970, Willy Brandt became the first West German Chancellor to refer to the *de facto* existence of the GDR as a separate German state within the German nation. By this new formula of 'two German states in one German nation', Brandt insisted that since the GDR and the FRG were not states foreign to one another, the West German government would not recognise *de jure* the GDR as a fully independent sovereign state.[54] The continued commitment to the Basic Law's demand for eventual German reunification made impossible West German *de jure* recognition of the GDR.

Ulbricht insisted on West German *de jure* recognition of the GDR. However, the USSR was more willing to accommodate the FRG's *Ostpolitik* on account of West German interest in convening a European Security Conference to confirm the status quo of the political division of Europe. As a major step towards the convening of this conference the FRG concluded treaties of non-aggression with both the USSR and Poland in 1970. It was a major blow to Ulbricht that the USSR had not insisted on West German *de jure* recognition of the GDR as a precondition for signing the treaties. Brandt then made it known that the Bundestag's ratification of the USSR–FRG Non-Aggression Treaty and support for a European Security Conference was dependent on a settlement of the Berlin question. The West German leadership was concerned that the four occupying powers' rights and responsibilities with respect to Berlin should be reaffirmed in order to protect the access routes between the Western sectors of Berlin and the FRG.

However, the SED authorities believed that further discussions concerning Berlin's status were unnecessary. According to Ulbricht, the GDR had previously obtained sovereignty *de jure* although not *de facto* over Berlin in an exchange of notes which accompanied the GDR–USSR treaty of 1955.[55]

Ulbricht's attempts to forestall the *Ostpolitik* of Brandt on account of the FRG's refusal to recognise *de jure* the East German state resulted in a serious confrontation between the USSR and the GDR on the issue of Berlin culminating in the SED leader's removal from office. In his refusal to accommodate the USSR's willingness to negotiate a new Four Power Agreement on Berlin, Ulbricht overstepped the bounds of his freedom of manoeuvre within the strategy of affiliation by endangering the prospects of the European Security Conference – an issue of crucial importance to the USSR.

The previously successfully cultivated affiliation strategy had already been strained by other disputes, economic and ideological, immediately prior to Ulbricht's 'retirement'.

In the economic sphere, Ulbricht complained about what he perceived as the increasingly disproportionate burden of the GDR in supporting the Soviet economy, through increased exports of goods, in particular. In practice, the GDR continued to receive preferential economic treatment from the USSR. Nevertheless, an aggrieved Ulbricht must have antagonised the Soviet leadership by drastically reducing East German exports to the USSR in 1970 on account of a number of poor harvests and severe winters.[56]

Ideologically, in the late 1960s Ulbricht had begun to adopt a 'school-masterly approach' concerning the lessons of socialist development.[57] He lectured the states of the Soviet bloc, the USSR included, on the theme that because of the advanced, industrialised nature of the GDR, it was this socialist model which should be promoted as that most applicable to Western industrialised states in their future transition to socialism.[58]

It may seem paradoxical that in those months of tension which culminated in the breakdown of affiliation, the GDR finally secured diplomatic recognition from a number of African and other Third World states. Indeed, in chapter 2 it will be shown that Ulbricht's earlier successful pursuit of affiliation with the USSR in the 1960s had actually hindered the GDR's attempts to secure African diplomatic recognition. The GDR eventually obtained diplomatic relations with several African states prior to general international recognition. Despite international non-recognition, earlier subordinate status within the Soviet bloc, and economic constraints, as early as 1953 the African continent was targeted by the SED in an attempt to secure international recognition, boost East German prestige at home and abroad, and hence, secure some form of legitimacy. The extent of Soviet support for the GDR's quest for diplomatic recognition from African states requires examination (see chapter 2).

After Ulbricht's 'retirement', in his first years as new SED leader, Erich Honecker finally secured general international recognition of the GDR. In this period Honecker reaffirmed the GDR's close links with the USSR to repair the damage caused by Ulbricht. Fearful of the impact on the East German population of West German appeals to common German nationhood, and still concerned over the deficit in the legitimacy of the SED regime even after international recognition had been secured, Honecker adopted a policy of *Abgrenzung* with the

FRG and *Annäherung* with the Socialist Community. The objective of German reunification previously pursued by Ulbricht was sacrificed as Honecker aspired to become Moscow's *Musterknabe* (literally 'model boy').[59]

At the 7th SED Congress in June 1971 Honecker declared in his report that the GDR's alliance with the Socialist Community was 'inviolable'.[60] And, as previously noted, the third East German constitution of 1974 and the new GDR–USSR Treaty of Friendship in 1975 (drawn up before the expiry of the 1964 treaty it should be noted) further strengthened ties between Moscow and East Berlin.

Honecker immediately overturned Ulbricht's heretical ideological formulations in favour of a conceptualisation of socialism in strict accordance with Soviet doctrine. Hence, in 1972 almost all the remaining East German semi-state/private enterprises were nationalised, and the new SED Statute of 1976 underlined more clearly the leading role of the SED in GDR society. Externally, Honecker hoped that the intentions of the Comprehensive Programme of the CMEA (1971) to obtain economic integration would result in a spillover leading to enhanced political and ideological integration within Eastern Europe. In effect, the SED leadership endeavoured to assume 'a vanguard role for the Soviet hegemonial power'.[61] De-Germanising its constitution (discussed later, p. 24) and aspiring to an effective integration of the Socialist Community, the SED elite hoped to consolidate their position within the GDR and attain for the GDR the status of the USSR's most important junior partner. Affiliation was reimposed and pursued more emphatically than in any period since Stalin's death. The East German authorities were even concerned that the USSR might be prepared to strike a political deal with the FRG which could endanger East German interests.[62] The SED were fearful that the USSR might employ the German card by sending strong signals to Bonn to suggest that German reunification might be possible if the FRG distanced itself from its Western allies. Suhrke has referred to this phenomenon as the 'mistrust factor' concerning the difference in foreign powers, i.e., in 'unequal alliances' the fear of a smaller state that it may become expendable in a climate of détente between the leaders of two previously hostile alliances.[63]

Hence, in 1971–2 Honecker had had no alternative but to yield to the demands of Brandt for an agreement on Berlin and a treaty between the two Germanies which failed to secure West German *de jure* recognition of the GDR as an independent sovereign state. The Soviet leadership was eager to oversee the conclusion of these agreements in order to obtain the convening of the long-anticipated European Security Conference.

Honecker was able to find some consolation in the vague and imprecise wording of the text of the Quadripartite Agreement on Berlin of 3 September 1971 and its accompanying documents. Hence, after the signing of the agreement, Honecker could immediately claim that its provisions were only applicable to West Berlin.[64] More importantly for this study (and examined in detail in later chapters), the precise nature of the relationship between the FRG and West Berlin remained contentious.

According to the Basic Treaty signed by the two Germanies on 21 December 1972 relations were to be normalised, the inviolability of borders to be recognised, and the independence and autonomy of each state in internal and external affairs respected. However, instead of the commencement of full diplomatic relations and the exchange of ambassadors, the treaty merely referred to the development of 'good neighbourly relations' on the 'basis of equal rights', while only permanent missions were to be exchanged.[65] Furthermore, on the day of the signing of the Basic Treaty, the West German government addressed a letter to the East German authorities which stated that the 'political aim' of the FRG remained that of working for peace in Europe 'in which the German nation will regain its unity through free self-determination'.[66]

On account of the failure to secure full West German diplomatic recognition of the GDR, the SED leadership remained conscious of the challenge to their legitimacy. The West German authorities had not renounced their goal of German reunification, nor had they recognised East German citizenship. Moreover, already forced to conclude a number of agreements with Bonn to secure the effective functioning of the Quadripartite Agreement concerning the rights of access and transit between the FRG and West Berlin, the SED authorities were worried that an implementation of the Basic Treaty threatened to expose the East German public to contacts with the FRG which could endanger the stability and social cohesion of the GDR. Ironically, as a consequence of the Basic Treaty, the legitimacy of the SED's authority in the GDR as perceived externally was bolstered as a result of the wholesale international recognition of the East German state that ensued. Furthermore, the Helsinki Final Act of 1975 (i.e., the eventual European Security Conference) included in its provisions a general recognition of the inviolability of all European borders (i.e., including the borders of the GDR).

Through the policy of *Abgrenzung* the East German authorities, contrary to the spirit if not the wording of the Quadripartite Agreement, attempted to curb the number of visitors entering the GDR. For example, in October 1980 the minimum amount of currency required to be exchanged by West Germans and West Berliners entering the GDR was doubled. Honecker also sought to convince the East German public that 'Germany' no longer existed although there were Germans of the FRG and Germans of the GDR. The existence of two distinct German nations was stressed to challenge Brandt's formulation of two German states in one German nation. In the 1974 constitution the GDR described itself as 'a socialist *nation* [my emphasis] of workers and farmers'.[67] A de-Germanising campaign was initiated in which the words 'Germany' and even 'German' were eliminated (as in the 1974 constitution) and substituted by the term GDR, e.g., the German Union of Journalists was renamed the Union of Journalists of the GDR.[68]

Although the SED leadership soon suspended the de-Germanising campaign because of ideological contortions in attempts to explain the origins, development and progress of the 'socialist nation' of the GDR, the policy of *Annäherung* was a success. It was Honecker, who, in a mood reminiscent of Ulbricht's profound aversion for the Prague Spring, became a principal upholder of Soviet orthodoxy when cautioning the Polish leadership in their negotiations with Solidarity in 1980–1.[69] Significantly, Honecker was accorded the honour of the first East European party leader to address the Congress of the Communist Party of the Soviet Union (CPSU) in Moscow in 1981 – an honour traditionally reserved for the Polish 'party' leader.[70] Earlier, in June 1976, as a reward for the GDR's ideological trustworthiness, the Soviets had selected East Berlin as the venue for the second meeting of European communist and workers' parties.[71]

Honecker reinforced his strategy of affiliation in Europe by expanding GDR involvement in Africa in order to further both East German and Soviet interests. Until 1984 Honecker was a success as Moscow's *Musterknabe* and the GDR was established as a loyal junior partner of the USSR. In return the USSR backed the SED leadership with reference to the German question by refusing to play the so-called German card, and also extended to the GDR further preferential economic treatment. Soviet economic support was especially important as Honecker hoped to generate popular support within the GDR and thereby offset problems of legitimacy in connection with *Abgrenzung* by satisfying the consumer interests of the East German population.

According to Article 2 of the 1974 constitution: 'The continued improvement of the material and cultural standard of living of the people . . . is the decisive task of a developed socialist society.'[72] Hence, the GDR needed to import more Western consumer goods. The GDR and other East European states were also eager to increase technological imports from the West in order to modernise their economies. But imports of Western technological goods generated requirements for further technological imports, manufactured articles and raw materials from the West. The result was an East European trade deficit and hard currency debt on a substantial scale. By 1981 the total hard currency debt of the GDR ranked second in Eastern Europe behind Poland at $14,700 million.[73] The reservicing of this debt was complicated by unforeseen price rises of raw materials including oil in intra-CMEA trade in 1975.

According to established procedure the price for oil in intra-CMEA trade between 1971 and 1975 was based approximately on the price for oil on the world markets in the preceding five years. However, after the oil price increases in 1973–5, the USSR, the chief oil producer within the CMEA, was delivering oil to Eastern Europe at prices as little as one-fifth of the world market price, despite the pressures of its own continued oil imports from the Organisation for Petroleum Exporting Countries (OPEC). Hence, with Soviet pressure, the CMEA Executive Committee introduced a new price formula for fuels and raw materials in January 1975. Instead of fixing prices for a period of five years, according to the Bucharest Formula prices were to be revised annually to take into account the escalating cost of primary products on the world market. Moreover, the 1975 price rise was based on the average of world market prices in the previous three years only to avoid the lower price rises of 1970 and 1971. The 1976 annual readjustment reverted to a previous five-year average.[74]

The introduction of the Bucharest Formula would seem to have been especially burdensome on the East German economy because of the gap between its low fuel resources and its high industrial level. In this period the GDR, with Poland and Czechoslovakia, were the heaviest consumers of oil, and, on average, approximately 90 per cent of oil consumed by the GDR was imported from the USSR.[75] Therefore, after 1975 the GDR needed to boost its exports to the West in order to meet rising debt repayments and also, in theory, it needed to increase industrial exports to the USSR to offset a rising balance of trade deficit with Moscow produced by the rise in oil prices.

In spite of these problems Honecker continued to promote the consumer interests of the East German population to boost the legitimacy of the SED as perceived internally. Only in December 1979 was a three-tier pricing system introduced in the GDR which increased the prices of certain 'luxury goods' while still keeping stable the cost of basic consumer goods.[76] This was possible in part, due to the GDR benefiting considerably from 'inter-German' trade and a number of miscellaneous West German hard currency payments. The FRG's policy of subsidising the East German economy through preferential trade credits and commercial arrangements, which originated from Adenauer's insistence that Bonn should support the lot of their fellow Germans trapped in the 'Soviet Zone', was allowed to continue by the SED authorities in spite of *Abgrenzung* – and with good reason. According to the West German government, between 1970 and 1977 alone, West German trade credits and payments connected with tolls, transit fees, foreign exchange requirements, and financial support to improve the GDR's communications infrastructure, *inter alia*, were estimated to total DM 7,500 million.[77]

The GDR also benefited considerably from an extension of the preferential economic treatment accorded by the USSR. By so-called 'implicit trade subsidies', underpriced Soviet raw materials were exchanged for overpriced East European machinery and industrial goods in the CMEA's imperfect barter system. According to calculations by Jan Vanous and Michael Marrese, between 1972 and 1981 the GDR profited most from this arrangement with a subsidy from the USSR totalling $33,500 million in comparison with Czechoslovakia which received the next highest amount of $19,500 million.[78] It should be noted that the accuracy of these calculations has been questioned as they were based on controversial estimates of the extent to which prices paid by the USSR for East European manufactured goods allegedly exceeded world market prices.[79] But still, in spite of Soviet oil price increases, through the system of barter – on account of the absence of an efficient intra-CMEA price-setting mechanism – the GDR continued to purchase Soviet oil and petroleum products at most favoured prices within the CMEA. Thus, in the period 1976–80 the GDR purchased Soviet oil at a rate more than 25 per cent less than Hungary, the least favoured East European state.[80] The superior quality of East German industrial imports to the USSR in comparison with other East European states explains the price differentials in part, but the extent of this differential for East German and Hungarian imports of oil would strongly suggest that the GDR did receive considerable implicit trade subsidies although the exact figures quoted by Vanous and Marrese may still be questioned.

The GDR also secured from the USSR other advantageous deals. Although details are sketchy it appears that according to an agreement in 1967 the GDR received an amount of Soviet oil at a fixed price for the period 1971–84 in return for providing the USSR with industrial machinery and equipment.[81] Furthermore, the GDR also secured substantial explicit subsidies from the USSR. In 1981 the GDR received Soviet hard currency loans which totalled $292 million at very low rates of interest with flexible, if not non-existent, repayment schedules.[82] Between 1972 and 1981 the GDR also received rouble credits from the USSR which totalled the equivalent of $2,200 million. Only Poland obtained more rouble credits from the USSR in that period ($2,800 million).[83]

The USSR may also have alleviated the East German contribution (in terms of equipment deliveries and loan payments) to CMEA joint investment projects undertaken in the USSR in this period, notably the Orenburg gas pipe-line. Certainly, such investment projects were unpopular throughout Eastern Europe on account of their expense in machinery, finance and even manpower.

Nevertheless, the USSR was forced to export more of its oil to the West to obtain desperately needed hard currency in order to purchase Western technology to modernise the Soviet economy. Hence, Soviet oil deliveries to Eastern Europe needed to be controlled. In spite of favourable economic treatment even the GDR was affected. On 14 December 1979 Honecker announced that imports of oil from the USSR would level off at around 19 million tonnes, and that this would be taken into account in the 1981–5 plan.[84] At that time Western economists believed that the Soviet decision had created problems for the SED leadership, as it was estimated that by 1984 the GDR would need to consume 24 million tonnes of oil per annum (see chapter 5).

Certain Western scholars have speculated that the GDR, in order to continue receiving preferential Soviet economic treatment enabling East German consumer interests to be satisfied, (thereby generating more legitimacy for the SED internally), pursued an active *Afrikapolitik* which would favour the USSR's global interests. A possible linkage between this preferential treatment and East German military/security operations in Africa has also been suggested.[85] Croan has proposed that the GDR pursued an active role in Africa in the interests of the USSR in order to obtain more influence over Soviet policies in Europe, and, in particular, leverage over the German question.[86] Certainly, during this period Honecker was concerned that the USSR should support the policy of *Abgrenzung* and not develop a close relationship with the FRG.

Definite evidence linking preferential economic treatment and respect for East German policies in Europe by the USSR in return for an active GDR involvement in Africa is impossible to obtain. However, it is argued in this study that in the post-recognition period East German policy-makers would have used a policy of affiliation with the USSR in Africa, as in Europe, in order to become Moscow's model partner, so that the GDR's bargaining capabilities *vis-à-vis* the USSR could be enhanced. Through the exercise of these bargaining powers the GDR obviously would have hoped to secure preferential economic treatment and Soviet protection of East German interests in Europe.

Nevertheless, it should also be re-emphasised here that the GDR also had particular interests of its own for involvement in Africa in the post-recognition period. These interests were, in part, economic, but the SED authorities also hoped to boost their legitimacy externally and internally through a policy of *Abgrenzung* with the FRG in Africa.

The East German economy has recovered dramatically since 1984. A rise in national income has been accompanied by a reduction in debt to the West. According to one set of Western statistics, by 1986 the GDR's net hard currency debt totalled only $5,500 million.[87] These successes were achieved by restricting imports and increasing exports to the West. Extensive use has been made of 'inter-German' trade and general West German financial support. A policy of energy conservation and substitution and a search for alternative sources of oil (notably from the Middle East and north Africa) has also helped (see chapter 5). Moreover, the GDR continued to benefit from considerable subsidies from the USSR until 1984 at least, although Soviet oil prices rose and in late 1981 Moscow had unexpectedly announced that in the following year oil deliveries to Eastern Europe were to be reduced by 10 per cent. In April 1981 at the 10th SED Congress Honecker had boasted that the GDR obtained oil from the USSR at half the current price on the 'capitalist' market, and that the present supplies of Soviet oil at around 19 million tonnes would be maintained.[88]

From 1984 onwards, with the success of the East German economy the USSR no longer appeared to be offering the GDR extensive preferential treatment. The GDR began to obtain Soviet oil at a price greater than that on the world market. By 1986 the East Germans were actually purchasing Soviet oil at the cost of 172 transferable roubles (TR) per tonne in contrast to the equivalent world market price of

TR 95 per tonne[89] – although I suggest that through the GDR's re-export of Soviet oil imports in excess of East German consumption needs, the USSR has continued to subsidise the GDR economy despite cutbacks in these imports (see p. 170). In addition, by the terms of a trade agreement for 1986–90 the GDR has promised to increase exports of industrial goods and machinery to the USSR by 30 per cent to compensate for a previously acquired trade deficit, as Moscow had actually earlier allowed East German exports to the West to increase at the expense of deliveries to the USSR.[90] Honecker also indicated that the GDR will make a considerable contribution to new joint investment projects in the USSR connected with raw materials and energy production.[91]

Despite these developments, it should be remembered that through Honecker's conscious pursuit of an affiliation strategy with the USSR, the Soviet leadership had earlier provided invaluable assistance in order to enable the SED authorities to overcome serious economic problems in the late 1970s and early 1980s.

Nevertheless, even under Honecker's helmsmanship, contrary to the strategy of affiliation the Soviet–East German relationship was temporarily strained in 1984, as the GDR's attempts to improve relations with the FRG, in a change of policy, met with Soviet disapproval.

Détente between the superpowers collapsed in December 1979 with the Western decision to deploy cruise and Pershing missiles and the Soviet invasion of Afghanistan. However, by that time, both Germanies sought to improve their developing relations and prevent any negative spillover caused by the deterioration of superpower relations. Honecker's policy of *Abgrenzung* was in the process of revision. The SED leadership realised that although in the 1970s the number of visitors from the FRG and West Berlin to the GDR had risen dramatically, the East German population had not been dangerously 'contaminated' through these contacts, in spite of the scare of the mid-1970s. The considerable economic advantages for the GDR from close inter-German contacts have been previously noted. Closer relations with the FRG were also popular among the East German public, many of whom had relatives living in the FRG. Moreover, further legitimacy was conferred upon the SED through changing external perceptions as increased contacts with the FRG demonstrated to states less directly involved in the German issue that the GDR was no longer a pariah state but rather a permanent fixture in the European system.[92]

The East German authorities combined their new *Deutschlandpolitik* with *Friedenspolitik* (Peace Policy). Both German governments were aware that the deployment of more nuclear missiles on their territories would be unpopular domestically. From this linkage emerged talk among the SED leadership of the need for 'damage limitation' to the inter-German relationship and the notion of the 'special community of responsibility' between the two Germanies.[93]

Helmut Schmidt was the first West German Chancellor to make an official visit to the GDR in December 1981. The success of this inter-German summitry resulted in the further development of political, economic, social and cultural ties between the two Germanies. Honecker finally arrived in the FRG in September 1987. Although Honecker's trip was officially described as only a 'working visit', the SED General Secretary was received with protocol, and was entertained by both the West German Chancellor and President. The visit did enhance the international credibility of the GDR and conferred further legitimacy on the SED. Honecker reminded Chancellor Helmut Kohl that German reunification was not possible since capitalism and socialism were as incompatible as fire and water.[94]

This reception in Bonn made possible Honecker's official visit to Paris in January 1988, which was another major landmark in the endeavours of the SED leadership to secure more legitimacy. France was the first of the three Western occupying powers of Germany to receive the East German head of state. Honecker held talks with both Prime Minister Jacques Chirac and President François Mitterrand.[95] Prior to these visits the SED General Secretary's itinerary in recent years had included trips to Italy, Greece, the Netherlands and Belgium (all NATO states). By December 1988 the GDR had established diplomatic relations with 135 states (the FRG with around 160 states).[96] Prominent government officials and economic delegations from Western states regularly visited East Berlin. Clearly, the GDR had become an internationally recognised state.

However, the improvement in relations between the two Germanies had clashed with the GDR's pursuit of a strategy of affiliation with the USSR prior to Gorbachev's assumption to power. The GDR was compelled to toe the Soviet line when the USSR sought to penalise Bonn for approving the deployment of cruise and Pershing missiles in November 1983. Hence, under Soviet pressure, and appreciating 'the tacit rules of appropriate alliance conduct', Honecker postponed a proposed visit to the FRG in September 1984.[97] The independent movements of Soviet troops stationed in the GDR in the weeks immediately prior to September 1984 had also constrained the

SED leadership, and were a reminder to East Berlin that it was the USSR which dictated ultimately the limits of the GDR's freedom of manoeuvre.[98]

Nevertheless, Honecker was able to convince a new Soviet leadership under Gorbachev that an inter-German summit in the FRG would further both East German and Soviet interests. The largely successful pursuit of an affiliation strategy hitherto, with the exception of the problems in 1984, had convinced the Kremlin that the GDR was a partner and ally worthy of trust. Gorbachev was also aware that closer inter-German contacts in Europe could encourage the FRG to loosen its ties with NATO.

Under the Soviet leadership in the late eighties the GDR acquired considerable leeway in the conduct of its external and internal policy. Interestingly, the SED Politbüro member Kurt Hager, when questioned by a reporter of the West German magazine *Stern* about the consequences of Gorbachev's policy of *glasnost* on SED domestic policy, replied, that simply because a neighbour decided to redecorate his house, this did not oblige one to redecorate one's own house.[99] The SED authorities neither officially approved nor disapproved of *glasnost*. Honecker also indicated that on account of growth in national wealth and structural reforms in the East German economy in the early 1970s, the GDR did not need to emulate the process of *perestroika* (economic reconstruction) embarked upon in the USSR. However, in the sphere of foreign policy, according to the SED leadership, the GDR and the USSR remained in full agreement.[100]

Honecker's reluctance to follow Gorbachev-style reforms was on account of continued concern among the East German leadership about the legitimacy of their rule in the GDR. The SED authorities were still not prepared to countenance a relaxation of their monopoly of political control in the GDR through fear of allowing Western-backed (and, in particular, of course, West German-backed) 'opposition groups' to mount an organised challenge to their government. For instance, the SED reacted with some alarm and pointed an accusing finger at certain 'subversives' from West Berlin who had allegedly provoked disturbances – unprecedented it seems – at the annual rally in honour of Karl Liebknecht and Rosa Luxemburg in East Berlin in January 1988.[101]

Under Gorbachev's more relaxed control over Eastern Europe, East German officials became increasingly more assertive. Apparent differences of opinion between the GDR and the USSR concerning the issues of *glasnost* and *perestroika* indicated that Honecker was no longer as eager to play the role of a *Musterknabe*. Although the SED leadership remained aware that their survival was dependent ultimately on the continued support of Moscow, the strategy of affiliation appeared no longer to be pursued so unconditionally and the GDR's status as a most loyal partner of the USSR also seemed in need of re-evaluation. For example, in stark contrast to the GDR, Poland and Hungary became most receptive to Gorbachev's political and economic reforms. However, it should also be noted that Gorbachev's concern for the stability of the GDR (and the legitimacy of SED rule as perceived internally in the GDR was still clearly in doubt in the summer of 1989 with the exodus of thousands of East German citizens to the FRG via Hungary and Austria) resulted in no Soviet pressure upon the East German leadership to embrace economic and political reform.

How has the GDR's *Afrikapolitik* fitted in with this intricate pattern of recent developments outlined above? How, in particular, have inter-German relations in Africa been affected by increasing ties between the two Germanies? Were East German economic relations with African states of importance in the resurgence of the GDR economy in the late eighties, bearing in mind that cutbacks in the import of Soviet oil and its rising price appeared to necessitate a search for alternative sources of oil? With the gradual scaling down of Soviet preferential subsidies to the East German economy, and with the increasing international profile of the GDR, was an active *Afrikapolitik* necessary?

2 The development of GDR relations with Africa in the pre-recognition period

Introduction

On 10 February 1953 an East German delegation arrived in Cairo at the invitation of the Egyptian government. The visit led to the GDR concluding its first official treaty with an African state when on 7 March 1953 a trade and payments agreement was signed with Egypt.[1] Immediately prior to the treaty the Egyptian authorities had refused an offer of West German economic aid because of the conclusion of a reparations agreement between the FRG and Israel in the previous September.[2] According to the reparations agreement the West German government would pay Israel DM 3,000 million in annual instalments by the delivery of certain commodities and services to settle and rehabilitate Jews in Israel. A further DM 450 million was to be paid to the Conference on Jewish Material Claims against Germany. The Arab world feared that these reparations would encourage the development of a formidable Israeli war machine. Eager to acquire Arab support for recognition, East German officials were quick to seize the opportunity to exploit the furore caused by the reparations agreement by initiating contacts with Cairo.

It should be noted that the trade and payments agreement, which opened up possibilities for future East German credit support, was initialled at a time when economic problems were contributing to the June 1953 workers' uprisings in East Berlin and other cities in the GDR. Interestingly, the USSR did not conclude its first official trade agreement with Egypt until March 1954.[3] Moreover, the March 1953 agreement was concluded more than two years before the USSR granted the GDR sovereignty. Soviet officials were unwilling to obstruct this East German initiative which was obviously of significance to Moscow bearing in mind the strategic importance of the Suez Canal.

The East German resolution to ignore internal economic hardship and conclude the agreement with Egypt indicated the importance of the GDR's first official contact with an African state. The need to secure international credibility to legitimise the SED regime was paramount.

The events of March 1953 and the months prior to the signing of the treaty highlighted several features that would assume importance in GDR involvement in Africa. The military coup in July 1952, with the overthrow of the dynasty of King Farouk, suggested the importance of a realignment of political forces within the African sphere – although it was several months before Colonel Gamel Abdel Nasser established his own authority in Egypt. As a result of this realignment the GDR could establish initial official linkages through commercial contacts. In this instance, the GDR was able to overcome West German opposition by developing relations with an African state critical of particular policies of the FRG. A link with problems in the Middle East was also apparent. However, it seems that the USSR did not directly pressure the Egyptian government to initiate relations with the GDR.

Active 'German' involvement in Africa actually commenced in the final decades of the nineteenth century. Politicians, military officials, bankers, merchants, railway-builders and other sectors of Bismarckian society encouraged the new imperial regime to embark on an expansionist colonial policy. Territories in South West Africa, 'German' East Africa, Togo and the Cameroons were acquired. Native uprisings were mercilessly crushed – most notably the massacre of the Hereros in South West Africa (1903–6). However, with the dismantling of this empire after World War I, an infrastructure of improved communications, education, health services and local administration remained as a legacy of transient German imperial rule.[4]

The former German colonial territories held contrasting perceptions of the two Germanies after World War II. Once independent, Togo and Cameroon developed close political and economic relations with the FRG. Touring Africa in the spring of 1966 President Heinrich Lübke was welcomed at the Togolese village of Kuma by natives eagerly displaying a portrait of Kaiser 'Bill' in his spiked helmet. In Cameroon, Lübke was greeted by African veterans of the German Imperial Army in their original military uniforms.[5] Both Togo and Cameroon had prospered under a relatively peaceful administration, in contrast to German colonial rule elsewhere in Africa. However, in Tanzania (principally former German East Africa), scene of the rebellions of the Hehe and the Maji-Maji tribes at the turn of the century, the government of Julius Nyerere, remained, in general, favourably disposed to the FRG. Only in Namibia (former German South West Africa) were the East Germans able to exploit previous antipathy to the former German colonial rulers. Dissociating themselves from the deeds of earlier German colonialists, the East German authorities likened the Herero massacre to the 'neo-colonialist' policies of the FRG of the 1960s.[6]

African specialists in the GDR have preferred to commence their analysis of German interest in Africa from a more positive perspective. Hence, it was alleged that the German workers' support for peoples in the developing world dated from the nineteenth century, and, in particular, that the speeches of the German Communist Party chief of the inter-war years, Ernst Thälmann, created precedents for later East German pronouncements on the national liberation struggles in the Third World.[7]

Solidarity with workers in other states, i.e., proletarian internationalism, was first directly espoused in the Soviet Zone of Germany in the revolutionary programme of the newly created SED in April 1946: 'The Socialist Unity Party of Germany declares itself united with the class conscious workers of all countries. The party expresses solidarity with the peace-loving and democratic peoples of the whole world.'[8]

Immediately following independence the GDR Prime Minister Otto Grotewohl declared, in a statement on 12 October 1949, that the GDR was willing 'to establish peaceful and friendly relations with all states, that were prepared to live in peace and friendship with Germany and recognise our national interests'. The statement also stressed the necessity to develop trade relations with all states on an equal basis.[9]

Hence, apparently, the GDR, eager to acquire diplomatic recognition as soon as possible, and despite appeals to proletarian internationalism, was willing to establish relations with any state irrespective of possible ideological impedimenta. The proviso that states should 'recognise our national interests' suggested the importance, already at this time, for the GDR to acquire some form of external recognition. Bonn almost immediately mobilised the non-socialist world to deny such recognition through the policy of *Alleinvertretungsanspruch* (see Introduction).

However, until 1953, East German foreign policy towards the emerging independent national states was constrained by the inflexibility of the 'two-camp' doctrine. This doctrine, formulated in 1947 at the founding of the Cominform by Andrei Zhdanov, one of Stalin's

Central Committee Secretaries, had inhibited the USSR's freedom of manoeuvre in the Third World. According to this doctrine, imperialist national bourgeois elements had assumed power in new independent states in the developing world. Only months before his death Stalin launched a scathing attack upon these bourgeois groups, denouncing them as the chief enemy of the national liberation movement. Not until 1955–6 did Nikita Khrushchev drastically reassess the role of the bourgeoisie in the developing states.

Consequently, the East German trade agreement with Egypt in 1953 appeared to indicate some form of autonomous behaviour initiated by the GDR although sanctioned by the USSR. Originally, the military coup of Egypt in 1952 had been categorised by the East German authorities, in accordance with the 'two-camp' doctrine, as merely an alteration in the form of imperialist government.[10]

The USSR's involvement in Africa only commenced, in effect, in 1955 after the Bandung Conference of Afro-Asian nations convened in April of that year. By September 1955 (if not earlier) Khrushchev had promised Nasser arms deliveries via Czechoslovak intermediaries to counteract the Western-sponsored Baghdad Pact. The Bandung Conference, with its appeals for solidarity, neutrality and independence for Afro-Asian peoples, had convinced Khrushchev of the need to cultivate relations with the national bourgeoisie in the Third World. An East German commentary of 1955 regarded Bandung as a 'blow against imperialist forces', and, 'an important success for the forces of peace in Asia and Africa'.[11]

East German relations with Egypt had been further consolidated prior to 1955. An important precedent was set in January 1954 when an East German trade mission was allowed to establish a permanent GDR presence in Cairo.[12] In November 1955, the East German Minister for Foreign and Inner-German Trade, and Deputy Chairman of the Council of Ministers of the GDR, Heinrich Rau, visited Egypt (6–12 November) in order to conclude a long-term trade agreement (the first of its kind concluded by the GDR in the Third World) and hold discussions with Nasser.[13] Upon his return to East Berlin, Rau declared that it had been agreed to allow trade representations of both the GDR and Egypt to be granted 'consular rights and functions' in their respective capitals.[14] However, an Egyptian trade representation was only established in East Berlin in February 1958 after considerable East German pressure.[15]

This sequence of events certainly indicated increasing Egyptian *de facto* recognition of the GDR. The Israeli question, and the USSR's military support from 1955 onwards, must have influenced Egyptian policies.

Likewise, Moscow's interest in offering military aid to the Sudanese regime in 1955 prior to Sudan's official date of independence (1 January 1956) most probably influenced the successful negotiation of a payments agreement between East Berlin and Khartoum on 10 June 1955.[16]

Until most African states achieved independence, after 1956, only Egypt and Sudan were the subjects of Soviet interest in Africa, and this was, principally, an account of their importance for political developments in the Middle East rather than Africa. Certainly, in this period, the GDR also concentrated activity within the Arab world on account of the repercussions of the West German–Israeli reparations agreement. For example, in December 1953 and November 1955 the GDR concluded trade and payments agreements with Lebanon and Syria respectively. Hence, East German contacts were restricted to agreements of economic aid and commercial development. The four other independent African states at this time – namely, Ethiopia, Liberia, Libya and the Union of South Africa – were sensitive to West German opposition to any contact with the East German regime. GDR official sources only reported contacts with Emperor Haile Selassie of Ethiopia.[17] With increasing opposition in the UN to Pretoria's racial policies, East German diplomatic relations with South Africa would have been problematic, although South Africa only severed diplomatic relations with the USSR in 1956, and Czechoslovakia maintained a trade mission there until 1964.

East German relations with African states became more difficult when, in December 1955, Bonn promulgated what was later known as the Hallstein Doctrine.

The Hallstein Doctrine

In August 1955, as a result of Adenauer's visit to the Soviet capital, when 10,000 German prisoners of war were released in return for Bonn establishing diplomatic relations with Moscow, the USSR recognised both German states. Although Moscow did not accord sovereignty to the GDR until the treaty signed in September 1955, the first Soviet ambassador was received in East Berlin as early as September 1953. Many of Adenauer's advisers feared that diplomatic relations between the FRG and the USSR would encourage certain states in the Third World to establish diplomatic relations with both German states also, thereby, impairing the FRG's claim to sole representation of German interests (*Alleinvertretungsanspruch*). Adenauer's insistence on the unique nature of Bonn's relations with Moscow, on account of the USSR's position as a signatory of the Potsdam Treaty, which covered the rights and responsibilities of the Four Powers over all Germany, was not regarded in some quarters as an argument sufficient to prevent a possible wave of recognition of the 'Soviet Zone'.[18]

Increasing East German interest in Africa, and the growing concern of some developing states to express more independent policies after Bandung, coincided with a sudden need for the FRG to reassess the mechanics of the further implementation of the *Alleinvertretungsanspruch*. The result was the promulgation of a loose series of official statements and public utterances by West German officials that would later be collectively termed the 'Hallstein Doctrine'.

Immediately prior to Adenauer's departure for Moscow a paper was presented to the Chancellor by Erich Kaufmann, a legal official in the Foreign Office in Bonn. The paper re-emphasised the dependent nature of the East German regime on Moscow. The paper concluded that, in contrast to other Soviet bloc states, the 'GDR' had always been dependent on Moscow for its identity and continued existence,[19] i.e., an explicit denial of the autochthonous nature of the East German regime. Undoubtedly influenced by this document, Adenauer declared before the Bundestag, soon after returning from Moscow, that the recognition of the so-called GDR by a third state, with which the FRG already had diplomatic relations, would be regarded by Bonn as an 'unfriendly act'.[20]

Returning from his visit to Egypt and India, Foreign Trade Minister Rau reported on 18 November 1955 the imminent exchange of trade missions with Egypt and the relocation of the GDR trade mission in India from Bombay to the capital, Delhi. The West German ambassador in Egypt protested, and Bonn seriously considered reducing the status of its embassy in Cairo. Adenauer was compelled to acknowledge the possibility of Egypt and India recognising the GDR diplomatically which could trigger further acts of recognition.[21]

In response, an Ambassadors' Conference was convened in Bonn on 8–9 December 1955, in which the FRG's diplomatic representatives in European capitals, the US, Canada, Brazil, and, most importantly, Egypt and India, together with West German observers in the UN, participated. Here, Foreign Minister Heinrich von Brentano proposed that the West German government should immediately break off diplomatic relations with all states that recognised the government of the 'Soviet Zone'.[22]

On 11 December 1955, Professor Wilhelm Grewe, the head of the political department of the Foreign Office in Bonn, discussed the results of the Ambassadors' Conference in an interview with the government publication *Bulletin*. He indicated, more cautiously than von Brentano, that the developing of relations with the GDR would be regarded by Bonn 'as an unfriendly act', and would be met by a series of graduated measures that could culminate in the breaking off of diplomatic relations. However, diplomatic relations would only be severed in the most serious circumstances and after careful consideration.[23]

Von Brentano, in a speech to the Bundestag on 28 June 1956, declared that the recognition of the GDR by a third state with which the FRG had diplomatic relations would be regarded 'as an unfriendly act calculated to intensify and aggravate the partition of Germany. The Federal Republic would in such a case have to reconsider its relations with the state in question.'[24]

The above quotation is traditionally regarded as the cornerstone of what later came to be known as the Hallstein Doctrine, named after Walter Hallstein, then State Secretary in the Foreign Office in Bonn – an obvious misnomer: the von Brentano Doctrine was a more appropriate designation. Accordingly, the granting of diplomatic recognition to the GDR did not necessarily need to result in the curtailment of diplomatic relations by Bonn. However, the actual implementation of the Doctrine in 1957 against Yugoslavia, and in 1963 against Cuba, suggested that, in practice, diplomatic relations would be severed once a third state recognised the GDR diplomatically.

However, according to Grewe, it was not only diplomatic recognition of the GDR which could provoke such a retaliation from Bonn. Other acts of implied recognition could meet with a similar response. In a book published in 1960, Grewe categorised, in three sections, actions by third states which definitely implied recognition, did not imply recognition, and might imply recognition.[25] The first category included those actions by which diplomatic relations were granted at the level of ambassador, envoy, or *chargé d'affaires*; and in which consular relations were agreed upon with the request or grant of an exequatur. Acts which did not imply recognition comprised the conclusion of trade and payments agreements, the despatch of trade representatives, and the acceptance at a purely technical level of subordinate 'non-political' officials (e.g., media officials), where recognition was of a strictly conditional nature. The problematic category included the establishment of consular relations without requesting or receiving an exequatur, and the reception of a trade delegation at governmental level (which obviously included the establishment of trade missions).

Consequently, Grewe's analysis left several 'grey areas' of East German activity in third states open to doubt as to whether such activities would be regarded as an 'unfriendly act'. For third states the problem was how far they could venture in 'conditionally' recognising the GDR without seemingly according what may be interpreted by Bonn as an actual full-scale recognition of the GDR. However, in accordance with Grewe's earlier interview with the *Bulletin*, third states could also assume that certain acts of implied recognition could meet with a graduated series of reprisals from Bonn short of suspension of diplomatic relations. Hence, it was possible that certain 'grey areas' of activity, including Grewe's categories, could provoke certain graduated reprisals by Bonn. The only satisfactory means of resolving these problems of interpretation is to examine these theoretical pronouncements as implemented in practice.

The East German interpretation of the Hallstein Doctrine was decidedly unequivocal. One East German commentary typically asserted that the Doctrine was illegal, and marked 'a gross interference in the internal affairs of the GDR and third states'. It provided further proof of the contradictory and weak position of West German imperialism. In short, the so-called Hallstein Doctrine was 'a further example of the neo-colonialist policy of the Bonn regime'.[26]

In practice, prior to 1969 only Zanzibar (other than Cuba and Yugoslavia) temporarily established diplomatic relations at ambassadorial level with the GDR – a possible similar step taken by Guinea in 1960 will be discussed later. Pressure from Bonn resulted in the closure of the East German embassy in Zanzibar (see p. 66). The GDR, instead, established a consulate-general on the Tanzanian mainland (following the unification of Tanganyika and Zanzibar), and a consulate in Zanzibar – consulates preside over a smaller territorial unit and rank lower in status that a consulate-general. No exequaturs were bestowed upon the East German consular officials in these instances.

Egypt and Guinea (the latter in 1969 immediately prior to recognising the GDR diplomatically) were the only other African states which agreed to the establishment of East German consulates and consulates-general prior to full diplomatic recognition. Bonn was reported to have accepted the Egyptian declaration in the *Journal*

Officiel on 25 September 1959, which stated that the granting of an exequatur to the East German consul-general did not imply recognition *de jure* or *de facto*.[27] Egyptian officials insisted that the East German consul-general was to be accorded only limited privileges and would not be added to the consular list.[28] West German acceptance of this action was largely due to Bonn acknowledging the value of maintaining close relations politically and economically with the strategically important Egypt, although the FRG withdrew from financing the second phase of the construction of the Aswan Dam.[29] It may be inferred from this that the location of an East German consular official with an exequatur would be tolerated, provided that a statement was issued which declared that recognition was not intended. It may also be noted that the Egyptian representation in the GDR maintained the status of a trade mission until 1965 when a consulate-general was established in East Berlin following a visit to Cairo by Ulbricht. The FRG was unable to retaliate diplomatically since by then Egypt and other Arab states had severed relations with Bonn. Later, in February 1969, an East German consulate was also opened in Alexandria.

Grewe indicated that the establishment of trade missions at government level could be interpreted as a sign of recognition. In practice no West German reprisal resulted from the establishment of trade missions. This was in spite of the fact that the GDR established trade representations at government level with various qualitative rankings.[30] The lowest order was that of *Handelsrat* (trade councillor), granted for missions in the Sudan (from January 1956), Tunisia (from April 1960) and Morocco (from 1962). A higher ranking was accorded to trade missions under the title *Legationsrat* (legation councillor), in Mali (from April 1961) and Ghana (immediately prior to March 1966). By the protocol between the GDR and Guinea of 17 November 1958 to allow the establishment of trade missions, the East German head of the mission in Conakry was given the title 'consul-general', and, hence, accorded, to all intents and purposes, full consular rights. The GDR trade mission in Algiers (established in 1963) was originally ranked higher than was customary with the title *Gesandter* (envoy), but this procedure only operated for one year (1963–4). The GDR mission's principal representative in Libya (from May 1965) was entitled *Beauftragte* (literally 'deputy'), implying a special form of status. An East German trade mission was also opened in Zambia in April 1967.

According to one West German analyst, many of these trade missions enjoyed privileges usually reserved for diplomatic posts, including courier and code rights, inviolability of archives, diplomatic immunity of leading officials, the right to issue visas, and the possibility of flying the GDR flag on special occasions.[31]

The GDR journal *Junge Welt* stated in 1967 that the role of trade representatives in general had been modified in international relations since World War II: 'Therefore, for example, the trade mission need not necessarily protect only the economic interests of a state, but also may perform political, consular and cultural functions, if the mission is the only state representation of the sending state in the receiving state.'[32]

One should also differentiate between those African states which in reciprocation established trade missions in East Berlin. Only Egypt (later consulate-general, in 1965), Ghana (until 1966), and Guinea and Mali (both in 1967) were thus categorised. Although the presence of these missions served to legitimise the GDR further by implying more recognition of the East German regime, the FRG did not respond to these developments.

From the above one may conclude that the GDR enjoyed extensive relations with several African states by circumventing the Hallstein Doctrine. However, in practice, because of the equivocal nature of the Doctrine, Bonn could declare that, with the exception of Zanzibar, the Hallstein Doctrine was not breached. If one regards the Doctrine as simply a threat to suspend diplomatic relations with a third state if that state chose to recognise the GDR diplomatically, Bonn's self-congratulation would be justified (e.g., perhaps with Guinea in 1960, see pp. 62–4). However, if one interprets the Doctrine as a looser formulation of principles embodying a graduated set of reprisals for acts implying some unacceptable form of recognition, short of diplomatic relations, the Hallstein Doctrine encountered insuperable resistance in Tanzania and Egypt (pp. 64–70).

Nevertheless, continued East German frustration at failing to secure diplomatic recognition was ventilated against the Hallstein Doctrine. The GDR required nothing short of full diplomatic recognition to convince international public opinion and the East German population that the GDR was, indeed, a sovereign and independent state. Certainly, African states refused to recognise the GDR diplomatically through fear of provoking West German reprisals by an application of the Hallstein Doctrine.

West German economic muscle was an important factor which strengthened the operation of the Hallstein Doctrine. The GDR, although the most economically advanced state within the CMEA, could not compete with the FRG's extensive development aid programmes and commercial transactions with the developing world. African states would not have wished to jeopardise their economic contacts with the FRG and possibly other Western states by recognising the GDR diplomatically. In the pre-recognition period, of all African states, only in the case of Egypt was the GDR a more important outlet for exports than the FRG in certain years.[33]

According to official statistics, in 1970 West German trade turnover with African states totalled DM 13,300 million compared with a total trade turnover of the GDR with all developing states amounting to only 1,601.4 Valuta marks (VM) in the same year (for the East German figure see Table 1).[34] The FRG's substantial trade could be exploited to secure political leverage in the Third World at the GDR's expense.

The accumulated amount of West German development aid commitment to the Third World by 1969 totalled DM 51,735 million in contrast to the GDR's DM 530 million.[35] Moreover, unlike the FRG, by no means all of the East German credits promised to the Third World were actually granted. For example, the US State Department estimated that only $140 million in credits were actually granted by the GDR out of a figure of approximately $600 million promised by 1970.[36] The conditions of East German credits for capital aid were less attractive than West German equivalents. Credits allocated by the GDR were to be repaid in a shorter time (ten to twelve years in contrast to the usual twenty-six year period for West German capital aid credits) with no period of grace (the FRG usually allowed over seven years before repayments) although the interest payment was somewhat lower (2.5 per cent in contrast to 3.2 per cent with West German capital aid credits).[37]

Analysing these statistics the West German political scientist, Heinrich End, concluded that the GDR could only obtain diplomatic recognition in those states where West German development aid was inconsiderable, and where also the GDR's own development aid programme was reinforced by other political supports.[38] However, many African states after independence remained firmly in the Western camp, and would scarcely have wished to antagonise their British, French and American sponsors by recognising the GDR diplomatically.

In reality, because of their ability to cultivate contacts with the GDR at a commercial, and even consular, level, there was little incentive for all but the most radical of African heads of state or government to grant the GDR diplomatic recognition. Recognition would seriously endanger the non-aligned path that the more 'progressive' African

Table 1. *Percentage of trade with developing states in the total trade of East European States, 1960–1987*

Year	Official GDR figures (VM million)			Other figures						
	GDR	Total trade	Trade with developing states	GDR	Bulgaria	Czechoslovakia	Hungary	Poland	Romania	USSR
1960	4.3 (9.58)	18,487.4	791.3		2.9	10.4	5.5	7.6	8.6	7.8
1965	4.5 (6.74)	24,693.2	1,106.1		4.1	8.8	6.4	8.7	7.6	11.9
1970	4.0 (7.03)	39,597.4	1,601.4		6.7	7.6	6.3	6.7	8.2	13.5
1973	3.4	53,501.7	1.817.8							
1974	5.0	64,012.7	3,167.1							
1975	4.4 (6.60)	74,393.6	3,253.8		7.2	7.0	6.6	6.5	18.5	12.4
1976	4.6	85,456.5	3,918.3		6.8	7.3	9.1	6.0	18.6	11.5
1977	4.9	91,726.3	4,504.1		7.4	7.3	9.5	6.5	18.5	13.1
1978	5.2 (7.71)	96,879.4	5,027.7		7.3	6.6	9.1	6.4	17.4	12.2
1979	5.2 (7.45).	108,844.6	5,670.1		7.6	7.0	9.2	6.4	21.6	11.8
1980	6.1 (8.79)	120,100.8	7,331.2	6.9	10.0	7.6	7.5	10.2	25.6	16.7
1981	4.9 (7.37)	132,926.9	6,542.3	6.0	12.6	7.8	7.7	8.7	28.0	18.9
1982	5.7 (8.05)	145,109.3	8,429.6	6.7	13.1	7.1	8.6	10.7	27.9	18.8
1983	5.4 (7.54)	160,423.7	8,638.2	6.4	10.7	7.3	8.2	10.7	25.2	17.5
1984	4.7 (7.21)	173,902.5	8,243.2	6.3	11.7	7.0	8.7	9.8	23.0	18.3
1985	4.6	180,191.3	8,244.5	6.9	12.3	6.6	6.6	8.8	21.9	17.6
1986	4.4	181,970.2	7,938.4	6.2	10.0	5.8	5.2	9.3	16.8	16.7
1987[a]	3.8	176,556.3	6,683.5	6.3	9.0	5.2	4.7	8.5	12.6	17.0

Note: Figures in brackets refer to Hillebrand's revised estimates.

a = Preliminary figures.

Source: For official GDR figures see, *Statistisches Jahrbuch der Deutschen Demokratischen Republik* (Berlin [East]; Staatsverlag der DDR, various years). For Hillebrand's revised estimates see, Hillebrand, *Das Afrika-Engagement der DDR*, p. 134. For figures for 1960, 1965, 1970 and 1975–9 for East European states other than the GDR see, Siegfried Kupper, 'Die europäischen Bündnispartner der Sowjetunion und die Entwicklungsländer', *DA*, vol. 14, 7 (1981), p. 749, referring to various East European sources and West German computations. All non-official GDR figures for 1980–7 have been calculated by the author from, *International Trade 1987–1988 – General Agreement on Tariffs and Trade*, vol. 2 (Geneva; GATT, 1988), Table AA4, Appendix II.

states wished to pursue by placing those states firmly in the Soviet camp. The newly independent African states were concerned with securing their own recognition in the international system. The diplomatic recognition of the GDR would have imperilled their international standing.

In 1957 East German officials may have hoped that by establishing diplomatic relations with Yugoslavia other non-aligned states such as Egypt would immediately follow Belgrade's example. Certainly, Bonn had feared such developments.[39] However, at the first conference of non-aligned states in Belgrade in September 1961, East German officials were refused admission to observe the conference proceedings. Different viewpoints on the German question – ranging from such proposals as Egypt's appeal for a negotiated settlement, Ghana's demand for a recognition of two German states, and Ethiopia's call for immediate reunification – resulted in no conclusive final conference statement on the German issue.[40]

Commentators in the GDR attempted to evaluate the Belgrade proceedings more positively. In particular, Ghana's demand was depicted as a serious blow struck against the operation of the Hallstein Doctrine.[41]

Three years later an East German delegation was allowed to attend the second conference of non-aligned states in Cairo. Struggling to report conference proposals that favoured the GDR, one East German commentator could only write that the participants had recognised the need to solve the problem of divided nations by peaceful means without outside interference.[42] In fact, President Kwame Nkrumah of Ghana, retreating from his previous position in Belgrade, now emphasised the importance of national self-determination for the German people. His foreign minister, Kojo Botsio, later asserted that GDR recognition would have 'unduly upset our trading relationships', as well as 'burned the fingers' of Ghana in European politics.[43]

The failure to secure diplomatic recognition in Africa before 1969 – with the exception, temporarily, of Zanzibar – indicates that the GDR encountered unsurmountable difficulties in overcoming the Hallstein Doctrine. Several reasons for this failure have already been proposed. Also, the USSR was generally unable to press African states to recognise the GDR on account of Moscow's own specific problems in establishing a presence in Africa when confronted with traditional Western economic, political and military influence throughout the continent, and competition with Beijing following the repercussions of the Sino-Soviet split.

However, although the Hallstein Doctrine remained intact, the GDR endeavoured to initiate or maintain relations with African states at various levels in order to circumvent the Hallstein Doctrine, or, at least, partially compensate for not establishing full diplomatic relations.

Attempts to secure recognition

Clearly, the securing of diplomatic recognition was the primary objective of East German foreign policy in Africa prior to the early 1970s. Recognition would effectively squash repeated Western accusations that the so-called 'Soviet Zone' was merely an appendage of the USSR. In their quest for recognition the East German authorities automatically pursued a strategy of affiliation with the USSR in Africa. East German attempts to render redundant the Hallstein Doctrine by denouncing West German 'neo-colonialist' policies complemented Moscow's ambitions to acquire influence in the Third World by discrediting Western involvement in Africa. As already observed in the trade and payments agreement concluded between the GDR and Egypt in 1953, the USSR was willing to sanction East German initiatives in Africa which would further Soviet interests and also demonstrate the autonomous nature of East German activities on the continent.

In spite of the failure to secure general diplomatic recognition, the GDR was actively engaged in Africa throughout the 1950s and 1960s, with the development of consular relations and the establishment of trade missions in several African states. Moreover, in this period, in the endeavour to obtain diplomatic recognition, the GDR initiated and expanded ties with African regimes by other means. Links were also cultivated – including with national liberation movements – in the hope of harvesting potential rich rewards after diplomatic recognition was secured and the Hallstein Doctrine had ceased to function. Although the most pressing and immediate aim was recognition, East German officials were clearly aware of possible longer-term benefits that could emerge as a result of their condemnation of neo-colonialism and support of national and social liberation in Africa.

Rundfunkpropaganda (radio propaganda) was one vehicle through which the GDR communicated with African governments and peoples. Within the Warsaw Pact only Moscow's transmissions could compare with Radio Berlin International. Inter-German rivalry in overseas broadcasting provided an incentive to improve the GDR's international radio service. *Adressendiplomatie* was another medium employed, where the GDR's messages of greeting, sympathy, congratulations, etc., to African states were reported in the East German national press. East Berlin's recognition of African states' independence was one illustration of this policy. The GDR hoped to provoke a similar awareness among African people of the East German desire to secure recognition.[44]

Both *Rundfunkpropaganda* and *Adressendiplomatie* were aimed at audiences in Africa and in the GDR. The East German public was encouraged to believe that their state pursued an energetic policy abroad.

Gifts of solidarity were another means of initiating contact, although in this instance East German officials were received by African representatives. Medicine, clothes, food and agricultural equipment were distributed, often at times of national disaster, and occasionally to states with which the GDR had little or no contact. As well as being motivated by humanitarian concern, solidarity donations also enabled the East Germans to gain popular support in Africa.

Contacts also originated through the activities of East German trade unionists, journalists, youth officials, church groups etc., in Africa. Further meetings and exchange visits could prompt East German state delegations to travel to the country in question to commence negotiations on such issues as trade and aid. African commercial groups would then be invited to attend the bi-annual Leipzig trade fair. A trade agreement at official level could ensue, followed by the establishment of a permanent GDR trade mission in the African state. Beforehand, East German technical advisers and experts may have been invited to prospect for possible aid projects in the receiving state. After the founding of an East German trade mission, further contacts at trade union, youth, cultural and party level, *inter alia*, could be employed to consolidate the GDR presence.

In the above sequence the role of the so-called international front organisations should not be overlooked. Bodies such as the International Union of Students (IUS), the World Federation of Democratic Youth (WFDY) and the World Federation of Trade Unions (WFTU), among others, were closely affiliated with the Soviet bloc. These were connected with Soviet-influenced Afro-Asian and later Pan-African Federations of youth, trade unions, women, workers etc. A West German official publication of 1971 connected a number of SED-controlled bodies with the international front organisations, including the (East) German Journalist Union (Verband der Deutschen Journalisten – VDJ), the Free German Trade Union Federation (Freier Deutscher Gewerkschaftsbund – FDGB), and the Free German Youth (Freie Deutsche Jugend – FDJ).[45] Utilising these connections, the GDR was able to exploit numerous channels of communication with African officials, and take advantage of the Soviet bloc's dominance within the international front organisations.

For example, in the WFTU's competition with the Western-sponsored International Confederation of Free Trade Unions (ICFTU) for influence in African trade unionism, the FDGB played an important role which Moscow must have further encouraged. The intention was to infiltrate African trade union cadres to mould revolutionary elements sympathetic to the GDR (and the Soviet bloc). This objective was advanced by the foundation of trade union cadre training institutions in the GDR and in Africa. By 1960, major trade union schools operated by the FDGB at the Fritz Heckert University in Bernau, and the seminary for overseas trade unionists at the FDGB institute at Leipzig-Leutzsch were running courses for African labour leaders. And in Guinea, the FDGB established close relations with the trade union institutes at Dalaba and at the Université Ouvrière Africaine in Conakry (modelled on the Fritz Heckert University), where trade union students from throughout Africa attended.[46]

The FDGB proved an important ambassador for the GDR in Africa. Bonn's concern was manifested by a campaign of the (West) German Trade Union Federation to improve relations with African trade unions, embarked upon in August 1960 at the request of the ICFTU.[47]

Similarly, contacts with African journalists were also established through training programmes, delegation visits and cooperation agreements concluded by the VDJ. Prior to December 1966 the VDJ negotiated agreements with the journalists' unions of Nigeria (1964), Tanzania (1966) and Egypt (1966), and the GDR news agency, Allgemeiner Deutscher Nachrichtendienst (ADN) established official contacts with its counterparts in Dahomey (later Benin, 1963), Algeria (1963), Morocco (1966), and Mali (1966).[48] The importance of these links as a means of further influencing African elites was obvious.

The indoctrination of Africa's future political elite was part of a longer-term strategy to secure influence on the continent. Exploiting contacts with the WFDY and the IUS, the FDJ, for instance, in 1960 organised a special African course concerned with the role of youth in the ideological struggle at their high school in Bogensee, the Wilhelm Pieck Youth College. After 1961 youth cadre training in the

GDR was supplemented by similar courses operating in Africa as part of cultural agreements concluded with individual states.[49]

The importance of the FDJ's role in Africa was reinforced in 1964 when the first FDJ Friendship Brigades arrived in Algeria and Mali to develop construction projects and youth training schemes. However, before 1970, the activities of these brigades were confined to states in which the GDR had previously acquired official contacts: namely, Ghana, Guinea, Tanzania as well as Algeria and Mali.

In the cultural field the GDR–Arab Society (Gesellschaft DDR–Arabische Länder) founded in 1958, the GDR–Africa Society (Gesellschaft DDR–Afrika) founded in 1961, and the League for People's Friendship (Liga für Völkerfreundschaft) established in 1961, initiated contacts abroad. Official cultural agreements might ensue. Cultural activities were used as a means to denigrate the FRG's role in Africa. The East German Herder and West German Goethe Institutes were fierce rivals. However, by 1970 the FRG had established eighteen cultural institutions in Africa in comparison to the GDR's four.[50]

The Secretary-General of the Christian Democratic Union (Christlich–Demokratische Union – CDU) of the GDR, Gerald Götting, cultivated relations with African Christians. Götting would have received a less hostile reception in more 'conservative' African states than delegations led by SED officials. In 1960 alone Götting headed delegations to Senegal, Liberia, Togo, Dahomey, Nigeria, Cameroon, Gabon, Guinea and Ghana.[51] On these occasions the CDU leader emphasised to African officials the constructive role of East German Christians in the development of socialism in the GDR. Götting was received by both church and state officials on his African tours. He also exploited his personal contacts with the Albert Schweitzer mission in Lamborene (Gabon) in order to associate the GDR with Schweitzer's international reputation.[52]

Other non-SED officials played a prominent role in the GDR's activities in Africa in the pre-recognition period. Ernst Scholz, Chairman of the Democratic Farmers' Party of Germany (Demokratische Bauernpartei Deutschlands – DBD), and Rudolph Schulze (CDU), were Presidents of the GDR–Arab Society and the GDR–Africa Society respectively.

When the GDR's relations with a particular state flourished – albeit short of diplomatic recognition – these were intensified through the SED concluding agreements or developing official contacts with ruling African parties. As early as September 1959 an official SED delegation led by Alfred Kurella attended the 5th Party Congress of the Parti

Démocratique de Guinée in Conakry. Kurella also held discussions with delegations from other African states, including officials of Nkrumah's Convention People's Party (CPP).[53] The SED–CPP agreement in March 1965 was the culmination of extensive inter-party contacts.[54] In October 1967 the Politbüro member, Hermann Matern, headed an SED delegation to Cairo to exchange views with the Arab Socialist Union (ASU).[55] However, the overthrow of Nkrumah and the dissolution of the CPP in 1966 demonstrated the dependence of even the closest party relationships on the oscillating nature of African politics.

Hence, in the quest for recognition, East German contacts with African states were developed across a broad spectrum. Inter-German rivalry was invariably evident, and usually Bonn's involvement in Africa was more impressive in statistical terms. For instance, according to one statistical compilation, in 1965 the GDR had despatched to the Third World only 800 experts in various fields compared to 2,560 provided by the FRG. By 1971 over 3,000 scholarships were offered to students from the developing countries to study in the GDR. The FRG had received 10,588 students and apprentices from the developing world in 1965 alone.[56]

However, the GDR, with the support of Soviet-dominated international front organisations, could compete successfully with the FRG in such key areas as trade union activity and journalism. Nevertheless, full diplomatic recognition remained elusive in spite of the USSR upgrading its interest and involvement in Africa after 1956 in order to acquire influence at Western expense.

East German officials must have hoped to profit from Khrushchev's revised assessment of the Third World following his speech in February 1956 to the 20th CPSU Congress. The status of the developing world was elevated to form part of a 'Peace Zone' in which socialist and non-socialist European and non-European states formed an increasingly powerful counterforce to Western imperialism. The rehabilitation of the national bourgeoisie as an important dynamic in the revolutionary process worthy of support was confirmed. Also, the possibility of a peaceful parliamentary road to socialism was stressed under the rubric of peaceful coexistence. Three years later the 21st CPSU Congress underlined the importance of supporting movements of national liberation in the Third World.

In the 1960s Khrushchev further re-evaluated developments in Africa as a considerable number of states became independent. First, the concept of 'National Democracy' was introduced to depict certain progressive developing states. A broad national front of workers, peasants, national bourgeoisie, intelligentsia and communists was seen as necessary to carry out specific tasks essential for the construction of socialism. By 1963, encouraged by the success of the bourgeois nationalist leader, now self-declared Marxist–Leninist, Fidel Castro, in Cuba, Khrushchev spoke of revolutionary democratic statesmen in certain African states who were consciously pursuing a path of non-capitalist development. Khrushchev's increasing rapport with Nkrumah, Nasser, Ahmed Ben Bella of Algeria, Sekou Touré of Guinea and Modibo Keita of Mali was thereby vindicated. But with Khrushchev's removal from power in 1964, and the rapid demise of Ben Bella, Nkrumah and Keita, the Kremlin downgraded the importance of revolutionary developments in Africa, although the value of a non-capitalist path of development was maintained.

In line with these ideological reassessments, the USSR expanded its contacts in Africa with the more 'progressive' states such as Egypt, Algeria, Guinea, Ghana and Mali. The hostile international reaction to British, French and Israeli aggression at Suez in 1956 must also have encouraged Moscow to extend its interest in the Third World.

Thus, after 1956 East German involvement in Africa received official ideological sanction. Within the enlarged concept of peaceful coexistence the GDR could seek to establish relations with governments of all African states (with the exception of 'racist' South Africa, and, later, Rhodesia). The need to encourage the development of revolutionary forces and national liberation movements provided other compelling ideological motives for concerted East German involvement in the Third World. Nevertheless, the precocious nature of earlier GDR activity in Africa in both ideological and practical terms of reference must not be overlooked. It should be noted that in his 1956 speech, Khrushchev's 'Peace Zone' embraced only non-socialist Asian and European states and excluded Africa.[57]

Employing these ideological criteria East German officials emphasised their support for the anti-imperialist struggle in the Third World while attacking the FRG's policy of militarism and economic monopoly. The more ideologically 'progressive' African states, flattered by Soviet blandishments, were willing to develop relations with the Soviet bloc including the GDR. However, there is no clear evidence of the USSR attempting to force such African states to recognise the GDR diplomatically. As indicated briefly earlier, in spite of the USSR's enhanced involvement in Africa under Khrushchev, Moscow lacked the political and economic clout to pressure states to relinquish contacts with the West or diverge from the path of non-alignment. The USSR's failure to match rhetoric with deeds in the Congo crisis of 1960, which led to the collapse of the regime of Soviet-supported Patrice Lumumba, was one example of Moscow's impotence due to the inability to project Soviet power overseas at that time. In the immediate post-Khrushchev era Soviet economic aid to Africa (excluding Egypt) declined appreciably as Moscow's initial optimism concerning developments in the Third World receded. Africa's downgrading in importance in the perceptions of the Kremlin did not facilitate the GDR's quest for recognition. Moscow's reduced commitment to Africa was, in part, surprising, since the USSR was beginning to face increasing competition from Beijing in the Third World as a consequence of the Sino-Soviet rift.

The affiliation strategy with the USSR actually operated to the GDR's disadvantage in Africa where Beijing was able to secure increased influence at Moscow's expense. The problem was a serious one for the SED since Premier Zhou Enlai's African tour in December 1963 to February 1964 (to Egypt, Algeria, Morocco, Tunisia, Ghana, Mali, Guinea, Sudan, Ethiopia and Somalia) demonstrated that China was attempting to acquire leverage over the same 'progressive' states with which the GDR hoped to secure diplomatic recognition. The Chinese won popularity through their small-scale labour-intensive projects which were of more immediate relevance to the impoverished, rural states of sub-Saharan Africa than the USSR's larger and more capital intensive undertakings. Moreover, the Chinese were able to secure sympathy in certain quarters by their appeal to common Afro-Asian ties (dating from Bandung) in an effort to curtail Soviet and East European influence in Africa – although after 1967 a frustrated China withdrew from the Afro-Asian People's Solidarity Organisation Secretariat after the USSR had prevented the organisation convening in Beijing as was originally scheduled. By December 1966, China, in competition with Taiwan in another quest for diplomatic recognition, had established diplomatic relations with fourteen African states. The GDR's abysmal failure to establish and preserve diplomatic relations with African states before 1969 was in stark contrast. East Berlin was unable to exploit fully certain developments in Africa in this period and secure full diplomatic recognition.

Immediately prior to the Suez crisis rumours already circulated that Nasser had threatened to recognise the GDR on 4 April 1956 after diplomatic relations between the FRG and Israel appeared imminent with the establishment of a West German diplomatic mission on Israeli territory.[58] Until 1965 the FRG refrained from establishing full diplomatic relations with Israel through fear of provoking Arab states to grant the GDR full diplomatic recognition as a reprisal. Seeking Nasser's further support, the East German government's declaration on 10 August 1956 approved of his decision to nationalise the Suez Canal as an expression of Egyptian sovereign independence.[59] Failing to secure admission to the London conference (on the basis of the previous signature of a then united 'Germany' to the 1888 Suez Canal Convention) which discussed how to react to Nasser's unilateral action, Ulbricht condemned the FRG's participation as another instance of Bonn's alignment with the imperialist powers.[60] When Israeli troops intensified the crisis by launching an attack on the Canal Zone, before British and French military intervention, the East German authorities proclaimed solidarity with the Egyptian people and accused the West Germans of supporting the expansion of Israeli armed forces in recent years via the terms of the reparations agreement.[61]

Despite this sequence of events Nasser still refused to accord the GDR diplomatic recognition through fear of offending the FRG, which was becoming an important source of development assistance for the Egyptian economy. In 1958, in a further effort to challenge West German influence, the GDR granted Egypt two 'long-term' loans (the first offered by the GDR to an African state), to promote Nasser's programme of industrialisation.[62] Nasser finally rewarded the GDR by first allowing the establishment of an Egyptian trade mission in East Berlin, and then inviting the East German Premier Grotewohl to Cairo in January 1959. During Grotewohl's only visit to an African state it was agreed that the East German trade mission in the Egyptian capital should be elevated to the status of a consulate-general.[63] Thus, the GDR secured further international recognition, albeit short of full diplomatic relations, at the expense of the Hallstein Doctrine, and, Bonn responded by withdrawing support for the Aswan Dam. West German suspension of diplomatic relations with Yugoslavia in 1957 after Belgrade's full recognition of the GDR must have warned Nasser that the Hallstein Doctrine would most likely also be fully implemented if Egypt chose to recognise the GDR diplomatically. Hence, a cautious Nasser neither accorded the East German consul-general the customary privileges, nor promised to open an Egyptian consulate-general in East Berlin.

Did the USSR pressure Nasser to accord the GDR further recognition? No clear evidence is available. According to one West German report, in early 1958 the USSR and East European states had instructed their diplomatic missions in the Middle East to press for full recognition of the GDR.[64] But relations between Cairo and Moscow had deteriorated by January 1959 after Nasser launched an anti-communist purge. The fact that Grotewohl's successful mission proceeded in such circumstances appears to have indicated the USSR's toleration of East German autonomous foreign policy in Africa in order to secure recognition, although Moscow must have appreciated the visit's value in preserving Egypt's relations with the Soviet bloc. Grotewohl's reception also revealed that Nasser regarded East Berlin as not totally dependent on the Kremlin.

Elsewhere in North Africa East German relations were consolidated, assisted by the stationing of a special plenipotentiary (initially Ernst Scholz) in Cairo, in 1956, responsible for the Arab world and Africa.[65] After an East German trade mission was established in Khartoum only days after Sudanese independence, the Deputy Prime Minister of Sudan, Ibrahim el Mufti, became the first prominent African politician to visit East Berlin, in May 1956, as relations between the GDR and the Sudan strengthened.[66]

Numerous Soviet credits and earlier support in the war for Algerian liberation may have prompted Ben Bella to permit the opening of an East German trade mission in Algiers in April 1963, but the GDR failed to obtain closer ties. According to the GDR's Ministry of Foreign Affairs, in a statement on 1 November 1960, in the war the East Germans (obviously hoping for diplomatic recognition) supported the National Liberation Front (Front National de la Libération – FLN) with gifts of 'solidarity', hospital treatment for wounded freedom fighters, and provision for the training of Algerian students and workers in the GDR.[67] However, in line with Moscow, which sought to avoid an open confrontation with General Charles de Gaulle to encourage his increasing independence from the rest of the West, East Berlin had not endeavoured to procure recognition by providing military aid to the FLN. Despite Ben Bella's ties with the USSR, Bonn apparently thwarted the GDR's attempts to open a consulate-general in Algiers in 1964. It seem that the FRG checked East German ambitions by offering the Algerians more substantial credits (DM 74 million) than the GDR was able to offer.[68]

From 1958 onwards the GDR developed links with sub-Saharan Africa. As in North Africa, relations were initiated and furthered with states more well-disposed to the USSR. With Guinea, Mali and Ghana, in particular, delegation exchanges, trade agreements and cultural ties were promoted, and trade missions exchanged.

Immediately after a Western economic boycott was organised in sympathy with French fury over Sekou Touré's refusal to join the proposed French Commonwealth of African States, independent Guinea concluded its first international treaty with a trade and cultural agreement negotiated with the GDR on 17 November 1958. A Protocol also empowered the GDR and Guinea to open trade missions with consular rights in their capitals.[69] However, as in the cases of Egypt, Mali and Ghana upon the conclusion of similar agreements, and most probably through a reluctance to antagonise the FRG, Guinea refrained from opening a trade mission in East Berlin for several years. The West Germans were engaged in extensive trade and offered substantial loans to these 'progressive' African states. By contrast, East German commercial relations with the African continent were insignificant. According to official East German statistics, a large percentage of GDR trade remained concentrated on Egypt, with only Ghana and Guinea occasionally topping VM20 million in annual trade turnover until the late 1960s (see Table 2.).

Ghana was an important state for Ulbricht to target in the quest for recognition. Under Nkrumah's leadership Accra became a major centre of the pan-Africanist movement and later a focus for 'anti-imperialist' subversion throughout the continent. Soviet economic and military support for the Nkrumah regime must have encouraged the GDR to hope that recognition was possible. And these hopes must have been raised when Nkrumah himself visited East Berlin in August 1961 as part of an East European tour. This marked the first visit to the GDR by an African leader, although it was hastily arranged and not originally included in Nkrumah's itinerary. However, through fear of offending the FRG, when Bonn was considering offering a loan for the construction of a second bridge over the Volta, the Nkrumah visit was not designated 'official', and neither Ulbricht nor Grotewohl received the African head of state.[70]

Significantly, when Ghana eventually despatched an official trade representation to East Berlin in September 1963 in accordance with an agreement four years earlier, Bonn's Foreign Minister, Gerhard Schröder, swiftly reacted by upbraiding Kojo Botsio, his counterpart in Accra.[71]

The coup that deposed Nkrumah on 24 February 1966 underlined the fragility of the GDR's relations with African leaderships, regardless of the duration and intensity of previous contacts (a coup against the Keita regime in Mali in November 1968 re-emphasised this point). In March 1966 the new regime in Accra, the National Liberation

Table 2. East German imports, exports and trade turnover with African states and selected oil exporting states, 1960–1987 VM (million)

	1960			1965			1970			1973			1974		
	Exp	Imp	Total	Exp	Imp	Total	Exp	Imp	Total	Exp	Imp	Total	Exp	Imp	Total
Algeria	0.2	0.2	0.4	1.7		1.7	20.0	3.1	23.1	76.3	0.5	76.8	57.4	23.7	81.1
Angola															
Congo PR	1.0	1.8	2.8	0.2		0.2	0.3		0.3	1.8		1.8	0.8		0.8
Egypt	131.6	130.1	261.7	129.2	105.7	234.9	199.6	190.1	389.7	291.4	151.9	443.3	394.0	232.7	626.7
Ethiopia	0.3		0.3	0.4		0.4			0.6			0.4			0.4
Ghana	4.7	2.3	7.0	36.7	16.3	53.0			2.2			1.3			18.5
Guinea	23.2	15.2	38.4	7.8	11.1	18.9			8.9						
Libya			0.5			3.2			6.4			7.3			10.6
Morocco	5.2	5.5	10.7	5.0	4.6	9.6	8.7	11.6	20.3	4.5	16.3	20.8	7.1	34.4	41.5
Mozambique															
Nigeria			0.9	2.0	11.4	13.4			12.9			5.3			12.3
Sudan	2.9	8.2	11.1	4.4	5.5	9.9	17.1	7.9	25.0	5.5	3.4	8.9	5.9	23.1	29.0
Tanzania				2.0		2.0	3.3	3.3	6.6	0.9	9.2	10.1	0.5	3.5	4.0
Tunisia	0.2	0.1	0.3	7.6	4.1	11.7			10.3			4.8			9.3
Zambia									0.3						
Zimbabwe															
Iran	6.8	4.7	11.5	11.8	9.1	20.9	9.0	18.4	27.4	4.2	2.2	6.4	16.2	21.8	38.0
Iraq	9.3	5.4	14.7	12.7	2.0	14.7	46.4	2.3	48.7	122.5	63.6	186.1	148.1	499.9	648.0
Kuwait	0.8		0.8	2.2		2.2	8.9		8.9	10.2		10.2	27.8		27.8
Mexico	2.6	0.2	2.8	2.5	0.5	3.0	11.7	2.1	13.8	13.6	11.4	25.0	18.1	16.6	34.7
Syria	6.6	7.3	13.9	12.3	3.3	15.6	50.2	16.8	67.0	80.8	17.8	98.6	89.6	75.0	164.6

Table 2 (*continued*)

	1975 Total	1976 Total	1977 Total	1978 Total	1979 Total	1980 Total	1981 Total	1982 Total	1983 Total	1984 Total	1985 Total	1986 Total	1987 Total
Algeria	72.9	120.3	101.3	324.0	247.4	538.9	249.7	463.7	308.9	296.9	743.7	355.8	177.0
Angola			236.0	233.7	311.6	275.0	198.5	264.3	255.2	797.8	844.0	428.4	171.9
Congo PR	0.1	8.0	3.8	1.0	0.4	3.6	14.2	28.6	11.9	6.8	5.0	5.2	3.7
Egypt	639.6	559.2	546.3	442.2	520.7	306.8	295.0	342.7	334.2	650.4	689.0	714.0	465.1
Ethiopia	0.2	0.2	278.2	316.5	63.3	132.3	62.4	129.1	193.9	93.7	112.0	94.7	93.6
Ghana	13.7	9.1	17.7	15.5	4.7	49.5	46.4	74.7	115.7	112.5	189.8	236.8	263.2
Guinea	6.6					3.8			32.2	25.2	8.5	17.2	13.2
Libya	12.1	63.3	84.8	13.3	54.7	502.0	494.7	260.4	126.8	93.0	75.1	54.2	55.9
Morocco	48.6	37.6	47.1	71.2	52.0	61.4	39.5	38.6	48.5	38.3	60.7	91.6	67.3
Mozambique			24.9	130.5	227.3	274.5	368.0	411.8	222.7	109.0	93.9	66.8	78.4
Nigeria	3.3	19.4	19.3	14.4	31.3	47.5	148.3	137.9	14.6	9.5	13.2	74.8	4.0
Sudan	33.3	47.7	51.3	46.1	42.5	26.7	6.2	16.0	79.3	96.8	36.6	93.8	45.8
Tanzania	6.3	2.2	2.0	2.0	7.4	49.1	3.5	2.6	2.4	2.9	0.6	0.5	0.6
Tunisia	13.4	15.4	29.2	25.3	44.1	60.7	15.1	9.1	12.6	31.1	16.6	24.9	35.2
Zambia	0.1					95.5			33.8	33.7	31.7	104.6	68.8
Zimbabwe								0.5	37.4	53.8	106.6	62.1	29.8
Iran	62.1	96.9	120.8	159.5	156.0	548.2	608.4	1,210.5	1,733.8	1,710.7	1,181.5	475.9	593.3
Iraq	764.2	779.0	595.0	724.7	912.3	1,502.4	712.7	1,923.7	1,958.6	1,195.8	1,129.9	1,000.8	766.3
Kuwait	31.0	39.7	42.6	38.0	29.3	35.8	38.5	67.1	33.9	17.9	34.8	35.7	15.7
Mexico	35.8	33.9	44.2	49.6	87.9	210.7	263.1	147.6	95.0	53.1	50.0	20.2	34.8
Syria	211.2	348.6	344.4	405.7	436.6	388.3	429.8	571.9	651.6	330.9	326.4	331.7	309.9

Source: Statistisches Jahrbuch (various years).

Council, instructed the East German trade mission to cease operations and ordered the closure of Ghana's mission in East Berlin. The East German authorities protested that these actions were unwarranted.[72] There then followed the 'Krüger affair' when an East German espionage agent based in Accra, Kurt Krüger, was interned by the National Liberation Council. West German involvement was possible.[73] According to a statement released by the Ministry of Information in Accra on 25 May 1966, Krüger was released in exchange for 350 Ghanaian students and the staff of Ghana's trade mission who had been held hostage in East Berlin over the previous weeks.[74] This episode exposed one of the first instances of East German involvement in the security arrangements of an African state.

It was not the failure to exploit opportunities to discredit West German operations in Africa which prevented the East Germans from securing diplomatic recognition. For example, in the declaration by the East German Ministry of Foreign Affairs on 1 November 1960, it was stated that between 1955 and 1960 over 35,000 West German mercenaries, and more than 8,500 West German youth serving as foreign legionaries, together with veteran Nazi officers and soldiers, were employed against the Algerian liberation fighters. Moreover, the declaration noted that, interested in Algerian oil reserves, West German sources had provided in excess of DM 3,000 million to finance the French war effort in this period.[75]

In July 1957, the Soviet Institute of World Economy and International Relations released a report, later known as the 'Seventeen Theses' or the so-called 'Eurafrica project'. This stated *inter alia* that the FRG, in alliance with France, would take advantage of the newly established European Economic Community (EEC) and that organisation's association and special relations with the colonies to expand West German economic exploitation of Africa and circumvent previous international agreements to acquire atomic weapons under the Euratom scheme. In line with the 'Seventeen Theses', as early as 10 April 1957 the GDR's Ministry of Foreign Affairs had denounced the FRG's contribution to the EEC's European Development Fund (EDF) for offering West German 'monopolists' innumerable possibilities to exploit further colonial territories.[76] Although East Berlin did not refer directly to the West German–French connection through Euratom, Bonn's financial support and research in the development of the French 'Sahara Bomb' was condemned in order to generate further African support.[77]

Throughout the 1960s the East German propaganda campaign

against the FRG in Africa was intensified. In a declaration of the GDR's Ministry of Foreign Affairs on 15 July 1960, West German 'monopolists' were accused of supporting Katangan separatists in the struggle for power in the Congo. Bonn's decision to place West German airports and military facilities at NATO's disposal to intervene in the Congo was censured. On 14 April 1961 the ministry condemned West German military and financial aid employed against the pro-Soviet regime installed in Stanleyville in the Congo. Bonn's delivery of 10,000 machine guns to Portugal to assist in the suppression of the 'Angolan people's liberation struggle' was publicised in an East German memorandum to the UN General Assembly on 28 September 1961. The GDR's Ministry of Foreign Affairs, on 25 March 1960, denounced West German political support for the South African 'apartheid regime' after the Sharpeville massacre. In September 1964, revelations of nuclear cooperation between Pretoria and Bonn were published in a text by the East German Afro-Asian Solidarity Committee. ADN announced on 21 December 1965 that while the FRG continued to develop relations with Rhodesia following its unilateral declaration of independence, the GDR had suspended all economic relations with the 'racist' regime of Ian Smith in line with UN resolutions. The East German government on 12 November 1963 had similarly announced that trade with South Africa was suspended in accordance with the resolutions of the Conference of African Heads of State and Government that met in Addis Ababa in May 1963.[78]

This torrent of invective appeared to impress certain African national liberation movements. Solidarity with these movements was emphasised to influence groups which the GDR hoped were destined to lead future independent states, and also to make a positive impact on already established African regimes. Hence Amilcar Cabral, leader of the African Party of Independence for Guinea and Cape Verde (Partido Africano de Independência da Guiné e do Cabo Verde – PAIGC), a guerrilla movement based in Portuguese Guinea, had allowed his cadres to be trained in the GDR before 1960.[79] Cabral's opinion of the two Germanies was succinctly expressed to East German journalists: 'It is a fact, which is for us most important, that the GDR offers our freedom struggle full sympathy and solidarity. West Germany's role, with NATO support, for the tottering Salazar dictatorship has become clear to us.'[80]

Likewise, Uria T. Simango, Vice-President of the Liberation Front of Mozambique (Frente de Libertação de Moçambique – FRELIMO) when visiting East Berlin in 1963, attacked West German military and financial support for the regime of Antonio de Oliveira Salazar in Portugal.[81]

Significantly, in 1961, in the East German journal, *Deutsche Aussen-politik*, the GDR was the first state in the Soviet bloc to publish the statutes of the Popular Movement for the Liberation of Angola (Movimento Popular de Libertação de Angola – MPLA).[82] However, the Portuguese colonies only acquired independence a decade later.

In spite of this incitement of feeling against West Germany, the construction of the Berlin Wall in August 1961 undoubtedly damaged the GDR's image in Africa. Ulbricht was compelled to despatch special envoys to Gabon, Mali and Guinea (Götting), Ethiopia (Wolfgang Kiesewetter, then the East German plenipotentiary based in Cairo), Egypt (Ernst Scholz), and to other non-aligned states to explain the purpose of the Wall's construction.[83] According to one East German commentary, the Council of State of the GDR reported, on 7 September 1961, that the envoys had secured 'great understanding' with regard to this new development in the German question[84] – a statement suggesting at most only lukewarm support. However, the FRG clearly obtained a further propaganda victory in the more Western-oriented African regimes.

Elsewhere in Africa the GDR suffered other reversals. In September 1964 an initial agreement concluded in Cotonou to establish trade missions in Dahomey and the GDR failed to materialise.[85] East German relations previously cultivated with Jomo Kenyatta rapidly deteriorated after Kenyan independence.[86] Particularly damaging to East German prestige in Africa were events in the then Congo-Leopoldville (later Zaire). On 21 September 1961 the East German *chargé d'affaires* in Stanleyville, who had recognised the secessionist regime of Antoine Gizenga, was expelled by the Cyrille Adoula government based in Leopoldville. The USSR, which had also recognised Gizenga, was able to maintain representation in Leopoldville.[87] The Adoula government perceived that the need to continue relations with the USSR was by no means comparable with maintaining contacts with the ostracised GDR. Consequently, in February 1963, three East German representatives who had sought to participate in a session of the UN Economic Commission in Leopoldville were arrested and then expelled.[88]

In three specific instances in this period, the GDR's hopes of securing full diplomatic recognition were temporarily raised – and, indeed, in the example of Zanzibar, and possibly Guinea, momentarily achieved – before being ultimately frustrated.

After independence in 1958 Sekou Touré's Guinea was courted extensively by the Soviet bloc, including the GDR, although Conakry maintained links with the West and benefited from trade and investment ties with Bonn. There was nothing exceptional in the activities of the Touré regime. Yet, dramatically, it was announced on 6 March 1960 that Guinea had established diplomatic relations with the GDR.

Under the headline, 'Diplomatic Relations GDR – Republic of Guinea', *Neues Deutschland* reported that on 5 March the East German President, Wilhelm Pieck, received the newly appointed ambassador of Guinea to the GDR, Dr Seydou Conté (then Guinea's ambassador in Moscow). Conté handed over his letter of credentials to Pieck and in his ceremonial speech spoke of Touré's 'deep gratitude' to the East German government and people for their past support. Conté referred to himself as the first accredited ambassador of Guinea to the GDR. The report also added that the GDR's ambassador to Guinea, Klaus Nohr, had been already despatched to Conakry.[89] Conté's official reception by Pieck was recorded on East German television.[90] In the following days the East German press eagerly provided details of Conté's activities in the GDR.

The West German reaction was one of vacillation. Having held discussions with its ambassador, recalled from Conakry, and with Guinea's ambassador to France and the FRG, Bonn issued an ultimatum on 9 March which called upon Touré to explain the purpose and activities of Conté's mission in East Berlin. Failing a satisfactory response, Foreign Minister von Brentano was empowered to suspend diplomatic relations with Guinea.[91]

In an interview with *Der Spiegel*, on 10 March, Touré explained that the Conté mission was limited to discussing the possibility of a future exchange of ambassadors between Guinea and the GDR in order to facilitate the work of the East German official representation in Conakry. Conté was also briefed to inform the East German authorities that Touré was unable to come to the GDR on an official visit which was apparently previously planned. Referring to East German misinterpretation of events, Touré continued: 'Everyone makes a mistake once, or is a victim of some indiscretion. This is especially likely with a new state without diplomatic experience.'[92]

Attempting to sway Touré, a report in *Neues Deutschland* compared the extensive East German commercial relations and assistance programmes with Guinea with the less substantial West German aid and trade.[93] The implication was obvious. Ostensibly, the economic development of Guinea would not suffer if the FRG suspended diplomatic and economic relations on account of the diplomatic recognition of the GDR.

Although not satisfied by Touré's account in the *Der Spiegel* interview, Bonn refrained from suspending diplomatic relations with Guinea as previously threatened. Instead, at the beginning of April, the Head of the West German Foreign Office, Hasso von Etzdorf, was despatched on a special assignment to Guinea to obtain official clarification from Touré on the precise status of relations between Guinea and the GDR. On 7 April, Touré assured von Etzdorf that no diplomatic relations between the GDR and Guinea existed. The Conté incident was attributed to a confusion between the terms *lettre de récommendation* and *lettre de créance*. Only the latter, according to diplomatic protocol, signified the according of ambassadorial status. Conté had delivered to Pieck a *letter de récommendation* which intended to improve Guinea's relations with the GDR. This explanation satisfied von Brentano.[94]

Conté had returned to Guinea several days prior to von Etzdorf's meeting with Touré. By the end of April the GDR's 'ambassador', Nohr, had apparently secretly arrived back in East Berlin having been virtually imprisoned in a secluded villa somewhere in Guinea after Touré had refused to see him.[95]

After initial comprehensive reports the East German press suddenly ceased to refer to Conté's activities in the GDR. Most significantly, on 6 April, an article in *Neues Deutschland* listing details of East German commercial, youth and trade union contacts with Guinea omitted reference to diplomatic relations.

Had Touré decided originally to grant the GDR full diplomatic recognition only to be surprised by the force of West German opposition? Or did Conté, with East German incitement, exceed his brief? To attribute the incident to a series of misunderstandings and breakdowns in communication appears difficult to believe. The most plausible explanation was that Touré had intended to test West German resolve to determine whether diplomatic recognition of the GDR was possible without reprisal from Bonn. Touré would have wished to continue to secure economic aid from both East and West. This would account for Touré's delaying tactics throughout March– Conté was not immediately recalled, for instance – once the immediate threat posed by the FRG's ultimatum was counteracted by ambiguous statements from Conakry. When it became obvious that the FRG would suspend diplomatic relations, and most probably curtail economic support, Touré finally retreated, unwilling to become dependent on the Soviet bloc alone. The West German threat to implement the Hallstein Doctrine had alone proved sufficient to deter Touré's official sanctioning of Conté's actions of 5 March, and the GDR's quest for diplomatic recognition had suffered a serious reversal.

Only a month after independence, Zanzibar's Sultan was deposed by a group of 'revolutionary' army officers, on 12 January 1964, and six days later a People's Republic of Zanzibar was proclaimed. On 29 January, the Zanzibar Foreign Minister, Abdul Rahman Mohammed 'Babu', in a telegram to Ulbricht, announced Zanzibar's recognition of the East German government.[96] Apparently, Soviet and Chinese representatives in Zanzibar – in spite of the developing Sino-Soviet conflict – had encouraged the fledgling revolutionary government on the island to recognise the GDR.[97]

Although aware of the Babu telegram Bonn recognised the new Zanzibar regime having been led to believe that the island's President, Abeid Karume, would not actually take up diplomatic relations with the GDR.[98] However, on 21 February it was announced that the authorities in Zanzibar had authorised Günther Fritsch to start his duties as 'Ambassador of the GDR in the People's Republic of Zanzibar and Pemba', although Fritsch did not deliver his letter of credentials to Karume until early March.[99] Angered by Zanzibar's action, the FRG withdrew recognition and support for the Karume regime on 24 February.

Zanzibar had chosen to ignore the possible application of the Hallstein Doctrine and granted full diplomatic recognition to the GDR. The outcome was the presence of the first East German ambassador to take up permanent residence in a recognised African state. Moreover, with the withdrawal of Western support, the embryonic revolutionary state became an ideal testing-ground for East German technical, military and economic assistance abroad. The GDR assisted in the formation of a youth brigade; provided advisers in the fields of planning, finance and banking; despatched teachers and nurses; commenced a housing project; began to develop local radio and the press; and embarked upon fishing and fruit canning projects.[100] Seventy Soviet and East German instructors arrived to train and equip the 600-man revolutionary army of Zanzibar.[101]

However, on 27 April, by an Act of Union between Tanganyika and Zanzibar, the United Republic of Tanzania was created. Under the terms of the Union, Zanzibar was allowed to maintain a separate government and legislature, but the United Republic was responsible for questions appertaining to the national interest, including the fields of defence and external affairs. As President of the new Republic, Julius Nyerere was confronted with an immediate problem over the question of German representation as the West Germans had previously established an embassy in Dar-es-Salaam on the Tanganyikan mainland opposite Zanzibar. Hence, Tanzania hosted both a West German and East German embassy in separate locations.

Nyerere was opposed to full diplomatic recognition of the GDR. In a later background paper circulated to all African heads of state Nyerere explained why Tanzania did not recognise the GDR: 'In our view normal people can be forced by victors to accept the permanent partition of their country but they are not expected to rejoice in it nor participate in upholding it.'[102]

Thus, the embassy in Zanzibar needed to be closed although Nyerere realised that Karume would insist on some form of East German representation in Zanzibar which the FRG would have to accept.

Initially Nyerere was willing to downgrade the status of the East German embassy in Zanzibar to that of a trade mission. By July 1964 he had apparently decided to allow the opening of an East German consulate-general in Dar-es-Salaam as compensation for the intended closure of the embassy in Zanzibar.

As a Vice-President of Tanzania, Karume vigorously challenged any attempt to demote the status of the GDR in Zanzibar. Karume was impressed by East German assistance in the weeks of disunity and turmoil following the January coup. It has been suggested that the USSR had opposed the Union and had urged Karume to resist Nyerere in order to maintain Soviet and East German control in Zanzibar at the expense of Union if necessary.[103] Significantly, on 17 May, a Treaty of Friendship, Mutual Assistance and Increased Cooperation was signed by Fritsch and Karume on behalf of the GDR and the United Republic respectively.[104]

Bonn reacted to these developments by initially opposing Nyerere's intention to press Karume to downgrade the East German representation in Zanzibar to the status of a trade mission, preferring rather a less official chamber of commerce. By early May, the West German authorities stated that an East German trade mission in Zanzibar would now be acceptable, although no consulate-general should be established anywhere in the Republic. This was soon modified again to allow the possibility of a consulate-general in Zanzibar with jurisdiction over the island alone. However, through apparent misinterpretation, by July Nyerere believed that Bonn would accept as a final measure an East German consulate-general without exequatur in Dar-es-Salaam. Karume's obstinacy, coupled with East German and Soviet pressure, had compelled Nyerere to seek a compromise solution that would satisfy all parties concerned. Not surprisingly, the West German ambassador in Dar-es-Salaam had immediately protested when Vice-President Karume exceeded his personal brief by signing the treaty with the GDR on 17 May.

After several months of tension both Karume and the East German government yielded to Nyerere's terms. Present in Zanzibar for several weeks in January and February 1965, the GDR's Deputy Foreign Minister, Kiesewetter, failed to secure official East German consulate representation in Dar-es-Salaam, Zanzibar and in another town to compensate for the closure of the GDR embassy. Instead, in February 1965, Nyerere agreed to the establishment of an East German consulate-general without exequatur with jurisdiction over all Tanzania. Although the location was not fixed, it was hinted that a consulate-general would be based in Zanzibar and an East German trade mission opened in Dar-es-Salaam. With this official decision to allow the establishment of an East German consulate-general, the West Germans finally reacted by withdrawing military assistance forthwith, and also threatened to terminate economic aid. Bonn, having misinterpreted Nyerere's intentions as indicated earlier, retaliated on account of the intended territorial jurisdiction of the consulate-general, although its location was still not officially announced. Infuriated at the FRG's reaction, Nyerere declared that Tanzania would refuse further development assistance from the West German government, although ongoing projects could be completed.

On 17 March 1965 the Tanzanian government officially announced that an East German consulate-general was to be opened in Dar-es-Salaam, although no exequatur was to be bestowed, and even radio communications with Berlin were to be denied. The East Germans reacted by stating that this decision was the result of successful negotiations between Kiesewetter, Nyerere and other officials, and demonstrated how the GDR did not wish to encumber non-aligned, anti-imperialist states with the problems of inter-German relations.[105] However, by June 1965, as part of a final package agreement, the GDR had officially opened in Tanzania a consulate-general in Dar-es-Salaam and a consulate in Zanzibar.

Both Germanies had suffered setbacks. The GDR had acquiesced in the closure of its only embassy in Africa at that time. The FRG had failed to limit East German representation to the status at most of trade mission in Dar-es-Salaam and consulate-general in Zanzibar.

In general, Bonn had adopted a less accommodating stance concerning East German consular representation in the Third World after 1961. Before the construction of the Wall, East German consulates-general were tolerated in Cairo, Djakarta and Rangoon with only minor reprisals. However, in 1964, West German aid was withdrawn from Ceylon (later Sri Lanka) when the GDR opened a consulate-general in Colombo.[106] By early 1965, the commotion which resulted from Nasser's insistence that Ulbricht should visit Egypt further angered Bonn and must have influenced West German behaviour with Tanzania.

In accordance with Grewe's interpretation of the Hallstein Doctrine that Bonn should employ a series of graduated reprisals against states granting the GDR further recognition, the FRG had endeavoured to prevent Nyerere permitting GDR consular representation in Dar-es-Salaam by withholding military aid. In this instance, Nyerere refused to accommodate Bonn, although full diplomatic recognition of the GDR was never intended: 'I will not recognise East Germany just because Bonn is stupid' (Nyerere).[107] Moreover, Nyerere apparently rejected an East German offer of a $25 million loan for full diplomatic recognition.[108]

The aggravation caused by this extension of *les querelles allemandes* in Africa, naturally inclined other states on the continent to avoid rekindling the German question by granting diplomatic recognition, or more recognition, to the GDR.

On 27 January 1965, *Neues Deutschland* announced an impending state visit to Egypt by Ulbricht. This would be the first visit to an African state by the East German head of state. According to Nasser's close adviser, Mohamed Heikal, Ulbricht had asked to visit Aswan for reasons of health. West German over-reaction to Nasser's approval of Ulbricht's request, on account of Bonn mistakenly linking the acceptance to Nasser's recent outrage over revelations concerning the extent of recent West German military aid to Israel, had prompted Nasser to elevate Ulbricht's informal stay of convalescence into a formal state visit.[109]

Some officials in Bonn suspected that Moscow had encouraged Nasser to extend the invitation. One West German analyst reported that a high-ranking Soviet delegation under Alexandr Shelepin, a member of the Politbüro of the CPSU, had offered further economic and military support on a visit to Cairo in December 1964 – Nasser was engaged in the Yemeni Civil War backing republican forces – on the condition that Nasser received Ulbricht.[110]

The Yugoslav leader, Josif Broz 'Tito', may also have encouraged Cairo to welcome Ulbricht. Tito and Nasser had established a close partnership within the non-aligned movement. One commentator noted, in favour of this explanation, that relations between the GDR and Yugoslavia were cordial following East German consent to the payment of reparations in 1963. Moreover, Tito allowed Ulbricht the use of airport and naval facilities when en route to Egypt.[111] But another analyst argued that Belgrade was careful to avoid encouraging the Third World to recognise the GDR: 'It would only have raised doubts about the extent of Yugoslavia's independence.'[112] However, Tito could still have encouraged Nasser to receive Ulbricht – an act which fell short of full diplomatic recognition. Soviet pressure on Nasser was also feasible.

It appears that the prolonged presence of an East German trade delegation led by Deputy Trade Minister, Gerhard Weiss (6 January to 3 February 1965), which culminated in an offer to provide industrial equipment with promises of further credit guarantees, may have facilitated negotiations concerning Ulbricht's visit.[113] Contrary to Heikal's account, East German press reports did not refer to Ulbricht's health as a pretext for Nasser's invitation.

However, in talks on 31 January 1965 with Bonn's ambassador in Cairo, Nasser explicitly linked West German arms transfers to Israel with the question of East German diplomatic recognition: 'If the arms deal with Israel continues we shall reconsider our whole position and shall definitely recognise East Germany.'[114] Confronted with this ultimatum Chancellor Ludwig Erhard retreated and on 12 February declared that all West German weapons deliveries to areas of tension were prohibited. But in an official declaration three days later the West German government stated that if the Ulbricht visit still proceeded, Bonn would respond by terminating all economic assistance to Egypt.[115]

Bonn and Cairo then commenced a series of acrimonious exchanges. Nasser threatened to establish full diplomatic relations with the GDR if economic aid provided by the West German government was suspended. It was also reported that in such circumstances Ben Bella would follow Nasser's example.[116] On 17 February, in a speech to the Bundestag, Erhard warned Nasser that anyone seeking 'closer political relations with the tyrannous (East German) regime must expect the Federal Republic to draw economic and possibly also

political consequences therefrom'.[117] Nasser's determination to continue with the visit of Ulbricht, despite Bonn's threat to curtail
economic aid and perhaps break off diplomatic relations, suggested
that Moscow had indeed promised Cairo substantial economic aid as
West German sources indicated.

Ulbricht was finally received in Egypt (24 February to 1 March 1965)
and although the GDR did not secure diplomatic recognition the SED
leader was accorded full state honours throughout the visit. The final
Joint Declaration only referred to the German question briefly,
reiterating the statement of the Cairo non-aligned conference on the
need for a peaceful, lasting solution to the problem of divided states.
Nasser added that the issue of German unity was a matter for the
German people alone to address. A series of agreements on economic
and technical cooperation, scientific–technical relations, culture, and
trade and payments was announced. More importantly, Nasser
also accepted Ulbricht's invitation to visit the GDR at a date to be
arranged.[118] In an exchange of letters on 1 March an agreement was
also concluded to open an Egyptian consulate-general in East Berlin.[119]
Significantly, the Egyptian consul-general (received in July 1965)
would be accorded full diplomatic privileges in contrast to the limited
rights conferred upon the East German consul-general in Cairo.[120]
Also, on 1 March, in accordance with earlier pledges, the GDR granted
Egypt a long-term credit of $70 million and a short-term credit of
approximately $11 million.[121]

Failing to secure diplomatic recognition, nevertheless, the GDR had
scored a major psychological victory over the FRG. Despite West
German threats of reprisal the visit had taken place, and the efficacy of
the Hallstein Doctrine called into question. *Neues Deutschland* boldly
proclaimed: 'Die Hallstein Doktrin ist bankrott', as events in Cairo
belied the FRG's claim to alone represent the German people.[122]
Although Ulbricht's visit provided ample proof that Nasser had not
intended to recognise the GDR diplomatically, the Egyptian President's expressed lack of concern over the West German threat to curtail
economic aid, and, possibly, suspend diplomatic relations, enfeebled
the Hallstein Doctrine.

Nevertheless, Bonn finally retaliated. Ulbricht's visit, in effect, had
provided the GDR with 'more' recognition, and, hence, in accordance
with Grewe's version of the Hallstein Doctrine, appropriate reprisals
should follow. Suspension of diplomatic relations with Egypt could
have impelled Nasser to grant the GDR full recognition. Thus, in an
announcement, on 7 March, the FRG retaliated by suspending future

governmental aid programmes in Egypt, reviewing current projects there (although in practice these were continued until completed), and also establishing diplomatic relations with Israel.[123] This prompted a meeting of the Arab League's foreign ministers in Cairo, on 14–15 March, where it was reported that Egypt, Iraq, Yemen, Algeria, Syria, Sudan and Kuwait were in favour of recognising the GDR because of the West German decision to open diplomatic relations with Israel.[124] But when Bonn formally established diplomatic relations with Tel Aviv, on 12 May 1965, although all Arab League member-states with the exception of Morocco, Tunisia and Libya severed diplomatic relations with the FRG, none recognised the GDR.

Heikal alleged that the need to maintain Arab unity had precluded recognition of the GDR, since the conservative Arab states (notably Saudi Arabia) were opposed to the recognition of 'communist' East Germany.[125] Nasser may also have been influenced by his belief that the German question should be solved by national self-determination. However, a more cogent argument is that Egypt and other Arab states would have been reluctant to commit themselves irretrievably to the Soviet bloc by recognising the GDR diplomatically. Diplomatic recognition most probably would have resulted in the curtailment of all West German governmental development aid to Arab League member-states, which continued despite the severance of diplomatic relations with Bonn – with the exception of Egypt of course.

In the short term, the GDR's ambitions to secure diplomatic recognition were thwarted. In the long term, aroused by developing Bonn–Tel Aviv relations, the Arab world became increasingly sympathetic to the GDR's campaign for international credibility.

Ulbricht's immediate disappointment must have deepened when, as a substitute for Nasser, the Egyptian Vice-President Hassan Ibrahim was welcomed in East Berlin in August 1965. At a banquet held before his departure Ibrahim stated that Nasser had been hitherto unable to visit East Berlin on account of an overcrowded schedule.[126] However, it was reported elsewhere that in the course of his visit Ibrahim expressed his dissatisfaction with current East German economic support, alleged that previous promises were not being upheld, and requested increased investment and deliveries of equipment to boost Egypt's industrialisation programme.[127] Apparently, insufficient East German economic support also accounted for Nasser's reluctance to recognise the GDR diplomatically.

Undoubtedly, inter-German rivalry curtailed the expansion of East German activities in Africa in this period and prevented the GDR from securing international recognition. Employing the Hallstein Doctrine, Bonn's principal objective was to circumscribe the East German 'presence' in Africa to lend credence to the policy of *Alleinvertretungsanspruch*. Although the majority of African states never intended to grant the GDR more than the most limited form of recognition (via commercial contacts), some might have accorded the GDR more recognition without the operation of the Hallstein Doctrine. Problems of accurately defining the Doctrine have been encountered, but it appears to have encompassed a series of graduated reprisals that would match the granting of certain levels of recognition to the GDR by third states, with the real possibility of the suspension of diplomatic relations in line with the Yugoslav and Cuban examples. Nevertheless, both Nyerere and Nasser, in spite of their unwillingness to grant the GDR diplomatic recognition, refused to adapt their foreign policy on account of pressure from Bonn in accordance with Grewe's interpretation of the Hallstein Doctrine. In these instances, the Doctrine failed to prevent the GDR obtaining greater recognition.

It has been noted that the USSR was unable in general to directly encourage African states to recognise the GDR diplomatically on account of the limitations on Moscow's own freedom of manoeuvre in the African sphere when confronted with Western, and later Chinese competition. Moscow, however, being able to influence the policies of Egypt and Zanzibar, taking into consideration their internal and external situations in 1964–5, most likely encouraged the authorities there to demonstrate further support for the GDR through the promise of economic support. At other times the USSR was not prepared to jeopardise relations with African governments by demanding diplomatic recognition of the GDR, but rather allowed the East Germans to pursue a limited autonomous policy in Africa. This at least assisted Ulbricht's endeavours to project a visible 'East German' activity overseas. Nevertheless, East German popularity in Africa remained dependent on the pro-Soviet stance of certain 'progressive' African governments (e.g., Ghana, Mali, Guinea and Egypt [1964–5]). In its efforts to gain full diplomatic recognition the GDR had no viable alternative policy option but to pursue a strategy of affiliation with the USSR in Africa. Relations cultivated with African states and liberation movements in this period would prove of value in the GDR's involvement on the continent after recognition was secured.

Clearly, the realignment of internal forces within Africa was of importance for the GDR's *Afrikapolitik* in this period. The achievement of statehood in the majority of African states, by 1966, and the assumption of power by radical groups in Egypt, Ghana, Guinea and Zanzibar facilitated East German endeavours to secure contacts. However, a further transformation of internal political structures in Africa could similarly undo earlier East German accomplishments (e.g., in Ghana in 1966, and in Stanleyville in 1961).

Although ideological criteria after 1956 in particular were not in conflict with the goal of diplomatic recognition, it appeared that the GDR's *Afrikapolitik* was motivated primarily by the pursuit of this specific objective than by a genuine concern for national liberation and world revolution.

Diplomatic breakthrough

Following Sudan's example in June 1969, another eight African states established diplomatic relations with the GDR before November 1972 (see Table 3). In that month, the initialling of the Basic Treaty between the two Germanies then allowed other states to recognise the GDR diplomatically with impunity. Between May 1969 and October 1972 eighteen states recognised the GDR diplomatically; outside Africa these were, namely, Cambodia (later Kampuchea) Iraq, Syria, South Yemen, the Maldive Islands, Ceylon, Chile, Bangladesh and India. Thus, in this period, half of these states which recognised the GDR 'prematurely' were African.

Were developments in Europe which resulted in the modification of the Hallstein Doctrine largely responsible for this wave of recognition? How important were other possible factors, such as the GDR's attempts to build on earlier relations with African states accompanied by a heightened propaganda campaign against the FRG (particularly in communications with the UN), East German offers of credit support, tensions in the Middle East, and internal African factors? What of the role of the USSR, noting that all African states which recognised the GDR prematurely were the recipients of economic, and in some instances, military aid from Moscow, and that Leonid Brezhnev spoke of the need to support states of 'socialist orientation' in the Third World?

In a period of emerging détente the Hallstein Doctrine, originally a product of cold war politics, was revised under the chancellorships of Kurt Kiesinger and Brandt as part of Bonn's new *Ostpolitik* and *Deutschlandpolitik*. The FRG established diplomatic relations with Romania in January 1967 under the terms of the so-called *Geburtsfehlertheorie* (birth defect theory). According to this theory, Romania, as

Table 3. *Diplomatic recognition of the GDR by African states, 1964–1984*

Date	Country	Date	Country
Mar. 1964–Mar. 1965 (then consular)	Zanzibar	13 Apr. 1973	Burkina Faso
3 June 1969	Sudan	18 Apr. 1973	Togo
10 July 1969	Egypt	19 Apr. 1973	Mali
8 Jan. 1970	Congo PR	11 June 1973	Libya
8 Apr. 1970	Somalia	21 July 1973	Cameroon
18 Apr. 1970	Cent. Afr. Republic	22 Aug. 1973	Senegal
(broken 14 Aug. 1971: restored 16 Apr. 1974)		14 Sept. 1973	Benin
20 May 1970	Algeria	28 Sept. 1973	Liberia
9 Sept. 1970	Guinea	29 Nov. 1973	Madagascar
14 Apr. 1971	Equatorial Guinea	4 Apr. 1974	Gabon
6 June 1971	Chad	17 Apr. 1974	Guinea-Bissau
7 Dec. 1972	Burundi	29 Oct. 1974	Mauritius
13 Dec. 1972	Ghana	4 Mar. 1975	Niger
17 Dec. 1972	Tunisia	19 May 1975	Kenya
18 Dec. 1972	Zaïre	25 June 1975	Mozambique
(broken 2 May 1977: restored 20 Jan. 1979)		13 May 1975	São Tomé and Príncipe
21 Dec. 1972	Tanzania	5 Aug. 1975	Cape Verde Islands
21 Dec. 1972	Sierra Leone	11 Nov. 1975	Angola
29 Dec. 1972	Morocco	14 Feb. 1976	Comores
(broken 13 Nov. 1975: restored 5 Mar. 1976)		22 Mar. 1976	Lesotho
5 Jan. 1973	Uganda	3 July 1976	Seychelles
15 Jan. 1973	Gambia	13 May 1977	Botswana
22 Jan. 1973	Mauritania	30 June 1977	Djibouti
10 Feb. 1973	Nigeria	1 Nov. 1980	Zimbabwe
14 Feb. 1973	Rwanda	5 Oct. 1984	Ivory Coast
21 Feb. 1973	Zambia		

Source: Dokumente zur Aussenpolitik der DDR (Berlin [East]: Staatsverlag der DDR, various years) and *ND*.

part of its duty as a Soviet bloc state, reborn after the Second World War as it were, had originally no option but to recognise the GDR. Bonn now excused Romania for this previous act of recognition by establishing diplomatic relations with Bucharest. In effect, the Hallstein Doctrine had been modified. However, when the FRG re-established diplomatic relations with Yugoslavia in February 1968 this could not be accommodated by the *Geburtsfehlertheorie*, since Tito had voluntarily chosen to recognise the GDR diplomatically in 1957. Furthermore, because of Yugoslavia's leading role in the non-aligned movement, the possibility of other states such as Egypt recognising the GDR diplomatically was suddenly more real. Indeed, only days after the resumption of relations between Bonn and Belgrade the then East German Foreign Minister, Otto Winzer, on 16 February 1968 in a speech before the Foreign Affairs Committee of the Volkskammer (the GDR's legislature), urged other states to normalise their relations with the GDR and declared: 'The proof of the absurdity of the Hallstein Doctrine has been furnished.'[128] Third World states were not convinced and Winzer's plea was ignored. No immediate diplomatic recognition of the GDR ensued despite Yugoslavia's continued importance in the non-aligned world, and recognition became even more remote after Tito's denunciation of the invasion of Czechoslovakia.

The decisions of Iraq and Cambodia to establish full diplomatic relations with the GDR in May 1969 were of enormous importance for inter-German rivalry in the Third World. As Iraq had severed diplomatic relations with the FRG in 1965, Bonn could only retaliate against Baghdad by forestalling possible future economic assistance. Iraq's diplomatic recognition of the GDR increased pressure on other 'radical' Arab states to follow suit, in particular, Egypt, which aspired to lead the Arab world. With Cambodia, by the so-called 'Cambodia Formula', the West German ambassador was recalled, embassy activities in Phnom Penh frozen, and the same economic sanctions applied as in the Iraqi case, but Kiesinger refrained from implementing the Hallstein Doctrine to its fullest by not breaking off diplomatic relations – although the authorities in Phnom Penh severed diplomatic relations with Bonn and terminated West German aid programmes.[129] The West German severe punitive response against Cambodia clearly would have discouraged the recognition of the GDR by 'progressive' sub-Saharan African states.

In practice, the 'Cambodia Formula' was never applied against an African state. When, prior to the commencement of Brandt's chancellorship in October 1969, Sudan, Syria, Egypt and South Yemen recognised the GDR diplomatically, the FRG retaliated by employing the Cambodia Formula against South Yemen and followed the Iraqi example in the other three cases since these Arab states had also severed diplomatic relations with Bonn in 1965. However, it should be noted that West German economic reprisals were mitigated by the fact that trade relations were maintained, current aid agreements continued, and private investors could not be restrained by Bonn.

According to End, the Hallstein Doctrine had all but expired when Brandt became Chancellor and his foreign minister, Walter Scheel, formulated what later became known as the 'Scheel Doctrine'. Seeking to prevent premature recognition of the GDR before a comprehensive inter-German settlement was reached, Scheel despatched a note to West German missions overseas in November 1969 stating that recognition should be discouraged, although states recognising the GDR diplomatically would not necessarily suffer sanctions.[130] According to End, this note tacitly allowed states to recognise the GDR diplomatically with virtual impunity, as Scheel's instructions on the need to avoid recognition until an inter-German settlement was achieved were aimed principally at friendly and non-committed third states and not the radical or even non-aligned.[131] However, despite End's dismissal, under the guise of the Scheel Doctrine sanctions were still applied against states recognising the GDR diplomatically.[132] Hence, the original deterrent value of the Hallstein Doctrine remained as many third states were reluctant to forgo West German economic benefits by recognising the GDR.

In most instances, diplomatic recognition of the GDR resulted in Bonn declaring that any future official economic commitments with the recognising state would only be made according to West German interests (i.e., in effect, preventing further official development assistance). In the example of Guinea (and also Ceylon and Chile), official West German development aid was reduced but not halted. Surprisingly, when the Central African Republic (CAR) recognised the GDR diplomatically, Bonn reacted with less forbearance by also recalling the West German ambassador leaving only a *chargé d'affaires* to preside over the mission in Bangui until October 1971.[133]

In December 1971 the Scheel Doctrine was revised when the FRG decided to resume diplomatic relations with Algeria and Sudan, followed seven months later by the restoration of relations with Egypt. After the CAR's diplomatic break with East Berlin in August 1971 (examined below, p. 77), a more confident Bonn would have regarded the modification of the Scheel Doctrine as a means of inflicting further diplomatic reversals on the GDR by depriving Honecker of the benefits of sole German representation in these north African states.

As early as 12 November 1969 the Chairman of the GDR Council of Ministers, Willi Stoph, in a speech at the University of Rostock, attacked the Scheel Doctrine by insisting that Bonn's foreign minister was attempting 'to continue to practise the bankrupt Hallstein Doctrine in a new form'.[134] In June 1970, in his report to the thirteenth plenum of the SED Central Committee, Ulbricht vehemently attacked the Scheel Doctrine's economic proscriptions as tantamount to gross interference in the internal affairs of sovereign states, where 'fulfillments of aid are misused for purposes of manipulation by blackmail by Bonn against the GDR'.[135]

Increasingly reluctant to relinquish political and diplomatic influence to the benefit of the GDR through a possible rigid application of the Hallstein Doctrine in its most extreme form, or by employment of the Cambodia Formula, Bonn modified its reactions to diplomatic recognition of the GDR by the Scheel Doctrine, although economic reprisals were maintained; one exception was the West German decision to embark on a new programme of official aid to Egypt in April 1971.[136] Certain African states which may have contemplated recognising the GDR (although, admittedly, it is not clear which) could have been deterred through fear of West German economic retaliation continued under the Scheel Doctrine. Thus a modification of the Hallstein Doctrine, by which a suspension of diplomatic relations by Bonn need no longer be feared, did not appear to account for the premature recognition of the GDR by a number of African states prior to 1972.

Clearly, calculations of economic gain and loss impinged on the perceptions of African state leaders. The more extensive West German programmes of development aid in comparison with the GDR have already been noted. In 1967 one East German publication noted the problem of African states possibly demanding greater financial assistance from both Germanies, by exploiting inter-German rivalry through conveying the impression that a recognition of the GDR might be imminent.[137] At a time of economic upheaval in the GDR, offers of credit support to Sudan, Algeria, Egypt, Guinea, Mali, Tunisia and Tanzania in 1969–70 in order to reward diplomatic recognition or encourage the establishment of diplomatic relations with East Berlin appear to have been an exercise in risk-taking.[138]

However, the GDR's failure to disburse fully promised credits was noted earlier.

Certainly, the CAR's decision to suspend diplomatic relations with the GDR in 1971 on account of economic grievances underlined East German financial shortcomings. Colonel Jean-Bedel Bokassa, the CAR's head of state, had established diplomatic relations with the GDR in April 1970 as part of his sudden interest in cultivating ties with the Soviet bloc on account of disillusionment with what he perceived as inadequate French development aid.[139] After recognition, in September 1970, the GDR and the CAR concluded agreements on economic, scientific, technical and cultural cooperation.[140] But, on 13 August 1971, Bokassa declared that diplomatic relations between the two states were suspended, stating: 'The aid which the Soviet Union has given to us is completely ridiculous. As for East Germany, its aid is non-existent. We have signed many agreements with these countries but these agreements are not respected.'[141] Significantly, in the same speech, past West German aid programmes were praised. It should also be noted in passing that in spite of his complaints Bokassa did not also suspend diplomatic relations with Moscow.

Although the example of the CAR was atypical – no other African state suspended diplomatic relations with the GDR through lack of economic support – other African states would have expected East German and Soviet development aid as a reward for recognition and compensation for West German economic reprisals. However, bearing in mind previously noted East German economic constraints the GDR could scarcely have 'bought' recognition. Even the erratic Bokassa it seems, had initially granted diplomatic recognition in an outburst of fury directed against the West, and in particular France, and was not enticed by East German offers of economic aid *per se*. However, with Bokassa's act of suspension, Honecker's quest for further diplomatic recognition suffered a serious reversal as the GDR's inability to guarantee the extension of economic and other benefits previously promised was suddenly exposed.

Many African statesmen were most likely disinterested in the complexities of *Deutschlandpolitik*. In general, they were prepared to bide their time until an inter-German settlement was eventually reached. This was in spite of East German efforts to generate more African interest in the German question through UN channels.

Starting in February 1966, over the next five years the East German authorities applied eleven times to obtain admission to the UN, failing on each count to secure majority approval in the General Assembly.

East German support of the invasion of Czechoslovakia in 1968 seriously impaired the GDR's efforts to poll votes. Only eight states voted in favour of East German admission in December 1968 compared with thirty-two states in October 1966.[142] Immediately following the invasion, the governments of Congo-Kinshasa (later Zaire), Ethiopia, Ghana, Kenya, Tunisia, Nigeria, Senegal, South Africa, Tanzania, Uganda and Zambia had condemned the action. Only Mali openly supported the invasion. Sudan displayed mixed feelings, while Egypt referred to the 'complicated' nature of events.[143] The GDR's eager pursuit of its affiliation strategy with the USSR had stalled the recognition campaign.

Even if enough support could have been mustered in the General Assembly, the Western states in the Security Council would have automatically vetoed East German admission. But through these repeated overtures to the UN, a number of African states were goaded into expressing their judgement on the German Question by the registration of their votes (unless they abstained or were absent at the time of voting) when the GDR applied to join the General Assembly and certain specialised bodies of the UN. Nevertheless, states such as Mali and Tanzania at times supported East German applications but did not recognise the GDR prematurely.[144]

Continuing previous practice, in numerous communications with the UN the GDR supported resolutions on issues concerning Rhodesia, South Africa, the Portuguese colonies, the Middle East and Namibia, and censured West German political, military and economic backing for Israel and the 'racist' and colonial regimes in southern Africa. The East German authorities paid scrupulous attention to the observance of UN-declared days of 'Struggle against Race Discrimination'. Declarations in favour of disarmament and its beneficial consequence for the Third World, the ending of racism (the East German success in the 'elimination' of Nazism was continually mentioned here), improved trade guarantees for the developing states etc., were issued regularly by the GDR and presented to appropriate UN bodies.

Through the medium of the UN, the SED leaders were most probably able to generate sympathy for the cause of East German recognition among the minority of African states already more favourably disposed towards the Soviet bloc, but the majority remained detached, or concerned about the application of the Hallstein/Scheel Doctrine. However, African national liberation movements such as FRELIMO, the MPLA, the PAIGC, the African National Congress (ANC), the Zimbabwe African People's Union (ZAPU), and the South

West African People's Organisation (SWAPO) – seeking independence for Mozambique, Angola, Portuguese Guinea, South Africa,
Rhodesia (Zimbabwe) and Namibia respectively – which were increasingly supported by the USSR, were likely impressed by the intensified
East German propaganda campaign in the UN.

In the late 1960s the GDR stepped up its support for liberation
movements by offering assistance (including military support) and
solidarity aid. Wounded guerrillas were treated in East German
hospitals; teachers despatched to educate the next generation of
'freedom fighters'; African apprentices trained in East German factories; propaganda publications printed in the GDR and school books
distributed in Africa. The PAIGC leader, Cabral, attended the 7th SED
Congress in 1967. Four years later Cabral and the leaders of the MPLA
(Agostinho Neto), FRELIMO (Samora Machel) and the Movement for
the Liberation of São Tomé and Príncipe (Movimento de Libertação de
São Tomé e Príncipe – MLSTP) under Manuel Pinto da Costa, visited
the GDR. Machel, Cabral and the ANC leader, Oliver Tambo, made
the trip in 1972.[145] Cabral concluded an agreement of further cooperation between the SED and the PAIGC Supreme Revolutionary
Council for 1973–74.[146]

Significantly, at the 8th SED Congress in June 1971 Honecker, now
First Secretary, referred to the 'movement for the national liberation of
peoples . . .' as a 'powerful revolutionary current . . .' in combination
with the socialist world system and the international workers' movement.[147] The USSR most probably encouraged heightened East
German relations with these movements to counter the major
Chinese-backed African guerrilla organisations, namely: the Revolutionary Committee of Mozambique (Comité Revolucionário de
Moçambique – COREMO), the National Union for the Total Independence of Angola (União Nacional para a Independência Total de
Angola – UNITA), the Zimbabwe African National Union (ZANU) and
the Pan-Africanist Congress of South Africa (PAC). The East Germans
must have hoped that by seeking favour among certain national
liberation movements, future African governments more sympathetic
to the GDR would be established should these movements obtain
power. The impact of Sino-Soviet rivalry in Africa on the GDR's
pursuit for diplomatic recognition will be discussed further shortly
(pp. 82–3).

Perhaps surprisingly, recognition was obtained as much as four
years after a part of the Arab world severed diplomatic relations with
the FRG, and two years after the devastating Arab defeat in the Six

Day War with Israel. During the war, and in the immediate weeks thereafter, the GDR issued declarations in support of Arab governments, and provided humanitarian relief in the form of medical supplies and blankets. On 8 June 1967 Ulbricht personally received the consuls-general from Egypt, Syria and Yemen based in East Berlin to inform them of West German assistance in the preparation of Israeli aggression.[148] In the aftermath of hostilities at a press conference in Cairo on 23 February 1968, Foreign Minister Winzer criticised West German neutrality for not demanding Israeli withdrawal from Arab territory occupied in the war.[149]

Defeat in 1967 increased Arab dependence on Soviet bloc support. Nasser, in particular, was the recipient of enormous arms transfers from the USSR. Nevertheless, Moscow's leverage over Cairo remained limited. Torn between the imperative of Arab unity and a personal desire to be recognised unanimously as leader of the Arab world, and sympathetic to the cause of self-determination for the German people, Nasser continued to avoid committing himself on the question of recognition of the GDR. The Egyptian leader was only spurred to act after the Iraqi decision to recognise the GDR. This decision was attributed to Iraq's desire to appease internal communist groupings, and to repay the debt owed to Moscow for Soviet aid in quelling Kurdish uprisings, i.e., connected to the USSR's support for Third World governments, however indirectly. An emboldened Radio Baghdad then demanded that Egypt, Syria and Algeria should follow Iraq's example and fully recognise the GDR.[150]

Sudanese recognition of the GDR was encouraged by the Iraqi example, although the military coup of 25 May 1969 led by General Jaafar Nimeiry provided the immediate catalyst. In a press interview on 29 May Nimeiry declared: 'We cannot ignore any longer the East German Republic which cooperates with Sudan, providing economic aid, and which backs the Arab states in their conflict with Israel.'[151]

Brandt attributed eventual Egyptian recognition to direct Soviet pressure following the visit of Foreign Minister Andrei Gromyko to Cairo between 11 and 12 June.[152] Further arms deliveries may have been promised. *Al Ahram*, the semi-official mouthpiece of the government in Cairo, implied that the Egyptian decision to recognise the GDR diplomatically was connected with the attitude of East Berlin and Bonn towards the Arab–Israeli conflict.[153] The Algerian government, less dependent on the USSR, delayed recognition of the GDR for almost another twelve months.

In north Africa eventual diplomatic recognition of the GDR was triggered by the Iraqi initiative. Until Baghdad's decision Soviet military and economic support and the position of the two Germanies on the Arab–Israeli question had failed to convince Arab leaders of the need to recognise the GDR.

The sub-Saharan African states which established diplomatic relations with the GDR before 1972 were all seeking to cultivate relations with the USSR to lessen traditional economic, political or military dependence on their former colonial masters. In turn, Soviet interest in acquiring strategically important naval facilities in Guinea, Somalia, Equatorial Guinea and the Congo PR (and also in Algeria and Egypt) resulted in offers of military and economic support from Moscow. Consequently, the USSR may have applied some influence on the policies of these states that could have operated to the GDR's advantage. As in the Sudanese example, military coups in the Congo PR and Somalia resulted in new leaderships willing to improve relations with the Soviet bloc. Bokassa's disillusionment with the West was previously noted to account for the CAR's recognition of the GDR.

Guinea's recognition of the GDR in September 1970 appears exceptional as it seems to have resulted from specific problems in Bonn's relations with Conakry. Touré's fury over the FRG's refusal to extradite a diplomat in the Guinean embassy in Bonn suspected of subversive activities, most probably led to the decision to recognise the GDR diplomatically.[154] On 30 January 1971, Touré suspended diplomatic relations with Bonn after suspecting that the West Germans were implicated in the abortive invasion of Guinea from Portuguese Guinea two months earlier. Thus, until May 1975 the GDR enjoyed a monopoly of German diplomatic representation in Guinea. In February 1971, at the UN, the FRG accused the GDR of fabricating false documentary evidence concerning the attempted invasion to incriminate Bonn. A stern East German rebuttal followed in the form of a declaration by ADN.[155]

Overall, the USSR's presence and influence in Africa – although still limited – appears to have contributed to the eventual East German diplomatic successes, but other factors, such as the GDR's efforts to generate favourable publicity, particularly through communications with the UN, and specific developments in the Middle East and Africa, need also to be considered. However, the GDR's strategy of affiliation with the USSR occasionally obstructed the quest for recognition in Africa. The uproar over the invasion of Czechoslovakia in 1968 was previously cited (pp. 77–8). The repercussions of Sino-

Soviet rivalry in Africa on East German involvement on the continent requires further discussion.

China exercised greatest influence in Africa in the strategically important frontline state of Tanzania where several national liberation movements were based. After the inter-German problem of 1964–5 Nyerere had turned to Beijing. By 1971 China was by far the largest aid donor to mainland Tanzania providing 56 per cent of all assistance, i.e., a total of $244.6 million compared with the $20 million offered by the USSR.[156] A large proportion of Chinese assistance was extended to cover the construction of the Tanzam railway, Beijing's most ambitious project in Africa. The railway's primary purpose was to enable Zambia to use Dar-es-Salaam as a port of exit for its goods rather than remain dependent on Rhodesian and South African facilities. Relations between Tanzania and China were strengthened by Nyerere's visits to Beijing in 1965 and 1968. By 1970, with the departure of Soviet and Canadian personnel, only Chinese military advisers remained in Tanzania.

On account of substantial Chinese economic and military aid the GDR could not buy Tanzanian diplomatic recognition. Increased Soviet bloc hostility to China in the late 1960s – Chairman Mao Zedong condemned the invasion of Czechoslovakia, and border clashes between Soviet and Chinese troops intensified – seriously impeded East German recognition efforts in Tanzania due to Nyerere's close alignment with Beijing. Zambia was also inevitably indebted to China for the launching of the Tanzam project. The Chinese even established a firm foothold in Zanzibar through their simple and cost-effective assistance programmes. By contrast, by December 1970, Karume had suspended all East German development projects on the island on account of their expense and inadequate nature, although the original success of the GDR's aid to Zanzibar was previously noted (p. 64). Failures in the GDR's aid programme had resulted in the expulsion of the East German consul from the island in June 1970.[157]

Chinese involvement in Africa was an unwelcome complication to the GDR's pursuit of recognition, although China's influence was constrained by Western and Soviet bloc competition, and remained limited on the continent in general. Even Beijing's substantial economic and political investment in the Congo PR, Somalia and Guinea did not prevent those states recognising the GDR diplomatically. Moreover, in spite of Chinese influence in Dar-es-Salaam, with the exception of ZANU, those national liberation movements backed by China were soon to lose out to their Soviet bloc-sponsored rivals (although FRELIMO and the PAIGC enjoyed close relations with both Beijing and Moscow). Thus, the GDR would ultimately benefit from its consistent support for certain guerrilla groups in Africa.

In the years immediately prior to the international recognition of the GDR the majority of African states remained favourably disposed to Bonn and maintained only minimal contacts with East Berlin. Limited East German resources were not squandered in regions of Africa where recognition was least likely.

Despite an eventual diplomatic breakthrough the GDR suffered a number of policy reversals in Africa in the late 1960s and early 1970s of which Bokassa's volte-face was only one – albeit the most grievous – example. Thus, in spite of Soviet bloc support for the federal government in Lagos in the civil war, Nigeria did not jeopardise traditional close ties with the FRG by recognising the GDR. In early 1970, after the conclusion of hostilities, Kiesewetter, accusing Bonn of previously supporting the Biafran separatists by political, economic and military means, unsuccessfully appealed to Lagos to 'develop further relations' with East Berlin.[158]

More serious was Zambia's decision to close the East German trade mission in Lusaka in September 1971. President Kenneth Kaunda had suspected the officials from the mission (apparently opened in 1967) were collaborating with former Vice-President Simon Kapwepwe to stage a coup. Rumours also circulated that the GDR had offered funds to Kapwepwe's breakaway party – the United Progressive Party – for possible seditious purposes, and, in addition, had incited radical students in the University of Zambia to protest against government policy.[159] Whatever the reasons for the closure, Kaunda's decision damaged – temporarily at least – the GDR's status among the frontline states and must have hindered communications with liberation groups which used Zambia as a rear-base for their operations.

In the Sudan and Egypt the GDR encountered problems in consolidating relations after diplomatic recognition was obtained. East German relations with Sudan deteriorated as a result of the abortive communist coup against Nimeiry in July 1971. Re-established in power, Nimeiry accused the Soviet bloc of conspiring with communist elements in Sudan. Fearful of losing diplomatic recognition, the East German authorities, in contrast to the USSR, exercised considerable restraint in their condemnation of the atrocities perpetrated against communists in Sudan in the aftermath of the failed coup.[160] Nevertheless, although Sudan did not suspend diplomatic relations, the GDR's cultural centre in Khartoum which had only opened the previous year was closed in July 1971, East German security officials expelled, and Nimeiry refused to accept new offers of credit assistance offered by East Berlin.[161]

Egyptian support for the reinstatement of Nimeiry reflected the GDR's declining influence in Cairo after Nasser's death in September 1970. Relations suffered further in 1972 when President Sadat expelled Soviet (and probably East German) military personnel.

By December 1972 the future prospects of the GDR's *Afrikapolitik* were uncertain. Inter-German rivalry remained intense. After two decades of confrontation this rivalry would not automatically disappear after international recognition. The majority of African states which had benefited from substantial West German development assistance, and which had refused to recognise the GDR prior to December 1972, would not necessarily be eager to cultivate extensive contacts with the Honecker government once diplomatic relations commenced. Nevertheless, the East Germans had developed and consolidated relations with several African regimes and liberation movements. Also, issues of contention in the Middle East and southern Africa were not to disappear in the post-recognition period. However, it was by no means clear by the end of 1972 whether the GDR would wish to maintain an active *Afrikapolitik* after obtaining international recognition.

3 The GDR in Africa in the 1970s

Introduction

East German foreign policy in Africa in the post-recognition period became motivated by factors not, at first sight, immediately akin to the quest for diplomatic recognition which had so dictated the GDR's manoeuvrings on the continent prior to 1972. Nevertheless, the continuing perceived need for Honecker to establish more firmly the legitimacy of the 'socialist' GDR remained a key determinant in the GDR's *Afrikapolitik*. Involvement in Africa also provided a means of influencing more favourably the USSR's estimation of the GDR through a strategy of affiliation.

Once general recognition was secured, the GDR, in line with the USSR, had concentrated attention in the years between 1973–5 on the European environment, where negotiations on issues of fundamental importance concerning political and military security were conducted in Helsinki (Conference on European Security and Cooperation) and Vienna (talks on Mutual Balanced Force Reductions in Central Europe). Visible participation in these conventions served to enhance East German prestige. The Helsinki Final Act, which confirmed the political and territorial status quo in Eastern Europe, was of over-whelming importance in further establishing the legitimacy of the GDR.

The liberation of the Portuguese colonies in southern and west Africa, the enforced oil price rise within the CMEA, and the progress of the Ethiopian revolution, shifted East German attention back to the African continent. With the implementation of détente in Europe (including a measure of 'enforced' inter-German détente with a series of agreements concluded after the Basic Treaty), events in Africa offered the USSR further opportunities to acquire increased leverage in the Third World without – Moscow hoped – jeopardising détente.

Honecker was eager to assist the USSR's revived interest in Africa in order to impress upon the Kremlin the importance of the GDR's contribution to the wider policy objectives of the states of the Socialist Community. More than two decades of carefully cultivated relations by the GDR with a number of African states and liberation movements would aid Honecker in this endeavour to upgrade further East German contacts with the African continent. Furthermore, East German specialisations in such spheres of activity as cadre training, journalism, trade union involvement, and, most importantly, military/security services, encouraged Honecker's ambitions. More specifically, with the rising costs of Soviet raw material exports to the GDR from 1975 onwards, the GDR sought to impress upon the USSR the importance of East German bonds of solidarity and friendship with certain African states, in order to obtain preferential Soviet economic treatment. In this context, the GDR pursued an active *Afrikapolitik* and military/security operations, in Africa in particular, were expanded. Moreover, the East Germans became eager to import increasing supplies of oil from north Africa and the Middle East in order to limit economic dependence upon the USSR.

Hence, one may note in Honecker's *Afrikapolitik* a need to continue to legitimise the East German regime by guaranteeing economic stability. Opportunities to enforce the policy of *Abgrenzung* from the FRG in Africa were also exploited (especially with reference to the 'Land Berlin Clause') as part of a campaign to consolidate the legitimacy of the 'socialist' GDR.

Within the period 1973–9 the GDR expanded relations with a number of states throughout the Third World. Honecker toured Vietnam (where a Treaty of Friendship and Cooperation was signed), North Korea and the Philippines in December 1977, and travelled to India in January 1979. Political and economic links with Latin America were intensified. Nevertheless, it was in Africa that opportunities were presented for the GDR to enhance its reputation. Overlap between the pre-recognition and post-recognition periods of East German involvement in Africa was apparent in policy motivation, and also in tools of policy cultivation.

One must not conclude from these observations that Honecker's *Afrikapolitik* in this period was an untrammelled success. Setbacks occurred in Somalia and Egypt, and problems arose in relations with Zaire and Morocco. The GDR's policy in Africa in this period was one of deepening previously developed relationships and initiating and diversifying contacts with other governments.

This chapter's analysis of the GDR's policy in Africa extends to 1979, when Honecker visited the continent on two occasions. Despite official East German pronouncements which suggested that a new era in GDR relations with Africa was inaugurated, I contend that Honecker's tours marked the culmination of the most successful phase of East Berlin's *Afrikapolitik* in the post-recognition period. In the 1980s, problems soon emerged with the independence of Zimbabwe, while the economic and political expense of continuing to support certain African governments and liberation movements became increasingly questioned throughout Eastern Europe.

The purpose of this chapter is to provide an overall perspective on East German foreign policy in Africa in the period 1973–9, with an emphasis on inter-German rivalry, and an analysis of the significance of Honecker's African tours. Chapters 4 and 5 will then discuss in greater detail GDR military/security and economic involvement in Africa.

However, before commencing a detailed analysis of East German activities in Africa in the immediate post-recognition period it is necessary first to consider what may be termed the 'ideological justification' for the GDR's support for national liberation movements and Third World states seeking political and economic independence from colonial or post-colonial powers in the 1970s. A vast amount of East German literature and several Western commentaries have already been published on this subject and need not be reviewed in detail here.[1] But it is important to note in passing how increasingly optimistic East German authoritative statements on the progress and heightened significance of socio-economic developments in the Third World, and in Africa in particular, were a reflection of the GDR's enhanced profile on the African continent.

The 'towering importance' of the natural alliance between states of the Socialist Community, the national liberation movements and recently independent developing states, and their objective interest in peace, security, disarmament and the struggle against racism and colonialism, were repeatedly emphasised.[2]

More so than in previous party congresses, in Honecker's report to the 9th SED Congress in 1976 the revolutionary potential of the developing states and liberation movements was stressed. 'Anti-imperialist solidarity' with peoples struggling for national and social freedom was ranked as an important foreign policy goal.[3] However, the report also cautioned that social progress for the developing states would be a long and arduous path. A considerable number of states were embarked on a path of socialist development, although this would involve 'complicated internal and external disputes'.[4] Expanding upon this theme, an East German article published later in the same year noted the possibility of reversals in socio-economic development in the Third World.[5] The East German leadership were already mindful of previous setbacks, e.g., the collapse of the Nkrumah government.

Nevertheless, in general, positive developments in Africa were stressed. In two major speeches in 1978 Honecker referred to Africa specifically as a continent in which peoples were substantially contributing to the continuing change of the international balance of power in favour of socialism.[6]

East German commentators and politicians in their publications and addresses were, in general, in agreement with the article produced by Deputy Foreign Minister Klaus Willerding in 1976. This stated that progressive socio-economic developments in the Third World, known as 'socialist orientation', involved a two-stage process, i.e., the achievement of a 'national democratic' revolution by a broad, heterogeneous, anti-colonial front including bourgeois groupings, and a later 'revolutionary democratic' phase where a 'left revolutionary wing' intensified the process on a non-capitalist path of development.[7]

Within the Third World the GDR supported the development of 'vanguard parties' in the revolutionary democratic phase of socialist orientation, and the formation of 'national fronts' of various parties and organisations in the national democratic phase. In the former, the party functioned as a Marxist–Leninist vanguard in which the working classes were ostensibly becoming the predominant element. In the ex-Portuguese colonies of Mozambique, Angola and Guinea-Bissau, in particular, revolutionary-democratic vanguard parties were reported to have formed by 1977.[8] These parties were not regarded as fully fledged 'socialist' parties.

With reference to the 'national fronts' in Africa, the GDR, unlike the USSR, could exploit its own experience in the formation of a 'National Front' to develop relations with regimes reluctant to cooperate closely with communist parties, for example, the National Revolutionary Council of Benin held talks with the National Council of the National Front of the GDR in East Berlin in 1975.[9]

In the post-recognition period the GDR proceeded to institutionalise contacts often only tentatively commenced in the pre-recognition period by concluding agreements of cooperation with parties, national fronts and liberation movements. For example, from reports in *Neues Deutschland* between 1974 and 1979, the SED concluded official agreements with the ruling parties in Algeria (1977), Angola (1974, 1976 and 1978), the Cape Verde Islands (1977 and 1979), the Congo PR (1974, 1976 and 1979), Egypt (1974), Ethiopia (1977), Guinea (1979), Guinea-Bissau (1977 and 1979), Libya (1977), Madagascar (1979), Mali (1979), Mozambique (1974, 1977 and 1979), São Tomé and Príncipe (1977), Somalia (1977) and Zambia (1977 and 1979). Undoubtedly, the extensive nature of East German contacts with African political parties in this period was of importance for the propagation of Marxism–Leninism throughout the whole of the African continent in the interest of the Soviet bloc. The GDR was the first East European state to conclude party-level agreements with FRELIMO and the MPLA.[10] Precise details of the nature of these and other party agreements is difficult to ascertain, although it may be assumed that party connections were employed to increase East German leverage over the internal and external policies of the states in question. It appears that an emphasis was placed on the training of party cadres in the SED-run 'Karl Marx' educational institution in the GDR, and in establishments opened in Africa with SED assistance.[11]

According to one East German source, party relations were the source of 'impulses not only for inter-state cooperation but also for ties with social organisations'.[12] Indeed, despite relations with vanguard parties or national fronts, the GDR was determined to consolidate and build upon contacts with such groups as trade unions, women's and youth organisations, and peasant associations, with an emphasis on the training of cadres. One particular traditional means of influence still employed by the GDR in Africa – doubtless with Soviet bloc encouragement – was *Medienpolitik*. Again from reports in *Neues Deutschland*, it appears that in the period 1973–9 the VDJ concluded agreements with journalists' unions in Algeria, Ghana, Guinea, Egypt, Guinea-Bissau, Somalia, the Congo PR, and São Tomé and Príncipe. ADN concluded agreements with news agencies based in Algeria, Tunisia, Ghana, Chad, Egypt, Guinea-Bissau, Somalia, Libya, Mozambique, Madagascar, Angola and Ethiopia. Radio and/or television broadcasting agreements were concluded between the GDR and Algeria, Tunisia, Egypt, Guinea-Bissau, Libya, the Congo PR, Mozambique, Angola, Ethiopia and Zambia. Journalists were trained in courses and seminars organised by East German specialists in Africa, or undertook training at the renowned Internationales Institut für Journalistik, Werner Lamberz, near East Berlin. In the sixteen years up to 1979, 432 journalists from 39 Asian and African states were reportedly trained at the Institute.[13]

This exercise of what one Western source has referred to as 'applied Proto-Leninism', to exert increasing East German and Soviet bloc influence through party contacts and organisational ties, was for the GDR fundamentally an extension and continuation of policies commenced in the pre-recognition period.[14] But with international recognition after 1973, and with the development of inter-state relations with a wide cross-section of African regimes of various political and ideological orientations, Honecker's confident and expanding *Afrikapolitik* bore increasingly less resemblance to Ulbricht's earlier more tentative power projection on the African continent.

The increased East German role in Africa

Honecker could boast at the 9th SED Congress in 1976 that the GDR maintained diplomatic relations with 121 states.[15] By December 1979 in Africa only Malawi, Swaziland, South Africa, Rhodesia-Zimbabwe, and the Ivory Coast had not established diplomatic relations with the GDR (see Table 3). Zaire and Morocco had earlier temporarily abandoned diplomatic relations on account of the Shaba crises (discussed in chapter 4) and the West (Spanish) Sahara problem respectively.

East German support for national liberation movements was enhanced by the opening of offices of quasi-diplomatic status for ZAPU, SWAPO and the ANC in East Berlin in 1978.[16] No other East European state at that time officially accommodated all three guerrilla groups in their capital.[17] The GDR had cooperated with each of these movements for several years.

Joshua Nkomo, Sam Nujoma and Oliver Tambo, the respective heads of ZAPU, SWAPO and the ANC, figured prominently in the ranks of leading African dignitaries and heads of state who visited the GDR between 1973 and 1979. Prior to independence the MPLA and FRELIMO leaders had also travelled to East Berlin (see Table 4).

Important East German delegations were present in Africa more frequently from December 1976 onwards following the independence of the former Portuguese colonies and internal upheavals in Ethiopia. Previously, high-ranking East German party officials visited north Africa. Until his death in March 1978, Werner Lamberz, the SED Secretary for Agitation and Politbüro member, had established himself as an indispensable troubleshooter despatched to Africa on

Table 4. *Visits by leading African officials to the GDR, 1973–May 1989*

	1973	1974	1975	1976	1977	1978	1979
Nujoma (SWAPO)			X[a]		Nov.+Dec.	Oct.	Nov.
Tambo (ANC)						May	
Nkomo (ZAPU)					Mar.+Oct.	Jan.+May	June
Mugabe (Zimbabwe)							
Machel (Mozambique)		Dec.					
Chissano (Mozambique)							
Pinto da Costa (São Tomé and Príncipe)	X[a]						
Neto (Angola)		May			Apr.		
Dos Santos (Angola)							
Pereira (President of Cape Verde Islands)							May
Luiz Cabral (Guinea-Bissau)				Nov.			June
Touré (Guinea)							Oct.
Ghaddafi (Libya)						June	
Mengistu (Ethiopia)						Nov.	
Yhombi-Opango (Congo PR)					Oct.		
Sassou-Nguesso (Congo PR)							
Kaunda (Zambia)							
Chief Jonathan (Lesotho)							

Table 4. (continued)

	1980	1981	1982	1983	1984	1985	1986	1987	1988	1989
Nujoma	Aug.	Jul.+Aug.	Feb.+Nov.	Sept.	Aug.		Aug.	Sept.	June	
Tambo	Oct.		July					Nov.		
Nkomo										
Mugabe				May						
Machel	Sept.			Mar.						
Chissano										May
Pinto da Costa		June	June	Apr.					July	
Neto		Oct.								
Dos Santos										
Pereira										
Luiz Cabral										
Touré										
Ghaddafi										
Mengistu					Dec.		Apr.			May
Yhombi-Opango										
Sassou-Nguesso						May				
Kaunda	Aug.									
Chief Jonathan			Sept.							

Note: a=No date given. From von Löwis of Menar, 'Das politische und militärische Engagement', p. 32.
Source: Except for a, from *Dokumente zur Aussenpolitik der DDR* (various years) and *ND*.

several occasions. The East German Minister of National Defence, General Heinz Hoffmann, was also active in Africa, indicating the GDR's increasing military interest on the continent (see Table 5). Not surprisingly, East German party and government delegations were concentrated, in general, on states with which the GDR enjoyed, or sought to enjoy, favourable relations.

Once formally admitted into the UN in September 1973, the GDR continued – as in the pre-recognition period – to use this international forum to present an anti-colonial and non-racist profile, whilst openly condemning the imperialist activities of the West (including the FRG). Annual sessions and other special convocations of the UN General Assembly in New York enabled the East German Foreign Minister (from 1975, Oskar Fischer) to meet regularly with African and other Third World official counterparts who might be reluctant to arouse possible controversy through a visit to East Berlin. Moreover, UN-sponsored training courses and seminars organised in the GDR, and often attended by Third World delegates, provided the East German authorities with an opportunity to impress.

In fact, the GDR was able to exploit the UN and its specialised committees to present a favourable image at little financial expense. Although official East German data with reference to UN contributions are not available, it appears that in this period financial support usually only covered statutory quotas. By 1979 the GDR's quota only amounted to 1.3 per cent of the total UN budget (c. $5.4 million), in contrast to the 7.7 per cent quota of the FRG (c. $38 million).[18] Between 1976 and 1980 (inclusive) the contributions of the two Germanies to the UN Development Programme amounted to $272,054,135 for the FRG and only $5,651,817 for the GDR.[19]

However, in spite of inadequate East German financial support of the UN, the GDR, and the Soviet bloc in general, was able to score a number of propaganda victories over the West through frequently securing UN General Assembly majority support for equivocally worded and wide-ranging anti-colonial policy goals.

Prior to the independence of the Portuguese colonies in 1975 there was a noticeable hiatus in East German activity in sub-Saharan Africa once diplomatic recognition was achieved. This was because the GDR's attention was rather focused on Europe, and in the Third World, on north Africa and the Middle East where opportunities to reassert East German influence arose with the 1973 Yom Kippur War. Nevertheless, in sub-Saharan Africa relations with Zambia suddenly improved following a speech on 10 January 1973, in which Kaunda

Table 5. *Visits to Africa by SED Politbüro members and Foreign Minister Fischer, 1973–May 1989*

	1973	
Egypt	Mar.–Apr.	Friedrich Ebert
	1974	
Algeria	Oct.–Nov.	A. Neumann
Egypt	Feb.	G. Grüneberg
	1976	
Egypt	Dec.	O. Fischer
Ethiopia	Dec.	O. Fischer
Kenya	Dec.	O. Fischer
Madagascar	Dec.	O. Fischer
Mozambique	Dec.	O. Fischer
Somalia	Sep.–Oct.	W. Stoph
Tanzania	Dec.	O. Fischer
	1977	
Algeria	Oct.	G. Mittag
	Nov.	Konrad Naumann
	Dec.	H. Sindermann
Angola	June	W. Lamberz
	Dec.	H. Sindermann
Congo PR	Jan.+June	W. Lamberz
Ethiopia	Feb.+June+Dec.	W. Lamberz
Guinea-Bissau	Nov.	K. Naumann
Libya	Oct.	H. Axen
	Dec.	W. Lamberz
Mozambique	Feb.	W. Lamberz
Niger	Dec.	H. Sindermann
Nigeria	June	W. Lamberz
	Dec.	H. Sindermann
São Tomé and Príncipe	Dec.	H. Sindermann
Somalia	Jan.–Feb.	W. Lamberz
Zambia	June	W. Lamberz
	1978	
Algeria	May	H. Hoffmann
Angola	May	H. Hoffmann
Congo PR	May	H. Hoffmann
Ethiopia	Sept.	W. Krolikowski
Guinea	May	H. Hoffmann
Libya	Mar.	W. Lamberz
Nigeria	May	H. Hoffmann
Tunisia	May	H. Hoffmann

	1979	
Algeria	Oct.–Nov.	H. Sindermann
Angola	Feb.	E. Honecker and delegation
	Sept.	W. Stoph
Ethiopia	May	H. Hoffmann
	Nov.	E. Honecker and delegation
Libya	Feb.	E. Honecker and delegation
	Aug.–Sept.	H. Tisch
Mozambique	Feb.	E. Honecker and delegation
	May	H. Hoffmann
Zambia	Feb.	E. Honecker and delegation
	May	H. Hoffmann
	1980	
Algeria	Mar.	G. Mittag
	Oct.	H. Sindermann
	Nov.	O. Fischer
Benin	Dec.	O. Fischer
Nigeria	Nov.	O. Fischer
Tunisia	Dec.	O. Fischer
	1981	
Algeria	May	H. Tisch
Angola	Oct.	K. Naumann
Congo PR	Oct.	K. Naumann
Ethiopia	Nov.	H. Dohlus
	1982	
Angola	May	O. Fischer
Congo PR	May	O. Fischer
Mozambique	Apr.	H. Sindermann
Tunisia	June	H. Sindermann
Zambia	May	O. Fischer
	June	H. Dohlus
Zimbabwe	May	O. Fischer
	1983	
Libya	Sept.	H. Sindermann
Mozambique	Apr.	W. Krolikowski
	1984	
Algeria	Mar.	O. Fischer
	Oct.	Gunther Kleiber
	Dec.	E. Honecker and delegation
Congo PR	July	H. Dohlus
Ethiopia	Sept.	H. Dohlus
	Sept.	E. Honecker and delegation

Table 5 (*continued*)

	1985	
Algeria	Jan.	O. Fischer
Angola	Dec.	W. Krolikowski
Djibouti	Jan.	O. Fischer
Egypt	Jan.	O. Fischer
	Apr.	G. Kleiber
Ethiopia	Feb.	H. Tisch
	1986	
Libya	Feb.+Aug.+Sept.	G. Kleiber
Mozambique	Oct.	W. Krolikowski
	1987	
Ethiopia	Sept.	H. Sindermann
	Nov.	H. Dohlus
Mozambique	Mar.	G. Kleiber
Tunisia	Mar.–Apr.	O. Fischer
	1988	
Algeria	Sept.	H. Tisch
Angola	Sept.	H. Tisch
Ethiopia	Mar.	H. Tisch
Mozambique	Oct.	G. Kleiber
	1989	
Ethiopia	Mar.	H. Dohlus
Morocco	May	O. Fischer

Source: Neues Deutschland.

spoke of the history of friendship between Zambia and the GDR and regretted the interruption of contacts in 1971.[20]

Diplomatic relations almost immediately ensued. This improvement in relations with Zambia facilitated East German contacts with liberation movements in southern Africa in the following years. The opportunities presented by the coup in Lisbon in April 1974 and the repercussions for the Portuguese colonies in Africa could not have been envisaged in East Berlin. The GDR, Cuba and the USSR were able to maximise earlier contacts with the MPLA and FRELIMO in order to influence the internal and external policies of the strategically important new independent states of Angola and Mozambique. The wholesale withdrawal of Portuguese expertise facilitated the efforts of the socialist states to establish influence in the immediate post-independence years.

Guinea-Bissau, the Cape Verde Islands and the small archipelago of

São Tomé and Príncipe also secured independence in these years and became the targets of several prominent East German party and state delegations through which numerous cooperation agreements were negotiated. The GDR had likewise previously established connections with the PAIGC and MLSTP prior to independence.

Before Angolan independence (11 November 1975) a further visit by Neto to East Berlin (7–9 May 1974) had resulted in a cooperation agreement between the MPLA and SED for 1974–5.[21] In the following months of internal struggle in Angola between competing guerrilla factions East German solidarity support and military assistance for the MPLA intensified. Independence was greeted with a sequence of congratulatory front-page headlines in *Neues Deutschland*. A high-level East German delegation under the special envoy Werner Dordan attended the independence celebrations in Luanda. Diplomatic relations between the GDR and Angola were immediately taken up.[22] The fact that no West German officials were invited to attend the independence celebrations on account of the FRG's traditional support of its Portuguese NATO partner must have been welcomed with considerable satisfaction in East Berlin. The GDR's earlier vociferous support of the liberation cause in Angola was vindicated.

In June 1976 relations between the SED and the MPLA were consolidated by a further cooperation agreement[23] – although the MPLA remained technically a movement and not a political party until the First Congress of the MPLA–Party of Workers (MPLA–Partido de Trabalho – MPLA–PT) in December 1977.

The GDR assisted in the infrastructural development of the Angolan state, particularly in the spheres of economic management and planning, health work, agriculture, port development, cadre training and military/security cooperation.[24] However, certain problems arose. For instance, under the management of harbour specialists from Rostock and Warnemunde, the port of Luanda became one of the most chaotic and congested in the world.[25]

Furthermore, possible East German foreknowledge of an attempted coup to depose Neto in May 1977 (see chapter 4), and in December 1978 the demotion of Prime Minister Lopo di Nascimento (with the abolition of the post of Prime Minister), a regular visitor to East Berlin and close friend of the GDR, suggested that relations between East Berlin and Luanda were not entirely smooth.[26] Significantly, in December 1977 at the MPLA PT's First Party Congress, the GDR ranked only seventh in the list of states Neto specifically praised for their support in the development of Angola since independence.[27]

The sole German delegation in attendance at the independence celebrations for Mozambique was also one headed by an official of the SED Central Committee. Diplomatic relations between Mozambique and the GDR immediately commenced.[28] SED–FRELIMO contacts had been reinforced earlier through an agreement on Machel's third visit to East Berlin in December 1974.[29] The FRG had failed to exploit negotiations held in August 1973 between a FRELIMO delegation and West German politicians and industrialists.[30] According to one East German commentator, these negotiations failed on account of Bonn's refusal to curtail military support to Portugal and suspend financial backing for the construction of the Cabora Bassa Dam,[31] which was regarded as a symbol of Portuguese colonial rule in Mozambique. The SED authorities had apparently regarded with intense suspicion FRELIMO's original acceptance of the West German government's invitation to visit Bonn.[32]

Contacts between the GDR and Mozambique expanded and agreements proliferated in the following years up to 1979. The GDR provided assistance in such areas as education, communications, economic management, cadre training and military/security operations.[33] Party relations were solidified through a further agreement of cooperation concluded by Lamberz in Maputo in February 1977 for the years 1977 and 1978.[34]

The end of imperial rule in Ethiopia in September 1974 also could have not been envisaged by the GDR. Although all Socialist bloc states assiduously cultivated relations with the military regimes in the strategically and politically important Ethiopian state, several difficulties soon emerged.

One problem concerned the Soviet bloc's traditional solidarity with the struggle of Eritrean liberation movements against the central government in Addis Ababa. Moreover, developing the strategically important port of Berbera, the USSR wished to preserve close relations with Somalia (in July 1974 the Soviets had concluded a Treaty of Friendship and Cooperation with Somalia) although the Somali leader, Said Barré, aspired to fulfil irredentist ambitions by seizing the Ogaden from Ethiopia. Finally, the turbulent nature of domestic Ethiopian politics produced complications, but also opportunities.

In spite of the proclamation of a New Democratic Revolution in Ethiopia (April 1976) with various land reforms and a programme of nationalisation, the Soviet bloc feared that the ruling military junta would refuse to relinquish power eventually to a Marxist–Leninist vanguard party. It appears that the GDR assumed an important role for the Soviet bloc in cultivating relations with the ruling military authorities in Addis Ababa, and in influencing the development of the Ethiopian revolution on a course favourable to the USSR's political and strategic interests.

In December 1976 Fischer had held a 'cordial meeting' in Addis Ababa with Brigadier-General Teferi Benti, at that time chairman of the ruling military body, the Provisional Military Administrative Council (PMAC).[35] In early February 1977 Benti was murdered in a bloody coup which resulted in Lt.-Col. Mengistu Haile Mariam, First Deputy Chairman of the PMAC, seizing the post of PMAC chairman on 11 February 1977. It was significant that Lamberz, in the course of his African tour, arrived in Addis Ababa on 10 Febuary and held talks immediately with Mengistu.[36] The East German authorities exploited this opportunity to strike up close relations with Mengistu. Lamberz assured Ethiopia of the GDR's full revolutionary solidarity and support.[37] Upon becoming new PMAC chairman, Mengistu received a telegram of personal congratulations from Honecker.[38] Benti was now posthumously denounced as a 'Trojan horse' by Neues Deutschland.[39]

In total, Lamberz visited Ethiopia on three occasions in 1977 and concluded a number of agreements, including one foreseeing the strengthening of cooperation between the SED and PMAC in June 1977.[40] When Lamberz died in a helicopter crash in Libya in March 1978 the entire Ethiopian military leadership went into mourning.[41]

Given the good fortune for East Berlin that Lamberz was immediately on hand to solidify contacts with Mengistu after the February coup, the GDR certainly endeavoured to establish an influence over the course of internal events in Ethiopia, which served the interests of the Soviet bloc in general. Nevertheless, despite the conscientious work of Lamberz, Mengistu was reluctant to allow the formation of a workers' party which would challenge the political supremacy of the ruling military junta.

Even Honecker attempted to pressure Mengistu on the occasion of the Ethiopian leader's first visit to East Berlin in November 1978. While praising the progress of the national democratic revolution, Honecker reminded his guest that the road of revolution was not an easy one, and added: 'Persevering and determined work is necessary to safeguard power under the leadership of the revolutionary party and create a state that is closely linked to the people.'[42]

Although Mengistu failed to react to Honecker's explicit reference to the need for a 'revolutionary party', inter-state relations were strengthened by both leaders agreeing to a Declaration on Principles of

Friendship and Cooperation between the GDR and Ethiopia.[43] By this time East German experts were especially active in Ethiopia in the fields of journalism, education, planning and security work. Moreover, advisers from the GDR were involved in training political cadres at the 'Yekatit 66' school of politics in Ethiopia, in the hope that Mengistu would approve the founding of a genuine workers' party.[44] But, in spite of the activities of East German and Soviet bloc advisers, only a Provisional Bureau for the Affairs of Mass Organisation had been established with PMAC approval prior to developments late in 1979.

Concerning the problem of the Eritrean liberation movements, the GDR attempted to assist in finding a comprehensive settlement on behalf of the socialist bloc. Contacts were established in East Berlin with the Eritrean People's Liberation Front (EPLF) by the end of 1977.[45] In 1978 further meetings with representatives of the Addis Ababa government and EPLF and the Eritrean Liberation Front–Revolutionary Council (ELF–RC) were held in East Berlin, but no agreement on a peaceful solution to the Eritrean question was finalised.[46]

In the war between Ethiopia and Somalia (1977–8), Moscow's decision to support Ethiopia militarily resulted in a serious deterioration of relations between Somalia and the USSR. However, Barré's relations with the GDR remained cordial. Indeed, the GDR assumed an important role for the Soviet bloc in maintaining contacts with the Somali government.

In the months immediately preceding the conflict in the Horn of Africa, ties between the GDR and Somalia at party and state level had expanded considerably. Indeed, an agreement of cooperation between the SED and the Somali Revolutionary Socialist Party was concluded as a result of a visit by Lamberz.[47] Therefore, when by the end of November 1977 Somalia had abrogated the Treaty of Friendship and Cooperation with the USSR, expelled Soviet, Cuban and North Korean advisers, and reduced the USSR's diplomatic staff in Mogadishu, the FDJ Friendship Brigade initially despatched in November 1974 remained in Somalia and top-ranking ambassadors were maintained in both East Berlin and Mogadishu.[48] Barré, in the presence of Stoph, had earlier showered tributes upon the work of East German advisers in Somalia and specifically commended the activities of the FDJ.[49] This sequence of events, as well as emphasising the importance of the GDR's presence in Somalia, also provided evidence that one African state believed that the GDR exercised a foreign policy independent of that of the USSR.

In this period the GDR continued to offer solidarity aid in various forms (including weaponry) to certain national liberation movements. SWAPO, ZAPU and the ANC were major recipients. The independence of Angola and Mozambique, and the previously noted improved relations with Zambia, facilitated East German contacts with these movements. For instance, at the 3rd FRELIMO Congress in Maputo in February 1977, Lamberz held meetings with Tambo, Nujoma, Nkomo, and also the ZANU leader, Robert Mugabe.[50] In Lusaka, in June 1977, at the time of signing of a Protocol of Cooperation between the SED and the ruling United National Independence Party (UNIP) of Zambia, Lamberz received ZAPU and ANC officials.[51] These and other contacts assisted the USSR's attempts to restrict China's influence over the national liberation cause in Africa.

In the 1970s, relations between East Berlin and Beijing continued to stagnate. At the SED Congress in 1976 Honecker referred to China's 'great power chauvinism' and 'anti-Soviet' policies which damaged the interests of world peace and security.[52] In February 1979, Honecker exploited his first African tour to secure from certain African statesmen condemnations of the Chinese invasion of Vietnam.

However, after the completion of the Tanzam railway, in 1976, China's influence in Africa noticeably declined. Machel's gradual dissociation from Beijing was manifest in the absence of a Chinese delegation at the 3rd FRELIMO Congress. This was probably on account of Machel's support for the MPLA government in Angola. Machel had successfully prevailed upon Nyerere to withhold arms shipped to Dar-es-Salaam from China and intended for use by the guerrilla groups in Angola opposed to the MPLA.[53]

In southern Africa, in general, Beijing could not compete with the quantity of socialist bloc military assistance. By 1979, ZANU remained the only liberation movement in the region under Chinese influence. Elsewhere in Africa China's involvement was minimal.

As more promising opportunities appeared in the Horn of Africa and southern Africa in the post-recognition period, the traditional importance of the north African region in the GDR's *Afrikapolitik* diminished. To a large extent, the GDR had been a victim of the policy failures of the USSR, particularly in Sudan and Egypt. Improved relations with Libya and other radical Arab states in North Africa and the Middle East, together with a developing relationship with the Palestine Liberation Organisation (PLO), helped to offset partially these policy failures for the Soviet bloc.

In this period the GDR continued to stress anti-imperialist solidarity with the Arab nations, demonstrated in annual weeks of International Solidarity with Arab Peoples, and regular declarations of support in the UN and Organisation of African Unity (OAU) for the Arab League and for the anti-Zionist campaign.

The progressive deterioration in East German–Egyptian political relations formed part of Sadat's realignment with the West. Dissatisfied with the quality, quantity and terms of Soviet arms deliveries, Sadat looked to the West for arms imports. As a consequence, the Soviet–Egyptian Treaty of Friendship and Cooperation (originally signed 27 May 1971) was abrogated in March 1976, Soviet use of Egyptian naval facilities was terminated, the Egyptian government suspended debt repayments owed to Moscow, and, finally, seeking closer relations with Israel, Sadat visited Jerusalem unexpectedly in November 1977.

Problems between Egypt and the GDR had been evident from November 1974 onwards when a tour of the Middle East by Horst Sindermann, then Chairman of the Council of Ministers of the GDR, had failed to include the customary call in Cairo.[54] Prior to this, relations between East Berlin and Cairo had momentarily improved after the Yom Kippur War of 1973. In January 1974 the SED and ASU concluded an agreement of cooperation for the years 1974 and 1975.[55] The following month the SED Politbüro member, Gerhard Grüneberg, had held talks with Sadat in Cairo 'in a friendly and open-minded atmosphere'.[56]

Relations between the GDR and Egypt deteriorated after November 1974 despite Fischer's brief visit to Cairo in December 1976.[57] No Egyptian ASU delegation attended the 9th SED Congress. Instead, the Libyan ASU delegation was conspicuous by its presence.[58]

The closure of the East German consulate in Alexandria, and two cultural centres in Alexandria and Cairo, by Egypt in December 1977 was labelled as 'nothing other than an unfriendly act' by the GDR.[59] Sadat ordered other East European consulates and cultural centres to be closed in reaction to Soviet bloc disapproval of his Jerusalem initiative. Thereafter, for several years, the GDR basically maintained only economic contacts with Egypt.

In a later East German article Egypt was singled out, with Ghana and Mali, as examples of regimes whose paths of 'progressive' development and ties with the Socialist bloc were severed due to the nationalist degeneration of political leadership, subjective mistakes, and a continued imperialist support of counter-revolutionary forces.[60]

Despite problems with Sadat, the GDR's policies in north Africa and the Middle East in these years were of importance in furthering Soviet bloc interests in the region as part of the affiliation strategy. Indeed, the GDR assumed a crucial role for the Soviet bloc in coordinating policies with the Libyan-sponsored 'Arab Front of Steadfastness' – composed of Libya, Algeria, Syria, South Yemen and the PLO – which was formed in Algiers in February 1978 in reaction to Sadat's Jerusalem initiative.[61] Moreover, economic imperatives, and in particular oil, had also attracted increasing East German interest in Libya.

As a result of a trip by the Politbüro member Hermann Axen to Libya in October 1977 it was agreed to expand further bilateral state and party relations – in the latter instance, between the SED and the General People's Congress – and the Libyan authorities finally consented to the despatch of an ambassador to East Berlin.[62]

The momentum was continued by the visit of Lamberz two months later – after the closure of GDR missions in Egypt – when further measures to develop bilateral relations were agreed upon.[63] The Libyan leader, Muammar Ghaddafi, visited the GDR in June 1978, as part of an East European tour. A Ten-Year Agreement on Political, Economic, Scientific and Technical Cooperation was signed. Moreover, a 'Joint Statement on the Strengthening of Friendship and the Deepening of Cooperation between the GDR and Libya' was issued. The Joint Statement stated that a new stage in relations between the two states had been reached. Ghaddafi extended to Honecker an invitation to visit Libya.[64]

However, Ghaddafi had embarrassed his hosts in East Berlin by provocatively declaring that he was in favour of German reunification. East German press accounts omitted all reference to Ghaddafi's appeal for reunification.[65]

Elsewhere in north Africa, the GDR developed ties with Algeria, but contacts with Sudan remained minimal after the abortive 1971 coup attempt. More interestingly, for several months the GDR appeared to endanger the USSR's interests in acquiring access to the extensive phosphate deposits in Morocco. Here, unusually, the East German authorities miscalculated in their enthusiasm to promote Moscow's interests.

On 13 November 1975 the Moroccan government severed diplomatic relations with the GDR after a systematic anti-Moroccan campaign had been conducted in the East German press in connection with the West (Spanish) Sahara issue. Rabat also issued a warning to Moscow.[66] On 12 November 1975 *Neues Deutschland* had reported that the governments of Spain and Morocco, in collusion with overseas companies such as the West German combine, Krupp, in order to protect their economic interests, had plotted to thwart the aspirations of Algeria and the Popular Front for the Liberation of Saguia el Hamra and Rio do Oro (POLISARIO) who were seeking self-determination for the former Spanish Sahara. East German eagerness to support POLISARIO and its Algerian sponsors had momentarily threatened to disrupt the USSR's economic interests in Morocco.

The situation was finally resolved on 5 March 1976 when diplomatic relations between East Berlin and Rabat were restored. The East German government had assured the Moroccan authorities that they wished to normalise relations on the basis of mutually advantageous cooperation and non-interference in the internal affairs of other states.[67]

With the decline of Soviet bloc leverage over Egyptian policies in the 1970s the GDR became more involved in sub-Saharan Africa where more promising opportunities could be exploited. However, in this period, improved relations with Ghaddafi were of significance, especially since Libya, together with Algeria, maintained connections with the PLO in the potentially explosive situation in the Middle East. In north Africa, in general, the GDR remained actively involved in the military/security sphere. Commercial contacts with the region were also of importance.

Nevertheless, in the 1970s the GDR gradually focussed attention more on sub-Saharan Africa. Hence, Honecker visited only one north African state, Libya, when he travelled twice to the continent in 1979.

Continued inter-German rivalry

With diplomatic recognition of the GDR in Africa and else-where the Hallstein Doctrine and its successor doctrines had become redundant. Inter-German relations in the 1970s in Africa coincided, to a large extent, with the GDR's general policy of *Abgrenzung*. For instance, according to one report, members of FDJ friendship brigades stationed in developing states were instructed to avoid fraternisation with their West German relief counterparts.[68]

In the ex-Portuguese colonies, and in Mengistu's Ethiopia, the GDR endeavoured to maintain a prominent presence at the expense of the FRG. In other states – notably Guinea, Somalia and also certain north African regimes – the GDR tried in vain to prevent the re-emergence of West German preponderance. Bonn recovered diplomatic relations with Conakry in May 1975, following the earlier release of three West

German citizens previously arrested after the attempted invasion from Portuguese Guinea in 1970. The FRG had issued a statement condemning interference in the internal affairs of other states prior to recovering full relations with Guinea.[69]

In Somalia, following the events of 1977, relations between Bonn and Mogadishu improved as part of Barré's re-orientation to the West, although it appeared that both Germanies at one time furnished aid for the national police force.[70]

An authoritative East German analysis of West German involvement in Africa by Gertraud Liebscher was published in 1978 in the journal *Deutsche Aussenpolitik*.[71] Quoting recent West German statistics, the author, not surprisingly, condemned the volume of the FRG's foreign trade and capital investment concentrated in South Africa (i.e., 21.9 per cent of all West German trade with Africa and an investment of DM 10–12,000 million by West German *Konzerne* in 1976). The strategic, political and economic interests of the FRG (and of the EEC and NATO) in the preservation of a sympathetic regime in South Africa was emphasised. More interestingly, as well as mentioning an increasing West German appetite for raw materials from certain key African states, reference was made to a twin-track strategy ostensibly pursued by the FRG. According to this analysis, pressure was being applied upon the South African (apartheid) regime to ease popular oppression through encouraging, for instance, the formation of trade unions for the purpose of coopting the labour movement into the capitalist system in order to perpetuate Western economic and political preponderance in the region. A similar 'soft' approach was adopted towards the liberation movements of Namibia and Zimbabwe, while credits were offered to the frontline states of Zambia and Tanzania. Even socialist-oriented states were tempted by economic enticements. Tools of assistance included the use of mass media, development of scientific-cultural relations, and aid in agricultural production. By this twin-track strategy a short-term policy of opportunism was combined with the long-term goal of neo-colonialism. According to Liebscher: 'All these activities are employed at the same time to increase the standing of the FRG with the firmer incorporation of these states into the capitalist world economic system and to stabilise in these states pro-capitalist financial, ideological and political tendencies.'[72]

Ironically, several of Liebscher's allegations (apart from references to South Africa) have been cited by Western political analysts to partly account for East German involvement in Africa (substituting 'socialist' for 'capitalist').

The above analysis accounted for the FRG's activity in the Western Contact Group, charged with responsibility for seeking a peaceful solution to the Namibian question. This was interpreted as part of a policy of only partially modifying the nature of the South African regime by removing the most obvious and grossest forms of apartheid's iniquities.[73]

On 22 January 1979, Politbüro official, Alfred Neumann, condemned the Contact Group's 'endless rounds of negotiations' with South Africa which only retarded the process of independence and, by sham elections in December 1978, had actually installed 'willing stooges' of Pretoria in power in Namibia.[74]

To what extent did inter-German rivalry continue in Africa in the post-recognition phase, given the GDR's continued pursuit of the affiliation strategy with the USSR, Honecker's policy of *Abgrenzung* and the problems of legitimacy for the SED leadership as long as the FRG refused to relinquish officially the ultimate goal of a reunified Germany? Certainly, in the UN, East German representatives often portrayed the GDR as the *bessere Deutschland* (better Germany).[75] As early as December 1973 the then Foreign Minister Winzer, in his report to the 11th Plenum of the SED Central Committee, noted how the FRG often abstained or voted against resolutions which the GDR and the majority of Third World states favoured, particularly on questions of racism and apartheid. According to Winzer, this demonstrated to peoples of the developing nations 'in the most illuminating way . . . how deceitful' the FRG's notion of the unity of the German nation was.[76]

However, the most interesting manifestation of continued inter-German rivalry in Africa in the post-recognition period, and one little explored, concerned the status of Berlin following the ratification of the Quadripartite Agreement. The GDR and the USSR continued to refer to the text originally prepared on the day before the Agreement was initialled in September 1971, in which the Soviet term *svazy* (ties) was translated into German by the imprecise *Verbindungen*, and not the more forceful *Bindungen* which was eventually used to refer to the 'ties' between the FRG and West Berlin.[77] These ties were to be 'maintained and developed, taking into account that these sectors [i.e., West Berlin] continue not to be a constituent part of the Federal Republic of Germany and not governed by it'[78] (Annex II – Three Powers Communication to the USSR).

The FRG was allowed to represent the interests of West Berliners abroad, with the exception of 'matters of security and status' which were to remain the responsibility of the Western Powers. Moreover, international agreements concluded between the FRG and other states 'may be extended to the Western sectors of Berlin provided that the extension of such agreements and arrangements is specified in each case' (Annex IV. 1.2.a and c).

According to the later East German interpretation of the text, the GDR (with Soviet approval) endeavoured to sever official connections between the FRG and West Berlin and regarded West Berlin as a separate unit.[79] The GDR censured certain international agreements and arrangements incorporating West Berlin with the FRG. Here, the GDR could not evade the change of hypocrisy since from the 1951 Berlin Agreement onwards West Berlin was automatically included with the FRG for purposes of inter-German trade. Moreover, other Soviet bloc states had concluded trade agreements with the FRG which also covered West Berlin.[80]

Following the conclusion of the Quadripartite Agreement, all Soviet bloc states, including the GDR, continued to negotiate successfully a series of agreements with the FRG which incorporated West Berlin. Here the Frank–Falin formula operated (named respectively after an under secretary in the West German Foreign Office and the Soviet ambassador in Bonn). Quite simply, according to this formula, a clause was inserted in the publication of agreements between the FRG and Soviet bloc states which declared: 'In accordance with the Quadripartite Agreement of 3 September 1971, the present agreement shall apply to Berlin (West) in conformity with the established procedures.'[81]

In other words, attention was once again drawn to the vague wording of the Quadripartite Agreement which affirmed that the FRG 'may' conclude international agreements that included West Berlin, but, in practice, in order for this to be actualised, the Frank–Falin formula needed to be negotiated and inserted.

Evidently trade agreements did not appear to compromise the security or status of West Berlin. The Frank–Falin formula was employed in the trade agreement concluded between the USSR and the FRG in July 1972.[82] However, in the following years, the USSR, supportive of the GDR's endeavours to decouple West Berlin from the FRG, only approved of the insertion of the Frank–Falin formula in other treaties with the FRG, whenever a treaty was of practical importance for the 'Western sectors' of Berlin.[83] Hence, between 1972 and 1978 a number of negotiated agreements between Bonn and Moscow on such issues as culture, science and tourism were not concluded on account of the USSR's refusal to consent to the insertion of the Frank–Falin formula.[84] Other agreements in these years between the FRG and East European states which did appear to be of relevance to West Berlin were concluded with the employment of the Frank–Falin formula.[85]

Important treaties between the two Germanies also employed the Frank–Falin formula to incorporate West Berlin. With reference to the Basic Treaty, it was decided that arrangements envisaged between the two Germanies in the Supplementary Protocol of Article 7 would be extended to West Berlin in accordance with the Quadripartite Agreement, provided consent could be obtained in each individual case.[86] Hence, in this period the GDR refused to sign certain agreements with the FRG on such issues as legal aid, economic and technical cooperation, and culture on account of the FRG's insistence that West Berlin should be incorporated. According to the GDR, these agreements were of no relevance to West Berlin.[87] The fact was that automatic agreement on the extension of arrangements to include West Berlin by the addition of the Frank–Falin formula was by no means guaranteed. It was the intention of the USSR and the GDR to ensure that the relevant clause had to be negotiated anew on each occasion. Nevertheless, the GDR did conclude a number of agreements with the FRG which included the Frank–Falin formula. Bonn had insisted that the FRG was fully entitled to represent the wishes of West Berliners in the UN, otherwise the West was willing to veto the GDR's application to the UN.[88] Moreover, the Frank–Falin formula was inserted as part of the Protocol on the establishment of Permanent German Representatives as envisaged in the Basic Treaty with reference to the authority of the West German plenipotentiary in the GDR.[89]

However, the FRG insisted that states, other than those within the socialist bloc and Finland, should not seek to include the Frank–Falin formula in any agreement concluded with Bonn. Instead, the West German government insisted that agreements with these other third states should be extended to incorporate the 'Land Berlin Clause',[90] i.e., not specifically restricted to the Western sectors of Berlin as under the terms of the Quadripartite Agreement and, hence, the Frank–Falin formula. This was implemented in accordance with a ruling of the West German Constitutional Court of July 1973 which declared that the Quadripartite Agreement had not altered the legal status of Berlin as defined under the Basic Law which had referred to 'Greater Berlin' (although the Western occupying powers had insisted that the Western sectors of Berlin remained under their jurisdiction).[91] Hence, in order to emphasise and consolidate the close linkages between the FRG and West Berlin, the West German authorities insisted that African states should accept the *Land* Berlin Clause in any agreement concluded with Bonn, and not the more conditional Frank–Falin formula.

This was of particular importance with reference to the EEC Lomé Conventions. According to Annex XXIV of Lomé I, signed in February 1975: 'The ACP [i.e., African, Caribbean, Pacific]–EEC Convention of Lomé shall apply equally to *Land* Berlin . . .'[92] Almost the exact wording was employed in the Lomé II Convention signed in October 1979.[93] Moreover, according to Annex XXIII of Lomé I (and also the similar text of Annex XXXIV of Lomé II), it was stipulated that: 'All Germans within the meaning of the Basic Law for the Federal Republic of Germany shall be deemed to be nationals of the Federal Republic of Germany.'[94]

The insertion of these annexes obviously would have antagonised the GDR. However, most interestingly, on several occasions African states refused to sign the Lomé II Convention, or conclude economic aid agreements with the FRG, thereby depriving themselves of substantial development assistance, on account of not wishing to offend East German sensitivities by agreeing to the inclusion of the *Land* Berlin Clause.

Here, intriguing questions are immediately raised. Was an East German variant of the Hallstein Doctrine in force in this post-recognition period whereby certain African states, over which the GDR (together with the Soviet bloc in general) wielded significant economic, military and political leverage, were persuaded, cajoled or even compelled to resist West German economic and political overtures because of the inclusion of the *Land* Berlin Clause? Had East German government circles recognised an opportunity to reap some form of vengeance against the FRG remembering the rigid enforcement of the Hallstein Doctrine only a few years previously? Certainly, African loyalty to the GDR in specific cases with reference to the *Land* Berlin Clause was clearly manifest, albeit somewhat surprising. In contrast to the Hallstein Doctrine, the GDR's economic resources were considerably less extensive than those of the FRG. Consequently, the maintenance of East German predominance in certain states would appear, at first sight, more difficult to preserve given the GDR's economic constraints. Moreover, the tools of reprisal the East German authorities possessed at hand scarcely realistically included the potential ultimate weapon of the Hallstein Doctrine, i.e., the withdrawal of diplomatic recognition. Even the renunciation of economic support by the GDR and other CMEA states (although the latter would have been extremely reluctant to support their socialist German brothers by such drastic means on account of the *Land* Berlin Clause issue alone) was not an obvious deterrent considering the likelihood of the substitution of Western assistance. Finally, and importantly, as noted above, the GDR and other Soviet bloc states were not themselves adverse to accepting the inclusion of West Berlin in agreements with the FRG, albeit through the Frank–Falin formula and not the *Land* Berlin Clause. If the FRG had not insisted on the *Land* Berlin Clause with reference to other non-socialist bloc states, but adopted the Frank–Falin formula, would the GDR have succeeded to the same extent in securing propaganda victories over the FRG in Africa?

In reality, one may not justifiably equate the problems engendered by the question of the *Land* Berlin Clause with the ramifications and innumerable difficulties caused by the application – or threat of application – of the Hallstein Doctrine. Certain African states appear to have conducted a policy favourable to the GDR out of some concept of loyalty which may have actually hindered and delayed their own economic development. It should be acknowledged that, in contrast to the Hallstein Doctrine, the states over which the GDR exercised influence with reference to the *Land* Berlin Clause were few in number – namely, Angola, Mozambique, Ethiopia, São Tomé and Príncipe, and Guinea-Bissau.

Perhaps the most grotesque application of the invalidity of the *Land* Berlin Clause was in May 1978 when the PAIGC government of Guinea-Bissau refused to accept two urgently needed gifts of rice for the poverty-stricken local populace. The shipment was already in transit when President Luiz Cabral insisted that the West German authorities should renounce the incorporation of the *Land* Berlin Clause in the aid agreement. Pressure on Cabral from the East German Ambassador Kurt Roth, who would have been able to manipulate a Cabinet largely sympathetic to the East German cause – many of them had studied in the GDR, and Cabral's personal secretary was East German – seems highly probable. Owing to this pressure one shipment of rice was finally unloaded in Gambia instead. A second gift was unceremoniously tossed into the harbour with toxic chemicals upon arrival at Guinea-Bissau. Only in 1979 was a quantity of rice finally received by the Cabral government from Bonn although only one-third of the host administration attended the handing-over ceremony which was not reported in the local press or radio.[95]

Despite close official relations between East Berlin and Cabral's government, Guinea-Bissau desperately needed increased technological aid and development assistance for which the PAIGC administration might have looked to the West. According to one Western source, almost the only machinery that remained operative on the island of Bissau was a ground-nut peeling unit originally stationed there by the Germans when Kaiser Wilhelm was in power![96] Refusal to receive humanitarian aid on account of the *Land* Berlin Clause appeared a self-defeating policy, especially as Guinea-Bissau had commenced negotiations to enter the Lomé Convention immediately after independence and ranked as one of the signatories of Lomé I when it came into force in April 1976.[97]

In Mozambique a West German government delegation arrived in Maputo in February 1978 to finalise a development aid agreement which would provide, in total, $11 million of assistance to the FRELIMO government. The technical details of the agreement were already fixed when the Mozambican authorities objected to the inclusion of the *Land* Berlin Clause and refused to sign the agreement.[98]

For similar reasons both Mozambique and Angola steadfastly refused to sign the EEC Lomé II Convention by October 1979, although both states had sent observers to the negotiations. It should be noted that the FRG remained adamant that extensive EEC aid should reach neither Mozambique nor Angola until both agreed to adhere to the Lomé Convention, although both states were in receipt of some EEC development aid as non-signatories of the Convention. However, as relations steadily improved the FRG established diplomatic ties with Mozambique and Angola in July 1976 and August 1979 respectively.

Interestingly, the Joint Communiqués issued following Honecker's tours of Angola and Mozambique in 1979 noted the need for 'strict observance of the Quadripartite Agreement',[99] i.e., in line with East German interpretations. However, no reference was made to the Berlin question in the Treaties of Friendship and Cooperation concluded with these states, in contrast to similar treaties concluded by the GDR with other third states (see chapter 6).

Apparently, in this period São Tomé and Príncipe refused to conclude an agreement with the FRG which included the *Land* Berlin Clause, although the small west African state had entered the Lomé I Convention by an agreement of 28 March 1977 with effect from 1 November 1978.[100]

Like Guinea-Bissau and São Tomé and Príncipe, Ethiopia initially had joined Lomé I, but with the later assumption of power of Mengistu, the authorities in Addis Ababa were reluctant to conclude bilateral agreements with the FRG on account of the *Land* Berlin Clause. According to Mengistu, the division of Berlin was a 'propaganda strong-point and centre of provocation' against the GDR.[101] Consequently, as in the instances of Angola and Mozambique, the Joint Communiqué issued on the occasion of Honecker's visit to Ethiopia, in November 1979, referred to the need to observe the Quadripartite Agreement, although, again, the Treaty of Friendship and Cooperation also concluded on the visit did not address this issue.[102]

Relations between the PMAC and the West German government had earlier reached their nadir in January 1978 when the West German ambassador in Addis Ababa, Christian Lankes, was expelled. Hans-Jürgen Wischnewski, Minister to the Chancellor's Office, complained in vain to the East German permanent representative in Bonn, Michael Kohl, that the expulsion was due to machinations on the part of the GDR.[103]

Certainly, according to an article published in the East German journal *Horizont*, the GDR expressed satisfaction with this 'second expulsion' (the first was Lankes' expulsion from Guinea in 1971 when he was the West German ambassador in Conakry!), which struck a massive blow against West German neo-colonialist interests in the Horn of Africa. The article also alleged that the 500 West German citizens living in Ethiopia were conspiring with internal and external imperialist forces in opposition to the 'progressive' regime.[104] Only in June 1979 did Bonn appoint a new ambassador to Addis Ababa.[105]

The expulsion was perhaps attributable to an agreement signed in Bonn on 17 January 1978, shortly before Lankes' enforced departure, when the West German government granted Somalia two substantial credits. The Ethiopian Deputy Foreign Minister, Major Dawit Wolde Ghiorgis, denied this linkage, and stated that Lankes' personal conduct had resulted in the expulsion. According to Ghiorgis, Lankes had forwarded to Bonn biased reports on the situation in the Ogaden. Several days earlier, the Ethiopian authorities had already requested the FRG to withdraw its military attaché, and had decided to close the (West) German school in Addis Ababa.[106] Relations between Bonn and Addis Ababa had worsened as early as August 1977 when the FRG had decided to suspend (provisionally, at first) aid and military equipment destined for the Ethiopian police, as the West, in general, reoriented its policies in favour of Mogadishu.[107]

The authorities in Bonn were aware of the problems of an anti-West German feeling in Africa whipped up by the GDR through UN channels, and via the issue of the *Land* Berlin Clause in particular, in order to maintain *Abgrenzung* between the two Germanies in Africa. In these circumstances, according to a Bundestag report, the FRG's official policy was to counter East German allegations by propagating the authentic version of events.[108]

According to a statement by Bonn's Permanent Representative at the UN, Rüdiger von Wechmar, on West German radio on 23 December 1979, the majority of states in the UN were uninterested in the problems and complexities of the German question and would remain so until after innumerable preliminary discussions with delegates behind closed doors would have effect, i.e., the late 1980s![109] Many African states at the UN were more concerned with such issues as creating a New International Economic Order (NIEO), and related topics concerning neo-colonialism, economic exploitation, and the abolition of racism, rather than with the German question *per se*. However, GDR governmental officials – with the customary assistance of trade unions, youth movements, journalist bodies, education establishments, etc. – related these wider issues of more interest to Third World states to the German question. Certainly, with reference to one particular aspect of the German question – the *Land* Berlin Clause – the GDR secured in this period psychologically important victories over Bonn in a small number of African states.

The importance of 1979

Honecker's first two tours of Africa in 1979 – the first by an SED leader since Ulbricht's Egyptian visit in 1965 – and the conclusion of twenty-year Treaties of Friendship and Cooperation with Angola, Mozambique and Ethiopia (the Angolan treaty was the first of its kind successfully negotiated by the GDR with a state outside the Socialist Community), marked the pinnacle of success of East German involvement in Africa in this period, and arguably, of the whole of the GDR's *Afrikapolitik* hitherto. Certainly, in 1979, official East German circles hoped for and envisaged further triumphs in Africa, particularly with certain national liberation movements still seeking independence. Moreover, another important factor, within the context of Honecker's tours, was the fact that the GDR authorities, bolstered by the success and the accompanying prestige, were eager to stress the significance of these visits for the whole of the Soviet bloc's policy in the Third

World. This depiction of the importance of GDR activity in Africa was directed both at the East German public and at officials in the Kremlin as part of the affiliation strategy.

Addressing the *Volkskammer* on 28 June 1979, Fischer referred to the GDR treaties with Mozambique and Angola, of that February, with their emphasis on cooperation on the basis of proletarian internationalism and Marxism–Leninism, as part of that policy agreed at a session of the Political Consultative Committee of the WTO in Moscow in November 1978, at which the Soviet bloc was urged to develop relations with 'states of socialist orientation' in the Third World.[110]

One West German analyst was prompted to assert that the GDR had come to regard itself 'as a pacemaker [*Schrittmacher*] of the world revolutionary process by the side of the Soviet Union'.[111]

According to one East German report published shortly after the February tour, the first Honecker mission was portrayed as 'a highpoint in the history of the foreign policy of the GDR, especially its African policy' which impressively reinforced 'the bonds of solidarity of the GDR with those peoples of the African continent struggling for their national and social liberation'.[112]

In fact, Honecker's missions to Africa (and South Yemen) were the culmination of assiduously cultivated relations stretching over several years including pre-independence wars of liberation (Angola, Mozambique), or were an example of relations intensively pursued in a much shorter period (Ethiopia), or were attempts to expand contacts with non-socialist oriented states for certain strategic and/or economic motives (Libya, Zambia). The importance of sub-Saharan Africa in the GDR's *Afrikapolitik* by this time was manifest.

It seems that by the start of February 1979 a visit by the SED leader to Mozambique alone was in the process of being finalised. The announcement of a schedule to include also Zambia, Angola and Libya was only published on the day of Honecker's departure.[113] This already indicated potential difficulties with the first African trip which were realised eventually in Lusaka and Tripoli in particular. Indeed, a closer examination of the results of the tour reveal that it was by no means the unmitigated success certain East German commentaries have tended to suggest. The composition of the East German delegation – including Stoph, Axen, Fischer, and Günter Mittag (Secretary of the Central Committee of the SED responsible for economic policies) – had indicated hopes of party cooperation agreements and economic deals.

The first call in Honecker's schedule, Libya, (15–17 February) was in return for Ghaddafi's visit to East Berlin the previous summer. No treaty of friendship and cooperation resulted, although one was promised for the near future. The Joint Declaration released at the end of Honecker's visit also stressed the importance of consolidating bilateral relations and reaffirmed solidarity with African liberation movements in the struggle against racism and colonialism. Ghaddafi was invited to visit East Berlin again.[114] Earlier, in a toast speech, Honecker praised Ghaddafi's role in the Arab Front of Steadfastness and called Ghaddafi 'comrade'. In contrast, Ghaddafi's speech ignored reference to Honecker's sweeping condemnations of NATO.[115]

Honecker achieved little in Tripoli apart from an agreement on economic, scientific and technical cooperation.[116] In the next months no marked increase in delegations between the two states was observed, although the SED Politbüro official Harry Tisch attended the celebrations of the tenth anniversary of the Libyan Revolution at the end of August.[117] Nevertheless, economic linkages had been consolidated and military/security cooperation also probably intensified.

The visit to Angola (17–20 February) was considerably more successful. A Treaty of Friendship and Cooperation was signed, based, according to its preamble, on 'Marxism–Leninism and proletarian internationalism'.[118] This wording was employed also for the Treaty of Friendship and Cooperation concluded with Mozambique only days later, and also with similar treaties concluded about this time with Vietnam (December 1977), Kampuchea (March 1980), and North Korea (June 1984). On the other hand, the Treaties of Friendship and Cooperation concluded by the GDR with Mongolia (March 1977) and Cuba (May 1980) were based on the more advanced 'socialist internationalism', which stressed close inter-state (as well as inter-party) relations within the Socialist Community.[119]

Article 3 of the GDR–Angola Treaty referred to the importance of expanding cooperation between political and social organisations. Thus, further contacts between political parties, trade unionists, youth movements, women's organisations, etc., were secured.

Western analysts have noted the omission of a clause concerned with military cooperation in contrast to the GDR–Mozambique Treaty (Article 5).[120] Unlike the GDR–Mozambique Treaty, the preamble to the Angolan Treaty failed to note the 'natural anti-imperialist alliance between the socialist states and the national liberation movement'. Moreover, the wording of Article 8 of the Angolan Treaty, in connection with the consent to hold 'regular consultations on international issues' of mutual interest, conveyed the impression of a more distant relationship than the equivalent Article (9) of the Mozambican Treaty which stressed the 'harmonising' of foreign policy actions.[121]

It appears that Neto was reluctant to jeopardise improving political and economic relations with the West (especially Portugal) by openly aligning Angola more closely with the GDR. This was further testified to by obvious differences in the toast speeches at a state banquet in which Neto underlined his predominant concern for Africa, while Honecker addressed himself to the wider importance of the global anti-imperialist struggle.[122]

However, the importance of Honecker's two visits to Luanda in February 1979, should not be overlooked – a second brief visit on 24 February was used to report to Neto the results of the trips to Zambia and Mozambique, and also included a meeting with the President of São Tomé and Príncipe.[123] Several bilateral agreements were concluded. These included a Programme on the Further Development of Economic, Scientific and Technical Cooperation, an Action Programme for Agriculture, and an Arrangement to cooperate in the Development of the Angolan Textile Industry.[124] Moreover, both Honecker and Neto in their banquet speeches, and in a Joint Communiqué, condemned the Chinese attack launched against Vietnam at that time.[125] Angola had not established diplomatic relations, principally on account of Beijing's earlier support for the National Liberation Front of Angola (Frente Nacional de Libertação de Angola – FNLA) and UNITA guerrilla factions who had opposed the MPLA in the civil war at the time of Angolan independence.

In Luanda, Honecker also held discussions with the SWAPO leader, Nujoma, to whom a solidarity gift of an undisclosed nature was given.[126] Contacts with SWAPO were further deepened following Nujoma's meeting with Axen in East Berlin in November 1979.[127]

Only a Joint Declaration was issued following Honecker's three days in Zambia (20–2 February).[128] Indeed, the Joint Declaration did not even refer to Honecker's visit as one of official friendship.[129] On account of Kaunda's reluctance to offend China, the Joint Declaration omitted any condemnation of the invasion of Vietnam. At the state banquet, Kaunda had failed to refer to events in South East Asia. In contrast, Honecker spoke of the 'shameful aggression' launched by the Chinese leadership against the 'valiant people' of Vietnam.[130] This prompted the Chinese counsellor to leave the banquet forthwith.[131]

Nevertheless, the Honecker delegation succeeded in concluding a number of agreements in Lusaka concerned with radio broadcasting, economic, scientific and technical relations, and an Executive Programme on Cultural and Scientific Cooperation.[132] Honecker also held talks with the ZAPU leader, Nkomo, in which both condemend China's aggression in Vietnam.[133] A solidarity gift, valued at 5 million East German marks, for ZAPU was announced.[134] Kaunda's harbouring of ZAPU guerrillas in conflict with the Smith regime in Rhodesia to a large extent explained the GDR's interest in intensifying relations with Zambia. Furthermore, in the following months, the GDR developed further contacts with ZAPU and the Zambian government. Military delegations between the GDR and Zambia were exchanged, and a SED–UNIP cooperation agreement concluded in September 1979.[135] Kaunda also accepted Honecker's invitation to visit the GDR (made public in the Joint Declaration) and travelled to East Berlin in 1980.

In Mozambique (22–4 February), as previously noted, Honecker concluded another Treaty of Friendship and Cooperation in which various clauses, when compared with the Angolan Treaty, indicated that the GDR had developed closer relations with Mozambique. According to a Joint Communiqué, other agreements were signed including a party agreement between the SED and FRELIMO for 1979–80, and a programme on long-term economic cooperation to 1990 (the first programme of its kind concluded by the GDR with an African state).[136] No such agreements were concluded in Luanda. Machel also received a solidarity gift from Honecker worth 5 million marks.[137]

Both Honecker and Machel condemned China's aggression against Vietnam in the Joint Communiqué.[138] This was significant, since, although FRELIMO had sought closer relations with the USSR and distanced itself from Beijing (as noted earlier), relations between Mozambique and China had remained close enough for Machel to be warmly received in the Chinese capital as recently as May 1978.[139]

It should also be noted that the Joint Communiqué issued in Maputo stated that the Principles of the Helsinki Final Act formed the basis of inter-German relations and not past treaties between the two Germanies (i.e., the Basic Treaty) as noted in the Luanda Communiqué. This indicated that Mozambique assessed the German Question more in accordance with the GDR's interpretation.[140]

As in Lusaka and Luanda, talks were held with national liberation movement leaders in Maputo. Both Honecker and ANC chief Tambo condemned China's aggressive policies, while Axen received the ZANU leader Mugabe.[141]

Addis Ababa was not included in the timetable of Honecker's first African tour. One Western commentator attributed this to the recent mutual assistance pact concluded between Ethiopia and the pro-Western Kenya.[142] However, in the months prior to Honecker's visit to Addis Ababa, in November 1979 (12–15 November), and to South Yemen, military and economic contacts between Ethiopia and the GDR had considerably expanded. This was reflected in the numerous agreements signed in Addis Ababa upon Honecker's arrival, together with the SED General Secretary's publicised inspection of the military camp at Tatek. A programme (and protocol) on the further development of economic, scientific and technical cooperation to 1985 was signed. Also agreed upon were documents relating to cooperation in mining, geology and agriculture.[143]

The GDR's third Treaty of Friendship and Cooperation with an African state was signed in Addis Ababa. In contrast to the two previous treaties, on account of the absence of a vanguard party in Ethiopia, the treaty's preamble referred to only the 'traditional close relations of friendship, cooperation and anti-imperialist solidarity' between the two states and peoples.[144] The terms 'Marxism–Leninism' and 'proletarian internationalism' were excluded. Policies were not to be 'harmonised' (the emphasis was rather on 'consultation' – Article 8); no article referred to military aid directly; and on account of the Eritrean problem, no mention was made of the need to support a people's right of self-determination.[145]

Throughout his visit, Honecker was careful to avoid Mengistu's past claims with reference to the Ethiopian regime's espousal of the principles of Marxism–Leninism and proletarian internationalism, without the functioning of a vanguard party.[146] Nevertheless, Ethiopia's intention to form a vanguard party in the future was cautiously noted by Honecker to be a 'logical step on the road of the Ethiopian revolution'.[147] It should be noted that under Article 1 of the Treaty of Friendship and Cooperation with reference to the need for further political cooperation, the GDR maintained its interest in influencing the progress of the Ethiopian revolution.

Significantly, Article 5 of the Treaty referred to the need of both sides to contend with 'hegemonism'. Here, China's policies were denounced, as the Joint Communiqué stated that both Ethiopia and the GDR 'condemned the hegemonistic, aggressive policy of the Chinese leadership'.[148] However, in line with Angola and not Mozambique, the Communiqué did not declare that the Helsinki Final Act should be regarded as a basis for current inter-German relations.

In order to bolster East German prestige, publicity about the Addis Ababa visit was maximised. Hence, upon laying the foundation stone of a monument dedicated to Karl Marx in the Ethiopian capital, Honecker proclaimed, that what Marx had sought for with revolutionary fervour, 'has become a reality during the thirty years of the German Democratic Republic, the first socialist workers' and farmers' state on German soil'.[149]

In talks between Honecker and the OAU Secretary-General Edem Kodjo, at OAU Headquarters in Addis Ababa, the latter declared that the GDR had made a 'valuable contribution to the freedom struggle in Africa'.[150] Again making full use of the occasion, Honecker praised the positive role of the OAU in international relations, stressed the successful struggle of the 'socialist German state' (i.e., in contrast to the FRG) in eradicating the evils of fascism and racism, and, in a possible appeal directed to the Ivory Coast (and even Malawi and Swaziland?), reiterated, 'the GDR's readiness to pursue friendly and mutually beneficial cooperation with all OAU member states'.[151]

In spite of the above critical account, the importance of Honecker's two African tours in 1979 must not be underestimated. The tours were manifestations of the degree of success of the GDR's *Afrikapolitik* hitherto. For the GDR, the beneficial consequences from the tours in the context of increased military, political and economic contacts were considerable. This was, in part, in contradiction to an official West German report which declared that although in Mozambique and Angola, 'the expected political fruits were delivered', the mission to Libya and Zambia ostensibly produced 'no indication of an intensification of current relations'.[152]

The treaties of friendship and cooperation were by no means pioneering successes for the Soviet bloc. The USSR had earlier concluded similar treaties with Angola, Mozambique and Ethiopia (on 8 October 1976, 31 March 1977, and 28 November 1978 respectively). Nevertheless, in spite of expected overstatements and exaggerations by East German officialdom on the significance of the two Honecker tours, this summitry diplomacy conducted by the GDR was of benefit to the Soviet bloc's political, and especially military, involvement in Africa. The GDR's pursuit of its affiliation strategy with the USSR was clearly evident.

On account of the timely nature of Honecker's first African tour in particular, the GDR played an important role in securing immediate disapproval of China's policies in South East Asia from a number of key African statesmen and liberation leaders. Only one month prior to

Honecker's arrival in Luanda, Angola had announced that it had accepted an invitation from China to begin talks aimed at securing diplomatic relations.[153] Honecker's mission assisted in checking a possible improvement in relations between Angola and China at the Soviet bloc's expense.

By December 1979 the GDR's *Afrikapolitik* appeared successful. The FRG had suffered a number of reversals in connection with the *Land Berlin* Clause, Honecker had consolidated relations with a number of African states as his two tours demonstrated, and, indeed, the GDR could now be regarded as an important junior partner of the USSR on the African continent. Although Guinea and Algeria had not been on Honecker's itinerary, President Touré had attended the thirtieth anniversary celebrations of the GDR in East Berlin (despite Guinea's drift to the West in recent years), while the SED Politbüro members, Tisch and Sindermann had led two delegations to Algiers and held talks with the recently appointed President, Chadli Bendjedid.[154] Moreover, in October 1979 the GDR was voted in as a non-permanent member of the UN Security Council – although the FRG had previously acquired this position in 1977–8.

Having examined East German involvement in Africa in the period 1973–9 from a broad perspective, specific economic and political imperatives to help account for the magnitude of GDR activity on the continent must now be analysed. Here, the GDR's military/security operations in Africa were of importance.

4 East German military/security involvement in Africa

Introduction

As previously noted, Western analysts have suggested that an increased East German military/security involvement in Africa from the mid-1970s onwards was connected with the GDR's desire to secure preferential economic treatment from the USSR and maintain Moscow's support with regard to the German question. Although, of course, these linkages are impossible to verify, it is argued here that, especially after 1971, in line with its affiliation strategy with the USSR, the GDR was eager to despatch military and security 'advisers' and military 'technicians', in particular, to Africa. But some sources have also referred to deployments of combat units of the GDR's National People's Army (Nationale Volksarmee – NVA) in Africa in this period. Other reports have indicated substantial East German arms exports to the African continent. It will be demonstrated that these claims also have some substance, especially with reference to arms transfers from the GDR.

Undoubtedly, with the destabilisation of southern Africa and the Horn of Africa in the 1970s, opportunities for military intervention by states of the Socialist Community were presented, and in these circumstances the USSR appreciated the value especially of East German and Cuban assistance. The USSR could pursue its specific goals in Africa at this time – such as enlarging influence at Western and Chinese expense, gaining international recognition of its superpower status, and acquiring refuelling and repair facilities for its blue-water navy – at reduced economic and military manpower costs, and with less political danger of antagonising the West.

However, the value of an East German military/security profile in Africa as a legitimising tool was circumscribed. An appreciation of this role was reserved solely for policy-makers in the Kremlin. It was understood in East Berlin that world public opinion would not regard favourably a prominent East German military presence in Africa considering the general propensity to equate Prussian/German traditions with militarism. In the late 1970s even the East German public through the local media expressed their unease concerning Western reports of the GDR's military involvement in Africa.[1] This was even though the East German authorities always had at their disposal ideological arguments which could be employed to justify military intervention in the Third World.

For example, at a time of détente, in his report to the 11th Plenum of the SED Central Committee on 15 December 1973, the then Foreign Minister, Winzer, emphasised the need to support 'the legitimacy of the armed struggle of peoples for freedom from colonial and foreign dominance . . .'[2] Seven years later East German military interest in Africa was justified under the rubric of preventing the export of counter-revolution by imperialist forces. Honecker informed an international conference of Third World delegates which convened in East Berlin in October 1980, that Warsaw Pact 'support' for national liberation movements 'had nothing in common with the export of revolution . . .' but was aimed primarily against the export of counter-revolution by the West.[3] Hence, military aid to Mozambique, Angola and Ethiopia, each in conflict with certain internal guerrilla factions receiving outside support, could be justified.

The East German public could also compare accounts of socialist support for national liberation forces with the allegedly aggressive, fascist and militarist policies of the West as exemplified by the FRG and its armed forces.

As noted earlier, East German condemnation of nuclear cooperation between the FRG and South Africa dated from the 1960s. Later commentaries reported West German support for mercenaries and racist police and military units. One such report, written in 1974, declared that the African continent had come to occupy 'a territorial centre of gravity in the militaristic arms and training assistance programme of the FRG'.[4] West German military and security support to Guinea and Somalia was denigrated. The expulsion of West German army pioneers from Guinea in November 1970, as tensions deepened between Bonn and Conakry, was depicted as a success for the German people and 'a defeat for the subversive activities of West German military advisers'.[5]

Bonn's response to these attacks was in general muted, although in a rare display of anger in May 1978 Chancellor Schmidt described GDR support for African governments as merely one of 'officers, arms and ideology'.[6]

At this point, the role of the NVA in its duty towards 'socialist internationalism' should also be noted. With obvious implications for the role of NVA combat units, one East German commentator, Klaus-Ulrich Schloesser, declared that the military cooperation between socialist states and recently independent developing states involved the delivery of arms and equipment; assistance in the formation of a domestic defence industry; the training of military cadres; the issue of licences for arms production; and aid in the combat drill and expansion of armed units. The temporary presence in liberated countries of troop contingents from certain socialist states was also permissible and in full conformity with Article 51 of the UN Charter whereby the host country called for the presence of external units for defence purposes.[7]

Such a bold pronouncement of the tasks of socialist armed forces abroad was unusual. A more characteristic use of terminology to describe East German military cooperation with the Third World was that used by the then Deputy Minister of Foreign Affairs, Willerding, in 1979: 'According to the wish of several [African states] cooperation has also been developed in the military field.'[8]

Hence, ideology could have been used to justify the GDR's military presence in Africa, although its role as an actual motivating force appears questionable. A more likely propulsive force determining the behaviour of the SED leadership, in addition to the strategy of affiliation with the USSR, was the perceived need to activate the East German military establishment. As Moreton has indicated, 'the experience gained by the NVA in overseas operations must be invaluable to an army mostly confined to its barracks'.[9] To lend further substance to this argument, it should be noted that the East German national armed forces were unique for their total subordination to the WTO's Soviet-controlled Joint Command. Also, since a reorganisation of the WTO in 1969, only the Defence Minister of the GDR has continued to be a deputy Commander-in-Chief while other WTO member states have filled this position with their deputy Defence Ministers.[10] Thus, active service in Africa probably played an important role in boosting morale within the East German military establishment. In this context, it should also be noted that a close network of prominent SED officials connected with the military/security establishment are likely to have had an increasing influence over the decision-making process of East German policy, particularly following the admission of Defence Minister Hoffmann to the Politbüro in 1973. These key officials have included Honecker himself, through his position as Chairman of the National Defence Council; the first Defence Minister and then Chairman of the Council of Ministers, Stoph; Hoffmann's appointed successor Heinz Kessler; other Polit-büro members such as Army-General Erich Mielke, Minister for State Security, and Egon Krenz, SED Central Committee Secretary in charge of security questions; and also Central Committee member Colonel-General Friedrich Dickel, Interior Minister and Chief of the German People's Police.

On account of the SED leadership's reluctance to divulge infor-mation concerning the GDR's military involvement in Africa – apart from brief news concerning the visits of military delegations – for the reasons noted above, specific details of the precise nature of the East German military/security role are difficult to obtain and, at times, a certain amount of speculation is unavoidable. Nevertheless, it is not impossible to form a general configuration of the nature of East German involvement in Africa in this sphere. Indeed, occasional speeches and commentaries by prominent East German officials bear testimony to a more substantial involvement in the military/security field than was usually officially admitted. Other reports, especially from South Africa or pro-South African sources, need to be approached with caution. Certain accounts of East German military intervention in Africa have been greatly exaggerated or distorted in order to attract Western support.

The importance of the military/security role of the GDR in Africa

Prior to 1971, East German military/security interest in Africa was sporadic, uncoordinated and amounted to a large extent to a policy of surreptitious manoeuvrings aimed primarily at securing diplomatic recognition of the GDR. Consolidation of relations with the recognising state was also pursued by these means. These activities, when successful, also served to further Soviet interests in Africa.

As indicated previously, before 1971 East Germans were involved in security operations in Ghana and Sudan, and possibly also Zambia before the closure of the GDR trade mission in Lusaka.

In Nkrumah's Ghana, the GDR apparently had been heavily involved in security operations culminating in the Krüger affair. East Germans were reported to be responsible for the tapping of hotel rooms and bar tables at the OAU Conference at Accra in 1965. Two East German officials had controlled a 'Special African Service' which provided Nkrumah's personal bodyguard.[11] These officials were, most probably, Krüger and Captain Stollmeyer, who had operated an espionage school under the guise of a scientific research institute in Accra.[12]

It appears that East German security officers had also established an early presence in Zanzibar, Egypt and Somalia. Prior to the expulsion of the GDR's consul from Zanzibar in June 1970, reports of East German assistance in the security services had led to complaints about the 'modern instruments for interrogation' that the Zanzibar security forces had learned to use.[13] In Egypt, when Sadat removed Vice-President Ali Sabri and Interior Minister Shaarawi Mohamed Gomoa in May 1971, it was revealed that East German and Soviet 'police advisers' had succeeded in establishing their own separate office within the Interior Ministry in Cairo.[14] In Somalia, in 1970, East German police advisers commenced the training of local police units previously undertaken by West German and Italian experts[15] – although (as noted in chapter 3) the FRG maintained an interest in the equipping and training of the Somali police. The GDR's support of the Somali police was further developed in later years prior to the Ogaden War. In May 1975 a commitment to provide regular aid for the Somali police force was reported.[16] Moreover, two years earlier the Somali prison authorities (the Custodian Corps) had received an East German gift of equipment worth almost 2 million Somali shillings.[17]

In the field of military training, East Germans had arrived in Zanzibar as early as 1964 to help organise the local armed forces (see p. 64). Those East German 'advisers' most probably expelled from Egypt together with Soviet military experts in July 1972, were likely security operatives and servicemen allegedly based in Egypt as early as February 1971 to train military telecommunications experts.[18] According to another report, by 1969, NVA officers were employed in FRELIMO camps in Tanzania.[19] Moreover, apparently immediately after the June war of 1967, 300 Egyptian officials were despatched to an NVA officers' school to receive instruction. The same source reported that the GDR had promised Nasser military aid worth 180 million Ostmarks, and that machine guns and pistols had been delivered to Egypt soon after the war.[20] According to other reports, by the late 1960s, East German infantry arms and munitions had been delivered to the MPLA and to FRELIMO.[21]

Most interesting of all, in the spring of 1969, replacing Egyptian

Table 6. *GDR–Africa, visits by military/security delegations, 1967–1988*

	1967	1968	1969	1970	1971	1972	1973	1974	1975	1976	1977
Algeria					GDR	GDR	AFR	GDR			
Angola									AFR	AFR[2a]	
Benin											
Cape Verde Islands											
Congo PR				GDR		GDR AFR	GDR		[b]		
Egypt			AFR		GDR[2]						
Ethiopia											
Guinea			AFR								
Guinea-Bissau											
Libya											
Mali	AFR										
Mozambique											
Nigeria											
São Tomé and Príncipe										AFR	
Somalia										AFR	
Sudan				AFR[2]							
Tanzania			AFR					AFR			
Tunisia											
Zambia											

Table 6. *continued*

	1978	1979	1980	1981	1982	1983	1984	1985	1986	1987	1988
Algeria	GDR										
Angola	GDR	GDR	AFR								
Benin		AFR			AFR				AFR		
Cape Verde Islands	AFR						AFR	AFR			
Congo PR	GDR		AFR		AFR		AFR	AFR		AFR	
Egypt											
Ethiopia		GDR	AFR							GDR	
Guinea	GDR	AFR	AFR			AFR					
Guinea-Bissau		AFR[2]	AFR	AFR				AFR			
Libya	GDR						AFR				
Mali											
Mozambique		AFR[3] GDR	AFR[2] GDR	AFR	AFR		AFR GDR				AFR[2] GDR
Nigeria	GDR AFR										
São Tomé and Príncipe						AFR		AFR		AFR	
Somalia											
Sudan											
Tanzania		AFR				AFR	AFR[2]	AFR	AFR		AFR
Tunisia	GDR										
Zambia	AFR GDR								AFR[2]		

Key: AFR=African delegation to the GDR

GDR=GDR delegation to African state

AFR^2 – denotes two visits by an African delegation to the GDR in that year

a=Delegation led by Commandante Tonha to the 9th SED Congress

b=Military agreement. From *Deutscher Bundestag*, 8 Wahlperiode, Drucksache 8/3463, 4 December 1979, p. 12

Note: The above only refers to specific military/security delegations led by defence or internal ministers, or army/security officials, and does not include visits by other leading members of party, government and national liberation movements where military/security matters would have been raised. Also military/security officials included within larger government delegations are not included.

Source: Dokumente zur Aussenpolitik der DDR (various years), and *Neues Deutschland* (except for *b*)

airmen, East German pilots were reportedly flying aircraft against the Biafran forces in the Nigerian Civil War.[22] This appears to be the first instance of direct East German involvement in combat action in Africa. At this time it was also reported that two MiG-19 fighters were 'delivered' to the Nigerian government by the GDR.[23]

The first East German military delegation to be received in an African capital was that led by a Colonel Heinrich Winkler in Brazzaville in the summer of 1970 on the fourth anniversary of the Congolese Armée Populaire Nationale.[24] Significantly, this visit followed the Congo PR's diplomatic recognition of the GDR earlier in that year. By contrast, several African military/security delegations had already been received in East Berlin (see Table 6).

In 1971 East German military involvement in Africa was upgraded. This followed the decision of the SED Central Committee and the National Defence Council to instruct Hoffmann, in accordance with the wishes of other WTO members, 'to take steps to raise military relations [with the Third World] to the same level as economic, scientific-technical and cultural relations which are already intensively cultivated'.[25]

This decision may be connected with the revelation of the Stockholm International Peace Research Institute (SIPRI) that at the conclusion of the 24th CPSU Congress in Moscow, in April 1971, an agreement was reached to establish a division of labour among WTO members to provide military training for national liberation movements and the armies of certain developing states. By the terms of this 'agreement', Czechoslovakia was entrusted with instruction in artillery and tank warfare; Poland with the training of air pilots and parachute-jumping exercises; Hungary with instructing infantry operations; and the GDR was to be involved in reconnaissance and air control.[26]

Although the GDR came to specialise in other spheres of military/ security activity, there can be no doubt that under Honecker a more prominent profile in Africa was consciously adopted from 1971 onwards as part of the affiliation strategy with the USSR.

Consequently, in October 1971, Hoffmann headed for the first time a full official East German military delegation to the African continent with a visit to Egypt as part of a tour of the Middle East which also included talks in Baghdad and Damascus. The impressions of the tour by Hoffmann and other senior NVA officers were published for the East German public to read. It was emphasised that military contacts needed further expanding despite the presence of military attachés in the states concerned, and that further visits for exchange of information and experience would be arranged.[27] Hoffmann's hopes of further military cooperation between the GDR and Egypt failed to be realised with Sadat's expulsions in July 1972.

Hoffmann had earlier actually briefly held discussions with Algerian army officers in Algiers when en route to Cuba in April 1971.[28] The following year (June 1972), Hoffmann returned to Algiers at the head of an official delegation of prominent NVA officers.[29] This visit resulted in an exchange of military delegations between the GDR and Algeria in the following years.

In sub-Saharan Africa the Congo PR was a target of Soviet bloc interest on account of the operations of the MPLA headquarters in Brazzaville. Winkler's 1970 visit to Brazzaville was followed up by a secret mission of Hoffmann in 1972 according to one West German commentator.[30] In the same year (in October–November), the Congolese Chief of General Staff, Joachim Yhombi-Opango, made an extended visit to the GDR and held talks with Hoffmann in a 'friendly and cordial atmosphere' about future military cooperation.[31] As a consequence of these contacts, the GDR's first publicised military agreement with an African state was announced on 19 March 1973 by Radio Brazzaville. The announcement of the signing of this agreement in Brazzaville by a visiting East German military delegation was not confirmed by the GDR authorities, no doubt mindful of East German public reaction to such news.[32] As conflict between rival guerrilla factions in Angola intensified, Brazzaville became a key centre of operations for Soviet bloc military support for the MPLA. According to one official West German source, the GDR signed another military cooperation agreement with the Congo PR in May 1975.[33]

East German military support for the MPLA in the months prior to Angolan independence cannot be separated from this presence in Brazzaville. Indeed, it has been suggested by one Western source that in 1973 the GDR had also concluded a military agreement with the MPLA, which covered training of MPLA units in the Congo PR, and provision for medical treatment in East Berlin for the seriously wounded. The absence of a military clause in the GDR Treaty of Friendship and Cooperation with Angola in February 1979 was supposed further evidence of a military agreement six years previously, although this argument appears largely founded on supposition.[34]

Nevertheless, the East Germans did support the MPLA more enthusiastically than the USSR prior to Angolan independence in 1975. Here, there are indications of East German autonomous behaviour as further evidence that the GDR was not a mere surrogate or proxy of the USSR. Early in 1972, at a time when Moscow had briefly suspended its arms deliveries to the MPLA, *Neues Deutschland* praised the MPLA as the only nationalist movement in southern Africa with a foreign policy closely oriented to the Socialist Community.[35] This promotion of the MPLA's cause may be attributed, in part, to the GDR's concern for recognition at that time. However, even after international recognition was secured, the East Germans continued to back Neto while Moscow's support remained lukewarm. Indeed, between 1972 and 1973, and again for several months in 1974, the USSR was channelling military aid to a splinter MPLA faction led by Daniel Chipenda, who had emerged as a powerful rival to Neto.[36] Moreover, until June 1975, the USSR continued to support an interim coalition government of the various guerrilla groups in Angola set up under the Alvor Accord earlier that year. At around this time two East Germans were expelled from Angola as subversives by this interim government, while in May and June 1975 alone, at least two East German shiploads of arms were delivered to the MPLA.[37] Interestingly, the Cubans also preferrred to continue to support the MPLA in the first months of 1975.[38]

The above evidence does not necessarily suggest major differences in policy between the GDR and the USSR. Indeed, while exploring other diplomatic possibilities, Moscow may well have recognised the possible advantages of maintaining links with Neto's MPLA through Cuban and East German contacts. It may be assumed that the Soviet leadership would have neither approved nor tolerated East German activities if they were deemed to undermine the USSR's geopolitical interests. However, in the Angolan example, while not negating the affiliation strategy, the East Germans for a time were able to pursue their own interests in Africa which did not appear to coincide 'completely' with those of Moscow.

Undoubtedly, the USSR, Cuba and the GDR played major military roles in the eventual establishment of the MPLA government in Luanda in 1975–6, and in support of Ethiopia in the conflict with Somalia in 1977–8. Some Western analysts have referred to this powerful combination of intervening forces as evidence of a tripartite division of labour in the military sphere between these three states in the Third World after 1975. This division of labour has been depicted as a 'tripod' of a Third World offensive conducted by the USSR; a quasi-alliance of mutual interest; and, in a more tongue-in-cheek vein, an illustration of 'Captain Russia, Adjutant Cuba, Sergeant

Germany'.[39] In the late 1970s, the US State Department believed that the three elements of this division of labour consisted fundamentally of a combination of Soviet logistics and arms deliveries, Cuban manpower and East German technical skills and sophisticated equipment.[40]

An examination of this tripartite cooperation need not be restricted to the two above-mentioned military operations. According to Dunér, in his analysis of military interventions by the socialist states in the Third World, the Soviets, Cubans and East Germans have cooperated in at least four other separate ventures in Africa since the late 1960s. These were, namely: support of FRELIMO prior to Mozambique's independence; assistance to ZAPU forces in Rhodesia before the establishment of Zimbabwe; aid in SWAPO's campaign to liberate Namibia, particularly after 1975; and in Ethiopia, reinforcing Mengistu's efforts to suppress the Eritrean guerrilla movements after the conclusion of the Ogaden War.[41]

Statistics from other sources may be employed to provide what seems to be further evidence of some form of coordination between the USSR, Cuba and the GDR in the military sphere in Africa. Thus, it appears that military contingents from these three states were present in perhaps up to seven African countries in 1981 (namely, Algeria, Angola, the Congo PR, Ethiopia, Guinea, Mozambique and Tanzania) and in at least three in 1988 (namely, Angola, Ethiopia and Mozambique) (see Table 7).

As Dunér has correctly observed, and contrary to the US State Department's views in the late 1970s, the tripartite cooperation was not restricted to a rigid clear-cut specialisation of tasks which would suggest a very close Soviet coordination of activities with the implication that the Cubans and East Germans acted only as proxies. Rather, for example, the GDR provided at various times not only technicians and equipment, but also military planners, military instructors, security and intelligence service operatives, and even pilots and possibly combat units.[42] East German military/security activities in Africa were diverse even prior to international recognition of the GDR. However, as Dunér has also acknowledged, the more the GDR (and, indeed, Cuba) became involved in military interventions in Africa, the closer was the cooperation with the USSR.[43] Nevertheless, despite the lack of a precise functional specialisation in this tripartite military cooperation in Africa, there was still a division of labour of sorts in which each socialist state appeared to concentrate on its particular operational strengths. In the GDR's case, as will be exam-

Table 7. Numbers of Soviet, Cuban, and East German troops and military advisers in Africa, 1978–1988

	May–June 1978		1981			1988		
	Cuba	GDR	Cuba	GDR	USSR	Cuba	GDR	USSR
Africa	39,200–38,380	1,550–1,700	16,450	1,525	14,630	53,900	1,925+	8,850[a]
North Africa								
Algeria			170	250	8,500		250	1,100
Libya		100–125					400	2,000
Sub-African Africa								
Angola	21,000	100	8,000	450	700	50,000	500	1,200
Congo PR	300	100	950	15	850	500		100
Ethiopia	17,000	1,000	5,900	550	2,400	2,800	550	1,700
Guinea	200–300	50–100	280	125	375		125	
Guinea-Bissau	70	50–100	55		370			
Madagascar	30							
Mali				20	635			200
Mozambique	300	100	1,000	100	500	600	100	850
Nigeria		50–100						
Sierra Leone	100–125							
Tanzania	20–30		95	15	300			
Uganda	20–30							
Zambia	70	100					b	

Key: a = Includes 900 military advisers whose country of stationing was not specified
b = Some GDR instructors reported

Source: For figures for 1978, ostensibly military forces 'without advisers', see Robinson, 'Eastern Europe's Presence', p. 10; figures for the remaining years include estimates of Cuban troops, although the sources assume that the Soviet and East German contingents consist of military 'technicians' and 'advisers'. For figures for 1981 see, *Dokumentation über Beziehungen der DDR zur Dritten Welt*, Nov.–Dec. 1981 (Bonn: Gesamtdeutsches Institut, 1982), for the *Pentagon Study Report* (Washington DC: 1981). For figures for 1988 see, International Institute for Strategic Studies, *The Military Balance, 1988–89* (London, 1988), pp. 44, 49 and 194.

ined later, this lay especially in the sphere of military training and security operations.

With the possible exception of the above-mentioned Angolan example prior to 1975, the East Germans have intervened militarily in Africa only when the Soviets were themselves directly involved. On the other hand, the Cubans have clearly operated independently in Africa at times: for example, against the Portuguese-sponsored invasion of Guinea in 1970, and in the Western Sahara.[44] Moreover, the East Germans and Soviets have also cooperated militarily in Africa without the Cubans: for example, in the Nigerian Civil War, and in support of the Libyan occupation of northern Chad in the early 1980s.[45] Thus, in comparison with Cuba, the GDR, in line with its affiliation strategy, appears to have pursued a closer military cooperation with the USSR in Africa.

As further proof, Coker has cited three particular instances of the GDR's willingness to promote Soviet policies in Africa through offering military support; an unsuccessful effort to forestall a peace settlement for Zimbabwe–Rhodesia by pledging military aid to Mozambique in the event of Rhodesian or South African aggression if the Zimbabwean liberation movements declared a legal government from territory on the Rhodesian–Mozambican border; in 1982, an East German offer to replace Cuban units in Angola with NVA troops should the USSR wish (and also succeed to persuade) to transfer the Cubans to Mozambique; and East German military assistance in the abortive Shaba I and II uprisings against the Mobutu regime in Zaire in 1977 and 1978.[46] The GDR's involvement in the Shaba rebellions will be examined later.

It must be emphasised again that the GDR acted as an affiliate and not as a proxy or surrogate of the USSR in Africa. The East Germans volunteered to upgrade their military/security involvement in Africa after 1971 initially, and then more so after 1975 on account of their own specific interests, which also reinforced Soviet strategic objectives.

The employment of NVA combatants in Africa

It is particularly difficult to differentiate an actual deployment of regular NVA combat units in Africa from the stationing of military/ security advisers, technicians and training units.[47] The acknowledged presence of substantial numbers of Cuban troops would appear to diminish any urgent need for manpower inputs from other socialist states. Furthermore, the likelihood of NVA troop contingents in Africa attracting adverse world-wide attention would also serve to dissuade the GDR from embarking upon such a high-profile engagement. The previously mentioned article by Schloesser specifically referred to the legitimate presence of Cuban troops in Angola, although, theoretically, the presence of NVA combat units would also be justified, employing Schloesser's argument, provided Angola had appealed for East German troop deployment.[48]

'In reality, there are no and never have been any units of our National People's Army in any African country' declared Hoffmann, in a rebuttal of Western allegations of thousands of East German troops stationed in Africa to impede the West's access to raw material supplies.[49] Previously, Hoffmann had asserted that military aid to frontline states in the face of heightened aggression from Rhodesia and South Africa would not include 'the contingents of troops that the Western popular media impute to us'.[50]

An official West German pronouncement on East German involvement in Africa in 1979 also conceded: 'The presence of whole GDR military formations in African states cannot be established as yet.'[51]

However, in Lagos in June 1977, Lamberz had stated that the GDR was prepared to despatch troops to southern Africa should the 'competent authorities' in those states so request.[52] Such pronouncements could have encouraged certain circles in the West to claim that the East German military involvement in Africa was massive. For instance, in 1981 a former *Fraktion* leader of the conservative parties in the Bundestag was convinced that Western intelligence sources indicated a GDR presence of over 30,000 officers, soldiers and military advisers in the Third World – an obviously exaggerated figure since the NVA in toto was composed of around only 150,000 troops.[53]

Difficulties in ascertaining the reliability of certain details of accounts referring to a substantial number of NVA troops in Africa make more difficult the problem of accurately determining the nature of East German involvement.

For instance, following Angolan independence, reports proliferated (chiefly South African) of East German Mig-21 and helicopter pilots, and NVA officers and combatants engaged in MPLA sorties and major offensives against UNITA forces.[54] However, these reports must be viewed with caution on account of the infamous story of the GDR's 'Willi Saenger' parachute battalion. In the final months of 1978 the West took alarm at the news that East German paratroopers were apparently stationed in southern Angola within fifty miles of the Namibian border.[55] It was then revealed that the 'Willi Saenger' parachute battalion was not stationed in Angola but in Ethiopia. Finally, it was confirmed that the battalion had actually remained based in the GDR throughout this period.[56]

In 1978, Honecker himself had denounced reports of NVA combat units engaged in Angola as 'fabrications that only serve to poison the atmosphere'.[57] Hoffmann later dismissed such accounts as *Geschwatz* (idle talk).[58] Indeed, the extent of the reliability of such reports of East German military involvement must be seriously questioned.

In the Horn of Africa, as early as 8 November 1977, an Ethiopian defector to the Somali invaders had insisted that East German troops were participating in the hostilities.[59] In May 1978, Mengistu informed Reuter that: 'Progressive comrades from the Soviet Union, Cuba, South Yemen, and the GDR live, fight and die side-by-side with us.'[60] In 1979 a spokesman of the Eritrean Liberation Front (ELF) declared that 5,000 additional East German 'specialists' were placed at Mengistu's disposal with the intention of 'exterminating the Eritreans'.[61] Considerable Cuban reluctance to engage in direct conflict with Eritrean insurgents may suggest that additional East German military units were summoned to assist the Ethiopian government.[62] However, previously noted GDR efforts to secure peace between the secessionists and the central government in Addis Ababa indicated the unlikelihood of a substantial East German troop contingent. The problem of differentiating military advisers and technicians from regular combatants is once more apparent.

As well as spearheading attempts to conclude a peace settlement in Ethiopia in the interests of the socialist bloc, the GDR also played a predominant role in enlisting and coordinating the activities of a number of South Yemeni troops in support of the Ethiopian counteroffensive against the Somali aggressors. In other words, with the GDR securing military backing from Aden, there was still less incentive for regular NVA troops to be deployed against the Somali forces in the conflict in the Ogaden.

East German military/security links with South Yemen were inaugurated after diplomatic recognition. Western intelligence sources reported 2,000 East German advisers organising South Yemen's security service, which included the management of concentration camps.[63]

The coordination of battalions of troops from South Yemen for the Ogaden front was organised by Lamberz. Preparatory training was provided by NVA instructors in Aden.[64] Most probably, Lamberz was assisted in this enterprise by Hoffmann. In October 1977 in Aden, Hoffmann conducted talks with the then Defence Minister and Chairman of the Council of Ministers, Ali Nasser Mohammed, and the General Secretary of the United Political Organisation National Front, Abdel Fattah Ismail.[65] In his role as special ambassador of Honecker, empowered to conduct talks on current developments in the Horn of Africa and the Middle East, Lamberz arrived in Aden less than two months later, having previously visited South Yemen in June 1977.[66] On 5 December, Lamberz held discussions with Ali Nasser Mohammed and the Chairman of the Presidial Council, Robaya Ali.[67] Significantly, Lamberz then arrived in Addis Ababa the next day and was received by Mengistu on 7 December.[68] On 9 December Lamberz had returned to Aden for talks with Abdel Fattah Ismail to whom Honecker's *Kampfgrüsse* (revolutionary greetings) were delivered.[69]

Undoubtedly, this sequence of events indicated that Lamberz was engaged in some operation which involved coordination between Aden and Addis Ababa. Furthermore, between 11 and 16 January 1978, Ali Nasser Mohammed headed a delegation from South Yemen to East Berlin which included the Chief of Staff of the South Yemeni armed forces and Mohammed's personal military adviser. Talks were held with Honecker, Stoph and Lamberz.[70] Following the retreat of Somali forces from Ethiopian territory in March 1978, it was reported that the forces from South Yemen were withdrawn on account of a reluctance to clash with the Eritreans.[71] Consequently, Honecker and Hoffmann most likely failed to secure guarantees of further military assistance in Ethiopia when the new Minister of Defence of South Yemen, Lt.-Col. Antar, arrived in East Berlin at the end of May 1978.[72] Nevertheless, the withdrawal of Aden's military support need not have necessitated the despatch of NVA contingents to confront the Eritreans.

It would appear that the above analysis has offered no hard evidence to substantiate fears among alarmists of the presence of 'considerable' numbers of NVA combatants in Africa. Still, certain observers could point suspiciously to military cooperation clauses and military protocols officially acknowledged by the GDR which were concluded with Mozambique and Ethiopia.

Article 5 of the GDR–Mozambique Treaty of Friendship and Cooperation spoke of military cooperation in the interests of 'strengthening' the 'defence capabilities' of the two states. According to Article 10, should a situation arise 'threatening or violating peace', both states should immediately contact one another 'in order to harmonise their positions regarding the elimination of the looming danger or the restoration of peace'.[73]

In accordance with Article 5, a Protocol on Military Cooperation was agreed on 26 May 1979 when the officiating Minister of National Defence of Mozambique, Armando Emilio Guebuza, visited East Berlin.[74] In an ambiguous statement, Guebuza was reported to have declared that: 'This agreement is going to contribute greatly to the reinforcement of our fight against imperial aggression.'[75] The following year Deputy Defence Minister Werner Fleissner, on a mission to Maputo (25 March to 1 April 1980), reportedly signed another Protocol to widen military cooperation.[76]

A Military Protocol was also agreed in Addis Ababa with Hoffmann's delegation in May 1979. The actual signatories were Fleissner (Head of Technology and Armaments) and the Chief of Supply of the Ethiopian Defence Ministry, Colonel Wolde Mariam, suggesting an agreement of at least a logistical nature.[77]

Also, as noted previously, it was rumoured that a military cooperation agreement was decided with the MPLA as early as 1973. Moreover, unconfirmed official reports from Bonn also referred to a military cooperation agreement between the GDR and the Cape Verde Islands in 1978.[78]

Certainly, the USSR's Treaties of Friendship and Cooperation with Angola, Mozambique and Ethiopia all contained clauses which spoke of furthering cooperation in the military field and stressed the need for immediate consultations if peace was endangered.[79]

However, the published military clauses in treaties between the USSR and the GDR with individual African states by no means promised a definite military commitment of troops in the event of conflict. An extension of the applicability of the so-called Brezhnev Doctrine to the African continent in the name of socialist internationalism was exceedingly remote. As early as May 1970, when skirmishes on the Sino-Soviet border had prompted the USSR to endeavour to extend WTO obligations beyond the European theatre of operations, Stoph had declared that the NVA was only prepared to combine with the USSR to guard peace at the western borders of the Socialist Community.[80] Unconfirmed reports later indicated that Soviet feelers for WTO military support against China's offensive in Vietnam and for Moscow's invasion of Afghanistan in the late 1970s were consistently rejected.[81] In this context, it would seem that even Honecker's policy of affiliation with the USSR was only operational within certain defined bounds.

Thus, an application of the Brezhnev Doctrine to the African continent in connection with the deployment of East German troops was most unlikely. Even ideologically, the 'socialist' nature of African regimes remained open to question. The GDR's military contribution involved more covert operations.

The work of East German military/security advisers and technicians

Exact data on the numbers of East German military/security advisers and technicians active in Africa at a given date are impossible to obtain on account of the problems caused by the GDR's obvious reluctance to supply statistical information, the insuperable difficulties involved in accurately distinguishing between the role of civilian and non-civilian technicians and experts (e.g., in vehicle maintenance, telecommunications and construction work) and, the usual aggregation of East European 'military technicians' abroad in Western data. Nevertheless, a number of immediate observations may be deduced from an examination of various, albeit conflicting, sources of data concerning the nature and extent of the East German military/security presence in Africa, although, again, the problem of precisely differentiating advisers from participants in military operations is impossible without close reference to individual states (see Table 7).

Estimates of the total numbers of East German advisers in particular states and throughout the continent vary immensely, although one may assume the presence in Africa, on average, of around 2,000 military and perhaps another 2,000 security advisers from the late 1970s onwards.[82] Not surprisingly, advisers were active in African states which were traditionally close associates of the Soviet bloc, or in states which were eager to diversify their external sources of support. The East German presence was considerable when taking into account the number of African states in which advisers were reported.

In general, the GDR came to specialise in such fields as security and intelligence services, paramilitary training and organisation, telecommunications, airfield construction, port development, pioneer-work, military engineering, tank-warfare instruction and training in parachute operations. The value of East German expertise for the Soviet bloc was not restricted to air control and reconnaissance as SIPRI had suggested. In a rare admission in 1979, in response to a question concerning how to combat Rhodesian and South African acts of aggression against frontline states, Hoffmann had replied, in part, by stressing the need to train experts, engineers, technicians, military officers and non-commissioned officers from the states concerned.[83]

Precise details of the nature and extent of GDR security operations in Africa are particularly difficult to obtain. The visit to East Berlin of the commander of the Angolan police forces, Andre Petroff, in May 1976 (30 April–7 May), to hold discussions with the GDR Chief of Police and First Deputy Minister of the Interior, General Ewald Eichorn, laid the foundations for the later intensive East German security involvement in Angola.[84] In 1976, the FNLA leader, Holden Roberto, accused East Germans in Angola of organising the Department of Information and Security of Angola (DISA), and of managing 'concentration camps'.[85] Given such links with DISA, the possibility of the GDR possessing foreknowledge of the attempted coup in Luanda by former Internal Minister, Nito Alves in May 1977, must be considered. This was in spite of Lamberz' arrival in Angola a few weeks later with a personal message from Honecker for President Neto which expressed satisfaction with the failure of the 'malicious' putsch.[86] Indeed, rapid changes of personnel within the Angolan internal security services and the dissolution of DISA in July 1979, appeared to indicate that East German control over intelligence operations had limited success.[87] Nevertheless, following further internal security reorganisation in Angola in 1983, it was reported that East German officials orchestrated the activity of new security officers and army political commissioners, as well as providing support for the paramilitary People's Defence Organisation.[88] As recently as January 1985, the UNITA General Secretary, Tito Chingunji, spoke of the presence in Luanda of around 2,000(!) East German officers and experts, many of them in the security sphere.[89] .

East German security personnel have been reported active also in Mozambique, Ethiopia, Guinea-Bissau, Libya; Uganda, Equatorial Guinea and the Congo PR. In Mozambique, contacts with the National Service of Popular Security were developed, and according to the West German press, up to 600 East German security advisers were active in the mid-1980s.[90] Around 1,500 security personnel from the GDR were apparently employed in Ethiopia in 1979.[91] Despite a coup against the Soviet-backed Luiz Cabral government in Guinea-Bissau in November 1980, the successor regime still evidently made use of Soviet and East German personnel.[92] The Libyan intelligence service 'Mukhabarat' was allegedly connected with its East German counterpart.[93] According to Egyptian sources, advisers from the GDR played a key role in the suppression of a military coup directed against Ghaddafi in Tobruk in August 1980 where several hundred insurgents were believed killed.[94]

Less successful was the GDR's support in the security sphere of the ruthless dictatorships of Francisco Macias Nguema and Idi Amin in Equatorial Guinea and Uganda, both of whom were deposed in 1979. It seems that two East German officials who died in the GDR's embassy in Kampala at the time of the Tanzanian-backed invasion of Uganda in 1979, immediately before their deaths had been desperately endeavouring to remove all compromising materials which linked the GDR with the operations of the notorious Ugandan secret police and Amin's 'State Research Bureau'.[95] Nevertheless, recent West German press accounts refer to East German security advisers in Uganda helping to train the secret police force under President Yoweri Museveni.[96]

In the Congo PR the overthrow of the then President Yhombi-Opango in February 1979 and his replacement with the East German trained Defence and Police Minister Colonel Dennis Sassou-Nguesso, was attributed to possible subversive GDR involvement.[97] This was plausible when considering rumours that upon his visit to East Berlin in October 1977 Yhombi-Opango had demanded financial compensation for the previous use of Brazzaville as a base of operations in the Angolan civil war.[98] More up-to-date information referred to East German aid in the police and state security services in the Congo PR, the training and equipping of the Congolese people's militia, and the installation by the GDR of the most modern coastal radio network system in Africa.[99]

A precedent having been established in the training of Nkrumah's praetorian guard, according to various sources East German advisers were active in recruiting and organising the personal bodyguards of Machel, Mengistu, Jose Eduardo dos Santos (Angola's second President) and Ghaddafi. East Germans have reputedly served in Ghaddafi's bodyguard and saved the Libyan leader's life on two unspecified occasions.[100]

One Western analyst has correctly underlined the crucial role of these praetorian guards in protecting rulers sympathetic to the Soviet bloc. Only small numbers of well-trained security guards, placing the protected African leader in a kind of 'cocoon', may be all that was needed to sustain a government in power.[101]

On at least two occasions in the 1970s, the GDR was accused of conspiring to overthrow certain African governments. In Khartoum, in July 1976, the USSR, Libya and the GDR were implicated in an attempted coup against the Nimeiry government with the result that the East German ambassador was ordered to leave two months later on suspicion of liaison with the prohibited Sudanese communist party.[102] And in Ghana, the East German trade adviser, Horst Hartmann, was expelled with four Soviet diplomats in September 1978 for subversive activities.[103]

On account of lack of data it is not possible to calculate the numbers of African security and military personnel trained in the GDR. Official sources in Bonn noted that an undisclosed number of officers from Ethiopia were undertaking courses of instruction in the Wilhelm Pieck Police Officer's School at Aschersleben.[104] Tuition was reportedly also offered to officers from the former Portuguese colonies at the School.[105]

Details of training programmes in the GDR for African military units were a little more specific.

According to the Bundestag report of December 1979, Angolan tank and parachute units were involved in training on the island of Rügen; FRELIMO units had received courses in officer instruction in the GDR since 1975; and, from 1976, Congolese officers attended the NVA high school in Stralsund (the 'Karl Liebknecht' Officers' Training College of the *Volksmarine*), and the second parachute battalion of the Congo PR had received instruction at Rügen.[106]

The NVA authorities were reluctant to divulge any information concerning their training programmes for visiting Third World army officers and units. Consequently, upon his visit to the GDR in October 1977, the disclosure by President Yhombi-Opango of the presence of a number of Congolese troops receiving instruction in the GDR acutely embarrassed his East German hosts.[107] According to other reports, a military delegation from Mozambique observed FRELIMO units in training exercises in the GDR in July 1984.[108] By 1980 a number of Libyan officers were apparently based at Stralsund, and at the Air Force/Air Defence unit in Kamenz.[109] Other reports mention the training of officers from Zimbabwe, and instruction in guerrilla tactics for ANC and SWAPO cadres in the GDR.[110]

For the purpose of preparing NVA army instructors for their deployment in Africa – 'training the trainers' – an NVA language school specialising in the instruction of African languages was maintained in Naumburg/Saale.[111]

One reputable source alleged that the GDR's first properly organised military training assistance programme in the Third World commenced in Algeria (and in Iraq), when instruction in military engineering, signals and logistics was given. Apparently, at one time (no dates given), over 1,000 East German 'soldiers' were present in

Algeria until the authorities in Algiers claimed that the 'weaponry' and 'ammunition' delivered by the GDR was unfit for use![112] However, according to a number of press reports, East German military advisers remained active in Algeria in the late 1970s in connection with the training of POLISARIO guerrillas, and other sources have referred to a continued East German military presence in Algeria in the 1980s.[113]

Western accounts have referred to extensive training programmes offered by East German military advisers to national liberation movements stationed in Angola, Mozambique and Zambia. For example, according to these reports, in 1979, SWAPO, ANC and ZAPU guerrilla units were receiving military instruction in Angola; and in 1984 allegedly up to 3,000 East German advisers (an obviously inflated figure) were still offering military assistance programmes to the ANC and SWAPO.[114] Other sources noted East German military personnel based in Mozambique and Zambia in the late 1970s were training ZAPU and SWAPO units.[115]

Evidently, at a meeting of the WTO's Political Consultative Committee in November 1978, within the context of discussions on extending aid to national liberation movements and frontline states in southern Africa, it was decided to increase the East German military contribution in Africa.[116]

Certainly it is reasonable to assume that in Angola, Mozambique and Zambia, East German military advisers also offered support facilities to the regular armies of those states. The number of military delegation visits between the GDR and these African states also indicated the deepening of cooperation in this sphere. For example, in Maputo in the summer of 1979, Hoffmann promised FRELIMO that its armed forces would become 'one of the most modern and efficient in Africa' to counter the imperialist threat.[117] A year previously, certain intelligence sources linked to UNITA had announced that the East Germans had established a special command centre at the former Portuguese army base at Henrique de Carvalho where Cuban and Angolan troops received instruction.[118] In September 1985, according to one account, officers from the GDR were training pilots, radar operators and artillery crews in Angola.[119] More recently, an undisclosed number of East German military instructors were reported active in Zambia (see Table 7).

In addition to providing military training programmes, East German advisers and technicians have apparently performed a key role in the planning, organisation and logistical coordination of Ethiopian offensives in the Ogaden and Eritrea.[120] The highest ranking GDR military officer in Africa was prominent in the Ethiopian Command in the late 1970s.[121] According to the International Institute for Strategic Studies, 300 East German technicians and advisers were operating aircraft and heavy equipment in Ethiopia as recently as 1987.[122]

Moreover, when Libya invaded Chad in 1981, it was reported that up to 250 East German military technicians accompanied the invaders and were active in servicing Soviet-built planes and helicopters in the field.[123]

According to debates in the Bundestag in 1980, it was reported that approximately 3,000 East German military advisers were stationed in Africa. In the words of one deputy of the Social Democrats: 'This is indeed no Afrika-Korps, since there are no troop units; but there are in many corners military advisers, and these bring nothing positive to this continent, but contribute to more armament.'[124]

Other less official sources stated that the East German Deputy Foreign Trade Minister, Alex Schalk, was responsible for the operations of a State Secretariat which coordinated East German military involvement in Africa.[125]

Despite difficulties in obtaining precise data, it is possible to conclude from this summary that the East German contribution to the Soviet bloc and Cuban effort was considerable. Military and security experts from the GDR apparently possessed a comprehensive range of skills to offer. A reputation for expertise in these fields was acquired in the pre-recognition period. At times, more covert cooperation in the intelligence field contributed towards a number of policy reversals for the GDR's *Afrikapolitik*. However, significantly, the USSR was convinced that East German military/security 'advisers' could be entrusted to undertake a catalogue of diverse operations in Africa and in the GDR.

Arms exports and other forms of military cooperation

It is universally agreed that the USSR is responsible for a substantial percentage of total arms transfers to the Third World. According to statistics published by the US Arms Control and Disarmament Agency (ACDA), between 1982 and 1986 Soviet arms exports to Africa totalled $19,110 million (current) compared with American deliveries for the same period valued at only $4,640 million (current). The USSR was the principal exporter of arms to Algeria, Angola, Benin, Burundi, the Cape Verde Islands, the Congo PR,

GDR arms exports, 1972–86 (mill. $ current)

Year	1972	1976	1978	1980	1981	1982	1983	1984	1985	1986
Amount	50	20	80	180	140	160	210	390	550	220

Sources: US ACDA *World Military Expenditures and Arms Transfers 1972–1982* (Washington DC: US Government Printing Office, 1984), p. 69: and, US ACDA *World Military Expenditures and Arms Transfers 1987* (Washington DC: US Government Printing Office, 1988), p. 101.

Ethiopia, Guinea, Guinea-Bissau, Libya, Madagascar, Mali, Mozambique, São Tomé and Príncipe, and Tanzania. Czechoslovakia and Poland delivered respectively $1,450 million (current) and $150 million (current) worth of arms to African states in the same period.[126] No figures were given for East German arms transfers to individual African states.

The East German contribution to the transfer of weaponry by the WTO to the Third World is generally regarded as of little more than peripheral value. No official East German data is published for the obvious reasons outlined previously. However, according to ACDA, the GDR's total arms transfers in 1986 only amounted to $220 million (current) (see following table compared with a value of $1,100 million (current) each exported by Poland and Czechoslovakia.[127] Note though the sharp drop in East German arms exports after 1985. Still, these amounts appear to suggest that the GDR's arms transfers to Africa were of little significance. Indeed, the official view from Bonn in December 1979 was that the GDR played only a minor role in arms exports to Africa within a Warsaw Pact division of labour.[128]

However other sources have suggested that the East German arms contribution to non-communist states was substantial and played an important role in a Soviet bloc weapons transfer programme to the Third World. One West German report noted as early as 1976 that the GDR delivered arms to twenty-four non-communist Third World states coordinated by an Office for Technical Industrial Trade in East Berlin.[129] At around the same time the French military periodical TAM calculated that East German arms supplies ranked second in quantitative terms in the WTO behind the USSR.[130] SIPRI later alleged that the East German military assistance programme was substantial, overlapped with Soviet arms recipients in 90 per cent of cases, and that deliveries were also made to certain regimes in which the USSR was less concerned to play a prominent role, i.e., 65 per cent of non-communist states which received French military support also apparently obtained military aid from the GDR.[131]

It must also be emphasised that neither ACDA nor SIPRI data with reference to arms transfers are necessarily reliable. For example, ACDA's assessment of the 'pricing' and 'timing' of Soviet bloc arms exports is open to criticism, as is SIPRI's concentration on major weapons systems only.[132] Most importantly, neither refer to arms exports to national liberation movements, although the GDR appears to have performed a valuable function in supplying certain guerrilla groups with armaments.

Another complication in the assessment of the actual quantity of GDR arms deliveries to the non-communist Third World, in general, lies in the impossibility of separating military and civilian material aid. For instance, should one incorporate in military aid estimates the 1,200 W50 trucks delivered by the Ludwigsfelde automobile works to Angola, Mozambique and Ethiopia between 1976 and 1980?[133]

Despite these problems, some details of the qualitative nature of East German arms transfers have been compiled. In general, the GDR has specialised in the manufacture and export to Africa of light infantry arms, rifles, mortars, howitzers, military vehicles, steel helmets and uniforms, together with invaluable arms components such as sophisticated optical and electronic equipment.[134] Given the advanced technological and industrial base of the GDR within the Soviet bloc, one must assume that the provision of certain East German weapons components was of particular importance for WTO arms transfers.

The GDR has not played a role in the manufacture of heavy weapons systems such as tanks, artillery and aircraft. But, apparently, the East Germans have manufactured and delivered three P6 class fast attack gunboats, two SCHWALBE class coastal patrol boats, and two 50 ton patrol craft to Tanzania.[135]

Moreover, apart from the manufacture of certain arms equipment, the GDR may have also played an important role in the shipment and delivery to African states of arms transfers from other WTO states. According to the testimony of an East German naval captain who jumped ship in Hamburg, the GDR played a key role in the shipment of Soviet tanks and ammunition stores to Ethiopia, Tanzania and Mozambique, and his own vessel had transported 20 tanks and 3,000 tons of ammunition to 10 African ports for the use of liberation movements.[136]

Interestingly, on rare occasions key East German officials have publicly admitted the export of arms to Africa. Reviewing the forces of the militia training camp in Tatek, Ethiopia, in May 1979, Hoffmann had boasted that thousands of the sons of former slaves and landless peasants were now equipped with steel helmets and machine guns from the GDR.[137] Mengistu expressed his gratitude to the GDR Defence Minister for East German assistance in the building up of the revolutionary, socialist army of Ethiopia.[138] In November 1979, Honecker himself observed a military parade at Tatek and proudly proclaimed to his Ethiopian hosts that 'the GDR did not hesitate for an instant when it was a matter of sending you arms and bread to enable you to wage your war successfully'.[139]

In Hoffmann's mission to Zambia in May 1979, the East German Defence Minister assured his hosts that, as in the past, the GDR would continue to provide political, diplomatic, economic and military aid, 'until the final strongholds of reaction in southern Africa fell'.[140]

Such examples serve to make more sinister the popular NVA rhyme – 'Kalashnikovs not Coca-Cola bring self-determination to Angola.'[141]

Details of East German arms exports to Africa in the pre-recognition period were noted earlier. In the post-recognition period, one may assume that weapons originating from the GDR were delivered to Mozambique, Ethiopia and Angola, and to the liberation movements ANC, SWAPO and ZAPU, and perhaps also to Libya and Tanzania. This assumption may be made on the basis of the number of official and military contacts publicised, the frequent references to East German deliveries of unspecified goods of 'solidarity', and the apparent military/security training programmes organised by the GDR, all with respect to the above listed states and liberation movements. Furthermore, more specific references to East German arms exports to several of the above were also published by Western sources.

At least two 'military gifts' were handed over to the FRELIMO authorities by NVA officials in 1979 and 1980, possibly under the terms of the earlier Military Protocol and Treaty of Friendship and Cooperation.[142] Prior to the disclosures of Honecker and Hoffmann, on 3 May 1977, information of a consignment of 45,000 AK rifles and other small arms deliveries from Czechoslovakia, the GDR and Yugoslavia to Ethiopia was recorded.[143]

After Nkomo accepted the solidarity gift from Honecker in Lusaka in February 1979, the ZAPU leader claimed that the GDR was one of the largest contributors to the material requirements of his force.[144] Following Hoffmann's later meeting with Nkomo in Lusaka, and the ZAPU leader's stay in East Berlin in June 1979, it was reported that the

GDR had even taken over from the USSR as the principal exporter of arms to ZAPU.[145] This claim appeared exaggerated. More plausible were accounts of East German assurances of 'considerable military assistance' to ZAPU in the use of heavy armaments and anti-aircraft weaponry delivered by the USSR.[146]

Brief references to East German 'solidarity assistance' to African liberation movements are innumerable. For instance, on 18 January 1979 GDR sources spoke of deliveries of solidarity gifts in Luanda and Lusaka to representatives of SWAPO, and ANC and the Patriotic Front of Zimbabwe, i.e., the amalgam of ZAPU and ZANU forces.[147] Only days later, Honecker, in Luanda, personally offered Nujoma the solidarity gift of 'unknown size'.

East German arms exports to Libya were indicated as early as 1976.[148] Four years later, sources in Tunis referred to the confiscation of weaponry originating from the GDR after a Libyan attack on the Tunisian mining town of Gafsa.[149]

The Tanzanian armed forces that invaded Uganda to assist in the overthrow of Amin were apparently equipped with weaponry from the GDR and Bulgaria[150] – ironic, when earlier East German security cooperation with Amin is recalled.

All these details have indicated the diverse nature of an East German arms programme, involving a number of African states and liberation movements, which in quantitative and qualitative terms was of greater importance than ACDA statistics have suggested, although, of course, this programme in no way rivalled that of the USSR. Massive Soviet arms transfers were, in part, directed against Chinese (especially in the 1970s) and Western influence in the Third World, aimed to secure political leverage over the recipients of weaponry, and provided useful sources of hard currency exchange from Arab states until the decline of oil prices in the 1980s. In contrast, East German arms exports were not primarily intended to accumulate hard currency earnings. This chapter has indicated that certain national liberation movements were key recipients of weaponry from the GDR. These groups had few financial resources at their disposal. In such cases, arms were not exported for profit-seeking purposes. However, these exports would have enabled the GDR to develop more favourable relations with certain states and guerrilla groups, and also furthered Soviet objectives in Africa.

The large number of visiting military delegations between the GDR and several African states, together with other contacts between heads of state and government and key party officials and national liberation leaders, among whom military/security issues were most likely raised, were further evidence of the extent of East German military involvement. Almost all such delegation exchanges were noted with at least minimal reference by *Neues Deutschland*, as further testimony to the East German public of the active profile of the GDR in Africa. In practice, these delegation visits were of both political and military importance. Leading African military officials were often received by Honecker in East Berlin, while Hoffmann, or his deputies, were often welcomed by various heads of state in African capitals. These visits contributed to an improvement in relations between the GDR and the African state in question. Through the reception of internal ministers and police chiefs, the GDR also hoped to consolidate African regimes which viewed the Soviet bloc with favour.

The political importance of military delegations may be illustrated with reference to the two high-level NVA delegations to Africa at the end of the 1970s. Hoffmann was welcomed by heads of state in Guinea, Angola, Zambia, Mozambique and Ethiopia in 1978 and 1979.[151] Bilateral relations with Nigeria and Guinea further improved when leading military delegations from these two African states soon reciprocated Hoffmann's visit (see Table 6). In Brazzaville, Hoffmann was entertained by the future president, Sassou-Nguesso. Relations with Zambia further improved, resulting in Kaunda's visit to the GDR in August 1980. It is also of interest to note here that, within nine months of Hoffmann's reception in Lusaka, Zambia had concluded an arms deal with the USSR valued at $85.4 million.[152] In fact, of all the states included in Hoffmann's itinerary, only relations with Tunisia in the military/security sphere did not develop further.

Such military delegations would also have discussed the delivery of arms or security advisers, the training of African combat units, the coordination of armed manoeuvres and general tactics in times of conflict or liberation struggle – in short, all of the features of military assistance examined in this chapter. Moreover, exchanges of experience and occasional overtures to *Waffenbruderschaft* (comradeship in arms) were employed by the East German military as part of an important morale-boosting exercise for the benefit of their African guests or hosts.

Undoubtedly, from the mid-1970s onwards, and more particularly after Hoffmann's two major African tours in 1978 and 1979, East Berlin became an essential stopover in the itinerary of African military delegations which toured Eastern Europe.

Conclusion

There are problems in ascertaining the exact nature of East German military involvement in Africa. Generally, the GDR has succeeded in pursuing a strategy of affiliation with the USSR in the military/security sphere of activities, without attracting too much adverse world-wide publicity. It appears that the GDR has played an important contribution in what was, in practice, a loose division of labour among socialist states in Africa. In particular, the East Germans have performed invaluable services as military and security 'advisers' and 'experts' in a number of African states.

Interestingly, in the post-recognition period, only one African state has suspended diplomatic relations with the GDR on account of alleged proof of East German military activities against an OAU member-state. This occurred at the start of May 1977, when accusing the GDR of involvement in the invasion of Shaba province (Shaba I) by rebels of the National Congolese Liberation Front (Front de la Libér-ation Nationale Congolaise–FLNC), Zaire ordered East German diplomats to leave Kinshasa within forty-eight hours and recalled its diplomats from East Berlin.[153] Diplomatic relations were not restored between the two states until January 1979. A spokesman of the Foreign Affairs Ministry in East Berlin immediately refuted the 'untenable' and 'slanderous' accusations that the GDR had supplied weapons to the FLNC and, indeed, participated in the invasion.[154] However, according to one Western press account, the GDR had been given the task, by the USSR, of destabilising the regime of Joseph Mobutu in order to end Zaire's support for the FLNA guerrillas who were still opposing the MPLA regime in Luanda. Apparently, as early as 1976, an East German military mission had been despatched to Angola to train the FLNC rebels stationed there, and weaponry was also provided, including Soviet anti-aircraft missiles, although the East Germans were under specific instructions not to participate in the invasion.[155] One West German analyst has traced an East German and Cuban connection with the FLNC's leader, Nathaniel Mbumba, prior to the Shaba I invasion.[156] Although Shaba I was a failure, the East Germans apparently continued to train the FLNC rebels and were involved in the second invasion in May 1978 (Shaba II). Here, specifically, attention has been drawn to Hoffmann's visit to Angola immediately prior to the Shaba II invasion at a time when other Eastern European defence ministers were attending a session of the WTO's Military Council in Budapest.[157] Hoffmann ridiculed reports that his visit to three military bases in eastern Angola had triggered the 'starting shot' to the Shaba II invasion.[158]

What exactly the GDR's role was in the Shaba invasions is by no means clear. It seems likely that given their expertise in military training, East German advisers would have offered some form of instruction to FLNC rebels based in camps in Angola. But to impute that the GDR actually masterminded the invasions, as some Western sources have alleged, is much more questionable. The presence of a West German-based company in Shaba province, 'Orbital Transport-und Raketen Aktiengesellschaft', seeking to develop payloads for commercial satellites, with potential military spin-offs, was not grounds enough to charge the GDR with responsibility for coordination of the invasions. This was in spite of East German accusations that through the research activities of this company, the FRG was seeking to test and develop nuclear weaponry which could be employed in future by South Africa and other 'reactionary' states in the region against the frontline states.[159] Even the official West German Bundestag report of December 1979 failed to confirm Mobutu's claims in a television interview on 24 May 1978 that East German weapons were captured from the FLNC rebels.[160]

Whatever the extent of East German military involvement, Mobutu's decision to sever diplomatic relations endangered the success of the GDR's *Afrikapolitik* hitherto, and, as far as the SED authorities were concerned, drew unwelcome attention to the GDR's military involvement in Africa. However, according to the affiliation strategy, the GDR would not have been forced to support the FLNC rebels. For a number of specific reasons cited previously, the GDR was willing to further the USSR's political and strategic interests in Africa. It is neither by accident, nor by Soviet coercion, that East German military/security involvement on the African continent has increased in the post-recognition period.

5   East German economic relations with Africa

Introduction

The official data of GDR foreign trade turnover are arguably the least comprehensive compilation of statistics of any major industrialised state. Possible political embarrassment for the East German government that may ensue with the disclosure of certain trade figures, in part, explains the inadequacy of these official records. Also, connected with this, is the customary reluctance of the security- and legitimacy-conscious SED elite to divulge information unnecessarily about political, economic and social development in the GDR, where 'positive' developments are open to question. Similarly, bold pronouncements in the 1980s concerning the expanding costs of East German aid programmes to developing states and national liberation movements aimed at securing political favour in the Third World, are also of dubious statistical value.

These preliminary statements immediately indicate the political importance of East German economic involvement in Africa. It will be observed that the economic imperatives of GDR activity in Africa are never completely divorced from their political significance.

Annual editions of the statistical yearbook of the GDR (*Statistisches Jahrbuch der Deutschen Demokratischen Republik*) furnish details of the totals of East German imports and exports from a select number of African states until 1974, after which only aggregate trade turnover figures with these states were provided. The method of statistical recording was revised by the SED authorities as a consequence, in part, of the sudden substantial GDR trade deficit of VM 608.5 million with the developing states in 1974 after a consistent trade surplus with these states from 1961 (inclusive).[1] Hence, with Iraq, an East German trade surplus valued at VM 58.9 million in 1973 was converted into a deficit of VM 351.8 million the following year as the GDR increased its oil imports (see Table 2). But even when in the 1980s according to Western statistics the GDR has maintained a constant trade surplus with the developing world (see Table 8), East German statistics have continued to refer only to aggregate trade turnover with individual states, presumably because of embarrassing trade deficits with the West.

East German statistics also fail to report trade turnover with many African states. These include those with which trade treaties or agreements of economic cooperation were signed. Moreover, also in this group were states with which the GDR enjoyed close political relations, i.e., Guinea-Bissau, the Cape Verde Islands, Benin and Madagascar; and in the former, Cameroon, Burundi, Liberia, Togo, Uganda, Sierra Leone and Zaire. Insignificant amounts of trade most likely account for these omissions. Interestingly, details of trade turnover with Zambia were listed for the first time in East German statistics in 1987, and then with figures dating back to 1970. Also in 1987, trade turnover data with Guinea were recorded for the first time in many years (see Table 2).[2] No data were provided on East German trade turnover with African states with which no previous economic agreements of cooperation at governmental level had been concluded. This was due to political factors, as will be demonstrated later (pp. 158–9).

Other deficiencies in the statistical yearbooks are the increasing inadequacy of a proper commodity breakdown of exports and imports from the few African states listed, and the failure to account for the quoted total East German imports of a key raw material – oil.

Finally, as a general cautionary observation, problems continually occur when attempting to convert the East German VM into US dollars, which is complicated by the fact that the GDR officially converts the VM with the West German DM at parity although the former is actually worth appreciably less.

Even when bearing in mind the unreliable nature of official foreign trade statistics, an analysis of East German economic involvement in Africa is still possible. In the pre-recognition phase of GDR foreign policy commercial contacts and credit offers to certain African regimes were primarily directed towards circumventing the Hallstein Doctrine with the ultimate goal of securing diplomatic recognition. One West German commentator has even alleged that in the hope of acquiring recognition the GDR was willing to import from the Third World non-essential goods, or was prepared to pay exorbitant prices for the purchase of specific products from the developing states.[3] However, in general, in the pre-recognition period, East German trade with the

Table 8. *Trade balance of the GDR and other East European states with the Third World, 1975–1987* (billion dollars)

Year	GDR Exp.	Imp.	Bal.	Bulgaria Exp.	Imp.	Bal.	Czechoslovakia Exp.	Imp.	Bal.	Hungary Exp.	Imp.	Bal.	Poland Exp.	Imp.	Bal.	Romania Exp.	Imp.	Bal.	USSR Exp.	Imp.	Bal.
1975	0.4	0.5	−0.1	0.5	0.2	+0.3	0.7	0.5	+0.2	0.4	0.5	−0.1	0.9	0.6	+0.3	1.0	0.7	+0.3			
1976	0.5	0.6	−0.1	0.4	0.2	+0.2	0.7	0.5	+0.2	0.4	0.5	−0.1	0.9	0.6	+0.3	1.1	1.1				
1977	0.8	0.7	+0.1	0.7	0.3	+0.4	0.8	0.7	+0.1	0.8	1.0	−0.2	1.0	0.7	+0.3	1.6	1.2	+0.4			
1978	0.6	0.7	−0.1	0.8	0.3	+0.5	0.9	0.6	+0.3	1.0	1.1	−0.1	1.1	0.9	+0.2	1.8	1.6	+0.2			
1980	1.3	1.2	+0.1	1.5	0.5	+1.0	1.4	0.9	+0.5	0.9	0.9		1.7	2.0	−0.3	2.2	4.4	−2.2	13.6	10.7	+2.9
1981	1.5	0.9	+0.6	2.0	0.7	+1.3	1.5	0.8	+0.7	1.0	0.8	+0.2	1.5	1.0	+0.5	3.3	3.5	−0.2	15.4	13.4	+2.0
1982	1.8	1.0	+0.8	2.1	0.9	+1.2	1.4	0.8	+0.6	1.2	0.9	+0.3	1.6	0.7	+0.9	3.1	2.9	+0.2	18.1	12.8	+5.3
1983	1.7	1.2	+0.5	1.7	0.9	+0.8	1.6	0.8	+0.8	1.1	1.0	+0.1	1.5	0.9	+0.6	2.4	2.8	−0.4	18.7	13.2	+5.5
1984	1.7	1.3	+0.4	2.0	1.0	+1.0	1.5	0.9	+0.6	1.2	1.0	+0.2	1.4	0.8	+0.6	2.3	2.8	−0.5	17.9	13.6	+4.3
1985	1.8	1.5	+0.3	2.0	1.3	+0.7	1.4	0.9	+0.5	1.1	0.6	+0.5	1.1	0.8	+0.3	2.1	2.9	−0.8	16.3	13.8	+2.5
1986	1.6	1.5	+0.1	1.6	1.3	+0.3	1.5	0.9	+0.6	0.9	0.7	+0.2	1.4	0.7	+0.7	1.8	2.0	−0.2	19.0	12.1	+6.9
1987[a]	1.9	1.5	+0.4	2.0	0.9	+1.1	1.4	1.0	+0.4	0.9	0.7	+0.2	1.2	0.8	+0.4	1.3	1.4	−0.1	21.2	13.3	+7.9

Key: Exp. = Exports; Imp. = Imports; Bal. = Balance

a = All figures for 1987 are preliminary

Source: Figures for 1975–8 from Roger E. Kanet, 'Eastern Europe and the World: The Expanding Relationship', in Sodaro and Wolchik (eds.), *Foreign and Domestic Policy in Eastern Europe in the 1980s – Trends and Prospects*, p. 236, calculated from CIA, East European and International Monetary Fund statistics. Figures for 1980–7 from, *International Trade 1987–1988 – General Agreement on Tariffs and Trade*, vol. 2, Table AA4, Appendix II.

Third World was modest in volume and exports to African states exceeded imports. According to GDR statistics, trade was concentrated on a small number of African states, of which Nasser's Egypt was clearly the most important through its exports of cotton and even oil.

In a speech to the 7th SED Congress in April 1967, Ulbricht declared that if relations between the GDR and the Third World states were normalised, the potential for economic exchange would be unbounded.[4] Is the allegation that Ulbricht's promise of commercial expansion remained unrealised following recognition justified?[5] Of what importance economically has Africa been for the GDR in the post-1973 period?

More specifically, of what significance for the GDR were certain African states endowed with substantial oil reserves, given the consequences of the escalating costs and decreasing quantities of Soviet oil supplies after 1975 (as noted in chapter 1)? Were certain African states also important sources of other key raw materials for the GDR in those years which were critical for the East German economy after the second OPEC price rise? And how should one assess the GDR's economic relations with Africa in recent years? Finally, what were the characteristics of inter-German economic interaction in Africa after the termination of the Hallstein Doctrine – continued conflict, compromise or cooperation?

In answering these questions in the context of the GDR's *Afrikapolitik*, the interplay between economic imperatives and political considerations must be continually borne in mind. This interplay did not exclude a number of fundamentally irreconcilable policy goals. On occasions East German economic interests in Africa clashed with the Third World's demands for a NIEO in global commercial relations. A reluctance to become alienated politically from the 'progressive' developing states led to carefully formulated speeches by leading SED officials at the UN, particularly at the sessions of the United Nations Conference on Trade and Development (UNCTAD). A continued perceived legitimacy deficiency compelled the GDR to seek political support from the 'progressive' Third World in order to differentiate further the generous, non-exploitative nature of the 'socialist' German state from the 'monopolist' and 'neo-colonialist' regime in Bonn. However, this differentiation became increasingly problematic given certain demands expressed by the Third World in UNCTAD sessions, e.g., concerning the issue of tripartite East–West–South economic relations. In this context, the GDR's *Afrikapolitik* became more complex in comparison with the more obvious foreign policy goals of the pre-recognition period.

General characteristics of East German economic involvement in Africa

According to GDR official statistics, the proportion of East German foreign trade turnover with the developing states is traditionally low both compared with other East European states' trade turnover with the Third World, and in relation to the overall size of the GDR's share of world exports. For instance, in 1983, the GDR's share in world exports was second in the rankings of CMEA member-states – only behind the USSR – at a value of VM 84,000 million, but according to official East German statistics, the percentage of GDR foreign trade turnover with developing states has only once exceeded 6 per cent in recent years in contrast to other East European states, and in particular, Romania.[6]

However, these figures have been disputed recently. Ernst Hillebrand had calculated that East German trade turnover with the African 'states of socialist orientation', namely Ethiopia, Mozambique and Angola, has been included in the statistical yearbooks under the category of 'socialist states' and not the category of 'developing states'. According to Hillebrand's calculations, if East German trade turnover with these three African states, and also turnover with other 'socialist' developing states (namely China, North Korea, Kampuchea, Laos and South Yemen) and developing states in the CMEA (i.e., Cuba, Mongolia and Vietnam) are added to the category 'developing states', then the proportion of East German trade with the developing states increases considerably. These statistics then compare more favourably with other East European states' trade with the developing world, and indeed, are more in line with trade figures published by the General Agreement on Tariffs and Trade (GATT) for the GDR. Furthermore, unlike official GDR figures those produced by GATT indicate no appreciable decline in the percentage of East German trade turnover with the Third World in recent years in contrast to other East European states with the exception of the USSR.[7]

Trade agreements at governmental level were concluded by the GDR with several African states prior to and immediately following diplomatic recognition. After 1973 such agreements were concluded for the first time with states such as Angola, Benin, Burundi, Cameroon, Ethiopia, Guinea-Bissau, Liberia, Libya, Madagascar, Mozambique, São Tomé and Príncipe, Togo, Sierra Leone, Uganda, Zaire and Zimbabwe. In general, these bilateral trade agreements included lists of goods to be exchanged, and provision for payments to be made in convertible currencies with prices based on those prevailing on the world market. Yearly protocols could be negotiated to amend the lists of goods to be exchanged. Trade agreements in the post-recognition period more often included provision for the formation of inter-governmental commissions to meet at regular intervals to discuss and promote further commercial contacts. Similar agreements on economic, industrial, scientific and technological cooperation were negotiated with Zambia, Tanzania and the Cape Verde Islands instead of trade agreements. Economic contacts were also developed by East German foreign trade enterprises with several African states although no official economic agreements at governmental level were signed. However, it appears that trade turnover with these African states was also included in the official GDR statistics under the category of 'developing states'.[8]

Trade expansion was promoted by regular representation by East German foreign trade enterprises at international fairs and exhibitions overseas and at the world-renowned bi-annual Leipzig Fair attended by many African delegations. Economic development in the Third World was promoted by the allocation of licences by the GDR to certain states.

The nature of bilateral trade agreements has perceptibly altered in recent years. In the pre-recognition period, in particular, GDR bilateral trade agreement with Third World states provided for more formal clearing settlements in which certain goods were exchanged for other goods on a definite barter basis. This was a mutually advantageous form of agreement whereby both states could trade in goods which might be more difficult to exchange in the competition of the open world market. The GDR was able to dump in Africa inferior industrial machinery which neither the West, nor the CMEA by the 1970s were willing to import (Eastern Europe by that time preferred to import Western goods, whenever possible). However, recently, the number of such formal clearing settlements has diminished, and although barter arrangements are maintained and Third World exports are secured as a form of repayment for East German credits (East German credit support will be examined in detail later, pp. 176–81) the GDR has increasingly demanded hard currency payments to make good trade deficits rather than transferring the deficit to a future trade accord. Previously, convertible currencies were little more than units of account.[9]

In view of this, has the GDR made extensive use of such bilateral trade agreements to acquire hard currency from the Third World, particularly in those years in which sources of hard currency were desperately sought to counter the rapidly expanding debt with the West? This question is impossible to answer satisfactorily. Apart from the oil-rich states of north Africa, other states on the continent, in general, are scarcely sources of a substantial hard currency reservoir. Indeed, Mozambique and Ethiopia, for instance, with which the GDR has had close economic relations, rank among the least developed of the Third World states. On the other hand, earlier East German payments agreements with developing states containing clauses for settlement in non-convertible currencies have disappeared, and payments in hard currency have been demanded instead.[10] More specifically, even with impoverished Mozambique, East German investment, equipment, and manpower involved in tantalite mining there were obtained by the FRELIMO government with the payment of hard currency. Furthermore, the GDR apparently enjoyed the exclusive rights of purchase at world market prices of Mozambique's tantalite reserves which could then be re-sold at similar cost to the FRG in exchange for further hard currency.[11] Similar procedures were also adopted with oil procurements from OPEC states (see pp. 170–1).

However, on account of political factors, and, in particular, the GDR's eagerness to court relations with the new socialist-oriented states of Mozambique, Ethiopia and Angola, and to exclude West German influence there, East German economic relations with Africa, according to official GDR statistics, did not automatically gravitate towards trade expansion with the most prosperous and well-endowed states on the continent. The statistical yearbook noted for 1985 that the GDR recorded its highest trade turnover in Africa with Angola (Table 2).[12] Despite Angola's economic wealth – particularly in diamonds, coffee and oil – the USSR's imports from the former Portuguese colony, for instance in the months January–September 1983, amounted to only the equivalent of £0.7 million in value.[13] This lends support to the hypothesis that the GDR was especially interested in maintaining a prominent economic profile in Angola to counter possible West German political *rapprochement* with Luanda. The possibility of the GDR importing oil from Angola will be raised shortly.

Similarly, in 1979, the percentage of Mozambique's exports and imports from CMEA states totalled 9 per cent and 15 per cent respectively, of which the GDR's percentage share respectively was 8 per cent and 9 per cent, in contrast to the USSR's 1.1 per cent and 0.1

per cent.[14] The Mozambique Information Agency reported in August 1984 that the GDR was the FRELIMO government's second most important trading partner. An official spokesman in Maputo added that the East German government had displayed a 'special understanding of Mozambique's potential'.[15] Coal appears to have provided a substantial portion of Mozambique's exports to the GDR until the early 1980s (see p. 171).

However, according to the statistical yearbooks, East German trade turnover with the impoverished economies of Mozambique and Ethiopia has declined markedly in recent years, suggesting that commercial links with sub-Saharan Africa are less influenced by political considerations. Certainly, the economic imperative of the GDR's *Afrikapolitik* should not be underestimated. Official East German trade statistics indicate the continued importance of Egypt as an economic partner of the GDR despite a deterioration in political relations in the late 1970s. The dramatic rise in trade turnover with Libya in the early 1980s suggested that Honecker was prepared to tolerate Ghaddafi's appeals for German reunification in order to acquire Libyan oil.

From an examination of trade statistics from non-GDR sources the economic importance of certain African states is further emphasised. Here, the evidence is particularly illuminating. For example, according to UN statistics, in the pre-recognition period between 1961 and 1966, Gambia imported more goods from the GDR than from the FRG. It was consistently recorded in this period that Gambia had the highest percentage of imports from the GDR of any sub-Saharan African state, reaching 3.3 per cent in 1961.[16] The reasons for this apparent anomaly are not known. One may conclude that East German trade turnover with the staunchly pro-Western state of Gambia was not specifically recorded in East German official statistics for reasons of political sensitivity.

Most interestingly, in contrast to official East German statistics which only registered trade with South Africa prior to 1960, and recorded no details of trade turnover between Rhodesia and the GDR, other sources have reported East German trade with these states. Contrary to previously noted East German assurances, South Africa continued to receive goods from the GDR throughout the 1960s.[17] This trade turnover continued in the post-recognition period. According to Pretoria, an overwhelming proportion of this trade turnover involved the import of East German machinery, although West German analysts have proposed that certain key South African raw materials were also exchanged.[18]

These reports lend some credence to Western accusations in the 1970s of East German commercial contacts with the Smith regime in Rhodesia in contravention of UN declared embargoes, and, hence, question the 'anti-imperialist' character of the GDR's *Afrikapolitik*.[19]

The importance of Africa as a source of raw materials

The precise importance of the African continent as a source of raw materials for the Soviet bloc in general has been in recent years a subject of lively debate among Western analysts, the protagonists being Christopher Coker and Colin Lawson.[20]

In Coker's opinion, following the oil price rises of the 1970s and the USSR's decision in 1975 to peg raw material commodities in general (not only oil) at the prevailing market price each year instead of, as previously, after five-year terms, there was triggered a CMEA attempt to seek markets for raw material imports from overseas, and, in particular, from Africa. As early as 1956 a research group funded by the USSR had proposed that Eastern Europe import raw materials from Africa. In response to the later price rises, the Soviet bloc eagerly seized upon the 1971 CMEA Comprehensive Programme's commitment to expand economic ties with the developing states in order to promote plan coordination with such states at a bilateral and multilateral level, and, in particular, to embrace such African states as Mozambique and Angola within the scope of the CMEA's Long Term Special Programmes for Fuel and Raw Material Industries, with the intention of facilitating the acquisition of raw materials.[21]

According to Lawson, economic investment in Africa as a result of developments in the overseas markets in the mid-1970s was quickly regretted by CMEA states, and by the start of the 1980s Eastern Europe demonstrated a renewed 'enthusiasm' to acquire raw materials from the USSR, which included participation in joint investment projects.

It will be demonstrated that both schools of thought in part contain elements of truth, although it should be remembered that the GDR was not eager to participate in costly projects in the USSR in the early 1980s (see Introduction).

Specific East German interest in acquiring raw materials from the Third World may be traced back to the first session of UNCTAD in 1964, when the GDR issued a Declaration concerning raw materials which was transmitted to the delegates at Geneva by the Czechoslovak delegation. The Declaration expressed the GDR's interest in expanding trade with the Third World to satisfy the raw material import needs of the East German economy.[22]

In 1979, in a speech at the 10th Plenum of the SED Central Committee, Gerhard Beil, the State Secretary in the East German Ministry for Foreign Trade declared that in the past decade imports from the developing states included approximately 1 million tonnes of fish-meal, 1.8 million tonnes of animal feed, 234,000 tonnes of coffee, 1.1 million tonnes of tropical fruits, almost 120,000 tonnes of rubber, and considerable quantities of metals, phosphates and cotton of value for GDR industry.[23]

More recently, it was officially conceded that the majority of East German imports from the developing states remained predominantly raw materials and agricultural products, that were of importance for the GDR which was not well endowed with such resources.[24]

From 1975 onwards East German official trade statistics no longer specified the annual amounts of imports and exports from individual African states, in part on account of a sudden trade deficit with the Third World (see pp. 152–3). In the following years up until 1980 the GDR, like Hungary, struggled to avoid recurring annual trade deficits with the developing states (see Table 8). The East German trade surplus with Third World states after 1980 immediately suggests that Africa's significance as a source of raw material imports has diminished in more recent years. In order to substantiate this, East German interest in the imports of African oil and other raw materials require more detailed analysis.

I have suggested that as a consequence of the readjustment in the quantity and cost of Soviet oil deliveries to Eastern Europe, especially in the post-1981 period, options open to the GDR to seek further economic growth to repay Western debts included energy conservation and substitution, and the use of alternative sources of oil imports (p. 28). Certainly, the CMEA bloc as a whole increased their proportion of total fuel imports from OPEC states from only 2.2 per cent in 1970, to a peak of 16.4 per cent in 1980, before declining to approximately 10 per cent in 1985.[25] How important for the GDR, in particular, was Africa as a source of oil imports, particularly in the post-1975 period?

Official GDR statistics alone again fail to provide enough data to answer this question satisfactorily. For example, according to these statistics, between 1981 and 1985 only details of oil imports from the USSR were registered, although in this period the origins of over 25 million tonnes of East German petroleum imports were 'officially'

Table 9. Sources of East German oil imports, 1960–1987 (metric tonnes, thousands)

Source	1960	1965	1970	1973	1974	1975	1976	1977	1978
USSR	1,811 (1,780)	4,908 (5,020)	9,233 (9,280)	13,025 (12,410)	14,135 (14,140)	15,097 (15,100)	16,012 (16,200)	17,007 (17,470)	17,760 (17,760)
Algeria								12.7 (50)	311 (310)
Egypt		115 (110)	932 (900)	132 (150)	105 (110)	187 (190)	180	135 (130)	179 (180)
Iran				2,610[a]	(220)[a]				
Iraq				913 (500)	1,760 (1,760)	1,454 (1,450)	1,576 (1,580)	1,072 (1,070)	1,057 (1,060)
Kuwait				(240)	(200)[a]	(20)			
Libya				(40)					
Syria			18 (20)	70 (100)	128	240 (240)	258 (260)	301 (300)	350
Tunisia									
Venezuela								(20)	
Asia								(350)	(260)
Europe									(200)
Unspecified									(70)
Actual Total	1,811 (1,780)	5,023 (5,130)	10,183 (10,200)	14,140 (16,050)	16,128 (16,430)	16,978 (17,000)	18,026 (18,040)	18,527.7 (19,390)	19,657 (19,840)
Published Total	1,941 (1,910)	5,132 (5,130)	10,334 (10,200)	16,045 (16,050)	16,434 (16,430)	16,977 (17,000)	18,036 (18,040)	19,042 (19,040)	19,925 (19,930)
Unaccounted for in GDR statistics[b]	130	109	251	1,095	306	19	10	514.3	268
Unaccounted for in UN statistics[b]	(130)							(350)[c]	(90)

USSR	18,536	19,011	19,036	17,709	17,051	17,068	17,075	17,067	17,072
Algeria	(18,540)	(19,010)	(18,600)	(17,709)	(17,051)	(17,300)[a]	(17,000)[a]		
Egypt		202							
Iran		(200)	(200)						
Iraq	1.095	1,430							
	(1,100)	(1,430)	(1,500)						
Kuwait				(1,000)[a]	(1,000)[a]	(1,000)[a]	(1,000)[a]		
Libya			(470)	(500)	(700)[a]	(700)[a]	(500)[a]		
Syria	268	(120)							
Tunisia									
Venezuela									
Asia									
Europe	(300)	(300)	(510)						
Unspecified	(490)	(820)	(1,450)						
Actual Total	19,899	20,643	19,036	17,709	17,051	17,068	17,075	17,067	17,072
	(20,430)	(21,880)	(22,730)	(19,209)	(18,851)	(19,000)	(18,500)		
Published Total	20,694	21,876	22,734	21,745	22,645	23,236	22,802	22,250	20.949
	(20,690)	(21,880)	(22,730)	(21,745)	(22,648)	(23,236)	(22,802)		
Unaccounted for in GDR statistics[b]	795	1,233	3,698	4,036	5,597	6,168	5,727	5,183	3,877
Unaccounted for in UN statistics[b]	(260)			(2,536)	(3,797)	(4,234)	(4,302)		

Key: Non-bracketed figures=GDR statistics

Bracketed figures=UN statistics

a=Estimates

b=Author's own calculations

c=Amount by which 'actual total' is higher than published total

Source: For official East German figures see *Statistisches Jahrbuch* (various years). For UN figures see *Energy Statistics Yearbook*, vols. 1962 and 1973–8 (New York: United Nations, Department of International Economic and Social Affairs, Statistical Office, 1966–79); and *World Energy Supplies*, vols. 1979–85 (New York: United Nations, Department of International Economic and Social Affairs, Statistical Office, 1981–87).

unaccounted for (see Table 9). In this same period the GDR, benefiting from preferential inter-German trade, imported 5.6 million tonnes of oil from the FRG, which the West Germans had previously purchased in hard currency from Third World states.[26] Deducting this amount from the total of 'officially' unaccounted for oil imports, a total of 19.6 million tonnes remains to be explained for the period between 1981 and 1985.

When UN statistics are employed, between 1981 and 1985 the origins of 15 million tonnes of oil remains unaccounted for, or 'unspecified'. These UN statistics have already also accounted for East German imports of oil from Algeria (until 1981), Iraq and Libya (see Table 9). Even after deducting oil imports from the FRG the source of over 9 million tonnes of oil imported by the GDR in this period remains unknown.

How much of this total of over 9 million tonnes of oil originated from Africa? The GDR's reluctance to provide complete details of oil imports after 1980 suggests that developing states were important sources of this key raw material.

In the so-called 'Manila Declaration' of 1976, the Third World had included in one of their demands that CMEA states should increase their proportion of semi-manufactured and manufactured goods in their imports from the developing states rather than concentrating only on raw material procurements.[27] Hence, the GDR was eager to demonstrate that an increasing proportion of its trade with the Third World involved imports of semi-manufactured and manufactured goods. According to one East German source, the percentage of imports of these categories of goods from the developing states ostensibly increased from 24 per cent in 1973 to as high as 40 per cent in 1984.[28] The admission of substantial oil imports from the developing states could politically compromise the GDR's support of the Third World's demands for a NIEO. Even in the early 1970s the GDR failed to disclose details of considerable imports of Iranian oil. Since the late 1960s UN data referred to East German oil imports from such states as Tunisia, Venezuela, Libya, Kuwait and Iran – none of which was included in GDR records – and the totals of imports from other states also differed from East German figures.

Nevertheless, one may conclude from the data at hand that GDR imports of oil from Africa, in general, were of marginal importance for the East German economy prior to the 1975 Bucharest Formula. An exception was in 1970, according to both UN and GDR statistics, when Egypt furnished approximately 9 per cent of East German total oil imports.

In the crisis between OPEC and the West in 1973–4, the authorities in East Berlin supported the sovereign right of the Arab peoples to dispose freely of their oil and other raw materials. Iraq, Syria and Libya were praised for their stand against the 'international oil monopolies'.[29] Was this an indication of the GDR's desire to initiate oil deliveries from Libya? Certainly, this championing of the OPEC states was seriously modified by 1980 on account of the improved relations between Western oil companies and Arab governments. One East German academic depicted OPEC as a divided organisation, in which anti-imperialist elements vied for control with other forces who were in league with the oil-military-industrial complexes of the US, Great Britain and the FRG.[30]

Did this reformulation affect GDR relations with African OPEC members (i.e., in particular Algeria, Libya and Nigeria)? The impact was probably minimal. Despite imports of oil from Algeria in 1977 and 1978, and substantially reduced amounts of Egyptian oil, Africa, by the late 1970s, was of little significance for the GDR in relation to oil.

A critical period followed the winter of 1979–80 when the USSR declared that its oil exports to the GDR would be levelled off at approximately 19 million tonnes for the coming five-year period. This sequence of events prompted Western analysts to speculate that by 1985 the East German economy would need to import at least 5 million tonnes of oil from non-Soviet sources to meet consumption needs. To meet this deficit, the African states of Algeria, Angola and Libya, together with Syria, Iraq and Mexico, were proposed as likely sources of oil imports. Oil from Iran could no longer be guaranteed. Indeed, after the Shah's deposition (by January 1979), Teheran's cancellation of a previously negotiated barter agreement involving the exchange of 1,000 railway carriages for a quantity of oil, resulted in serious oil shortages in the GDR which compelled the East German authorities to purchase oil on the very expensive Rotterdam spot market.[31]

The above account illustrates the extreme dependence of the East German economy on Soviet and potential Iranian oil exports in the late 1970s. In order to avoid further purchases on the Rotterdam spot market, a combined strategy of energy substitution and conservation, and the diversification of sources of oil imports, was embarked upon in earnest by the GDR. The reduction in Soviet oil imports and their spiralling costs in the 1980s further encouraged this combined strategy. This, in part, explains the total of over 9 million tonnes of oil unaccounted for in UN data in the period 1981–5. However, how much of this oil originated from such oil-rich African states as Egypt,

Algeria, Angola and Nigeria rather than from Syria, Kuwait and other states including, later, Iran?

East German trade turnover with revolutionary Iran remained consistently high. Oil imports by the GDR most probably covered a considerable percentage of this trade turnover, in spite of initial problems (with the important proviso that the value of trade turnover in this and other instances in the GDR statistical yearbooks, in part, reflects the increased prices of oil rather than an actual increase in the quantity of oil deliveries). Indeed, one West German source referred to an agreement concluded in Teheran in 1984 for the delivery of 1.5 million tonnes of oil to the GDR.[32]

On account of its relatively low trade turnover with the GDR, Kuwait was, most probably, of minor importance for East German oil imports, despite Honecker's tour of Kuwaiti petro-chemical plants and the exhibition centre of the national oil company on his visit in October 1982.[33]

Syria perhaps provided a more lucrative source of oil imports, although trade turnover was in decline by 1984, only two years after Honecker's stay in Damascus when a Programme on the Further Development of Economic, Industrial and Scientific–Technical Cooperation to 1990 was successfully negotiated.[34]

Likewise with Mexico, Honecker's trip there in 1981 failed to result in increased trade turnover. Negotiations on oil imports and on an earlier envisaged agreement, by which the GDR would refine Mexican oil for the CMEA market, were not reported.[35]

Consequently, it would appear that Syria, Mexico, Iran and Kuwait alone were exceedingly unlikely to have provided the whole of the over 9 million tonnes of oil unaccounted for in UN statistics in the 1981–6 period.

In Africa, UN statistics have referred to East German imports of oil from Libya since 1980. Certainly, upon the visit of Libyan Prime Minister Major Abdul Salam Jalloud to East Berlin in April 1975, a long-term trade agreement specifically included provisions for the delivery of Libyan oil to the GDR.[36] Further important economic agreements, upon the visits of Ghaddafi to East Berlin in June 1978 (Ten-Year Agreement on Political, Economic and Scientific–Technological Cooperation), and Honecker to Tripoli in February 1979 (Agreement on the Further Development of Economic, Scientific and Technical Cooperation), made no specific reference to oil imports.[37] However, in 1980 and 1981 trade turnover between the two states expanded substantially as the UN statistics began to record East

German imports of oil from Libya. These oil imports apparently increased, although trade turnover between the GDR and Libya surprisingly declined remarkably by the mid-1980s. Evidently, Libyan oil supplies were by no means guaranteed. It was reported that shipments of oil to the GDR were interrupted as early as 1978 and were then resumed for no apparent reason.[38]

Elsewhere in Africa, East German trade turnover with Egypt increased considerably in recent years, according to the statistical yearbooks, as political relations prospered, although there was no evidence of oil imports. For example, the long-term trade agreement between the two states signed in East Berlin in February 1980 referred only to East German imports of raw cotton, cotton products, rice, and semi-manufactured and manufactured goods.[39]

Likewise, one may only speculate that the high trade turnover with Algeria in 1985 included oil imports. Interestingly, Honecker's visit to Algeria in December 1984 included an inspection of the major oil centre at Hassi Messaoud which was responsible for 60 per cent of the north African state's total oil production.[40]

It has been previously noted that East German trade turnover with Angola ranked as the highest of all African states in 1985. Did East German oil imports account for a significant portion of this trade? Certainly, Angolan oil ministers visited the GDR on at least three occasions between 1979 and 1983.[41] Reports in February 1980 alleged that the GDR had expressed strong interest in importing Angolan oil to recoup losses in imports as a result of Soviet cutbacks and the Iran–Iraq war.[42] However, in 1982, it was calculated that 90 per cent of Angolan oil was exported to the West in order to provide hard currency which comprised 80 per cent of Angola's export earnings and 50 per cent of government revenue.[43]

A particularly illuminating case concerning the issue of East German oil imports from Africa was demonstrated in the example of Nigeria. According to the then Minister for Foreign Trade, Horst Sölle, the trade agreement concluded in Lagos on 15 October 1974 involved a mutual exchange of goods in which East German exports of machinery and equipment for the Nigerian oil industry, in part, would be covered by oil imports.[44] The later trade agreement of November 1980 signed by Fischer on a visit to Lagos included a most-favoured nation clause and again envisaged East German imports of oil.[45] Nevertheless, reports circulated in May 1983, at the conclusion of the second session of the Joint Economic Commission for Economic, Industrial, Scientific–Technological and Cultural Cooperation between the two governments, that Nigeria was dissatisfied with the persistent East German trade surplus which hindered the intensification of bilateral trade relations. The Nigerian Minister for National Planning pleaded for the overhauling of the trade deficit as soon as possible by East German imports of crude oil.[46] Continued low trade turnover recorded in recent years appears to indicate that no uptake of crude oil has occurred. This was in spite of a further long-term agreement signed in July 1983.[47]

Why was the GDR extremely reluctant to boost trade turnover with Nigeria by importing oil, especially at a time when the world market price for oil had become significantly less than prices charged by the USSR? No satisfactory answer is apparent. One may only speculate about possible East German caution or conservatism in commercial policies with a reluctance to expand trade with a relatively politically unstable African state in these years. It should be noted in passing that the FRG's most important trading partners in Africa included Nigeria, Libya, Algeria and Egypt. Hence, with the exception of Nigeria, the GDR may have suffered through competition from the FRG in securing raw materials from these more prosperous African states. It is reasonable to suppose that East German criticisms of West German raw materials policy in Africa reflected a fear that the GDR might be excluded from important African markets.[48]

On account of a shortage of hard data, firm conclusions concerning the importance of Africa as a source of oil imports for the GDR may not be made. However, one may speculate that in the 1980s, despite East German trade surpluses with the developing states, oil imports from the Third World, and to an extent from Africa, remained of some importance for the GDR. Initially, this resulted from the need to diversify sources of oil imports following the events of the winter of 1979–80. Indeed, with the continuing Iran–Iraq war, the GDR could not have risked seeking to acquire Third World oil imports from the Gulf region alone.

Intriguingly, in more recent years new developments in oil politics for the GDR have resulted in reassessments of the importance of oil for the East German economy. First, prices for Soviet oil imports to the GDR exceeded the world market prices from 1984 onwards (see Introduction). By 1986 the average world market price for a barrel of oil totalled $15 compared with the equivalent CMEA price of $28.[49] In these circumstances, East German imports of oil from OPEC states, including Algeria, Libya and Nigeria, seemed increasingly attractive. *The Economist* noted that while low world energy prices and surplus amounts of OPEC oil prevailed, states such as Libya, Iraq and Iran were content to permit CMEA states to obtain oil for goods or weaponry rather than hard currency.[50] Actual advantages for the GDR in this changed economic environment were questionable. It has been shown that prior to 1985 East German goods and equipment were already bartered for at least some oil imports according to the limited information at hand, although if the GDR had acquired oil from Angola, which seems unlikely given earlier cited statistics, Luanda would have insisted on hard currency payments.

Secondly, earlier forecasts in the winter of 1979–80, which predicted an East German consumption of up to 24 million tonnes by 1985, were grossly inflated. Energy substitution and conservation actually reduced oil consumption from 15.1 million tonnes in 1980 to only 9.6 million tonnes in 1984. This enabled the GDR to increase its exports of oil and refined petroleum products. These climbed from a figure of 2.4 million tonnes in 1976 to 6.6 million tonnes officially, and most probably unofficially, a total approaching 14 million tonnes in 1984.[51] Hence, it seem that a quantity of East German oil imports from the USSR were re-exported to third markets, presumably for hard currency earnings after possible previous refinement.[52] This could be regarded as further evidence of a Soviet subsidisation of the East German economy, perhaps as a reward for the GDR's affiliation in Africa.[53] If so, this throws into question my earlier assumption that after 1984 the GDR no longer received extensive preferential economic treatment on account of the increase in price of Soviet oil.

Similarly, oil imports from OPEC states could be re-exported. One West German source alleged that East German oil re-exports to states of the Organisation for Economic Cooperation and Development (OECD) were actually recorded in OECD statistics as originating from OPEC states.[54] Certainly, the USSR had employed the policy of re-exporting oil from OPEC states to Western Europe to boost hard currency earnings for several years.[55] However, it should be noted that the decline in oil prices in most recent years would also limit, to some extent, the amount of hard currency earnings acquired from reselling oil and petroleum products.

Vanous has questioned the above analysis for a number of reasons. These include the problem of the violation of a probable non-re-export clause in the agreement on oil deliveries between the USSR and the GDR; serious doubts on the ability of the East German refinery industry to handle all Soviet crude imports; and grave scepticism as to whether the GDR could re-export such quantities of oil and avoid international publicity.[56]

However, the unreliability of OECD statistics concerning commercial oil dealings has been noted; the USSR could choose to ignore any violation of an agreement with the GDR; and, presumably, East German refineries could find some means to process oil that would then be traded for hard currency. Certainly, the statistics indicate that the GDR was not consuming a substantial portion of its oil imports.

Consequently, it appears that an East German policy of enhanced diversification of oil sources in the early 1980s to support the GDR economy – at a possible cost of sales of quality goods and services, and possibly even hard currency purchases – had given way to an economic arrangement by which the luxury of re-exporting non-essential OPEC oil imports actually added to East German hard currency earnings. In both these instances, a limited number of African states most probably provided certain quantities of oil for consumption or re-export.

With reference to other raw materials, East German imports of pit coal from Mozambique, although appearing of little importance economically for the GDR, were a more vital component in the trade turnover of Mozambique, at least in the late 1970s, and were of definite political value as part of Honecker's cultivation of close relations with the frontline African states.

According to the statistical yearbooks, East German imports of pit coal from Mozambique were only recorded between the dates 1979 and 1982. Mozambique exported a maximum of 188,500 tonnes in 1981.[57] However, between 1980 and 1982 the GDR imported 16.9 million tonnes of pit coal, of which the USSR delivered 8.9 million tonnes.[58] Moreover, pit coal was not a key source of energy consumption in the GDR. For example, in 1981 it accounted for only 3 per cent of the GDR's primary energy consumption, while brown coal (lignite) and oil provided for 67 per cent and 17 per cent respectively.[59]

East German trade turnover with Mozambique dramatically declined after 1982, indicating that pit coal imports from the Moatize coalfields in Mozambique likewise stagnated. But an agreement of tripartite cooperation in the exploration of coal and tantalite reserves was concluded between the GDR, the USSR and Mozambique in September 1982.[60] The East German practice of the procurement of tantalite for re-export to acquire hard currency (as with oil re-exports) was previously noted, although this tripartite cooperation agreement suggested that the GDR may not have enjoyed sole purchase rights of tantalite as earlier stated.

Although pit coal imports appear to have declined, the GDR has continued to encourage the development of the coal industry in Mozambique. Bilateral agreements were signed concerning the training of Moatize mine workers, the management of coalfields and the improvements of safety standards in mines.[61]

Other East German imports of raw materials and also agricultural products originated from a number of African states. The statistical yearbooks of the GDR in recent years have reported that rice, oranges and cotton were imported from Egypt, tea, fruits and vegetables from Mozambique, knitted goods, animal hides, legumes and coffee from Ethiopia, and also coffee from Angola. According to Hillebrand, in 1984 the GDR purchased 61 per cent of Angola's total coffee exports at above average prices, although overpriced East German goods may have been received by Angola in return.[62]

Although no other precise details are available, it appears that other East German imports have included phosphates from Tunisia and Morocco, bauxite from Guinea, cocoa from Ghana and Nigeria, and copper from Zimbabwe and Zambia. Honecker's visit to Zambia in February 1979 resulted in a governmental Agreement on Economic, Scientific and Technological Cooperation which envisaged the East German provision of surface-mining equipment, railway rolling stock, and machinery for the agricultural and textile industry, in return for copper and tobacco imports.[63] Moreover, on 21 July 1980 the GDR was awarded a contract to receive 10 per cent of that year's copper production from the Zambian company 'Memaco' – evidently the GDR's first procurement of Zambian copper.[64] These copper imports were only obtained at the price of East German support – initially at least – for Kaunda's agrarian modernisation programme, as chapter 6 will examine.

To conclude, it would seem that oil and tantalite imports from Africa have contributed to the development of the East German economy through the provision of undisclosed amounts of hard currency earnings. Also, it appears that the GDR has imported an unknown amount of other important raw materials together with traditional African agricultural products. However, it would be an exaggeration to say that Africa is of major importance for the GDR in the provision of strategic raw materials.

Coker has noted that on account of a possible future critical shortage within the CMEA of important raw materials such as copper, phosphates, bauxite, aluminium, titanium, vanadium, chromite, etc., the GDR has an incentive to continue to seek raw material imports from the Third World.[65]

However, Lawson's assertion that CMEA states would rather seek raw material imports from the USSR, although not applicable to the GDR in the early 1980s, appears to be more accurate in recent years. According to Stoph's presentation of the five-year plan for 1986–90 at the 11th SED Congress in 1986, the GDR must increase its exports to the USSR by 30 per cent. Thus, East German imports of Soviet raw materials would probably increase, presumably at the expense of Third World imports, especially since the GDR is providing Moscow with equipment required for the extraction of raw materials.[66] Honecker's speech at the 11th SED Congress indicating increased East German involvement in joint investment projects in the USSR was noted earlier. Nevertheless, even in this scenario, the East German import and re-export of African oil and tantalite remains of value.

East German development assistance and the New International Economic Order

Since 1974 the developing states have increasingly demanded a radical reorganisation of world trade in their favour in a NIEO. At UNCTAD conferences the Soviet bloc has endeavoured to secure and maintain Third World political support by praising the NIEO Programme while simultaneously attempting to preserve an advantageous economic relationship with the developing states.

The GDR has aligned itself with the Group D Joint Statements addressed to more recent UNCTAD sessions which insisted that the Western industrialised states were alone responsible for past and present colonial and neo-colonial exploitation. Hence, it was stressed that the CMEA was not obliged to meet the demand of the NIEO Programme which insisted that at least 0.7 per cent of the Gross National Product (GNP) of the world's industrialised states should be employed for development assistance programmes.

East German spokesmen were also eager to propagate further the notion of the neo-colonialism of the FRG in contrast to the beneficial economic policies of the GDR. A Leninist critique of the West German aid policy in Africa has been presented, including references to the employment of cheap overseas labour, and the export of capital and investment to secure raw materials and profits in competition with other Western states.[67]

However, the Soviet bloc's proposals in connection with a NIEO have been received with increasing scepticism by the Third World. For example, the previously noted Manila Declaration of 1976, as well as demanding increased CMEA purchases of semi-manufactured and manufactured products from the developing states, also insisted that both East and West should expand their assistance programmes to meet the 0.7 per cent of GNP target, and that multilateral and tripartite forms of economic cooperation should be expanded in the interests of the Third World.[68]

Consequently, the GDR, in line with other Group D states, found the policy of maintaining economic advantage and political support within the context of the Third World's demands for a NIEO increasingly problematic. Therefore, leading SED spokesmen also presented specific GDR statements of policy to UNCTAD sessions, which were more recently employed to offer evidence of an expansive individual East German development assistance programme ostensibly in accordance with many of the Third World's economic, social and political objectives.

In the first three UNCTAD sessions – 1964 (Geneva), 1968 (New Delhi) and 1972 (Santiago) – East German memoranda and declarations were aimed preeminently at securing diplomatic recognition and actual membership of the UNCTAD body. No GDR delegation was invited to attend the inaugural Geneva session. However, East German statements of intent, in conformity with general Soviet bloc proposals, presented to the UNCTAD President via the Czechoslovak delegation, included references to the need to support the economic development of the Third World states by balancing trade, granting licences, despatching economic specialists, initiating extensive training programmes, and providing machinery and equipment for such economic sectors as agriculture, industrial machinery, chemicals, construction, and metallurgy.[69] A major shortcoming here was the failure of the GDR to fulfil the promise to expand trade threefold with the developing states 'in the coming years'. In fact, trade turnover failed to double between 1965 and 1973.[70]

An East German delegation was eventually permitted to attend the 1968 UNCTAD session. Both at New Delhi and Santiago, the GDR Declarations referred to a desire to develop further economic relations with the developing states in line with the 'General Principles on

Trade Relations and Trade Policy' presented at the first UNCTAD session.[71]

Having finally joined UNCTAD in February 1973, at the 4th UNCTAD session in Nairobi three years later Foreign Trade Minister Sölle presented for the first time specific details of East German assistance to the developing states which were not mentioned in the Joint Policy Statement of the Socialist Countries. Accordingly, Sölle underlined the fact that the GDR currently maintained government agreements concerning trade and scientific–technological relations with thirty-seven developing states. He added that, since 1955, 540 East German sponsored projects had been undertaken in the Third World, concentrating on the spheres of construction of textile mills, cement factories, rolling mills, steel foundries and the provision of agricultural machinery. Between 1971 and 1974 alone, approximately 2,600 specialists from the GDR were employed in the developing states to assist in the construction of industrial plants and provide training programmes for the local workforce.[72]

Sölle's presentation at the 5th UNCTAD session in Manila three years later was notable for the significance attached to the clauses of the GDR Treaties of Friendship and Cooperation with Angola and Mozambique which specifically referred to support for the NIEO.[73]

Prior to the 6th UNCTAD session in Belgrade in 1983, the GDR adapted a more critical assessment of the NIEO Programme in accordance with discontent expressed with it by the USSR, most probably on account of continued criticisms of the Soviet bloc's economic policies by the developing states after the Manila Declaration. Hence, the term 'Democratic Transformation of International Economic Relations' was employed in preference to NIEO. Third World states were reprimanded for failing to recognise that colonialist and neo-colonialist exploitation was attributable to Western imperialist states alone. This oversight weakened 'the forces of many developing states in the struggle for economic decolonialisation'. An appeal was made for the initiation of more internal social reforms and the elimination of antiquated political–social structures in developing states.[74]

However, after Belgrade, with the renewed hope of intensifying political support from the Third World as the debts of certain developing states to the major Western capitalist states escalated, the Soviet bloc returned to a more positive appraisal of the clamour for a more judicious international economic system, in which reference was once more made to the need to activate a NIEO.[75]

At Belgrade, the GDR statement to the 6th UNCTAD session had presented the most comprehensive account hitherto of East German assistance, training programmes, and other aid projects to the developing states and national liberation movements.[76]

Hence, in general, the GDR and the Soviet bloc as a whole, were enthusiastic advocates of a NIEO, provided political support for developing states' demands did not jeopardise CMEA economic interests in the Third World. The GDR was undoubtedly influenced by this dual imperative to maintain and advance political support and economic advantage from the Third World as analyses of East German credit assistance and the question of tripartite economic cooperation further demonstrate.

Even in the pre-recognition phase of GDR foreign policy, Bokassa had voiced stern criticism of the inadequacies of the East German development aid programme. Questions were also raised about whether pledges of credit assistance made in the early 1970s would be realised once recognition was secured.

These doubts were apparently justified in the first years of the post-recognition period. Between 1971 and 1977 the GDR provided only 8.8 per cent of pledged East European (excluding the USSR) economic assistance to non-communist developing states with only Bulgaria offering less (4.4 per cent). Assistance from Czechoslovakia – of similar industrial structure to the GDR – totalled 28.2 per cent. In the pre-recognition period of 1954–70, East German aid commitments had amounted to 22 per cent of East European outlay, i.e., second only to Czechoslovakia's 33.1 per cent contribution. In 1971–4 (inclusive) East German bilateral commitments of capital aid to non-communist developing states were especially low, totalling only $94 million.[77] According to OECD definitions and statistics, East European development aid was minimal. For example, between 1975 and 1976 East European aid (excluding the USSR and the GDR) formed only 0.9 per cent of the world's share of overseas development assistance (ODA) offered (using the dollar at 1983 prices and exchange rates), compared with a 6.6 per cent contribution by the FRG. According to these OECD statistics the East German contribution in these years was 0.3 per cent.[78]

Development assistance from the GDR continued to lag behind West German aid programmes. Between 1969 and 1978, according to an official West German source, the FRG's bilateral aid programme to Africa resulted in a commitment of $4,200 million in comparison to the GDR's offer of $440 million. A further $925 million was committed by Bonn in multilateral aid.[79] According to more recent OECD statistics,

East German pledged ODA for 1983–4 totalled $169 million (at 1983 prices and exchange rates) which amounted to 0.5 per cent of world ODA, and 0.16 per cent of the GDR's GNP. The corresponding figures for the FRG were $3,108 million providing 8.45 per cent of world ODA, and totalling 0.47 per cent of GNP.[80] Furthermore, it was estimated in 1980 that actual East German credit payments to non-communist developing states totalled only approximately one-third of original pledged aid.[81]

Confronted with such statistics, Honecker, in a speech at an international conference in East Berlin, in October 1980, accused the West of boasting about the extent of their development aid programmes while remaining silent on the size of their profits which accrued from investment and multinational corporation activity in the Third World which annually amounted to up to $100 billion.[82]

Hence, in the immediate post-recognition years, the GDR was apparently not prepared to expand commitments and payments of credit assistance to African states and to the Third World in general. It would seem that the political benefits that could result as a consequence of increased expenditure in the developing states were judged to be of less importance than Honecker's determination to satisfy the East German populace's appetite for Western consumer goods, and industry's demand for Western technology. Further oil price rises in the late 1970s, East European aid to prop up the Polish economy after 1980, and the economic crisis years for the GDR in the early 1980s, all suggest that new, expansive East German outlays of capital expenditure in the Third World were extremely improbable.[83] East German spokesmen referred to bilateral credit assistance from the GDR to the developing states 'in the scope of its [the GDR's] possibilities', or within 'its [the GDR's] limited means'.[84]

However, from around 1980 onwards, the GDR and the USSR adopted a new policy approach to secure Third World political support. Although still refusing to be bound officially by targets set by the developing states with respect to aid programmes, announcements of schemes of credit support which supposedly exceeded these targets were proclaimed. Careful manipulation of statistics enabled the GDR to be seen to be following assistance demands of the programme of the NIEO at little economic expense. By this strategem the dual imperative of political and economic support was not compromised and actual East German economic efforts could remain concentrated on reducing debts to the Western capitalist states with little distraction resulting from the commitment of funds to the

Third World. The developing states' criticisms of the lack of CMEA support for a NIEO most probably explained the adoption of this new policy.

This strategem could be employed by adhering to the Soviet bloc's definition of economic aid which embraced a whole range of other forms of cooperation in contrast to the OECD's more limited definition which usually covered only state development assistance in the form of grants, loans and technological cooperation.

Hence, the GDR also included such forms of assistance as solidarity gifts, humanitarian aid, commercial transactions (within the scope of compensation agreements where East German credits for the exports of machinery for industrial and agricultural development were repaid by goods in kind), the granting of scholarships, costs of sending experts overseas, favourable freight rates, and probable price subsidies (for example, to Cuba and Vietnam).[85] Most probably, a substantial portion of East German aid disbursements to the Third World were to such states as Cuba, Mongolia, Vietnam, North Korea, Afghanistan, Laos and Kampuchea, rather than to obviously non-communist developing states. Moreover, as noted previously, East German governmental loans were usually at higher rates of interest than equivalent West German credits with repayment periods (usually through exports of goods) covering a much shorter time-span.

Initial indications of the employment of this strategem were in evidence with the first real East German publication of more extensive details of the numbers of students and citizens from developing states educated and trained in the GDR (in 1970–9, 10,000 students and 39,000 citizens), together with the number of skilled experts from the GDR engaged in training programmes in the Third World (15,000 in 1970–9), and the extent of medical treatment offered to the sick and wounded from overseas (in 1970–9, 2,300 patients had received treatment in the GDR) – in fact, these were usually injured members of national liberation movements.[86]

Before the Second Committee of the UN General Assembly in October 1982, the GDR's Permanent Representative at the UN presented precise figures on the extent of East German material and financial aid to the developing states and national liberation movements – the first CMEA state to publish such details after a similar report offered by the USSR a few months before.[87] The East German aid figures were presented as a proportion of 'produced national income' or 'net material product' (NMP) – 0.78 per cent in this instance. This was, in effect, a method of expanding the aid percent-

Table 10. *Official development aid of the FRG and the GDR, 1970–1987*

| | OECD figures | | GDR figures | |
| | a | | b | |
	FRG (%)	GDR (%)	GDR (%)	Total (VM mill.)
1970	0.33	0.08		
1975	0.40	0.06		
1980	0.44	0.15		
1981	0.47	0.17	0.78	1,529.7
1982	0.48	0.15	0.79	1,528.7
1983	0.48	0.12	0.79	1,662.4
1984	0.45		0.82	1,820.0
1985	0.47		0.86	
1986	0.43		0.89	2,240.0
1987	0.39			2,322.9

Key: a=Relationship of net official development aid and gross national product
Key: b=Percentage of East German development aid from produced national income with total of percentage expressed in VM millions
Source: for a, *OECD Development Co-operation – 1984 Review* (Paris: Organisation for Economic Co-operation and Development, 1984), p. 210; and *OECD Development Co-operation – 1988 Report* (Paris: OECD, 1988), p. 187. For b, for figures for 1981, see *Dokumente zur Aussenpolitik der DDR*, 1982, vol. 30 (1985), p. 537, speech by Harry Ott, Permanent Representative of the GDR at the UN, 21 October 1982. For figures for 1982, see *Proceedings of the United Nations*, Sixth Session, vol. 1, p. 151, assistance given by the German Democratic Republic . . ., TD/304. For figures for 1983, see *Horizont*, Year 17, 12 (1984), p. 5. For figures for 1984, see Peter Dietze, 'Sozialistische Initiativen zur Umgestaltung der internationalen Wirtschaftsbeziehungen', *H*, Year 19, 7 (1986), p. 22. For figures for 1985, see *ND*, 19 November 1986. For figures for 1986, see *ND*, 29 October 1987. For figures for 1987, see Gunther Sieber, 'Bruder haben sie in aller Welt', *Einheit*, Year 43, 11–12 (1988), pp. 1036–41.

age by excluding sums devoted to capital depreciation and the contribution of the service sector which the calculations based on GNP included.[88]

In later years, further similar annual reports of increasing East German aid to developing states and national liberation movements were produced which far exceeded OECD estimates (calculated by gross social [national] product) (see Table 10). Bulgaria and Czechoslovakia followed the precedents established by the USSR and the GDR and also claimed aid contributions of over 0.7 per cent GNP or NMP.[89] According to OECD statistics, GDR aid as a percentage of gross social (national) product had only increased from 0.06 per cent in 1975 to a peak of 0.17 per cent in 1981.

Similarly, East German commentators have attempted to demonstrate that the GDR's aid commitments to the least developed countries (LDCs) have matched favourably with the demands of the special UN conference held in Paris in 1981. In line with these demands that industrialised states should provide 0.13 per cent of their GNP in aid commitments to the LDCs, the GDR has claimed to have offered 0.13 per cent and 0.12 per cent of its produced national income to the LDCs – many of which are African – in 1982 and 1983 respectively.[90]

Exact details of each individual credit pledge and payment to African states are impossible to compile on account of limited information supplied by the GDR, although a general impression of the nature of this credit assistance may be gathered. Thus, after 1975, considerable credits were offered to Egypt for electrification projects; Algeria received regular assistance for an industrial expansion programme including assistance in the construction of a large complex at Berrouaghia; road development and telecommunications projects were assisted in Madagascar; and other credits for a variety of programmes were offered to such African states as Ethiopia, Angola, Mozambique, the Congo PR, the Cape Verde Islands, Ghana, Zambia and Nigeria.[91]

In Egypt, also, considerable support has been granted to textile industry expansion. According to a recent report, since 1959 the GDR was involved in the construction of twenty textile enterprises in Egypt in which over 1 million spindles operated. Furthermore, as evidence of the import of more semi-manufactured and manufactured goods from the developing states, the report stated that since 1960 East German imports of raw cotton had declined in contrast to products from the textile spinning mills which had increased.[92] According to the statistical yearbook for 1987, imports of Egyptian raw cotton were reduced, approximately, from 16 million tonnes in 1960 to 4,236,000 tonnes in 1986, while in the same period, imports of textile products increased in quantity from 963,000 to 11,161,000 square metres.[93]

Also worthy of special mention is the East German assistance to the Ethiopian economy through three important projects: the construction of a textile factory at Kombolcha (with Czechoslovak support); a cement factory at New Mugher (with Cuban backing); and a food-oil factory in Bahr Dar.[94] Visiting the cement works at New Mugher in September 1984 – which would increase almost threefold Ethiopia's production capacity of construction materials when fully operational[95] – Honecker declared that the project was an example of 'proletarian internationalism in action'.[96]

Various Western sources have presented a contrasting image of East German 'support' for the Ethiopian economy. According to one report, in the late 1970s the GDR exchanged 580 East German lorries for 15,000 tonnes of Ethiopian coffee resulting in the exorbitant cost of approximately $100,000 for each lorry. Another account referred to an agreement of 1978 by which the GDR delivered 500 tractors for an unspecified amount of raw coffee which was promptly re-sold on the New York goods market at a discount of 15 per cent below the world market price, while the tractors themselves proved unsuitable for local conditions in Ethiopia.[97]

These appear to be isolated instances of wayward development aid. One may assume rather that bold East German announcements of expanding credit assistance and economic aid programmes were at least of some political propaganda value in the GDR's *Afrikapolitik*.

With reference to tripartite cooperation ventures in the Third World, these provided the most obvious irrefutable proof that the Soviet bloc had dispensed with Khrushchev's earlier emphasis on the division of the world economy into two opposing capitalist and socialist-based systems, and instead had substituted a more interdependent vision of an international division of labour in global commercial relations. These ventures typically provided East–West–South projects of cooperation in which industrialised capitalist states provided the most advanced technological equipment, the Soviet bloc assisted in the provision of fittings and materials at an intermediate level of technical sophistication, and the host developing state offered manpower and basic raw materials. The advantage for CMEA states lay in guaranteed access to African markets without Western competition. Rather, Western expertise and technology were tolerated as an alternative to possible massive capital investment in the Third World by the Soviet bloc.[98]

Third World states were enthusiastic about tripartite ventures which they hoped would expand their industrialisation programmes. The Manila Declaration, and later official statements by the developing states in UNCTAD sessions, underlined the need for the Soviet bloc to expand further their participation in such cooperation ventures which were also promoted as a 'positive means of extending trade turnover.[99] Joint Statements issued by the Socialist Countries to UNCTAD sessions and to the UN General Assembly recognised the need for an expanded multilateralisation of trade with the developing states which included tripartite forms of cooperation.[100]

The GDR had certainly embarked on a series of multilateral ventures in Africa involving cooperation with other CMEA states – e.g., cooperation between the GDR and Czechoslovakia and Algeria on the Berrouaghia complex.

But how enthusiastic was the GDR at embarking on a range of tripartite cooperation ventures with Western industrialised states given traditional East German condemnation of imperialist exploitation in Africa? More importantly, was the GDR willing to modify the policy of *Abgrenzung* with the FRG in Africa by agreeing to conclude tripartite cooperation ventures with Bonn in order to appease Third World states' pleas for enhanced multilateralisation in this sphere?

Between 1965 and 1975 the GDR had concluded only five agreements with Western states in tripartite cooperation ventures in third countries amounting to only 3.4 per cent of total East European ventures (including Yugoslavia). In the next four years the number increased to ten which was 11.1 per cent of East European ventures, i.e., evidence of a transformation by which the GDR, from being the least interested of all CMEA states in such activities, suddenly demonstrated more enthusiasm than Bulgaria, Czechoslovakia and even Romania.[101]

These tripartite cooperation ventures in Africa were concluded, for instance, with Italian, Austrian, Dutch, Swedish, French and Swiss enterprises in Algeria, Mauritania, Cameroon, Libya and Tunisia on projects such as oil refinery construction, and the building of chemical plants and cellulose factories.[102] The enlargement of East German interest in such projects accompanied an enhanced general East European concern to expand these forms of multilateral cooperation.[103] Most significantly, in line with this trend, in 1977 an agreement was concluded between the two Germanies to assist in Ethiopia's economic development.

In the late 1960s, Bonn had allegedly expressed interest in expanding economic cooperation with the socialist states in the Third World. The GDR rejected West German overtures, which were characterised as a great imperialist manoeuvre of deception directed against the political and economic interests of the national liberation movement, and an attempt to distract and divert developing states from correct ideological development.[104]

Official GDR policy was rapidly reversed. The DM 15 million agreement of 1977 (completed in 1981) between the East German foreign trade enterprise Unitechna-Textima, the West German firm Krupp, and the Ethiopian National Textile Corporation to build a textile mill in Ethiopia was being negotiated before Mengistu's seizure of power. After the bloody coup of February 1977, the East German enterprise replaced Krupp as consortium leader, although the West German firm most probably remained in *de facto* control of the project.[105]

The long-term agreement concluded in April 1975 between the GDR and Krupp by which the Essen-based enterprise would provide technology and know-how for certain projects to assist the East German economy, and by which the possibility of joint-marketing of products in third countries was envisaged, may have facilitated the Ethiopian deal.[106]

The Ethiopian contract provided incontrovertible proof of an enlarged East German interest in tripartite cooperation ventures in Africa. One article published in *Deutsche Aussenpolitik* in 1976 had already referred to the possible advantageous employment of Western technology and economic potential in the Third World if used judiciously and not for capitalist monopoly interests.[107] In the official speech of Foreign Trade Minister Sölle to the UNCTAD session in Manila in 1979, a more intensive development of multilateral and tripartite forms of cooperation in the Third World was promised, although it was added that traditional bilateral forms of assistance were to remain the GDR's principal means of aid commitment.[108] Honecker, himself, had earlier offered a more positive interpretation of the value of tripartite forms of cooperation by noting that such ventures were in the East German economic interest by raising the export capacity of the developing states in certain goods which the GDR was seeking to import.[109]

In May 1984, in an international symposium convened in East Berlin on the subject of 'Economic Cooperation between Socialist States and Capitalist Industrialised States in Third Markets', the need for the Soviet bloc to intensify economic and scientific–technological cooperation with Western states in the developing states and other third markets was forcibly expressed. The possibility of further expanding tripartite cooperation ventures was approved in such spheres of activity as the extraction and processing of brown coal (of importance to the East German economy); the installation of chemical, textile and cement plants; the provision of technical know-how; the establishment of centres in the Third World to provide necessary professional training for jobs in key economic sectors; the equipping of agricultural projects; and other related cooperation programmes.[110]

In view of such high-profile discussions and positive analyses of tripartite cooperation ventures overseas and in the Third World in particular, was the GDR willing to embark on further assistance projects with the FRG in Africa? Hitherto, apart from the Ethiopian deal, there appears to be only one other example of inter-German cooperation in Africa in this sphere of activity concerning a much less-publicised agreement between the East German enterprise, Kombinat Textima, and CCC Hamburg to construct a cotton-spinning mill in Port Sudan (Sudan).[111]

At the May 1984 conference in East Berlin a West German representative attended, and an East German commentary of the proceedings praised West German cooperation with East European states in third states, although inter-German cooperation was not referred to.[112] In fact, East German commentaries have avoided discussion of the Ethiopian contract of 1977. It seems that despite supporting Third World demands for increased tripartite cooperation, both verbally and in practice, in general, the GDR remains reluctant to compromise the policy of enforced *Abgrenzung* with the FRG in Africa. In this particular instance, the issues of potential economic advantage and political support from African states are subordinated to East German sensitivity to the dynamic of inter-German politics.

Conclusion

Although reliable statistical details and precise information about East German commercial relations and development assistance programmes are impossible to obtain, one may still conclude that, quantitatively, GDR economic involvement in Africa in trade and aid (although the two are interconnected) remained relatively inconsiderable in both the pre-recognition and post-recognition phases of East German foreign policy. Aware of the restricted trade turnover, a recent East German commentary attributed this to a world economic crisis in the 1980s in which the West demanded debt repayments from impoverished developing states, leading also to more constricted East German commercial relations with the Third World. However, this 'nevertheless did not exclude in the future a positive development with a number of states'.[113]

In this chapter I intended to demonstrate the complex intertwining of political and commercial considerations in the GDR's economic activity in Africa, and in this context, I have indicated various problems. For instance, the continued East German interest in importing raw materials, particularly oil from Africa, despite the restored trade surpluses with the developing states in the 1980s, ran counter to one of the most fundamental issues in the Third World's demand for a NIEO, i.e., a more judicious system of trade exchange in which the CMEA states were to import more semi-manufactured and manufactured products from the least-developed states to promote industrialisation and import-substitution programmes in the latter.

It has remained in the GDR's interest to seek the political support of African states within the programme of the NIEO, in order to secure further propaganda successes over the FRG, and thereby ease continued perceived East German legitimacy shortcomings. This support was more skilfully manipulated by the strategem adopted more recently in the 1980s in which exaggerated claims of East German development assistance were annually broadcast. In reality, aid commitments had only marginally increased since the nadir of the mid-1970s.

The question of tripartite industrial cooperation in Africa compromised the GDR's policy of non-cooperation with the FRG in Africa in economic affairs. Collective pressure from the Third World, and possible economic benefits, have compelled the inter-German agreements in Ethiopia and Sudan. But, despite official endorsement of further tripartite ventures, future cooperation between the two Germanies in this sphere in Africa remain doubtful. Moreover, such arrangements in the future have become more problematic given the developing states' increasing criticism of the absence of a genuine technology transfer process within the scope of tripartite ventures. In addition, CMEA states are facing increasingly stiff competition from more advanced Third World states such as South Korea and Brazil, which are now also capable of providing intermediate levels of technological support.

Certainly, the GDR's general economic problems in the late 1970s and early 1980s affected its commercial relations in Africa. However, although apparently there was little reduction in commitments of credit assistance to African states, the economic crisis ultimately appears to have resulted in enhanced East German exploitation of African oil in particular in order to supplement hard currency earnings. Nevertheless, despite economic difficulties, the actual size of East German development assistance remained woefully inadequate for the most advanced industrialised East European state. Moreover, the GDR could never match the scale of West German development assistance and trade with African states. For instance, in 1984 along Bonn's trade turnover with African states totalled almost DM 48,000 million.[114] In the post-recognition period, apart from the problems of the *Land* Berlin Clause, the FRG's economic superiority, and the importance of Bonn's contribution to the Lomé Conventions and the EDF, enabled the West Germans to maintain political influence over the majority of African states at the GDR's expense.

As chapter 6 will demonstrate, in the 1980s the GDR and other CMEA states even failed to prevent increased Western influence and involvement in African states traditionally regarded as close associates of the Soviet bloc, principally on account of the latter's reluctance to provide sufficient economic support in contrast to enthusiasm from the West. Consequently, the FRG secured key propaganda successes over the GDR. Mozambique and Angola were willing to accept the *Land* Berlin Clause in order to obtain desperately needed Western economic assistance.

6   The GDR in Africa in the 1980s

Introduction

The East German authorities had hoped that following Honecker's African tours of 1979 a new era in GDR–African relations would commence. But the Soviet invasion of Afghanistan in December 1979 resulted in a sudden enhanced Third World suspicion of Soviet bloc activities in developing states. Here, the GDR was particularly unfortunate. East German admission to the UN Security Council in January 1980 coincided with the first UN General Assembly votes in which the overwhelming majority of Third World states condemned the invasion. Among African states in the UN only Ethiopia, Mozambique and Angola initially supported the Soviet invasion. In the Security Council the GDR and the USSR were isolated. In this particular instance, close association with the USSR was detrimental to the GDR's *Afrikapolitik*.

The invasion of Afghanistan also resulted in the demise of détente between the superpowers. Consequently, with the cost of an escalating arms race following the NATO decision to deploy cruise and Pershing missiles, and with the prospect of expensive military, political and economic support to shore up the new regime in Kabul, the USSR was reluctant to expand upon earlier commitments in Africa. However, the political and military support of socialist-oriented regimes and national liberation movements (particularly SWAPO and the ANC) in Africa was important, in order to reinforce the USSR's claim to global power status, to continue to adhere to the ideological imperative to work to change the international balance of forces in favour of socialism, to prevent a damaging loss of international prestige and credibility especially among Third World states, and to continue to offset Western influence in the region.

With the arrival of Mikhail Gorbachev in the Kremlin in 1985 the

Soviet leadership has commenced a reassessment of the USSR's involvement in the Third World. Gorbachev's priorities lie in internal economic and political reforms, and the need to integrate the USSR into what is now perceived as an increasingly interdependent global economy, in order to transform the USSR into a modern industrial state. This would also serve to underpin the USSR's claim to super-power status. Hence, in this so-called 'new political thinking', the new Soviet leadership has sought to 'de-ideologise' relations among states and, in particular, improve ties with the US. Certainly, the signing of the agreement in December 1987 eliminating intermediate range missiles in Europe was clear evidence of a *rapprochement* between the US and the USSR. Moreover, in line with this new policy, Moscow has demonstrated an interest in seeking political solutions to longstanding regional conflicts in the Third World in order to improve further relations with the US, and curtail the expense of despatching arms and military advisers. In addition, in line with the more obvious pragmatic nature of Soviet policy in recent years, support for socialist-oriented states has been downgraded. Indeed, Gorbachev's advisers have been encouraging rather the development of ties with economically impor-tant 'national capitalist' states in the Third World.

How has this recent Soviet reassessment of the Third World affected the GDR's *Afrikapolitik*? The importance of the GDR's contribution in Africa in the military/security field as part of the affiliation strategy with the USSR has been examined earlier (chapter 4). And, as will be seen, in the 1980s inter-German rivalry in Africa continued as the dispute concerning the *Land* Berlin Clause illustrated. Competition with the FRG, and economic benefits from contacts with certain oil-rich African states in particular, were concerns specific to the GDR which accounted, in part, for continued substantial East German involve-ment in Africa. Certainly, before the arrival of Gorbachev these concerns did not clash with the GDR's interest in further pursuing the strategy of affiliation with the USSR. Indeed, they reinforced affili-ation. The USSR had come to recognise the importance of the GDR's role in Africa for Soviet bloc interests. Having by now acquired the status of an important junior partner of the USSR in Africa, the GDR could be confidently entrusted to conduct policies in Africa with the assurance that the East Germans would pursue objectives beneficial to the Soviet bloc. Affiliation in Africa was also maintained so that Honecker could continue to benefit from Soviet subsidising of the East German economy. Moreover, after 1980 Honecker became eager for the USSR to allow more freedom of manoeuvre for the GDR in inter-German relations – here, continued *Abgrenzung* between the two Germanies in Africa no longer corresponded to relations between East Germany and Bonn in Europe. Close affiliation with Moscow in Africa would strengthen the GDR's claim for enhanced autonomy elsewhere.

In the Gorbachev era it will be demonstrated that the GDR has endeavoured to maintain the strategy of affiliation with the USSR in Africa. However, it appears that the East German authorities are not completely at ease with the latest Soviet reassessment of the Third World. The SED leadership has invested much expertise and man-power (including military/security support) and extensively publi-cised its backing for 'progressive' African states and liberation move-ments. Still perceiving legitimacy shortcomings, Honecker has been eager to demonstrate to the East German population and world public opinion the contrast between the FRG's policies in the Third World and the GDR's *Afrikapolitik*. But these established precepts and pat-terns of behaviour are now challenged by Gorbachev's new political thinking.

Problems of the early 1980s

Before Gorbachev's appointment as General Secretary of the CPSU, East German commentaries were already becoming less opti-mistic about the progress of ideological development in the Third World. Certainly, prior to 1980, the possibility of reversals in the construction of socialism in the Third World had been openly acknowledged. But Honecker's reference in 1981 at the 10th SED Congress to the 'People's Revolutions' in Mozambique, Angola and Ethiopia was especially significant.[1] The use of this terminology coincided with those East German commentators who recognised problems in the social and political development of the socialist-oriented states. In their opinion, the 'Democratic People's Revo-lutions' (*Demokratische Volksrevolutionen*) in certain developing states needed to be differentiated from and accorded inferior status to the 'People's Democratic Revolutions' (*Volksdemokratische Revolutionen*) in Eastern Europe on account of the absence of proletarian hegemony in the former category of states.[2]

Nevertheless, between 1980 and 1988, the SED has negotiated a number of agreements of cooperation with African political parties in Algeria, Angola, the Congo PR, Ethiopia, Guinea-Bissau, Mozam-bique, São Tomé and Príncipe, Tunisia, Uganda, Zambia and Zim-babwe. Undoubtedly, the GDR has continued to maintain an important role for the Soviet bloc in developing relations at party level. The Politbüro member Horst Dohlus appears to have assumed the previous mantle of Werner Lamberz in endeavouring to solidify SED relations with African parties. It was Dohlus who castigated Ethiopian officials in 1981 for not having taken the necessary steps towards the creation of a genuine vanguard party after the formation of the Commission for Organising the Party of the Working People of Ethiopia (COPWE) in December 1979.[3]

The GDR exercised an important influence over the shaping of the Ethiopian revolution in the early 1980s. High-ranking COPWE officials and study delegations visited East Berlin prior to the founding of the Ethiopian Workers' Party (WPE) in September 1984. Dohlus participated at the WPE's founding congress, at which he even, surprisingly, enthusiastically proclaimed that the new vanguard party espoused Marxism–Leninism.[4]

The SED has also maintained close relations with FRELIMO and the MPLA–PT. For instance, in December 1985, the Politbüro member Werner Krolikowski attended the 2nd MPLA–PT Congress in Luanda and praised the achievements of the Angolan party and people in education, health, child-care and defence in particular.[5]

Undoubtedly, in the early 1980s before Gorbachev's accession to power, the Soviet bloc suffered a number of reversals in Africa. In November 1980 in Guinea-Bissau the pro-Soviet government of Luiz Cabral was overthrown by a military coup under Joao Bernardo Vieira (although as noted in chapter 4, this did not inhibit the work of East German and Soviet security advisers in Guinea-Bissau). Unlike previous Soviet treaties with Angola, Mozambique and Ethiopia, the Congo PR refused to include a military aid clause in its Treaty of Friendship and Cooperation with the USSR in May 1981. More significantly, in 1984 Angola and Mozambique were compelled to negotiate ceasefire agreements with South Africa in an endeavour to halt further raids by Renamo and UNITA guerrillas backed by Pretoria. The Lusaka Agreement (between Angola and South Africa on 16 February 1984), and the Nkomati Accord (between Mozambique and South Africa on 16 March 1984) were a consequence, in part, of shortcomings in Soviet bloc economic and military assistance programmes.

With reference to the Nkomati Accord one account has noted that the USSR intentionally reduced arms deliveries to compel Machel to conclude the settlement, and that the Soviet ambassador in Maputo openly welcomed the agreement.[6] The principal Soviet motive appears to have been the desire to cut back on the expense of equipping and training the FRELIMO forces.

Nevertheless, Pretoria's success in negotiating agreements with the GDR's closest associates in Africa must have perplexed the East German leadership. Thus, immediately after the Lusaka Agreement, Honecker promised President dos Santos of Angola (Neto having died in 1979), on the occasion of the fifth anniversary of the signing of the Friendship Treaty between the GDR and Angola, 'absolute solidarity' in the face of threats from the 'racist South African regime'. In the same issue of *Neues Deutschland*, a commentary referring to the Lusaka Agreement maintained (unconvincingly) that: 'As an outpost and bastion of the free peoples of Africa the People's Republic of Angola held firm to her policy principles.'[7]

On the other hand, a report on the Nkomati Accord the following month praised the emphasis on peace and good neighbourliness between Mozambique and South Africa. Even Prime Minister P. W. Botha was specifically named in a surprisingly positive account.[8]

In reality, the SED leadership would not have approved of these compromises with the 'apartheid regime'. Most probably, the East German Deputy Foreign Affairs Minister, Gerd König, would have informed the Angolan and Mozambican authorities of the official SED interpretation of the two agreements on his visits to Luanda and Maputo in April 1984. Interestingly, in Maputo König was reported to have promised members of the ANC National Executive Committee 'unswerving solidarity', although only weeks earlier, under the terms of the Nkomati Accord, the FRELIMO authorities had apparently raided homes of ANC members in Maputo to confiscate stocks of weaponry.[9] Fortunately for the GDR, neither UNITA nor the Renamo guerrillas abided by the ceasefire agreements, and both Mozambique and Angola continued to expand their arsenals and receive military training from East and West.

It is also of interest to note, in particular, the situation in Mali, Somalia, and Zimbabwe in the early/mid-1980s with reference to the GDR's *Afrikapolitik*.

In the pre-recognition period Keita's Mali had been a principal target-site in the GDR's endeavour to secure diplomatic recognition. But, in April 1985, according to one West German press report, the East German ambassador was still absent from Mali after a twelve-month holiday. The second secretary to the GDR's embassy in Bamako had not been replaced. East German teachers and youth brigade workers had left the country, and the network of twinning between towns in the GDR and Mali had been allowed to become moribund.[10] This impoverished and strategically unimportant West African state obviously possessed little attraction for the GDR in the post-recognition period.

President Barré of Somalia had originally diplomatically recognised the GDR many months before the Basic Treaty between the two Germanies was initialled. However, in March 1982, after the departure of the FDJ Friendship Brigade, Barré, mindful of the Soviet bloc presence in Ethiopia, announced at a press conference in Washington, that the principal threat to Somali security derived from the USSR, Cuba and the GDR.[11]

In Zimbabwe, East German hopes of influencing the post-independence regime were shattered by the overwhelming electoral victory of Mugabe and his ZANU party in 1980. Although Honecker did improve relations with Mugabe dramatically in later years, result-ing in the GDR establishing itself at the forefront of Soviet bloc relations with Zimbabwe, the indelible memories of 1980 must have compelled the East German authorities to adopt a more cautious approach to the evolutionary prospects of national and social liber-ation in Africa. Hence, the Zimbabwe episode merits examination in some detail.

I have referred (in chapters 3, 4) to the GDR's political and military links in the late 1970s with Mugabe's arch-rival, the ZAPU leader, Joshua Nkomo. Moscow had initiated contacts with Nkomo prior to 1960.[12] In the years immediately prior to Zimbabwe's independence the Soviet bloc had considerably expanded relations with Nkomo while the Chinese supported Mugabe militarily and politically. At the III FRELIMO Congress in February 1977 Lamberz had held discuss-ions with both Nkomo and Mugabe in a 'comradely atmosphere'. Both guerrilla leaders praised East German solidarity assistance.[13] There-after, the GDR channelled support solely to Nkomo's forces as divisions between the liberation movements deepened and Mugabe appealed for further Chinese backing.[14] In 1977 and 1978 alone Nkomo visited East Berlin on four occasions (see Table 4). Meanwhile, the GDR further dissociated itself from ZANU. In November 1978 Presi-dent Nyerere of Tanzania had arranged for ZANU's entire Central Committee to visit East Berlin. The mission was refused entry. The GDR also persuaded other Warsaw Pact states to withhold arms shipments to ZANU despite Castro's entreaties in favour of Mugabe.[15] As previously noted, at Lusaka in February 1979 both Honecker and Nkomo in a joint statement opposed Chinese aggression in Vietnam.

In Maputo shortly after, Honecker declined to meet Mugabe because of ZANU's refusal to censure Beijing's intervention in Vietnam. Consequently, Axen of the SED Politbüro confronted Mugabe and demanded a condemnation of the invasion.[16] According to certain sources, Honecker's contempt for Mugabe in these years led to the SED General Secretary at times calling the ZANU leader a 'black teaboy'![17]

However, most interestingly, towards the end of the guerrilla campaign the Cubans and the Soviets but not the East Germans were providing military support to the forces of both Nkomo and Mugabe.[18] This was further evidence of the GDR maintaining a measure of autonomy in the conduct of its *Afrikapolitik*. Rather than coordinating their activities with Cuba and the USSR the East German authorities labelled ZANU as a 'splinter group' and demanded that Mugabe's forces should rejoin Nkomo's ZAPU units.[19] Nevertheless, in partial contradiction of the above, it should also be recalled that Coker referred to an East German proposal to encourage the formation of a joint ZAPU–ZANU government on the Rhodesia–Zimbabwe and Mozambique border (see chapter 4).

Consequently, it was not totally unexpected when Mugabe, as Prime Minister of an independent Zimbabwe, omitted to extend an invitation to the GDR to send a delegation to participate in the independence celebrations in April 1980. The GDR's disappointment was deepened by the presence of a delegation from the 'pro-apartheid' West German state, and the immediate commencement of diplomatic relations between Zimbabwe and the FRG on 18 April 1980. The GDR established diplomatic relations with Zimbabwe on 1 November 1980, apparently only after Honecker had implored Machel to influence Mugabe.[20] This sequence of events must have seriously damaged the GDR's prestige in southern Africa at that time.

However, soon aware that Mugabe was a key statesman in the struggle for national and social liberation in Africa, the GDR swiftly improved relations with Zimbabwe. It should be noted that the GDR established diplomatic relations with Zimbabwe before the USSR and many other East European states.[21] By the end of 1981 a trade agreement and measures to develop cooperation between the SED and ZANU were agreed upon. Economic and political relations were further intensified through a number of delegation visits (see Tables 4 and 5).

Mugabe was warmly welcomed by Honecker in East Berlin in May 1983 as part of an East European tour which included Czechoslovakia and Hungary (but not the USSR). In his speech in Mugabe's honour, Honecker made no reference to the activities of ZAPU and Joshua Nkomo. On the other hand, Mugabe seized the opportunity to denounce ZAPU as representing 'a band of criminal dissidents' who were out to destabilise the Zimbabwean government.[22]

While relations between Zimbabwe and the GDR flourished, the USSR only eventually succeeded in negotiating its first bilateral trade agreement with Mugabe on 18 January 1984.[23] The ZANU leader finally travelled to Moscow in December 1985, but this was in effect only a courtesy call prior to Mugabe assuming chairmanship of the non-aligned movement.[24] Hence, the USSR would have appreciated the prospering of relations between the GDR and Zimbabwe.

The East Germans must have taken immense satisfaction at West German official protests to a statement delivered by Zimbabwe's Minister of State for Security, Emmerson Munangagwa, in August 1986. The minister had categorised the FRG with Britain and the US as the 'major imperialist powers supporting South Africa'. However, Mugabe could not afford to antagonise one of the largest aid donors to the Zimbabwean economy. Consequently, in the same month, on a visit to Bonn, he alleged that 'new thinking was emerging in West Germany over sanctions [against South Africa] as a result of the Commonwealth Summit in London'.[25]

East German relations with Zimbabwe have continued to prosper. The GDR officially supported the decision made in December 1987 to merge ZANU and ZAPU.[26] In April 1988, Günther Sieber, an SED Central Committee official, signed in Harare another SED–ZANU agreement on cooperation for 1988–91.[27] Perhaps Sieber was a little embarrassed when at a banquet given in his honour, Dr Nathan Shimuyarira, the Foreign Minister of Zimbabwe, praised the GDR's longstanding support for his people which dated back to the time of the liberation struggle![28]

The Zimbabwean episode illustrated how the confident East German expectations concerning Africa of the late 1970s failed to materialise fully in the early 1980s. However, despite initial setbacks, the GDR has continued to play an important role for the USSR in southern Africa in this period. Inter-German rivalry once more acquired prominence in the above sequence of events. The following sections examine further the nature of inter-German and East German–Chinese rivalry in Africa in the 1980s, and also the value to the USSR of the GDR's *Afrikapolitik* before and after Gorbachev's accession to power.

East Berlin's rivalry with Beijing and Bonn

In both the pre-recognition period and in the immediate years following general international diplomatic recognition, pursuing a policy of affiliation with the USSR, the GDR had competed with China for influence in certain African states as the repercussions of the Sino-Soviet conflict extended overseas. However, more recently, the warming of relations between the USSR and China (symbolised in Gorbachev's welcome in Beijing in May 1989), has in turn, it seems, resulted in a revision of the traditional rivalries between the GDR and China in Africa.

Direct East German references to Chinese involvement in Africa in the 1980s are difficult to obtain. This is, in part, attributable to China's inactivity on the continent in recent years. Between December 1982 and January 1983 the then Chinese Premier, Zhao Ziyang, on a tour reminiscent of that of Zhou Enlai in the mid-1960s, had undertaken an extended trip to ten states in northern and sub-Saharan Africa. But by 1986 Beijing's interest in Africa was relegated to the lowest order of Chinese foreign policy priorities, apparently accorded the same status as China's concern for events in Central America.[29] The Chinese authorities appear to be channelling their resources to programmes of economic modernisation at home at the expense of an active role in the Third World.

However, it is interesting to note that in August 1986 an article in *Neues Deutschland* praised China's role in the construction of the Tanzam railway in the 1970s through favourable credit terms.[30] One should remember that the interests of Presidents Kaunda and Nyerere in China's generous economic assistance programmes had accounted, in part, for the GDR's failure to secure early diplomatic recognition from Zambia and Tanzania. This article was perhaps produced as part of a publicity build-up before Honecker's official visit to Beijing in October 1986.

In contrast to the GDR and China, inter-German rivalry in Africa has continued despite the improvement in relations between the two Germanies in Europe. For example, the SED leadership, seeking to boost further their legitimacy internally and externally, has continued to aim to secure propaganda points from Bonn's continued economic and political linkages with South Africa. Moreover, by 1980, although the Hallstein Doctrine had not been operative for several years, the problem of the interpretation of the *Land* Berlin Clause remained as the GDR endeavoured to maintain leverage over certain African states at West German expense.

In general, East German references to West German 'neo-colonialist' involvement in Africa were now more oblique than the bludgeoning approach employed in the Ulbricht era. The SED authorities preferred to dissociate themselves from past imperial German history in an attempt to differentiate themselves from the current regime in Bonn.

Addressing the international conference convened in East Berlin in October 1980 to discuss the national liberation movement, Honecker boldly proclaimed: 'Nobody today is unaware of the fact that the German Democratic Republic has broken with the German imperialist past once and for all and that it successfully develops friendly relations on an equal footing with the African, Asian and Latin American countries.'[31]

Five years later *Neues Deutschland* drew attention to the fact that an international conference on Africa held in East Berlin in 1985 (6–8 February) entitled 'Colonialism, Neo-colonialism and the Path of Africa to a Peaceful Future', was the antithesis of Otto von Bismarck's colonial Congo Conference in Berlin 100 years before.[32]

As in earlier years, West German involvement in Namibia and South Africa was denounced. Again, typically, West German economic investment (around 10 per cent of all foreign investment in South Africa) and military cooperation (including research on nuclear weaponry) with Pretoria was condemned.[33] More generally, it was noted that West German officials were cleverly endeavouring to disguise their 'neo-colonialist exploitation' in the Third World by the peddling of slogans such as 'support of the social reform programmes' and 'modernising of the economy'.[34]

However, East German officials were again embarrassed by the public statement of a visiting African dignatory demanding the removal of the Berlin Wall. In 1980, Kaunda's references to German reunification echoed Ghaddafi's proposals made on an official visit to East Berlin in 1978. Following the precedent set by the Libyan leader, *Neues Deutschland* judiciously omitted any reference to Kaunda's personal appeals. It was reported that when receiving an honorary doctorate at Humboldt University, 'the President also extensively dealt with the political situation in Europe and its effects on Africa'.[35] But, according to the West German press, referring to the need to overcome the political division in Europe in order to strengthen world peace, Kaunda declared: 'Your little wall is the perfect symbol of the dangerous division of Europe.'[36]

Ghaddafi himself, in an interview for the Koblenz magazine *Wir*

Selbst, published in its August/September 1983 edition, had demanded the demolition of the Wall. Speaking in favour of German reunification, Ghaddafi declared that neither East German nor West German governments were genuine representatives of the German state and people. Apparently, the Libyan leader had argued similarly about German reunification on his first visit to Moscow in April 1981.[37]

Such statements from leading African statesmen with whom the GDR had cultivated extensive contacts in recent years must have aroused considerable discomfort among East German officials.

Concerning the *Land* Berlin Clause, it should be remembered that in the 1970s certain African states had refused to sign agreements with the FRG which included reference to the *Land* Berlin Clause (i.e., agreements which referred to the extension of the provisions of the agreement to incorporate Berlin also), and Ethiopia had expressed its stern disapproval. However, unlike the earlier Treaty of Friendship and Cooperation concluded with Vietnam (1977), none of the similar treaties agreed upon with Angola, Mozambique and Ethiopia (1979) referred to the GDR's interpretation of the Quadripartite Agreement with reference to West Berlin. Hence, the possibility of those African states later accepting the FRG's views with reference to the *Land* Berlin Clause was by no means excluded.

From 1980 onwards the GDR concluded Treaties of Friendship and Cooperation with Kampuchea (18 March 1980), Cuba (31 May 1980), Afghanistan (21 May 1982), Laos (23 September 1982) and North Korea (1 June 1984). With the exception of Afghanistan, in all these instances attention was again drawn to the GDR's interpretation of the Quadripartite Agreement with reference to West Berlin.[38]

Principally on account of the desperate need for economic assistance from the FRG (and from the EEC with reference to Mozambique and Angola), and because of inadequate aid programmes from the GDR specifically, and the Soviet bloc in general, Mozambique, Angola and São Tomé and Príncipe have eventually concluded agreements with Bonn incorporating the *Land* Berlin Clause.

Maputo's refusal to accept the *Land* Berlin Clause had jeopardised substantial EEC aid pledged to the Southern African Development Coordination Council (SADCC), of which Mozambique was a founder member.[39] A large portion of the approximately $900 million in aid, promised to the SADCC in November 1980 by the EEC for use in the next five years, was earmarked for regional transportation projects involving Mozambique. The failure of Mozambique to join the forthcoming Lomé III Convention (thereby implicitly recognising the validity of the *Land* Berlin Clause), threatened to result in EEC states withholding funds for the transportation programme.[40] The pressure upon Mozambique and the other relevant SADCC member, Angola, was intensified when in November 1980 the West German government rejected a compromise wording proposed by the European Commission concerning the *Land* Berlin Clause, which would have secured the admission of these two African states to the Lomé Convention.[41]

The economies of Mozambique and Angola were further squeezed by the withholding of EEC funds allocated to them under the 'non-associates' budget for 1981 and 1982. This pressure coordinated by the FRG finally succeeded. Following a tour of southern Africa by the EEC Commissioner for Development Cooperation, M. Edgard Pisani, in July 1982, it was agreed that both Mozambique and Angola should henceforth receive aid due to them under the 'non-associates' budget. This was envisaged as an interim measure as part of an implicit understanding that both African states should participate in the negotiations for Lomé III.[42] After agreement was reached on these terms, by the end of 1982 around 8.5 million European Currency Units were assigned to Angola alone.[43] It must be remembered that both Angola and Mozambique had participated in the negotiations for Lomé II in the late 1970s without finally signing the convention. However, by 1982, the economic plight of both African states had intensified. Indeed, in the summer of 1982, Mozambique had actually explicitly accepted the *Land* Berlin Clause in agreements with the FRG ensuring Maputo's participation in Lomé III.

The precise timing of Mozambique's acceptance of the *Land* Berlin Clause is debatable. One source refers to two relatively minor agreements concerned with industrial and food aid concluded between Mozambique and the FRG in June and July 1982.[44] According to the official West German *Bundesgesetzblatt*, an agreement on financial cooperation in industrial development was signed in Bonn on 28 September 1982. Article 7 of this agreement referred to its validity 'for the *Land* Berlin'.[45]

Angola was the final sub-Saharan African state to enter the Lomé Convention, belatedly joining Lomé III (signed by members at the end of 1984) on 30 April 1985.[46] Earlier, in May 1983, Lopo di Nascimento, then the Planning Minister of Angola, had confirmed to Pisani that Angola intended to join Lomé III. Angola had been a full participant in the preparatory negotiations held in Brussels in September 1983.[47] Hence, like Mozambique, the precise date of Angola's explicit acceptance of the *Land* Berlin Clause remains in doubt, unless the date of Angola's signature to Lomé III is taken.

Through aid agreements in December 1984 São Tomé and Príncipe openly declared a willingness to accept finally the *Land* Berlin Clause and receive aid directly from the FRG (although it should be remembered that the former Portuguese colony had earlier joined the Lomé Convention and, hence, technically accepted the *Land* Berlin Clause in November 1978).[48]

One crucial factor that explained Machel's decision to accept the *Land* Berlin Clause in the summer of 1982 was the failure of Mozambique's repeated requests to join the CMEA. Granted observer status to the CMEA in 1979, the following year on a visit to Moscow in November, Machel apparently pressed his hosts to support Mozambique's application for full admission into the economic organisation.[49] But the Soviets and East Europeans were unwilling to subsidise the enormous investment necessary to expand Mozambique's economy if it entered the CMEA. The commitment to 'level up' the woeful Vietnamese economy following Hanoi's admission in 1978 was already provoking considerable friction within the CMEA at a time of economic hardship in the Soviet bloc. Moreover, if admitted to the CMEA, Mozambique's unsteady socialist orientation would have been effectively upgraded into one of an 'irreversible' socialist development.[50]

Did the GDR sponsor Mozambique's endeavours to join the CMEA in order to forestall an increasingly likely acceptance of the *Land* Berlin Clause? Certainly, references to East German support of Mozambique's endeavours have been cited elsewhere. One source has reported that in November 1980 the FRELIMO authorities officially thanked the GDR for its support in backing Mozambique's efforts to secure admission to the CMEA.[51] But East German sources have downplayed their connections with Mozambique's efforts to join the CMEA. The problem of levelling-up the economy of any African state possibly intending to join the organisation has been acknowledged.[52] A renowned East German commentator on African events at a conference discussing current issues in the national liberation movement in May 1983, argued that no developing 'states of socialist orientation' could join the CMEA in the foreseeable future. The continued economic dependence of these states on the imperialist camp was cited as an underlying reason. Hence, admission to the CMEA was impracticable since, as a consequence, 'certain contradictions' would develop.[53]

The East German reservations outlined above must be regarded with a degree of scepticism. They were published after Mozambique's earlier acceptance of the *Land* Berlin Clause. They do not necessarily prove that the GDR did not promote Mozambique's application to join the CMEA prior to the summer of 1982.

With reference to Ethiopia, the signing of the Lomé Convention by the imperial government has enabled Mengistu's regime to receive essential EEC aid to overcome the catastrophic problems of famine in the mid-1980s. Thus, Mengistu is not forced to conclude bilateral agreements with the FRG incorporating the *Land* Berlin Clause. Indeed, relations between Bonn and Addis Ababa have remained almost frozen as Mengistu has maintained a close alignment with the GDR and the Soviet bloc in general.

East German prestige must have suffered with the eventual recognition of the *Land* Berlin Clause by Angola, Mozambique and São Tomé and Príncipe. Here, the GDR was a victim of the lack of economic development aid offered by the Soviet bloc to socialist-oriented African states.

Inter-German rivalry in Africa has persisted. Although details are difficult to ascertain, it would seem that the GDR attempted to involve other East European states in supporting East German rivalry with the FRG. East German sponsorship of Mozambique's admission to the CMEA in order to prevent FRELIMO's acceptance of the *Land* Berlin Clause would have required general support within the Soviet bloc to succeed. If, indeed, the GDR supported Mozambique's application, East German autonomy in involvement in Africa could only operate within certain constraints. For example, in this particular instance, the USSR was not willing to incur the additional problems that would ensue with the admission of an African state to the CMEA.

The GDR's continued prominent profile in Africa

Between 1980 and May 1989 a number of high-ranking delegations visited East Berlin and various African capitals. The majority of the African guests were already familiar to the SED leadership, although the visit of Chief Leabua Jonathan of Lesotho was perhaps less expected. The East German Foreign Minister, Fischer, travelled separately to Africa on six occasions in this period. Honecker headed delegations which visited Ethiopia and Algeria in September and December 1984 respectively (see Tables 4 and 5).

Twenty-seven African parties and national liberation movements

from twenty-two African states (including the 'South African' communist party) attended the 11th SED Congress in East Berlin in April
1986.[54] The Ivory Coast agreed to establish diplomatic relations with
the GDR in October 1984. In continental Africa, with the exception of
South Africa (and its 'independent' tribal homelands), only Malawi
and Swaziland had failed to establish diplomatic relations with the
GDR by December 1987. Nevertheless, both Swaziland and Malawi
were targets of East German *Adressendiplomatie* (through communications by telegram). Moreover, the GDR has developed contacts with
both African states through their membership of the SADCC.

The above details immediately convey the impression of an active
and expansive East German *Afrikapolitik*. It is of interest to note that
the establishment of diplomatic relations with the Ivory Coast was
announced with much less fanfare by the East German press in
comparison with previous acts of diplomatic recognition in the pre-
recognition period. *Neues Deutschland* merely stated that the Ivory
Coast was the 132nd state with which the GDR had established
diplomatic relations.[55] The contrast with the welcoming of diplomatic
relations with any state prior to the winter of 1972 could not be more
striking.

The GDR continued to sponsor actively Soviet bloc relations with
the frontline states and liberation movements in southern Africa as
tensions in the region were heightened. Military and political contacts
were maintained between the ANC and the GDR. Between October
1980 and November 1987 Tambo visited East Berlin on five occasions.
In line with Soviet bloc policy, East German officials demanded an end
to apartheid, the halting of collaboration with the South African
regime, comprehensive sanctions against Pretoria, and freedom for
Nelson Mandela and other political prisoners. Likewise, the GDR
maintained close contacts with SWAPO. Between August 1980 and
July 1988 Nujoma was received in East Berlin on at least eight
occasions. The GDR's reaction to the agreement of December 1988
referring to Namibian independence will be examined in the following
section.

The heads of government of Lesotho and the Congo PR were
welcomed in East Berlin in September 1982 and May 1985 respectively.
Chief Jonathan was received by Honecker, Stoph and Fischer and in
the course of his visit an Agreement on Cultural and Scientific
Cooperation was signed.[56] Unfortunately for the GDR and the Soviet
bloc, Chief Jonathan was deposed in a military coup in January 1986.
This did not prevent Stoph from despatching greetings in October of

the same year on the anniversary of Lesotho's independence to General-Major Lekhanya, the instigator of the coup.[57] The visit of Denis Sassou-Nguesso resulted in a number of agreements including a Protocol of Cooperation between the Foreign Affairs Ministries of the GDR and the Congo PR.[58] No treaty of friendship and cooperation was concluded (in contrast to that between the USSR and the Congo PR in May 1981). One may speculate that for Congolese officials the development of relations with the GDR was less of a foreign policy priority than consolidating ties with the USSR.

As well as establishing a comprehensive network of agreements with individual states and liberation movements in southern Africa, the GDR's role in expanding contacts with these states collectively within the SADCC was also of importance for the USSR. Indeed, it appears that the GDR was assigned the sole responsibility of overseeing CMEA interests in the SADCC for several years. The USSR was apparently confident that the East Germans could make use of their accumulated knowledge and expertise in southern African affairs to represent the Soviet bloc competently in the SADCC. Until 1987 the GDR alone liaised between the southern African regional organisation and the CMEA. A specific concern for the foreign economic policies of Mozambique and Angola probably also explained the GDR's enthusiasm for the SADCC. The GDR was deputed to participate in SADCC sessions on behalf of the CMEA.[59] As early as the second SADCC conference in Maputo in November 1980 an official East German delegation under Deputy Foreign Trade Minister Peter Schmidt was in attendance.[60] The East Germans were the sole East European contributors to SADCC projects, providing in 1985 $3.2 million in aid as part of a $90 million project to rehabilitate the Beira–Malawi railway.[61] Only in February 1987 did the first official CMEA delegation accompany a separate East German delegation to attend the annual session of the SADCC in Gaborone.[62] The Executive Secretary of the SADCC, Dr Simba Kamoni, has recently praised East German support in cadre training and assistance in transport, agricultural, educational and health projects in certain SADCC member states.[63]

In April 1987 the GDR's active involvement in southern Africa was recognised and praised by the Zambian Foreign Minister, Luke John Mwananshika, who led a delegation of eminent persons from a number of key frontline states. Addressing his East German hosts, Mwananshika referred to the 'cordial and friendly relations' between the GDR and the frontline states, and continued: 'We are grateful for the support that you have granted us through all these difficult times.

Your support for the freedom movement in South Africa and Namibia is a further proof of your concern for freedom and justice.'[64]

The GDR also continued to be actively engaged politically in certain north African states in order to advance East German and Soviet bloc policies. Several Arab states were concerned with the latest developments in the Arab–Israeli problem. These developments lie beyond the scope of this work. However, the GDR did continue to play an important role for the Soviet bloc in consolidating military and political relations with the PLO in a period of serious reversals for Yasser Arafat prior to the commencement of the Palestinian uprising or *intifada* in late 1987.[65]

In December 1984 Honecker finally visited Algiers – Algeria, surprisingly, had not been included on the itinerary of Honecker's African tours of 1979 – and held an 'extensive exchange of views' on bilateral and international issues with President Bendjedid in a 'cordial atmosphere'.[66] Apart from these typically ambiguous references little substantive progress was actually achieved according to the official Joint Communiqué. However, the GDR had consolidated relations with one of the most important African members of the non-aligned movement. Addressing journalists in Algiers before his departure, Honecker confirmed that he had invited President Bendjedid to visit East Berlin in order to continue their dialogue.[67] According to later press releases upon the occasion of the visit of the Algerian Foreign Minister to East Berlin in May 1986, and the trip to Algiers by the Central Committee member Gerhard Müller in December 1986, it was envisaged that President Bendjedid would visit the GDR in 1987.[68] By the end of December 1987 the visit had still not materialised. Significantly, when Bendjedid received the Deputy Chairman of the Council of State of the GDR, Dr Günther Maleuda, in July 1987, no reference was made to an impending visit by the Algerian President to East Berlin.[69] The reasons for Bendjedid's non-arrival are not known.

East German relations with Libya cooled in line with the USSR's concern, from 1984 onwards, to promote contacts with more moderate Arab states in order to secure backing for the reconvening of a Geneva Conference to discuss the Arab–Israeli problem. Ghaddafi's open statements concerning German reunification must also have infuriated East German officials. A number of high-ranking delegations from the GDR did visit Libya in this period. At the 11th SED Congress, Honecker condemned the American attack on Libya in April 1986 as a 'barbaric bombardment' and expressed sympathy and support for the Libyans.[70] Coordination between the military and security services of both states was also evident. But the task of consolidating political ties was left principally to the Friendship Societies of both states. Unlike Bulgaria, Romania and Czechoslovakia, the GDR has still to conclude a Treaty of Friendship and Cooperation with Libya, although it will be recalled that this was previously agreed upon in 1979. The USSR itself was reluctant to conclude such a treaty with Libya through fear of encouraging Ghaddafi to provoke further tensions with the US.

After Brezhnev's death the Soviet leadership was more eager to seek *rapprochement* with Hosni Mubarak's Egypt in order to obtain international recognition of Moscow's resurrected demands for equal participation in the faltering Middle East peace process.

Shortly before his assassination, Sadat had expelled over 1,000 Soviet technicians for reportedly recruiting Egyptian dissidents to subvert Egypt's 'national unity'. The departure of the Soviet ambassador was also demanded in September 1981.[71] *Rapprochement* between Moscow and Cairo only commenced after 1984 when negotiations resumed to reschedule (on generous terms over a twenty-five year period) the substantial Egyptian military debts owed to the USSR.[72]

Commercial transactions between the GDR and Egypt remained of importance throughout the latter half of the 1970s at a time when serious political problems arose. In the 1980s the GDR re-established, and thereafter swiftly expanded, political ties with the Egyptian government. Given the circumstances outlined above, the USSR would have approved of these developments. Before Moscow had even restored full diplomatic relations with Cairo, Fischer received in East Berlin Dr Boutros Boutrous-Ghali, the Egyptian State Minister for Foreign Affairs, in November 1983. Both officials were conscious of their ideological differences, although it was reported that this should not hinder the promotion of further contacts between both states as an example of peaceful and constructive cooperation between states of different social orders.[73] Hence, although the GDR acknowledged the reality that Egypt (once one of the most 'progressive' of African states) was not firmly in the Western camp, bilateral relations could still improve. In January and April 1985 Fischer and Politbüro member Günter Kleiber were received by President Mubarak. When an Egyptian Foreign Minister visited East Berlin for the first time in seventeen years in June 1986, Honecker spoke positively of Egypt's 'growing contribution' to the non-aligned movement and expressed satisfaction that in recent years bilateral relations had considerably improved.[74] Three months later, as further evidence of the new warmth in relations, a joint colloquium concerned with questions of foreign policy between the GDR and Egypt was convened in Cairo entitled, 'Dialogue, GDR–Egypt on Key International Questions'.[75]

In addition to East German monitoring of the political development of the regime in Addis Ababa, and further support in the military/ security sphere, the personal relationship between Honecker and Mengistu appeared to flourish in the 1980s. Mengistu visited the GDR on three occasions. The first visit witnessed the signing of an agreement of cooperation between the SED and the new WPE.[76] The second visit was also of note because of Mengistu's personal presence at the 11th SED Congress – the only African head of state or government in attendance. It was also noteworthy that Honecker was the only East European party chief to participate in the tenth anniversary celebrations of the Ethiopian revolution in Addis Ababa.[77] Only minimal details of these visits were provided by the East German press.[78] But Mengistu's third visit to East Berlin in this period in May 1989 was abruptly cut short on account of an attempted military coup.

In chapter 5 I suggested that the extent of genuine East German programmes of development assistance to the Third World should be played down. Although in overall quantitative terms this assessment was accurate, in particular spheres of activity the GDR has on occasion provided substantial support to African states. This support may prove beneficial to African economies, although East German interest in consolidating and expanding Soviet bloc influence in the states in question was also another factor accounting for GDR aid as in previous periods. It will be recalled that in the pre-recognition period of East German foreign policy in Africa contacts with trade union and youth officials, journalists, educational and cultural representatives were essential components of the GDR's efforts to secure increased recognition. In the 1980s, similar contacts were employed as part of the East German strategy of affiliation with the USSR in order to enhance Moscow's estimation of the role played by the GDR in Africa.

In the GDR's official statement to the UNCTAD VI session in Belgrade in 1983 the most comprehensive statistics of the East German development programme hitherto published were submitted. According to this statement, at the beginning of 1983, 29,249 persons from the developing states were undergoing professional training or upgrading of their job qualifications in East German enterprises and institutions in such sectors as industry, mining, agriculture, education, health care and economic planning. In 1982, 4,222 cadres had completed their training bringing the total of citizens from developing states who had completed their job training in the GDR since 1970 to over 54,000.

Since 1970, 14,500 persons from the developing states have completed their studies at an East German higher or technical education institute. In 1983 5,951 citizens from the developing states were enrolled on educational courses in the GDR covering such fields as engineering, economics, transport and agronomy. Since 1970 reportedly the GDR has funded the assignment of more than 10,000 experts in developing states, concentrating on the training of economists, engineers, teachers, vocational instructors and medical personnel. Between 1970 and 1982 over 3,500 patients from developing states received medical treatment in the GDR.[79] These statistics have been regularly updated since 1983.[80]

In education, institutions in the GDR such as the Herder Institute, Die Deutsche Hochschule für Korperkultur, Die Hochschule für Ökonomische Studien, Bruno Leuschner, and others have expanded their recruitment of Third World students in recent years. President Machel, when visiting the School of Friendship at Stassfurt in March 1983, praised the institution as a 'shining' example of solidarity between the GDR and Mozambique.[81] The school provided a course of general education and professional training for around 900 youths from Mozambique. At inter-university level the Karl-Marx University (Leipzig) and the Humboldt University (East Berlin), in particular, have established cooperative arrangements with African universities, including those in Cairo, Luanda and Addis Ababa.

The FDJ has continued to develop relations with African youth organisations. Between 1964 and 1984 fifty-five FDJ Friendship Brigades had been active in twenty-two developing states.[82] In February 1987 eight brigades were employed, or preparing for work, in Angola, Ethiopia, Guinea-Bissau, the Congo PR, Mozambique, São Tomé and Príncipe, Tanzania (providing aid for the ANC), and Zimbabwe to assist in the professional training of bricklayers, plumbers, electricians, builders, mechanics, joiners and experts in transport and agriculture.[83] Invaluable projects were apparently organised by these brigades.

The Internationales Institut für Journalistik, Werner Lamberz, in Friedrichshagen has become one of the major training centres in the Soviet bloc for overseas journalists. *Neues Deutschland* reported in 1983 that there were currently 700 journalists from 51 states (of which several would be African) enrolled on a six-month course of further training at the Institute. A further 2,400 journalists had undertaken courses abroad under supervision of VDJ members. Specialist courses were organised for journalists from Angola, Mozambique, the Congo PR and for ANC and SWAPO members.[84]

The FDGB has also consolidated ties with African trade union groups. The 11th WFTU Congress was assembled in East Berlin in September 1986 at which workers' representatives from 154 states were present. In a Declaration of the Congress to the Working People of the GDR, the 'unshakeable international and revolutionary spirit' of the FDGB was praised.[85] The importance of East Berlin as a centre of trade union activity was again illustrated in April 1987 when twenty-eight delegations from twenty-four African states and two trade union confederations participated at the 11th FDGB Congress.[86]

However, the East German view of the state of trade union development in Africa in August 1987 was not very positive. The first sentence of an article published in that month began: 'The African trade unions operate in extremely complicated and at the same time very different conditions.'[87] The article went on to state that on account of problems of the socio-economic development of sub-Saharan Africa in particular, and with the continuation of exploitative relations under influential imperialist monopolies, the African trade movement in general remained in a formative stage of development. One wonders what actual progress had been made in the African trade union movement according to the GDR since the initial East German tentative contacts with trade unionists from the continent in the late 1950s.

The impact of Gorbachev on the GDR's *Afrikapolitik*

In this address to the 27th CPSU Congress in February 1986 and in the new party programme introduced at the meeting, the intended application of Gorbachev's 'New Political Thinking' to the Third World was indicated. Five years earlier, Brezhnev's speech to the 26th CPSU Congress had specifically praised the treaties of friendship and cooperation concluded by the USSR with Angola, Ethiopia and Mozambique, and had referred to the need to provide economic aid and support to strengthen the defence capabilities of the socialist-oriented states in the Third World.[88] By contrast, Gorbachev's speech in 1986, emphasising the importance of political solutions to regional conflicts, merely offered his 'sympathy' to 'liberated countries' in the Third World and did not refer to African states by name.[89] This alarmed the Cuban, Ethiopian and Angolan delegates at the Congress and prompted them to plead for more definite commitments of Soviet support.[90] The new party programme also scarcely mentioned the role of the socialist-oriented states in the Third World. Attention was rather focused on the possibilities of building ties with certain national capitalist developing states hostile to imperialist aggression and expansionism.[91]

At both the 10th and 11th SED Congresses in 1981 and 1986, Honecker listed as one of the foreign policy priorities of the GDR: 'Active anti-imperialist solidarity with all peoples fighting for national and social liberation . . .'[92] As well as referring to the American attack on Libya, Honecker in his speech in 1986 singled out the GDR's close relations with Angola, Mozambique and Ethiopia when referring to problems in the consolidation and defence of their economies from 'counter-revolutionaries'. Moreover, an end to imperialist aggression against Angola, Mozambique and other frontline states was demanded.[93] No mention was made of expanding contacts with capitalist states in the Third World.

The differences between these major speeches of Gorbachev and Honecker are striking. The East German leadership has experienced some discomfort in attempting to accommodate the revised Soviet policy in the Third World. Nevertheless, in order to maintain close affiliation with the USSR such accommodation has been necessary. Thus, analysts and commentators in the GDR have become increasingly optimistic on the role of national capitalist developing states and even more pessimistic with regard to socialist-oriented states. In line with Gorbachev's emphasis on global interdependence, the GDR has also recommended to African states that they should accept Western aid and capital. Political solutions to regional conflicts in Africa have also been urged. Still, in spite of this official support for revised Soviet policies, an East German unease with these developments may be detected.

As examined earlier, the GDR's increasing pessimism concerning the progress of socialist-oriented states in the Third World pre-dated Gorbachev's 'New Political Thinking'. However, recent East German commentaries have paralleled Soviet writings with regard to growing concern over how these states would make the transition to 'real' socialism as exemplified by the USSR and East European states. Previously recognised problems of the absence of a broad proletariat base, illiteracy, and the intricacies of religious, ethnic and cultural divisions have been reiterated.[94] The 'slow, complicated historical process' has been emphasised with reference to the construction of socialism in the developing states. Over the past two decades the building of socialism in Africa had scarcely advanced, and the record showed that the conditions necessary for a socialist future could not be artificially imposed.[95] Even Honecker in his major speech in 1986 appeared to have acknowledged these problems when referring to Angola, Mozambique and Ethiopia as proceeding on a path of a 'socialist perspective', implying a lowering in immediate expectations of their political and social development.[96]

Although East German commentaries and spokesmen could accommodate themselves with little difficulty to a less optimistic portrayal of the revolutionary progress of African states, it was much more problematical to extol the value of receiving Western aid and investment. Insisting that the capitalist industrialised states were obliged to assist the Third World on account of their past colonial record was totally agreeable, but to admit that an enhanced scope for private enterprise and foreign aid and investment was essential for economic growth even in the socialist-oriented states must be somewhat disconcerting for the East German leadership. This must be particularly so bearing in mind continued East German condemnation of West German economic support for the Third World over the past decades. On the other hand, in spite of their statistical manipulation of aid programmes and verbal declarations of support for a NIEO the SED leadership must have realised that recommending and praising Western development assistance would prevent the GDR from being forced into making aid commitments which could not possibly be fulfilled.

To take one example, East German officials were most probably alarmed when President Kaunda, on a visit to East Berlin in August 1980, pleaded for substantial economic support. Referring to the prospects of a new era of fruitful economic cooperation between the GDR and Zambia, Kaunda declared that: 'The possibilities in agriculture, mining and industry are unlimited. The resources in our [Zambian] territory are practically unexploited in all branches. We need much understanding. We need good management cadres. We need equipment. We need technology and favourable financial support.'[97]

In practice, Honecker had no intention of dissipating enormous funds to subsidise Kaunda's ambitious Operation Food Production Programme which aimed at Zambian self-sufficiency. Some assistance was provided in the organising of state farms and agricultural cooperatives.[98] But, after 1982, with the declining prices of copper (Zambia's main export) it was the US which became Lusaka's largest bilateral foreign aid donor to assist in the expansion of private agricultural enterprises.[99]

More recently, East German commentaries have reported favourably on the efforts of Angola and Mozambique to expand their economies through policies which encouraged, *inter alia*, increased Western investment and the use of such institutions as the International Monetary Fund to reschedule debts.[100] The GDR, like the rest of the Soviet bloc, cannot afford the expenditure required to support the economies of these states.

In line with Gorbachev's emphasis on interdependence, addressing the UN General Assembly in October 1986, the GDR's Permanent Representative to the UN, Harry Ott, declared that the critical economic situation in Africa was a challenge for the whole international community.[101]

But the reluctance of the East Germans to embrace wholeheartedly these new formulations was also apparent. Some commentators have preferred to stress the need for increased African 'self-reliance' and omitted references to the positive role of Western development aid.[102] More significant was the progress of recent talks on international issues between the SED and the West German Social Democrats. A Joint Declaration of Goals entitled 'Conflicting Ideologies and Common Security' released on 27 August 1987 emphasised the need for cooperation to overcome the economic crisis and hunger prevalent in Third World states.[103] However, an East German commentary on a follow-up meeting within the framework of the Joint Declaration stressed that problems of poverty, debt and hunger were the result of neo-colonialist exploitation. The article added that although it was unavoidable that developing states should seek assistance from capitalist states, the general trend of development in the Third World remained on a path towards eventual communism.[104] A reluctance to approve of West German development aid programmes was clearly manifest.

Concerning Gorbachev's cultivation of relations with certain national capitalist states in Africa, East German analysts have encountered less problems. As early as the mid-1970s Karen Brutents, a prominent Soviet Third World specialist, had indicated that there were two types of capitalist developing states. Those which pursued a path of national–capitalist development were more critical of neo-colonialist practices and more sympathetic to the Socialist Community than dependent capitalist states. Several East German articles also adhered closely to Brutents' views at that time.[105] Hence, when Gorbachev was attracted to Brutents' positive appraisal of the national capitalist developing states it posed no major problem for East German commentators to assess more favourable the role of these economically more advanced states in the Third World. The revolutionary 'possibilities' of capitalist states led by the national bourgeoisie were noted. In contrast with dependent capitalist states led by the neo-comprador and bureaucratic bourgeoisie, the national capitalist states were seeking to strengthen their national, anti-imperialist interests by reducing their dependence on foreign monopoly capital.[106] Egypt was grouped with Argentina, Brazil, Mexico, India and Indonesia as examples of states where the national bourgeoisie were cooperating less with 'transnational monopolies'.[107] Hence, it should be noted in passing that only certain types of Western aid to Third World states was to be approved. The listing of Egypt was significant (East Berlin's relations with Cairo having improved in the 1980s). Clearly the GDR, as the USSR, is interested in expanding economic contacts with national capitalist states such as Egypt on account of their raw materials and intermediate technologies, although East German trade turnover with Egypt has surprisingly declined recently.

In view of the above, Honecker's omission of the role of the national capitalist developing states in his speech to the 11th SED Congress in 1986 appears more puzzling. One would imagine that Honecker's (or his successor's?!) address to the 12th SED Congress in 1990 would contain a positive reference to the activities of these states.

However, the most interesting issue for the East German leadership to address is Gorbachev's interest in political solutions to regional conflicts in the Third World, and the possible political repercussions this might entail. Here, the SED authorities have had to appraise the Angola–Namibia Accords of December 1988 concerning the independence of Namibia and the phased withdrawal of Cuban troops from Angola, as well as contemplate the possibility of a future coalition government in Luanda incorporating UNITA. The possibilities of a settlement in the Horn of Africa must also be considered. In addition, the East Germans must also ponder over the prospects of a genuine peace agreement between Mozambique and South Africa and a negotiated settlement between FRELIMO and the Renamo guerrillas. Connected with events in southern Africa, the GDR cannot discard the possibility that its public support for the ANC might have to be toned down as the USSR develops further its recent tentative contacts with the South African government.

Close military and political support for the regimes in Angola, Ethiopia and Mozambique, and for the ANC and SWAPO in their guerrilla campaigns, as well as differentiating the GDR's *Afrikapolitik* from that of the FRG's policies on the continent, have also formed important components of the East German leadership's pursuit of an affiliation strategy with the USSR in Africa. Hence, the SED authorities must be following recent Soviet interest in developments in Africa with some concern as the GDR's *Afrikapolitik* would require a radical re-assessment if settlements of all these problems eventually materialised.

According to one argument, the SED leadership could possibly welcome political solutions to longstanding conflicts in Africa. The USSR, Cuba and the GDR, having in the 1960s and 1970s supported a number of guerrilla movements against colonial powers, are now to an extent in favour of the status quo and are opposed to 'counter-revolutionary' guerrilla groups struggling to overthrow the present order. Less skilled in understanding how to combat guerrilla forces in contrast to regular units, the Cuban and Soviet bloc military advisers have encountered serious problems in attempting to deal with UNITA and Renamo groups in southern Africa, and the Tigrayan and Eritrean movements in Ethiopia. Indeed, in recent years the FRELIMO government has literally withdrawn the Warsaw Pact book of rules on military engagement and ironically turned to Portugal and Britain for military support – former colonial powers well-versed in the art of counter-insurgency.[108] Thus, the argument might follow that the East Germans would embrace Gorbachev's appeal for political solutions to these conflicts in order to save face and extricate themselves from what might seem to be an increasingly hopeless position. But in his efforts to check 'the export of counter-revolution', it should be emphasised that Honecker has contributed significant military/security support to these African regimes as a cornerstone of the GDR's strategy of affiliation with the USSR on that continent. Moreover, East German unease with the Lusaka and Nkomati Agreements of 1984, harbingers of the more recent diplomatic manoeuvrings, should also be recalled.

In theory, East German analysts have supported Soviet interest in seeking political settlements to regional conflicts in the Third World. It has been stated that these settlements make an essential contribution to world peace and security and upgrade peaceful coexistence between states provided that they are based on compromise and dialogue, and respect the rights of self-determination of all peoples.[109] As early as June 1985, in a speech to the 10th Plenum of the SED Central Committee, Honecker himself had cautioned that without the peaceful resolution of conflicts in regions such as southern Africa and the Middle East, the next world war could erupt from an escalation of tensions there.[110]

In practice, the GDR has expressed its cautious approval of the Angola–Namibia Accords of December 1988. Even the South African government was praised indirectly in the official East German press release immediately after the signing of the Accords. Regarding the agreements as an important step towards the political solution of the conflict in southern Africa, the participating states were commended for their realism and respect of legitimate interests. Significantly, another article in the same issue of *Neues Deutschland* declared that the Accords confirmed the correctness of previous policies of the GDR and other socialist states towards southern Africa.[111] But the East German authorities still voiced reservations concerning the settlement. Immediately prior to the Accords it was noted that Pretoria had only come to the conference table following the 'military débâcle' when South African troops supported by UNITA rebels had failed to seize the military base at Cuito Cuananvale in southern Angola.[112] After the agreement was signed the East German authorities continued to question South African motives. Pretoria was warned that SWAPO must be accepted as a serious partner, and that the implementation of the Accords should not be thwarted by trickery. Furthermore, together with concern over the future of the strategically important port of Walvis Bay, the East Germans expressed their alarm over the possibility that the South Africans alongside the US would continue to provide military support to the UNITA guerrillas and thus continue to destabilise the Angolan government.[113] Even by the summer of 1989, in spite of African attempts to obtain a tentative ceasefire agreement between UNITA and the authorities in Luanda, the prospects for a peaceful and lasting solution concerning Namibia and Angola were by no means guaranteed.

Connected to these developments, the East Germans are also having to prepare for a possible full peace settlement between Pretoria and Maputo. Relations between Mozambique and South Africa have improved following the meeting between Presidents Joacquim Chiss-ano (Machel having died in a plane crash in October 1986) and P. W. Botha in the Mozambique village of Sango in September 1988, and the reactivation in May 1988 of the Joint Security Commission of the two states originally instituted by the Nkomati Accord. In 1989 efforts were stepped up under African auspices to initiate negotiations between FRELIMO and the Renamo insurgents. Thus, on his first visit to the GDR as President of Mozambique in May 1989, Chissano, while referring to the terror instigated by the Renamo 'bandits', also spoke of his efforts to begin a dialogue with the South African backed insurgents. But, interestingly, Honecker, in the speech given at a banquet for his guests, made no reference to the Renamo problem.[114]

One must accept that East Berlin believed that the ending of apartheid would ultimately ensue as a consequence of a successful liberation struggle waged by the ANC supported politically (and militarily) by the Soviet bloc. But a new generation of Soviet Africanists, concerned that an escalation in the internal struggle between blacks and whites in South Africa would contribute to a renewed destabilisation in southern Africa as a whole, have begun to press more openly for a negotiated settlement to the apartheid issue in preference to a military solution. Still committed to supporting the ANC as the legitimate voice of the black majority in South Africa, and still demanding the imposition of economic sanctions against Pretoria until apartheid is finally dismantled, Soviet experts have indicated that the ANC should work out beforehand comprehensive guarantees for the whites for a future post-apartheid regime. Even the recent limited internal reforms in South Africa have been praised and alarm expressed for Botha's problems in dealing with the extreme right-wing Afrikaners.[115] Significantly, in April 1989, Vyachislav Ustinov led the first official Soviet delegation to visit South Africa since diplomatic relations were suspended between the two states in 1956. Although the visit was primarily connected with a meeting in Cape Town to review the progress of the December 1988 Accords – the USSR and the US having been appointed as joint monitors of the Accords – Ustinov, along with the Cuban and Angolan delegation leaders, paid a courtesy visit to the then still President Botha in his official residence at Tuynhaus.[116] Although information is difficult to obtain, one may assume that the East Germans are closely following these developments with some apprehension.

Much less problematic for the GDR is the question of the future of the Western Sahara. In a full centre-spread in the December 1988 issue of *Horizont* devoted to the issue of regional conflicts in the Third World, the official East German line was repeated. All UN initiatives for a peaceful settlement of the Western Sahara problem would continue to be supported.[117] The GDR has continued to follow Soviet policy in refusing to recognise the Saharan Arab Democratic Republic (SADR) although the OAU granted the SADR full membership in November 1984 provoking Morocco's withdrawal from the OAU. The import of phosphates from Morocco, and the relative insignificance of the Saharan region have dictated Soviet and East German actions. Fischer did receive Ould Salek, a member of the POLISARIO Politbüro in

December 1984. But the East German Foreign Minister could only assure Salek that the GDR had supported since 1981 all appropriate UN and OAU resolutions for a peaceful settlement of the Western Sahara issue.[118]

However, on account of the traditional close support for the Mengistu regime in Ethiopia, the East German leadership seems much more awkward when espousing a peaceful political solution to the conflict in the Horn of Africa. Thus, one report in *Neues Deutschland* in July 1988 condemned the murder and terror perpetrated by Western-backed secessionist groups and counter-revolutionaries in the provinces of Eritrea and Tigray, and defended Mengistu's efforts to 'defend the territorial integrity of Ethiopia'. But the same article also added that a political solution to conflict in the region was necessary.[119] The details of how a settlement could be reached without destabilising Mengistu's regime was not addressed. On account of the close ties between the current leaderships in Addis Ababa and East Berlin, it appears that the GDR no longer performs the role it pursued in the mid-1970s as a broker between the Ethiopian administration and the opposing guerrilla factions.

When Mengistu arrived in East Berlin in May 1989 *Neues Deutschland* in its front-page coverage referred to a four-day official friendship visit.[120] The following day the paper reported that Mengistu had concluded his visit after comprehensive talks with Honecker.[121] No reference was made to the attempted coup led by a number of senior military officers which had compelled Mengistu to cut short his state visit. The following month the Ethiopian Foreign Minister arrived in East Berlin to hold talks with Axen and Fischer.[122]

Despite these attempts by the East German authorities to present an image of a stable and secure government in Ethiopia with whom business was as usual, the long-term future of Mengistu's rule must be questioned. In addition to serious strains on the Ethiopian economy and humiliating military defeats in the field which had triggered the attempt coup, the current leadership in Addis Ababa faces the likelihood that the USSR will no longer replenish the Ethiopian army with further arms exports when the current arms agreement expires in 1990. With the easing of tensions in the Gulf region and Indian Ocean following the end of the Iran–Iraq war and the Soviet withdrawal from Afghanistan, the Horn of Africa has lost much of its original strategic importance. Moscow appears to be increasingly regarding Mengistu as an expensive liability and a hindrance to the progress of a lasting and peaceful settlement in the Horn.[123] Significantly, in July 1989 the

Deputy Soviet Foreign Minister, Anatoli Adamshin, for the first time held discussions in London with EPLF officials.[124]

Clearly, the ongoing Soviet reassessment of relations with the Third World has raised serious questions over the future role and significance of the GDR's *Afrikapolitik*. But the East Germans must be reluctant to disengage themselves from Africa given the accumulated prestige reaped from an active profile on the continent in past years. Speculation concerning the future character of East German involvement in Africa is offered in the final chapter.

7   Conclusion

The importance of Africa for the GDR

In this book I have set out to demonstrate that an examination of the GDR's *Afrikapolitik* enables one to appreciate the broader significance and consequence of the development of East German foreign policy *in toto* and, indeed, of the GDR as an entity *per se*.

In the pre-recognition period of East German foreign policy African states and liberation movements were selected as important targets in the GDR's quest to secure diplomatic recognition or at least obtain some form of recognition as an independent state. Recognition was imperative in order to boost the legitimacy of the SED-controlled state as perceived internally and externally. Bonn's refusal to renounce the goal of German reunification and recognise the legitimacy of the GDR – Adenauer's original *Alleinvertretungsanspruch* – was mobilised on an international scale through the Hallstein Doctrine.

Developments in Africa (and in the connected region of the Middle East) in this period had encouraged the GDR to concentrate attention on the African continent in an attempt to break loose from the shackles of international isolationism imposed by the FRG. Inter-German rivalry in Africa mirrored the overall competition and hostility between the two Germanies. Within a consciously chosen strategy of affiliation with the USSR, intense East German support of Soviet objectives in Africa was directed towards securing policy successes over Bonn in Africa and elsewhere, and was cultivated as a means of ensuring Moscow's assistance in obtaining diplomatic recognition worldwide. The USSR's overriding stake in the consolidation of the SED regime in order to suppress possible West German attempts to secure reunification on Western terms enabled Ulbricht to utilise the bargaining powers of the weak and profit from a certain autonomy in the GDR's *Afrikapolitik* in these years. Despite the operation of the

217

Hallstein Doctrine the GDR's *Afrikapolitik* was by no means totally inhibited. Through innumerable channels of contact, an active East German engagement in Africa was observed in the pre-recognition period.

Consequently, before 1972–3 international recognition was the primary purpose of the GDR's *Afrikapolitik*. The pursuit of a strategy of affiliation with the USSR was directly connected to the SED's concern for its own legitimacy and that of the East German state (although the two could scarcely be separated). Foreign policy was an important tool which could be employed by the SED to legitimise their authority within the GDR.

On account of the German question, the SED leadership encountered serious problems in obtaining international recognition, which they regarded as essential in their domestic struggle for legitimacy. If external recognition boosted the legitimacy of SED rule within the GDR, acceptance at home, in its turn, would encourage external powers to recognise the GDR. Insofar as international recognition may be considered to confer substantive acceptance by a community of states, it amounted to a gain of legitimacy at the international level. In this sense the domestic and international aspects of legitimacy were closely linked.

Africa's importance for the GDR in the post-recognition period has become more complex, and, for this reason the significance of certain developments in the Gorbachev era will be addressed separately later. Although, undoubtedly, the obvious legitimising function of an active and successful East German foreign policy had diminished somewhat once global diplomatic recognition was obtained, and the statehood of the GDR sanctioned internationally, the continued West German cherishing of the Basic Law's demand for ultimate German reunification and non-recognition of East German citizenship resulted in a maintained inter-German rivalry in Africa. In these circumstances, the Honecker regime's continued legitimacy shortcomings compelled the GDR to exploit advantageous opportunities offered in Africa in the mid-1970s to differentiate the foreign policies of the two Germanies in the Third World in order to boost further the international stature of the East German state both internally and externally. A number of propaganda victories over the FRG in Africa were also obtained by Honecker with reference to the *Land* Berlin Clause. Certainly, in the 1970s, *Abgrenzung* in Africa corresponded with Honecker's emphasis on *Abgrenzung* in Europe in connection with inter-German relations in spite of the ratification of the Basic Treaty.

Moreover, Honecker's policy of *Abgrenzung* was coupled with the promotion of an intensified policy of affiliation with the USSR whereby the GDR attained the status of the USSR's most important junior partner. This rise in status was epitomised by Moscow entrusting East Berlin with a key role in further developing relations between states of the Socialist Community and Africa. Here, East German self-congratulatory articles and speeches concerning the success of Honecker's tours of Africa in 1979 and their relevance to socialist bloc interests in Africa and the Third World were to an extent vindicated. In practice, innumerable exchanges of prominent delegations of leading party and state officials between East Berlin and several African capitals were complemented by much more furtive operations in the military/security sphere. Here, an ever-expanding autonomous role was accorded to the GDR in Africa by the USSR.

Consequently, contrary to the views of certain Western analysts, the GDR has not acted as a surrogate or a proxy. Through the strategy of affiliation with the USSR the GDR has conducted an autonomous foreign policy in Africa. Hence, in its *Afrikapolitik* the GDR has pursued certain foreign policy goals separate from those of the USSR, e.g., diplomatic recognition, international prestige, propaganda victories over the FRG. At least until Gorbachev's accession to power, these goals had coincided with the USSR's geopolitical ambitions. The GDR's traditional hostility to the FRG in Africa complemented the desire of the USSR to secure further influence in the Third World at the West's expense.

Fearful of their legitimacy shortcomings the East German authorities have sought to impress upon the Soviet leadership the importance of the GDR as a dependable ally of the USSR. Although the GDR has its own particular interests to be involved in Africa, nevertheless, as a dependable ally the GDR would also have to share the costs and risks (as well as the successes) of the USSR's strategic involvement on the continent. Moscow has maintained an overall control of socialist bloc activity in Africa. In these circumstances, the GDR has become an important but still junior partner of the USSR in Africa. Certainly, before Gorbachev, Moscow would have neither approved nor tolerated East German activities on the continent that might have undermined the USSR's geopolitical interests.

Almost ironically, the GDR has aspired to and obtained a measure of autonomy in its policies in Africa by stressing the interdependent nature of the Soviet–East German relationship. Through its advisers in Africa, particularly in the military/security sphere, the GDR has been able to gain direct access to and therefore some influence on the principal decision-makers in these countries without Moscow as an intermediary. Furthermore, East German officials based overseas may be expected to have some discretion and act on their own initiative in the day-to-day conduct of affairs in the field.

The GDR's strategy of affiliation appears to have brought its rewards. East Berlin received considerable and invaluable preferential economic treatment from the USSR, especially in years of serious difficulty for the East German economy. Also, the Soviet leadership in recent years has entrusted the GDR with a certain amount of leeway in the development and maintenance of closer inter-German relations in Europe. Firm and demonstrable proof to correlate Soviet economic and political rewards for East German services rendered in Africa is impossible to collect. However, at least until most recently, the pattern of USSR–GDR relations within the strategy of affiliation would suggest that a positive correlation was apparent.

Nevertheless, the importance of East German activities in Africa in their own right must not be overlooked. Rivalry with the FRG in Africa has continued to influence East German involvement on the African continent even in the 1980s in spite of improved relations between the two Germanies in Europe. Movements towards harmonising inter-German relations in Africa would compel a fundamental reassessment of one of the traditionally important legitimising functions of the GDR's *Afrikapolitik* i.e., that based on antagonistic relations between the two Germanies. Perhaps, after decades of inter-German rivalry in Africa it would seem improbable that this rivalry could be suddenly transformed into more cooperative interaction. Tripartite cooperation ventures between the two Germanies in Africa remain rare. But, perhaps, rivalry could be modified into some form of coexistence between the two Germanies in Africa at some future date.

It is significant that the Joint Communiqué released in Bonn on the occasion of Honecker's visit in 1987 made only fleeting references to the Third World in general. In the Joint Communiqué, it was agreed to work to strengthen the UN in order to find solutions to pressing global political, economic, social and humanitarian problems. The importance of the non-aligned movement as a factor for international stability was also praised.[1]

More interesting perhaps was the publication of an article in the East German journal *IPW-Berichte* in 1988 which offered a surprisingly positive appraisal of certain popular movements and organisations in the FRG which appealed for solidarity with the Third World. Bodies such as the Anti-Apartheid Movement and the Anti-Imperialist Solidarity Committee were singled out for praise, while the activities of Communists, Social Democrats, trade unionists and women's and youth groups *inter alia* were also commended.[2] This was a far cry from the Ulbricht regime's usual blanket denunciations of West German interest and involvement in the Third World. Nevertheless, the SED has continued the policy of *Abgrenzung* between the two Germanies in Africa and the reason is clear. The current East German authorities still seek an ultimate goal that Ulbricht had also pursued, namely, official West German repudiation of German reunification, and thereby, West German recognition of East German citizenship.

Commerce has also motivated the GDR's *Afrikapolitik*. The importance of oil imports from certain African states in the 1980s has been examined. Some of these oil imports have been re-exported to the West to provide the GDR with alternative sources of hard currency.

Once the primary objective of international recognition was secured, it would have appeared likely that the GDR could concentrate more on regular commercial dealings with African states. But the GDR's trade turnover with the Third World as a whole has remained low when compared with several other East European states. Moreover, even in the post-recognition period economic interests cannot be totally separated from political interests as the relatively high East German trade turnover with 'socialist-oriented' states has demonstrated. Likewise, East German development aid programmes have remained to some extent subordinate to political interests.

However, to return to the question of legitimacy, has active GDR involvement in Africa *per se* strengthened the support of the East German public for the SED? Here, the problem of gauging the success of any strategy used to generate legitimacy is evident. According to Croan, the so-called 'African Elixir' boosted the NVA's prestige – acutely needed on account of continued inferiority with the ranks of the WTO in Europe – and also 'energised' lower-ranking SED officials in their difficult task of providing 'potent ideological arguments' to offset the more mundane domestic complaints of the East German public. A continued emphasis on the importance of the GDR's role in Africa in furthering the world revolutionary process was intended to facilitate SED propaganda spokesmen and local party cells in their work in offering East German citizens ideological guidance.[3] According to Coker, an emphasis on the ideological importance of the East German support for national liberation and revolutionary struggle boosted the legitimacy of the SED by compensating for a 'revolution-

222 The foreign policy of the GDR in Africa

ary sclerosis' that was threatening to take firm hold in the average East German citizen.[4]

Another related argument refers to the ostensible educational function of East German assistance and solidarity support of Third World states. Such activities served to expunge once and for all within the GDR previous racial prejudices, and effect a *volte-face* in earlier received German perceptions of their international role. According to this line of thought, East German support for the national and social liberation struggle in Africa also played an important role in the GDR's own nation-building endeavours. Solidarity with Africa would eradicate the final vestiges of any remaining fascist, colonialist and imperialist sympathies within the GDR.[5]

One may reason that a motivating element for the GDR's *Afrikapolitik* was the need perceived by the SED elite to assuage the onerous legacies of responsibility for two recent world wars and their accompanying horrors. Such a policy was intended to command the attention of a receptive public in both the GDR and abroad. However, the success of such a policy must be seriously questioned. It has already been noted that the East German public were shielded from information concerning the GDR's military/security operations in Africa on account of their possible hostile reaction to such accounts, and also that critical international reaction needed to be considered. These operations themselves were scarcely a means of erasing memories of the activities of Rommel's Afrika Korps. Moreover, it has been alleged that the East German public regard GDR involvement in the Third World as a dissipation of limited resources.[6] On the other hand, continued solidarity donations in organised campaigns designed to secure further public support for the Third World appear to indicate that East Germans remain mindful of their internationalist duties. One may only speculate whether this is actually rather more through force of habit than genuine concern. It is perhaps reasonable to presume that the majority of East Germans, including lower-ranking SED members, remain indifferent to their government's activities in Africa. If so, passive acceptance by the masses, although hardly contributing positively, does not operate to the detriment of the SED's endeavours to generate further legitimacy through an enlarged *Afrikapolitik* from which beneficial spin-offs have been obtained.

One must not draw the conclusion that East German involvement in Africa has consisted simply of cheap propaganda exercises and obscure military/security dealings with some of the least salutory African regimes. The temptation to focus almost exclusively on tales of

the escapades of a new East German Afrika Korps has proved
overpowering for several more conservative Western journalists and
commentators. Genuine East German assistance programmes in education, job-training (professional, skilled and semi-skilled), journalism, and disaster relief, *inter alia*, are often overlooked or cited as
examples of the GDR's attempts to ingratiate itself with certain African
states, most often at the expense of the FRG. One may rather contend
that, overall, the GDR's involvement in Africa has incorporated
elements of both altruism, a need for the re-education of the East
German public (although by no means to the extent that official SED
spokesmen would impute), and more self-interested politically and
also economically (to a lesser extent) motivated behaviour couched in
ideological terms.

Certainly, in its *Afrikapolitik* and indeed, in general, the GDR's
actions are conditioned by a range of various constituents, historical, political and economic. In Africa, these have provided for a
foreign policy not akin to the external activities of other East European states on the continent. For instance, Hungary has no inter-
Hungarian factor to determine its overseas policy. No other East
European state (including the USSR/Russia) can match the historical
tradition of past German governments' interest in Africa. Of all East
European states, with the exception of the USSR, it is only maverick
Romania which is as actively engaged as the GDR in Africa.
Romania's peculiar interests in the Third World form part of a foreign
policy traditionally less in accordance with the USSR's global perceptions, i.e., almost the opposite of the GDR's affiliation policy in
Africa. Romania's close connections with the Third World through
membership of the Group of 77 have also influenced Bucharest's
policies. Poland, Hungary and Bulgaria perform little more than
normal diplomatic and economic relations with African states – their
military/security role is almost minimal. Likewise, Czechoslovakia
may also be bracketed in this category when, after 1968, Czechoslovak arms exports to the African continent came under stricter Soviet
observation. Despite these contrasts, clearly, a better understanding
of GDR foreign policy in Africa would be of benefit in expanding
the existing comparative dearth of Western, and particularly, Anglo-
American academic interest in East European (i.e., non-Soviet) relations with the Third World.[7]

But what of the GDR's strategy of affiliation with the USSR in the
Gorbachev era bearing in mind certain changes in the GDR–USSR
relationship? And, how have these recent developments affected the

significance of the GDR's *Afrikapolitik*? As indicated in the Intro-duction, the East German authorities, still somewhat paranoid con-cerning the question of their legitimacy, have been most reluctant to embrace political and economic reforms of the type introduced in the USSR and taken up by the leaderships of Hungary and Poland. Indeed, the GDR has been grouped along with Czechoslovakia, Bulgaria and Romania as a member of the so-called 'Gang of Four' opposed to initiating genuine *glasnost* and *perestroika* in their respective political systems. With regard to domestic policy, Honecker no longer appears to be Moscow's *Musterknabe*. Moreover, with improving East–West relations in Europe and Gorbachev's latest appeals to a 'common European home', the SED leadership is less able to exploit previous Soviet concern over the exposed position of the East German state bordering a 'hostile' Western alliance. Instead, perhaps, some East German statesmen may be once again alarmed that the USSR might be tempted to play the German card in order to entice the FRG away from its NATO allies. Under the present circumstances the GDR's bargaining capabilities *vis-à-vis* the USSR appear to have declined considerably.

But the present SED leadership does not have the confidence to strike a truly independent path. The strategy of affiliation with the USSR is still pursued, but within certain bounds. For example, the GDR has become more willing to participate in joint investment projects in the USSR in recent years in order to emphasise to the Soviets the indispensability of the East German economy. In the sphere of foreign policy in general – with the possible exception of the German question in Europe – the East German authorities may continue to support actively Soviet initiatives. Hence, Honecker has endeavoured to reinforce Gorbachev's important proposals for chemi-cal, nuclear and conventional arms reductions in Europe.

Yet in Africa, in particular (as noted in chapter 6), the East German leadership has again encountered certain problems in accommodating itself to Gorbachev's new policies. The GDR's *Afrikapolitik* in the past decades with its emphasis on rivalry with the West (embodied in the FRG), and close military/security and political support of national liberation movements and earlier adjudged ideologically 'progressive' socialist-oriented regimes, is difficult to square with Gorbachev's 'New Political Thinking'. It is too early to say that the GDR no longer pursues a strategy of affiliation with the USSR in Africa, but the next years should prove significant.

The GDR and Africa in the future

Crystal-ball gazing is always a difficult and dangerous exercise to undertake. Any attempt to predict the nature of the future role and involvement of the GDR in Africa – even assuming, of course, that there will be a continued East German interest in African affairs – is especially fraught with difficulties. Internal developments in Africa, particularly in southern Africa and in the Horn, would, in part, dictate East German responses. Moreover, a change of leadership in Moscow or in East Berlin could fundamentally alter the future nature of the GDR's *Afrikapolitik*. Although Gorbachev at present appears to have consolidated his position domestically, serious problems remain concerning the state of the Soviet economy, and ethnic tensions have been exacerbated in recent years. Honecker's tenure as SED leader must draw to a close in the foreseeable future, and at this time it is impossible to envisage how the policies of a possible new generation of SED statesmen could affect the GDR's relations with the Third World.

Dunér has attempted to predict East German and Cuban behaviour should the USSR seek to disengage itself 'militarily' from the Third World. In those circumstances, would the East German and/or Cubans also disengage, or would they continue 'their military activism'? According to Dunér, if the latter proved to be the case 'this would be a really interesting development'. This could 'indicate a great degree of allied independence', or it could indicate a 'proxy relationship' as the Soviets 'may be tempted to bring some kind of pressure to bear on its allies, to act in its place, and these may feel more inclined than earlier to anticipate Soviet wishes . . .' Dunér tends to dismiss the proxy relationship argument and speculates that a Soviet military disengagement could lead to much closer cooperation between East Berlin and Havana in the Third World with both combining and maximising use of their more limited resources.[8]

In his analysis Dunér was primarily concerned with Cuban and Soviet bloc military interventionism in the Third World. Nevertheless, the above line of thought is also of relevance for speculating on the future role of the GDR in Africa from a broader political perspective. However, it should be pointed out that since Dunér's work was published the Cubans and East Germans have accepted the, in part, Soviet-sponsored Angola–Namibia Accords of December 1988, which when fully implemented would lead to a substantial reduction in the Cuban military presence in Africa.

If Gorbachev continues to downgrade the importance of a visible and active Soviet 'presence' in Africa in preference for his vision of global interdependence and concern for domestic political and economic reforms – as, indeed, seems likely at the present moment – then the future role of the GDR in Africa must be seriously questioned. According to the analysis employed in this book it would seem unrealistic to suppose that the USSR would compel the East Germans to downgrade their operations in Africa, although, of course, with less or no Soviet logistical support the GDR would find it difficult to maintain the scale of its current involvement in Africa even with Cuban backing. In this book, I have emphasised throughout that the GDR is no surrogate or proxy of the USSR. But, on the other hand, if the East Germans, with possible Cuban support, attempt to maintain a presence in Africa regardless of a Soviet downgrading of interest, disengagement or even withdrawal, then the GDR's *Afrikapolitik* would no longer form part of a strategy of affiliation with the USSR. East Berlin could still continue to denounce Bonn's activities in Africa and emphasise its support for national and social liberation on the continent, but one of the principal aims would no longer be to impress the authorities in the Kremlin.

Nevertheless, as indicated earlier, a downgrading of the GDR's role in Africa would demand a fundamental reallocation of East German resources and would appear to make nonsense of previously accumulated contacts with certain states and national liberation movements, trade union bodies, journalistic groups, youth organisations etc. Thus, it would seem that the SED leadership – the current one at least – would only most reluctantly disengage from Africa. One possible scenario is that the East German authorities would attempt to prolong their political and military involvement in Africa – of course, commercial relations would still continue – by convincing Moscow that the GDR could perform an invaluable role in protecting Soviet interests in this important period of transition on the continent. Certainly, present conflicts in southern Africa and in the Horn would not necessarily immediately be extinguished even after the conclusion of a negotiated settlement, as the continued tensions in Angola–Namibia at the time of writing indicate. This scenario would allow the East Germans to play for time and to maintain the strategy of affiliation with the USSR in Africa, with the possibility that in the not too distant future the current group in power in the Kremlin, if not ousted, may have at least been forced to revise their policies on account of certain developments in Africa.

But whatever the future may hold, it seems likely that in the next years at least the SED leadership will continue to experience the recent discomfort caused by the impact of Gorbachev's 'New Political Thinking' on the GDR's long-established *Afrikapolitik*.

Notes

1 Introduction

1 E.g., in 1987 alone two comprehensive West German works on East German relations with Africa were published, namely: Ernst Hillebrand, *Das Afrika–Engagement der DDR* (Frankfurt, Bern, New York and Paris: Verlag Peter Lang, Münchner Studien zur internationalen Entwicklung, vol. 5, 1987); and Hans-Joachim Spanger and Lothar Brock, *Die beiden deutschen Staaten in der Dritten Welt – Die Entwicklungspolitik der DDR – eine Herausforderung für die Bundesrepublik Deutschland?* (Opladen: Westdeutscher Verlag, 1987).

2 David E. Albright, 'Introduction', in David E. Albright (ed.), *Africa and International Communism* (London and Basingstoke: Macmillan, 1980), p. 5.

3 Andrew Gyorgy, 'East Germany', in Vaclav Benes, Andrew Gyorgy and George Stambuk (eds.), *Eastern European Government and Politics* (New York, Evanston and London: Harper and Row, 1966), p. 100.

4 Zbigniew Brzezinski, *Alternative to Partition* (New York, Toronto and London: McGraw-Hill, 1965), p. 140.

5 See Albert P. Blaustein and Gisbert H. Flanz (eds.), *Constitutions of the Countries of the World*, Binder 6, *The German Democratic Republic* (Dobbs Ferry, New York: Oceana Publications, 1987), pp. 89–120, for the full text of the GDR constitution of 7 October 1974.

6 See Günther Doeker, Jens A. Bruckner and Ralph Freiberg (eds.), *The Federal Republic of Germany and the German Democratic Republic in International Relations*, vol. 3, *The Federal Republic of Germany and the German Democratic Republic in International Relations and Organisations* (New York and Alphen aan den Rijn: Oceana Publications and Sijthoff and Noordhoff, 1979), pp. 106–7, for full text of the GDR–USSR treaty of 7 October 1975.

7 James N. Rosenau, 'Pre-theories and theories of foreign policy', in R. Barry Farrell (ed.), *Approaches to Comparative and International Politics* (Evanston: Northwestern University Press, 1966), p. 65.

8 N. Edwina Moreton, 'The impact of détente on relations between the member states of the Warsaw Pact: efforts to resolve the German problem and their implications for East Germany's role in Eastern Europe, 1967–1972' (University of Glasgow: unpub. Ph.D. thesis, 1976), p. 31.

9 Peter Bender, *East Europe in Search of Security*, trans. S. Z. Young (London: Chatto and Windus, 1972), pp. 31–4.

10 Melvin Croan, *East Germany: The Soviet Connection*, The Washington Papers, vol. 4, 36 (Beverly Hills and London: Sage Publications, for the Center for Strategic and International Studies, Georgetown University, Washington DC, 1976), pp. 13–14.

11 Christopher Clapham, 'Clientelism and the state', in Christopher Clapham (ed.), *Private Patronage and Public Power – Political Clientelism in the Modern State* (London: Francis Pinter, 1982), pp. 28–9.

12 The two relevant works here are, Siegfried Kupper in cooperation with Alparslan Yenal and Roswitha Zastrow, *Die Tatigkeit der DDR in den nichtkommunistischen Ländern – VI arabischen Staaten und Israel* (Bonn; Forschungsinstitut der Deutschen Gesellschaft fur Auswärtige Politik, 1971); and in the same series, Sibyl Reime, *VIII – Schwarzafrika* (1972).

13 E.g., Hans Siegfried Lamm and Siegfried Kupper, *DDR und Dritte Welt* (Munich and Vienna: R. Oldenbourg Verlag, 1976); and numerous articles in the journal *Deutschland Archiv* (DA) by Henning von Löwis of Menar and Bernard von Plate in particular.

14 E.g., see Stephen T. Hosmer and Thomas W. Wolfe, *Soviet Policy and Practice toward Third World Conflicts* (Lexington, Mass. and Toronto: Lexington Books, D.C. Heath, 1983).

15 *The Role of the Soviet Union, Cuba and East Germany in Fomenting Terrorism in Southern Africa*, Hearings before the Subcommittee on Security and Terrorism of the Committee on the Judiciary, United States Senate, 97th Congress, 2nd Session, March 1982, vol. 1 (Washington DC: US Government Printing Office, 1982), p. 1.

16 Andrzej Korbonski, 'Eastern Europe and the Third World; or "Limited Regret Strategy" revisited', in Andrzej Korbonski and Francis Fukuyama (eds.), *The Soviet Union and the Third World – The Last Three Decades* (Ithaca and London; Cornell University Press, from the Rand/UCLA Center for the Study of Soviet International Behaviour, 1987), p. 107.

17 Maqsud Ul Hasan Nuri, 'The Soviet–Cuban military intervention in Sub-Saharan Africa; proxy or partner relationship?', *Pakistan Horizon*, vol. 50, 2nd Quarter (1987), p. 61.

18 Brian Crozier, 'The surrogate forces of the Soviet Union', *Conflict Studies*, no. 92 (1978).

19 Michael Sodaro, 'The GDR and the Third World; supplicant and surrogate', in Michael Radu (ed.), *Eastern Europe and the Third World – East vs. South* (New York: Praeger, 1981), esp. p. 106.

20 John M. Starrels, *East Germany – Marxist Mission in Africa* (Washington DC: The Heritage Foundation, 1981), see Introduction.

21 Hosmer and Wolfe, *Soviet Policy and Practice*, pp. 101–2.

22 Gordon H. McCormick, 'Proxies, small wars and Soviet foreign policy', in John H. Maurer and Richard H. Porth (eds.), *Military Intervention in the Third World – Threats, Constraints and Options* (New York, Philadelphia, Toronto, Hong Kong, Tokyo, Sydney and Eastbourne: Praeger, 1984), pp. 48–9.

23 Bertil Dunér, 'Proxy intervention in civil wars', *Journal of Peace Research*, vol. 18, 4 (1981), p. 46.

24 N. Edwina Moreton, 'The East Europeans and the Cubans in the Middle East: surrogates or allies?', in Adeed Dawisha and Karen Dawisha (eds.), *The Soviet Union in the Middle East: Policies and Perspectives* (London: Heinemann, for the Royal Institute of International Affairs, 1982), p. 81.

25 Christopher Coker, 'Pact, pox or proxy: Eastern Europe's security relationship with Southern Africa', *Soviet Studies*, vol. 40, 4 (1988), pp. 575–6.

26 K. J. Holsti, *International Politics – A Framework for Analysis* (Englewood Cliffs, New Jersey: Prentice-Hall International, 4th edition, 1983), p. 119.

27 Although it should be noted that according to Holsti, the role of a faithful ally derived from 'weak capabilities' *inter alia, ibid.*, p. 316.

28 Astri Suhrke, 'Gratuity or tyranny: the Korean alliances', *World Politics*, vol. 25, 4 (1973), p. 509.

29 Zbigniew Brzezinski, *The Soviet Bloc – Unity and Conflict* (Cambridge, Mass: Harvard University Press, 2nd edn, 1971), pp. 433–55.

30 See Blaustein and Flanz (eds.), *Constitutions of the Countries of the World*, Binder 6, The Federal Republic of Germany, pp. 43–98, for the full text of the Basic Law of 23 May 1949 with amendments.

31 William Zimmerman, 'International regional systems and the politics of system boundaries', *International Organisation*, vol. 26, 1 (1972), p. 26.

32 See Guenther Roth and Claus Wittich (eds.), *Max Weber – 'Economy and Society – An Outline of Interpretative Sociology'*, vol. I (New York: Bedminster Press, 1968), pp. 212–301.

33 Joseph Rothschild, 'Political legitimacy in contemporary Europe', in Bogdan Denitch (ed.), *Legitimation of Regimes – International Frameworks for Analysis* (Beverly Hills and London: Sage Publications, for the International Sociological Association, 1979), p. 49.

34 Charles Tilly, 'Western state-making and theories of political transformation', in Charles Tilly (ed.), *The Formation of National States in Western Europe* (Princeton: Princeton University Press, Studies in Political Development, vol. 8, 1975), pp. 608–9.

35 Alfred Meyer, 'Legitimacy of power in East Central Europe', in Sylvia Sinanian, Istvan Deak and Peter C. Ludz (eds.), *Eastern Europe in the 1970s* (New York and London: Praeger, 1972), pp. 59–61.

36 Joseph Bensman, 'Max Weber's concept of legitimacy: an evaluation', in Arthur J. Vidich and Ronald M. Glassman (eds.), *Conflict and Control – Challenge to Legitimacy of Modern Governments* (Beverly Hills and London: Sage Publications, 1979), p. 42.

37 See, Heinz Lippmann, *Honecker and the New Politics of Europe* (London: Angus and Robertson, 1973), pp. 160–1, for Honecker's desperate reactions to the Soviet proposals of August 1953, which spoke of possible free elections to form an all-German government.

38 David Childs, *The GDR: Moscow's German Ally* (London: Allen and Unwin, 1983), p. 64.

39 Terence Prittie, 'East Germany: record of failure', *Problems of Communism (P of C)* vol. 10, 5 (1961), p. 7.

40 Jean Edward Smith, 'The Red Prussianism of the German Democratic Republic', *Political Science Quarterly*, vol. 92, 3 (1967), p. 378.
41 A. James McAdams, *East Germany and Détente – Building Authority after the Wall* (Cambridge, London, New York, New Rochelle, Melbourne and Sydney: Cambridge University Press, 1985), p. 10.
42 Kurt Sontheimer and Wilhelm Bleek, *The Government and Politics of East Germany* (London: Hutchinson, 1975), p. 144.
43 According to recent Soviet pronouncements the 'Socialist Community' of states include the so-called Soviet bloc (i.e., its East European nucleus) and also Cuba, Mongolia and Vietnam, i.e., the members of the CMEA. See, Boris Meissner, 'The GDR's position in the Soviet alliance system', *Aussenpolitik* (English edition), vol. 35, 4 (1984), pp. 370–1.
44 See Doeker *et al.* (eds.), *The Federal Republic of Germany and the German Democratic Republic*, vol. 1, *Confrontation and Cooperation*, pp. 162–4, for the text of the GDR–USSR Treaty, Moscow, 20 September 1955; and, *ibid.*, vol. 3, pp. 102–5, for the full text of the GDR–USSR Treaty, Moscow, 12 June 1964.
45 Jürgen Radde, *Die aussenpolitische Führungselite der DDR – Veränderungen der sozialen Struktur aussenpolitischer Führungsgruppen* (Cologne: Verlag Wissenschaft und Politik, 1976), pp. 60–2.
46 Brzezinski, *The Soviet Bloc*, p. 79.
47 Martin McCauley, *Marxism–Leninism in the German Democratic Republic – The Socialist Unity Party (SED)* (London and Basingstoke: Macmillan, 1979), pp. 85–6.
48 Moreton, 'The impact of détente', pp. 34–5.
49 *Deutscher Bundestag, Stenographische Berichte*, 1 Wahlperiode, 13 Sitzung, Bonn, 21 October 1949, p. 308. In practice, successive West German governments have claimed to represent the interests of all Germans inhabiting territory governed by the Reich in December 1937 (although this was later modified by West German recognition of the Oder–Neisse line).
50 See Jan F. Triska (ed.), *Constitutions of the Communist Party–States* (Stanford: Stanford University Press, 1968), pp. 216–39, for the full text of the GDR constitution of 7 October 1949.
51 See Fred Oldenburg, 'Die Autonomie des Musterknaben – zum politischen Verhältnis DDR–UdSSR', in Richard Lowenthal and Boris Meissner (eds.), *Der Sowjetblock zwischen Vormachtkontrolle und Autonomie* (Cologne: Markus Verlag, 1984), p. 168, for this title bestowed on Ulbricht.
52 Moreton, 'The impact of détente', pp. 49–50.
53 Melvin Croan, 'Czechoslovakia, Ulbricht and the German Problem', *P of C*, vol. 18, 1 (1969).
54 See Auswärtiges Amt der Bundesrepublik Deutschland (ed.), *Die Auswartige Politik der Bundesrepublik Deutschland* (Cologne: Verlag Wissenschaft und Politik, 1972), pp. 701–6, for the text of Brandt's inaugural speech; and *DA*, vol. 3, 2 (1970), pp. 171–9, for the State of the Nation speech.
55 Moreton, 'The impact of détente', p. 260.
56 Peter Marsh, 'Foreign policy making in the GDR: the interplay of internal pressures and external dependence', in Hannes Adomeit and Robert

Boardman (eds.), *Foreign Policy Making in Communist Countries: A Comparative Approach* (Farnborough, Hants.: Saxon House, 1979), p. 96.

57 Oldenburg, 'Die Autonomie des Musterknaben', p. 169.

58 *Ibid.*

59 *Ibid.*, pp. 171–4.

60 *Dokumente zur Aussenpolitik der Deutschen Demokratischen Republik (Dokumente)*, 1971, vol. 19, pt. 1 (Berlin [East]: Staatsverlag der DDR, 1974), p. 62.

61 Boris Meissner, 'Die völkerrechtlichen Beziehungen zwischen der DDR und der Sowjetunion auf dem Hintergrund der Bündnisverträge', in Siegfried Mampel and Karl C. Thalheim (eds.), *Die DDR – Partner oder Satellit der Sowjetunion?* (Munich: Gesellschaft für Deutschlandforschung Jahrbuch 1979, Politica Verlag, 1980), p. 162.

62 N. Edwina Moreton, 'Foreign policy perspectives in Eastern Europe', in Karen Dawisha and Philip Hanson (eds.), *Soviet–East European Dilemmas: Coercion, Competition and Consent* (London: Heinemann, for the Royal Institute of International Affairs, 1981), p. 179.

63 Suhrke, 'Gratuity or tyranny', pp. 512–13.

64 *Neues Deutschland (ND)*, 5 September 1971.

65 See Doeker *et al.* (eds.), *The Federal Republic of Germany and the German Democratic Republic*, vol. 1, pp. 395–6, for the full text of the Basic Treaty.

66 *Ibid.*, p. 397.

67 Blaustein and Flanz (eds.), *Constitutions of the Countries of the World*, Binder 6, The GDR, p. 92, Article 1.

68 See Ronald Asmus, 'The GDR and the German nation: sole heir or socialist sibling?', *International Affairs*, vol. 60, 3 (1984), pp. 408–11, for an excellent background discussion.

69 Angela E. Stent, 'Soviet policy towards the German Democratic Republic', in Sarah Meiklejohn Terry (ed.), *Soviet Policy in Eastern Europe* (New Haven and London: Yale University Press, 1984), p. 56.

70 Eric G. Frey, *Division and Détente – the Germanies and their Alliances* (New York, Westport, Connecticut and London: Praeger, 1987), p. 102.

71 McAdams, *East Germany and Détente*, pp. 151–2.

72 Blaustein and Flanz (eds.), *Constitutions of the Countries of the World*, Binder 6, The GDR, p. 92.

73 Paul Marer, 'East European economies: achievements, problems, prospects', in Teresa Rakowska-Harmstone (ed.), *Communism in Eastern Europe* (Manchester: Manchester University Press, 2nd edition, 1984), p. 313. Calculations mostly based on Wharton Econometrics.

74 Marshall I. Goldman, *The Enigma of Soviet Petroleum – Half-Full or Half-Empty?* (London: Allen and Unwin, 1980), pp. 100–2.

75 Anthony Staacpole, 'Energy as a factor in Soviet relations with the Middle East', in Dawisha and Dawisha (eds.), *The Soviet Union in the Middle East*, p. 96. More extensive details on East German oil imports are given in chapter 5 of this book.

76 Ernst Kux, 'Growing tensions in Eastern Europe', *P of C*, vol. 29, 2 (1980), p. 31.

77 Michael J. Sodaro, 'External influences on regime stability in the GDR: a linkage analysis', in Michael J. Sodaro and Sharon L. Wolchik (eds.), *Foreign and Domestic Policy in Eastern Europe in the 1980s – Trends and Prospects* (London and Basingstoke: Macmillan, 1983), pp. 87–8.

78 Jan Vanous, 'East European economic slowdown', *P of C*, vol. 31, 4 (1982), p. 7.

79 Thomas A. Baylis, 'Explaining the GDR's economic strategy', *International Organisation*, vol. 40, 2 (1986), p. 420, n. 122.

80 John P. Hardt, 'Soviet energy policy in Eastern Europe', in Terry (ed.), *Soviet Policy in Eastern Europe*, p. 206.

81 *Ibid.*, p. 193.

82 Valerie Bunce, 'The empire strikes back: the evolution of the Eastern bloc from a Soviet asset to a Soviet liability', *International Organisation*, vol. 39, 1 (1985), p. 17. Two East European states received more substantial Soviet hard currency loans in 1981 – Poland ($1,900 million) and Czechoslovakia ($344 million).

83 Vanous, 'East European Economic Slowdown', p. 7.

84 Ronald Asmus, 'The East German search for oil', *Radio Free Europe Research*, RAD Background Report/187 GDR (25 July 1980), pp. 2–3.

85 Hardt, 'Soviet energy policy', p. 207: Jiri Valenta and Shannon Butler, 'East German security policies in Africa', in Radu (ed.), *Eastern Europe and the Third World*, pp. 142–68; and George A. Glass, 'East Germany in Black Africa: a new special role?', *The World Today*, vol. 36, 8 (1980), p. 310.

86 Melvin Croan, 'Two Germanies at 30(1), "new country, old nationality"', *Foreign Policy*, no. 37 (1979–80), pp. 152–3.

87 Maria Haendcke-Hoppe, 'Die DDR-Aussenwirtschaft am Beginn des Fünf-jahrplanperiode 1986–1990', *DA*, vol. 20, 1 (1987), p. 53. According to these statistics, in 1981 the GDR's net hard currency debt had totalled $10,000 million.

88 Erich Honecker, *Report of the Central Committee of the Socialist Unity Party of Germany to the X Congress of the SED* (Dresden: Verlag Zeit im Bild, 1981), pp. 77 and 82.

89 Haendcke-Hoppe, 'Die DDR-Aussenwirtschaft', p. 51.

90 *Ibid.*, pp. 51–2.

91 Erich Honecker, *Bericht des Zentralkomitees der Sozialistischen Einheitspartei Deutschlands an den XI Parteitag der SED* (Berlin [East]: Dietz Verlag, 1986), p. 43.

92 Fred Oldenburg, 'East German foreign and security interests', in N. Edwina Moreton (ed.), *Germany between East and West* (Cambridge, London, New York, New Rochelle, Melbourne and Sydney; Cambridge University Press, in association with The Royal Institute of International Affairs, 1987).

93 For detailed analyses, see Ronald Asmus, 'The dialectics of détente and discord: the Moscow–East Berlin–Bonn triangle', *Orbis*, vol. 28, 4 (1985); and A. James McAdams, 'The new logic in Soviet–GDR relations', *P of C*, vol. 37, 5 (1988).

94 *ND*, 8 September 1987.

95 Johannes Kuppe, 'Staatsbesuch in Frankreich', *DA*, vol. 21, 2 (1988), pp. 113–16.
96 Details of states recognising the GDR may be obtained from various editions of *ND* and *Dokumente* (various years). For the FRG, see *Vertretungen der Bundesrepublik Deutschland im Ausland*, Stand: November 1986 (Bonn, Bundesanzeiger).
97 McAdams, 'The new logic', p. 55.
98 Oldenburg, 'East German foreign and security interests', pp. 110–11.
99 *ND*, 10 April 1987.
100 Dirk W. W. Rumberg, 'Glasnost in the GDR? The impact of Gorbachev's reform policy on the German Democratic Republic', *International Relations*, vol. 9, 3 (1988).
101 *ND*, 26 January 1988.

2 The development of GDR relations with Africa in the pre-recognition period

1 *Dokumente*, 1949–54, vol. 1 (1954) pp. 505–6. Note that until 1963, vol. 11 (1965), this series of documents was known as *Dokumente zur Aussenpolitik der Regierung der Deutschen Demokratischen Republik* and published by Rütten and Loening, Berlin (East).
2 *Keesing's Contemporary Archives* (*Keesing's*), p. 12893.
3 Walter C. Laqueur, *The Soviet Union and the Middle East* (London: Routledge and Kegan Paul, 1959), p. 195.
4 Robert Cornevin, 'The Germans in Africa before 1918', in L. H. Gann and Peter Duignan (eds.), *Colonialism in Africa 1870–1960*, vol. 1, *The History and Politics of Colonialism 1870–1914* (Cambridge: Cambridge University Press, 1969), pp. 383–419.
5 Arnold Zeitlin, 'Hegelian re-entry – the Germans are back in Africa', *Africa Report*, vol. 12, 2 (1967), p. 37.
6 *Dokumente*, 1963, vol. 11 (1965), p. 277, Declaration of the government of the GDR concerning the 'Declaration on the Granting of Independence to Colonial States and Peoples', 12 November 1963.
7 See Günter Sieber, 'Brüder haben sie in aller Welt!', *Einheit* (*E*), Year 43, 11/12 (1988), pp. 1036–41; and Hans Piazza, 'Die Grundlegung der Bündnispolitik der SED mit den Völkern Asiens, Afrikas und Lateinamerikas (1946 bis 1949)', *Asien, Afrika, Lateinamerika* (*AAL*), vol. 4, 3 (1976), p. 334.
8 *Dokumente aus den Jahren 1945–1949 – Un ein antifaschistisch-demokratisches Deutschland* (Berlin [East]: Staatsverlag der DDR, 1968), p. 262, in 'Principles and goals of the SED', 21 April 1946.
9 *Dokumente*, vol. 1, p. 30.
10 Hans-Joachim Spanger, 'Die beiden deutschen Staaten in der Dritten Welt I', *DA*, vol. 17, 1 (1984), p. 31.
11 Siegfried Baerwald, 'Die Länder Asiens und Afrikas einig im Kampf um den Frieden', *E*, Year 10, 5 (1955), pp. 494 and 497.
12 Kupper *et al.*, *Die Tätigkeit der DDR in . . . arabische Staaten und Israel*, p. 31.
13 *Dokumente*, 1955–56, vol. 3 (1956), pp. 620–2.

14 *Ibid.*, pp. 622–3.
15 Kupper *et al.*, *Die Tätigkeit der DDR in . . . arabische Staaten und Israel*, p.36.
16 See Stockholm International Peace Research Institute (SIPRI), *The Arms Trade with the Third World* (Uppsala: Almqvist and Wiksells, 1971), p. 648, for reference to the USSR's offer of military aid to Sudan in 1955. See *Dokumente*, vol. 3, p. 660, for reference to the payments agreement between the GDR and Sudan.
17 See *Dokumente*, vol. 3, p. 671, for reference to Selassie receiving the trade official, Kurt Wolf, on 19 November 1955.
18 Rudolph Schuster, 'Die "Hallstein-Doktrin" – Ihre rechtliche und politische Bedeutung und die Grenzen ihrer Wirksamkeit', *Europa Archiv*, vol. 17, 18 (1963), p. 675.
19 Heinrich End, *Zweimal deutsche Aussenpolitik – Internationale Dimension des innerdeutschen Konflikts, 1949–1972* (Cologne: Verlag Wissenschaft und Politik, 1973), pp. 34–6.
20 *Deutscher Bundestag Stenographische Berichte*, 2. Wahlperiode, 101 Sitzung, Bonn, 22 September 1955, p. 5647.
21 Schuster, 'Die "Hallstein Doktrin"', p. 677.
22 *Frankfurter Allgemeine Zeitung (FAZ)*, 10 December 1955.
23 *Bulletin des Presse- und Informationsamtes der Bundesregierung (Bulletin)*, 233, 13 December 1955, p. 1193.
24 *Deutscher Bundestag Stenographische Berichte*, 2. Wahlperiode, 155 Sitzung, Bonn, 28 June 1956, p. 8422.
25 See, Wilhelm Grewe, *Deutsche Aussenpolitik der Nachkriegszeit* (Stuttgart: Deutsche Verlags-anstalt, 1960), p. 148, for the full list of the three categories. The 'actions' reported in the text are those of particular relevance to this study.
26 Peter Klein *et al.*, *Geschichte der Aussenpolitik der Deutschen Demokratischen Republik – Abriss* (Berlin [East]: Dietz Verlag, 1968), pp. 384–6.
27 *The Times*, 24 February 1965. Note that Egypt was officially known as the United Arab Republic between 1958–71 after a political and economic unification with Syria (actually terminated in 1961). For convenience the term 'Egypt' will be used throughout the text.
28 *Die Welt*, 17 September 1959.
29 Kupper *et al.*, *Die Tätigkeit der DDR in . . . arabische Staaten und Israel*, p. 148, n. 91.
30 See Radde, *Die aussenpolitische Fuhrungselite*, for the following details.
31 Harold Ludwig, 'Die "DDR" in Afrika (I) – Der Einfluss der SBZ auf die unabhängigen afrikanischen Länder', *SBZ Archiv*, 6 (1965), p. 84. Here particular attention was drawn to the trade missions in Algeria, Ghana, Guinea, Mali and Sudan.
32 Radde, *Die aussenpolitische Fuhrungselite*, p. 35, citing, *Junge Welt*, 10 August 1967.
33 According to UN statistics, in the years 1960, 1961, 1966, 1967 and 1969 in the period 1960–9. See, *Yearbook of International Trade Statistics (Yearbook)*, *Trade by Country, 1965*, vol. 1 (New York: United Nations, Department of

International Economic and Social Affairs Statistical Office, 1966), p. 777, and *Yearbook*, 1969, vol. 1 (1971), p. 866.

34 See Volker Matthies, 'Die Staatenwelt zwischen Sahara und Sambesi', in Hans-Peter Schwarz (ed.), *Handbuch der deutschen Aussenpolitik* (Munich and Zurich: R. Piper Verlag, 1975), p. 327, for the West German figure. Note that the VM is a unit to convert to Western currencies. For 'inter-German' trade purposes DM 1=VM 1, although in practice the VM is worth considerably less.

35 End, *Zweimal deutsche Aussenpolitik*, p. 127.

36 See Matthies, 'Die Staatenwelt', pp. 134–5.

37 The GDR also offered short or medium term supply credits at 2.5–6 per cent with a time span of 5–8 years, see *Bericht der Bundesregierung und Materialien zur Lage der Nation, 1971 (Bericht der Bundesregierung . . . 1971)* (Bonn: Bundesministerium für innerdeutsche Beziehungen), p. 56.

38 End, *Zweimal deutsche Aussenpolitik*, p.129.

39 Lamm and Kupper, *DDR und Dritte Welt*, p. 57.

40 G. H. Jansen, *Afro-Asian and Non-Alignment* (London: Faber and Faber, 1966), pp. 299–304.

41 Günter Pötschke, 'Die Belgrader Konferenz nichtpaktgebundener Staaten – ein Sieg der Kräfte des Friedens', *E*, Year 16, 10 (1961), p. 1158.

42 Klein *et al.*, *Geschichte der Aussenpolitik*, p. 400.

43 W. Scott Thompson, *Ghana's Foreign Policy, 1957–1966 – Diplomacy, Ideology and the New State* (Princeton: Princeton University Press, 1969), pp. 402–3.

44 Lamm and Kupper, *DDR und Dritte Welt*, pp. 59–69.

45 *Bericht der Bundesregierung . . . 1971*, p. 54.

46 Kurt Müller, *The Foreign Aid Programs of the Soviet Bloc and Communist China*, trans. Richard H. Weber and Michael Roloff (New York: Walker, 1967), pp. 284–9.

47 Anon., 'East and West Germany compete in Africa', *The World Today*, vol. 17, 2 (1961), p. 46.

48 See, *Dokumente*, relevant years.

49 Fritz Schatten, *Communism in Africa* (London: Allen and Unwin, 1966), pp. 301–10.

50 *Bericht der Bundesregierung . . . 1971*, p. 52.

51 Henning von Löwis of Menar, 'Das politische und militärische Engagement der Deutschen Demokratischen Republik in Schwarzafrika – Überblick von 1953 bis 1978', *Beiträge zur Konfliktforschung*, vol. 8, 1 (1978), p. 15.

52 Childs, *The GDR*, p. 112.

53 Fritz Schatten, 'Zur Afrikapolitik des deutschen Kommunisten – Grundlagen, Absichten, Schwerpunkte', *Der Ostblock und die Entwicklungsländer*, no. 19 (1965), p. 18.

54 Müller, *The Foreign Aid Programs*, pp. 73–4 and 76.

55 *Dokumente*, 1967, vol. 15, pt 2 (1970), Zeittafel, p. 1339.

56 Lamm und Kupper, *DDR und Dritte Welt*, p. 140.

57 *Current Digest of the Soviet Press (CDSP)*, vol. 8, 4 (2 March 1956), p. 6.

58 Inge Deutschkron, *Bonn and Jerusalem – The Strange Coalition* (Philadelphia and London: Chilton, 1970), p. 89.
59 *Dokumente*, 1956–7, vol. 5 (1958), pp. 13–14.
60 Joseph J. Malone, 'Germany and the Suez Crisis', *Middle East Journal*, vol. 20 (Winter 1966), p. 24.
61 *ND*, 4 November 1956.
62 Müller, *The Foreign Aid Programs*, p. 242.
63 *ND*, 8 January 1959.
64 'USSR und Volksdemokratien sagen Ostberlin Hilfe bei Bemuhungen um de-jure Anerkennung im Nahostraum zu', *Informationsbüro West*, 1 March 1958.
65 Kupper *et al.*, *Die Tatigkeit der DDR in . . . arabische Staaten und Israel*, p. 39.
66 *Dokumente*, vol. 3, p. 666.
67 *Dokumente*, 1960, vol. 8 (1961), pp. 258–61.
68 Theodore Hanf, 'Die Bedeutung der arabischen Staaten fur die Bundesrepublik', in Schwarz (ed.), *Handbuch der deutschen Aussenpolitik*, p. 321; and David Childs, *East Germany* (London: Ernest Benn, 1969), p. 255, n. 19.
69 *Dokumente*, 1958, vol. 6 (1959), pp. 309–11; and Schatten, 'Zur Afrikapolitik des deutschen Kommunismus', p. 17.
70 *ND*, 2 August 1961; and, Michael Dei-Anang, *The Administration of Ghana's Foreign Relations, 1957–1965: A Personal Memoir* (London: The Athlone Press, for the Royal Institute of Commonwealth Studies, 1975), p. 52.
71 *Neue Zürcher Zeitung (NZZ)*, 10 November 1963.
72 *National Zeitung*, 25 March 1966.
73 Zdenek Cervenka and Mario R. Dederichs, 'The two Germanies in Africa', *Africa Contemporary Record (ACR)*, vol. 11 (1978–9), A. 104.
74 *Africa Research Bulletin*, Political, Social and Cultural Series *(ARB)*, vol. 3, 5 (1966), 542A. The security dimension of the GDR's involvement in Ghana will be discussed further in chapter 4.
75 *Dokumente*, vol. 8, pp. 258–61.
76 *Dokumente*, vol. 5, p. 107.
77 *Dokumente*, vol. 8, p. 259.
78 See respectively, *Dokumente*, vol. 8, pp. 167–8; *Dokumente*, 1961, vol. 9 (1962), pp. 23, 199–201; *Dokumente*, vol. 8, pp. 65–6; *Dokumente*, 1964, vol. 12 (1966), pp. 366–8; *Dokumente*, 1965, vol. 13 (1969), p. 754; and *Dokumente*, vol. 11, p. 276.
79 Erich Weidemann, 'Reibungslos lauft nur die Schalmaschine', *Der Spiegel (Sp)*, Year 34, 10 (3 March 1980), p. 58.
80 Gerhard Joswiakowski, '"Portugiesisch" – Guinea im Kampf gegen Salazar und NATO', *Deutsche Aussenpolitik (DAPK)*, vol. 7, 6 (1962), p. 705.
81 *ND*, 11 December 1963.
82 Noted by Sodaro, 'The GDR and the Third World', p. 116. The article in question was in *Deutsche Aussenpolitik*, vol. 6, 4 (1961), pp. 482–7.
83 'Übersicht über die Bemuhungen der "DDR" um die nichtpaktgebunden Staaten', *Informationsbüro West*, 26 February 1965, p. 1.
84 Klein *et al.*, *Geschichte der Aussenpolitik*, p. 396.

85 See *Dokumente*, vol. 12, pp. 728–30, for the agreement to establish trade missions.

86 The GDR's disappointment with Kenyatta was personally expressed in a private interview by Herr Horst Brasch, member of the Central Committee of the SED and Honorary Vice-President of the Liga für Völkerfreundschaft, in Berlin (East), 3 April 1987. Herr Brasch, when Chairman of the Afro-Asian Solidarity Committee of the GDR and Vice-President of the National Council of the National Front of the GDR, had headed the East German delegation which attended Kenya's independence celebrations. See, *ND*, 12, 16 and 20 December 1963.

87 *Keesing's*, p. 10350.

88 *ND*, 19 February 1963; and *Dokumente*, vol. 11, Zeittafel, p. 585.

89 *ND*, 6 March 1960.

90 Von Löwis of Menar, 'Das politische und militärische Engagement', p. 15.

91 *Le Monde*, 10 and 11 March 1960.

92 'Guinea erkennt die DDR an', *DA*, vol. 13, 10 (1970), p. 1097.

93 *ND*, 15 March 1960. UN statistics appear to confirm this in part. For example, in 1959 Guinea imported goods to the value of 385 million francs from the GDR compared with goods worth 189 million francs from the FRG. See *Yearbook*, 1964, vol. 1, p. 318.

94 *Le Monde*, 10/11 April 1960.

95 *Die Zeit*, 25 March 1960; *NZZ*, 25 March 1960.

96 *ND*, 30 January 1964.

97 Schatten, 'Zur Afrikapolitik des deutschen Kommunismus', p. 22.

98 Timothy C. Niblock, 'Aid and foreign policy in Tanzania, 1961–68' (University of Sussex: unpub. D.Phil. thesis, 1971), pp. 207–9. Unless otherwise cited, specific details concerning the GDR's relations with Zanzibar and the Tanzanian government in 1964–5 are from this source, especially, pp. 195–261.

99 *ND*, 21 February and 4 March 1964.

100 'Zanzibar – with Ulbricht's aid', *The Economist*, 12–18 March 1966, p. 993.

101 SIPRI, *The Arms Trade*, pp. 22–3.

102 Timothy C. Niblock, 'Tanzanian foreign policy: An analysis', *The African Review*, vol. 1, 2 (1971), p. 95.

103 Alaba Ogunsanwo, *China's Policy in Africa, 1958–1971* (London: Cambridge University Press, 1974), p. 137.

104 *ND*, 19 May 1964.

105 *National Zeitung*, 21 March 1965.

106 'Two Germanies, three worlds', *The Economist*, 6 March 1965, pp. 977–8.

107 *Ibid.*, p. 978.

108 William W. Marsh, 'East Germany and Africa', *Africa Report*, vol. 14, 3–4 (1969), p. 64.

109 Mohamed Heikal, *Nasser – The Cairo Documents* (London: The New English Library, 1972), pp. 294–8.

110 Arnold Hottinger, 'Die Hintergründe der Einladung Ulbrichts nach Kairo', *Europa Archiv*, vol. 19, 20 (1965), pp. 111–13.

111 McCauley, *Marxism–Leninism in the German Democratic Republic*, p. 227, n. 49.
112 Alvin Z. Rubinstein, *Yugoslavia and the Nonaligned World* (Princeton: Princeton University Press, 1970), p. 286.
113 *Keesing's*, p. 20740.
114 *Ibid.*, p. 20738; and *ND*, 9 February 1965.
115 *Bulletin*, 29, 17 February 1965, p. 225.
116 *The Times*, 22 February 1965.
117 Auswärtiges Amt der Bundesrepublik Deutschland (ed.), *Die Auswärtige Politik*, pp. 537–40.
118 *ND*, 2 March 1965.
119 *Dokumente*, vol. 13, p. 1057.
120 Harald Ludwig, 'Die "DDR" in Afrika (II) – Die Aktitivat in den arabischen Ländern', *SBZ Archiv*, 22 (1965), p. 354.
121 Müller, *The Foreign Aid Programs*, p. 243.
122 *ND*, 9 March 1965.
123 Auswärtiges Amt der Bundesrepublik Deutschland (ed.), *Die Auswartige Politik*, pp. 542–3.
124 Kupper *et al.*, *Die Tätigkeit der DDR in . . . arabische Staaten und Israel*, p. 29.
125 Heikal, *Nasser – The Cairo Documents*, p. 307.
126 *ND*, 28 August 1965.
127 *Ost-Spiegel*, 7 September 1965.
128 *Dokumente*, 1968, vol. 16, pt 1 (1971), pp. 195–6.
129 *Keesing's*, p. 23844.
130 *Frankfurter Rundschau*, 5 November 1969.
131 End, *Zweimal deutsche Aussenpolitik*, p. 69.
132 Ironically, End himself provided a useful table which charted West German sanctions against states prematurely recognising the GDR diplomatically: *ibid.*, p. 157.
133 'Diplomatie – nichts fur nichts', *Sp*, Year 25, 36 (30 August 1971), p. 44.
134 *Dokumente*, 1969, vol. 17, pt 2 (1971), p. 739.
135 *Dokumente*, 1970, vol. 18, pt 2 (1972), p. 886.
136 Lamm and Kupper, *DDR und Dritte Welt*, p. 60.
137 Peter Florin, *Deutsche Aussenpolitik, zur Aussenpolitik der souveränen sozialistischen DDR* (Berlin [East]: Dietz Verlag, 1967), pp. 67–8.
138 For references to the credit offers to these states, see, Lamm and Kupper, *DDR und Dritte Welt*, p. 136; and, End, *Zweimal deutsche Aussenpolitik*, p. 129.
139 'Interview avec Jean-Bedel Bokassa', *Jeune Afrique*, 510 (13 October 1970), pp. 48–9.
140 *Dokumente*, vol. 18, pt 1, pp. 549–52.
141 *ACR*, vol. 4 (1971–2), C34–5, for the text of Bokassa's speech, the Independence Anniversary Broadcast (Radio Bangui, 13 August 1971).
142 End, *Zweimal deutsche Aussenpolitik*, p. 145.
143 *ACR*, vol. 1 (1968–9), pp. 611–18.
144 For example, in October 1970 Mali and Tanzania voted in favour of East

German membership of the United Nations Educational, Scientific and Cultural Organisation, *Dokumente*, vol. 18, pt 2, Zeittafel, pp. 1153–4.

145 Von Löwis of Menar, 'Das politische und militärische Engagement', pp. 31–2.

146 *ND*, 1 November 1972.

147 *Dokumente*, vol. 19, pt 1, pp. 57–8.

148 *ND*, 9 June 1967.

149 *Dokumente*, vol. 16, pt 2, pp. 935–8.

150 Kupper *et al.*, *Die Tätigkeit der DDR in . . . arabische Staaten und Israel*, pp. 69–70. Cambodia's early diplomatic recognition of the GDR appears to have been connected with Phnom Penh's desire to pursue a policy of 'neutrality and reciprocity' with the two Germanies, see *Keesing's*, p. 23844.

151 *ARB*, vol. 6, 5 (1969), 1406A.

152 Thomas W. Kramer, *Deutsche-ägyptische Beziehungen in Vergangenheit und Gegenwart* (Tübingen: Horst Erdmann Verlag, 1974), p. 263.

153 *ARB*, vol. 6, 7 (1969), 1476B–C.

154 *ND*, 10 September 1970.

155 *Dokumente*, vol. 19, pt 2, p. 700.

156 George T. Yu, *China's African Policy – A Study of Tanzania* (New York and London: Praeger, 1975), p. 75, and elsewhere, for full details of Chinese assistance to Tanzania at this time.

157 'Zanzibar politics', *Africa Report*, vol. 15, 12 (1970), pp. 6–7; and, *ACR*, vol. 2 (1969–70), B197–200.

158 *ND*, 15 January 1970.

159 For reference to the opening of the trade mission, see, Wokalek, 'Zur Afrikapolitik der DDR', Paper of *Gesamtdeutsches Institut – Bundesanstalt für Gesamtdeutsche Aufgaben* (Bonn; 19 March 1979), p. 9. For other details, see *ACR*, vol. 4 (1971–2), B261; and, 'Schmütziges Werk', *Sp*, Year 25, 39 (20 September 1971), p. 119.

160 Compare the moderate tone of Ulbricht's correspondence to Nimeiry with an earlier TASS declaration. See *ND*, 31 and 28 July 1971 respectively.

161 For reference to the closure of the cultural centre, see Hans Lindemann and Kurt Müller, *Auswärtige Kulturpolitik der DDR – Die kulterelle Abgrenzung der DDR von der Bundesrepublik Deutschland* (Bonn–Bad Godesberg: Verlag Neue Gesellschaft, 1974), p. 111. For other details, see *Keesing's*, p. 24751; and, Horst Knape, 'Rückschlag für Ostberlin – warum die DDR in Afrika keinen Erfolg hat', *Stern*, Year 24, 44 (24 October 1971), p. 200.

3   The GDR in Africa in the 1970s

1 See Hillebrand, *Das Afrika-Engagement der DDR*; and, Spanger and Brock, *Die beiden deutschen Staaten in der Dritten Welt*.

2 Klaus Willerding, 'Die DDR und die national befreiten Staaten Asiens und Afrikas', *AAL*, vol. 2, 5 (1974), pp. 689 and 691.

3 Erich Honecker, *Bericht des Zentralkomitees der Sozialistischen Einheitsparti*

Deutschlands an der IX Parteitag der SED (Berlin [East]: Dietz Verlag, 1976), p. 27.

4 *Ibid.*, p. 10.

5 Klaus Willerding, 'An der Seite der Kämpfer gegen Imperialismus und Kolonialismus; für nationale Befreiung und sozialen Fortschritt', *AAL*, vol. 4, 6 (1976), p. 842.

6 *ND*, 18/19 February 1978, speech to *Kreis* SED first secretaries; and, *8 Tagung des ZK der SED*, 24/5 May 1978 (Berlin [East]: Dietz Verlag, 1978), p. 15, report for the SED Politburo, where Honecker said Africa was 'in the truest sense of the word a rising continent'.

7 Willerding, 'An der Seite der Kämpfer', p. 846.

8 Helmut Nimschowski, 'Probleme der Einheitsfront der anti-imperialistisch-demokratischen Kräfte in Staaten mit sozialistischer Orientierung', *AAL*, vol. 5, 4 (1977), p. 536.

9 Bernard von Plate, 'Aspekte der SED-Parteibeziehungen in Afrika und der arabischen Region', *DA*, vol. 12, 2 (1979), p. 145. For a full East German assessment of the role of National Fronts in the Third World, see, Nimschowski, 'Probleme der Einheitsfront'.

10 Von Plate, 'Aspekte der SED-Parteibeziehungen', pp. 134–5.

11 *Ibid.*, pp. 135–6.

12 Jürgen Zenker, 'Zusammenarbeit der SED mit revolutionär-demokratischen Parteien in Afrika und Asien', *DAPK*, vol. 22, 10 (1977), p. 105.

13 Henning von Löwis of Menar, 'SED–Journalismus als Exportartikel – die journalistische Entwicklungshilfe der DDR', *DA*, vol. 12, 10 (1979), p. 1016.

14 See Melvin Croan, 'A new Afrika Korps?', *The Washington Quarterly*, no. 4 (Winter 1980), p. 22 – for use of the term 'applied Proto-Leninism'.

15 Honecker, *Bericht . . . IX Parteitag der SED*, p. 10.

16 These offices, accredited by the GDR Solidarity Committee, were opened on 4 January, 13 October and 20 November respectively: see *ND*, 5 January 1978; and *Dokumente*, 1978, vol. 26, pt 2 (1983), Zeittafel, vol. 1241 and 1252. Note that an office for the Palestine Liberation Organisation was previously opened in East Berlin in 1973.

17 Glass, 'East Germany in Black Africa', p. 306.

18 Wilhelm Bruns, 'Uneinig bei den Vereinten – die beiden deutschen Staaten auf der 33. Generalversammlung der UNO', *DA*, vol. 12, 5 (1979), p. 492.

19 Sodaro, 'The GDR and the Third World', p. 136.

20 *Die Welt*, 14 January 1973.

21 *ND*, 11 May 1974.

22 *Ibid.*, 12 and 13 November 1975.

23 *Ibid.*, 26/7 June 1976.

24 See Hennig von Löwis of Menar, 'Das Engagement der DDR im Portugiesischen Afrika', *DA*, vol. 10, 1 (1977), pp. 35–6, for details of East German assistance in the early months after independence. Later chapters will discuss the GDR's role in the economic and military/security spheres in Angola.

25 Christopher Coker, *NATO. The Warsaw Pact and Africa* (Basingstoke and London: Macmillan, 1985), p. 187.
26 'Angola: puzzling both East and West', *Africa Confidential*, vol. 20, 2 (17 January 1979), pp. 1–2, suggests that di Nascimento's demotion was part of an attempt to remove a pro-Moscow faction as Neto increasingly looked to the West for economic support. Interestingly, a key Angolan official had to assure an East German radio correspondent that Angola was not moving away from the socialist bloc – 'in fact, the opposite is the case'.
27 Thomas Ammer, 'Zu den Beziehungen DDR–Angola', Paper of the Gesamtdeutsches Institut – Bundesanstalt für Gesamtdeutsche Aufgaben (Bonn: 22 March 1979), p. 7. The states listed before the GDR were the USSR, Cuba, Guinea-Bissau, Mozambique, Guinea and Algeria.
28 *ND*, 26 June 1975.
29 *Ibid.*, 11 December 1974.
30 Wokalek, 'Zur Afrikapolitik der DDR', p. 15.
31 Ilona Schleicher, 'Internationalistische Entwicklung der FRELIMO und ihre Beziehungen zur SED', *DAPK*, vol. 24, 7 (1979), p. 70.
32 Wokalek, 'Zur Afrikapolitik der DDR', p. 15.
33 See, von Löwis of Menar, 'Das Engagement der DDR', pp. 37–8, for details of early assistance programmes in independent Mozambique. Again, later chapters will discuss the GDR's role in the economic and military-security spheres.
34 *ND*, 10 February 1977.
35 *Ibid.*, 20 December 1976.
36 *Ibid.*, 11 February 1977.
37 'An Brennpunkt des revolutionären Prozesses in Afrika – Interview mit Werner Lamberz über die Reise einer SED-Delegation nach Mocambique, Äthiopien und Somalia', *Horizont* (*H*), Year 10, 9 (1977), p. 4.
38 Interestingly only printed in *ND*, 17 February 1977, i.e., after Mengistu's assumption to power appeared secure.
39 *Ibid.*, 19/20 Febuary 1977.
40 *Ibid.*, 18/19 June 1977.
41 *Ibid.*, 9 March 1978.
42 *Ibid.*, 27 November 1978.
43 *Ibid.*, 30 November 1978.
44 *ACR*, vol. 11 (1978–9), B257; and *ACR*, vol. 12 (1979–80), B213.
45 René Lefort, *Ethiopia: An Heretical Revolution*, trans. A. M. Berrett (London: Zed Press, 1983), p. 265.
46 *Ibid.*; *Keesing's*, p. 29357; and, Fred Halliday and Maxine Molyneux, *The Ethiopian Revolution* (London: Verso editions and NLB, 1981), p. 173.
47 *ND*, 2 February 1977.
48 Moreton, 'The East Europeans and the Cubans', p. 75.
49 *ND*, 2/3 October 1976.
50 *Ibid.*, 8 February 1977.
51 *Ibid.*, 25/26 and 27 June 1977.
52 Honecker, *Bericht . . . IX Parteitag der SED*, p. 136.
53 Thomas H. Henriksen, 'Angola, Mozambique and the Soviet Union:

liberation and the quest for influence', in Warren Weinstein and Thomas H. Henriksen (eds.), *Soviet and Chinese Aid to African Nations* (New York: Praeger, 1980), pp. 62–3.

54 Lamm and Kupper, *DDR und Dritte Welt*, p. 206.

55 *ND*, 24 January 1974.

56 *Ibid.*, 18 February 1974.

57 *Ibid.*, 20 December 1976.

58 Bernard von Plate, 'Der Nahe und Mittlere Osten sowie der Maghreb', in Hans Adolph Jacobsen *et al.* (eds.), *Drei Jahrzehnte Aussenpolitik der DDR* (Munich and Vienna: R. Oldenbourg Verlag, 1979), p. 697. In 1977 the Libyan ASU became known as the General People's Congress.

59 *ND*, 9 December 1977.

60 Egon Dummer and Emil Langer, 'Grundtendenzen der nationalen Befreiungsbewegung', *E*, Year 35, 1 (1980), pp. 9–16.

61 Indeed, the GDR played a key role for the Soviet bloc in developing relations with the PLO in this period. See Gareth M. Winrow, 'East German Foreign Policy and the Arab–Israeli Problem', *Journal of Economics and Administrative Studies* (Istanbul), vol. 2, 1 (1988), pp. 57–78.

62 *ND*, 5 October 1977, for reference to the Joint Communiqué on Axen's visit. See also, *ND*, 13 October 1977, for the eventual despatch of the Libyan ambassador. No Libyan embassy had hitherto been opened in East Berlin in spite of the establishment of diplomatic relations in 1973.

63 *Ibid.*, 15 December 1977.

64 *Ibid.*, 29 June 1978.

65 Thomas Ammer, 'Zu den Beziehungen DDR – Libyen', Paper of the Gesamtdeutsches Institut – Bundesanstalt für Gesamtdeutsche Aufgaben (Bonn: 6 September 1983), pp. 1–2.

66 *Der Tagesspiegel*, 14 November 1975.

67 *ND*, 6/7 March 1976.

68 'Wir haben euch Waffen und Brot geschickt', *Sp*, Year 34, 10 (3 March 1980), p. 56.

69 *Keesing's*, p. 27295; and Franz Ansprenger, 'Germany's Year in Africa', *ACR*, vol. 7 (1974–5), A60.

70 Details of the GDR's security operations in Somalia are provided in chapter 4. However, in April 1972 a West German delegation had concluded an agreement to provide an extensive programme of assistance for the Somali police, see, *ARB*, vol. 9, 4 (1972), 2450C. Hence, for several years both Germanies assisted the Somali police! A point not denied in a private interview with an official of the FRG's embassy in London, 12 February 1988.

71 Gertraud Liebscher, 'Die Afrika-Politik des BRD-Imperialismus', *DAPK*, vol. 23, 5 (1978), pp. 89–102.

72 *Ibid.*, p. 98.

73 *Ibid.*, p. 93.

74 *Against Racism, Apartheid and Colonialism – Documents published by the GDR 1977–1982* (Dresden: Verlag Zeit im Bild, 1983), p. 220. The elections were organised by South Africa in contravention of UN resolutions and led to

the instalment in office of the Democratic Turnhalle Alliance with little effective power.

75 Wilhelm Bruns, 'Organisation der Vereinten Nationen', in Jacobsen *et al.* (eds.), *Drei Jahrzehnte Aussenpolitik*, p. 766.

76 *Dokumente*, 1973, vol. 21, pt 1, p. 124.

77 McCauley, *Marxism–Leninism in the German Democratic Republic*, p. 164.

78 See Doeker *et al.* (eds.), *The Federal Republic of Germany and the German Democratic Republic*, vol. 1, *Confrontation and Cooperation*, pp. 267–73, for the text of the Quadripartite Agreement, 3 September 1971, and its accompanying documents.

79 E.g., *Dokumente*, 1977, vol. 25, pt 2 (1982), p. 946, Declaration by the Ministry of Foreign Affairs of the GDR opposing the decision of the West Berlin Senate to hold a conference of internal ministers of the West German *Länder* in West Berlin, 25 February 1977.

80 Angela Stent, *From Embargo to Ostpolitik – the Political Economy of West German–Soviet Relations, 1955–1980* (Cambridge: Cambridge University Press, 1981), p. 84 and elsewhere.

81 Joachim Nawrocki, 'Schwierigkeiten mit den "drei Z" – Die DDR und das Viermächte Abkommen über Berlin', *DA*, vol. 7, 6 (1974), p. 585.

82 *Bundesgesetzblatt*, nr. 48, pt 2 (9 August 1972), p. 844, for Article 10 of the agreement.

83 Ernst Renatus Zivier, 'Anwendung und Beachtung des Berlin – Abkommens aus ostlicher und westlicher Sicht', in Gottfried Zieger (ed.), *Zehn Jahre Berlin-Abkommen 1971–1981 – Versuch einer Bilanz, Symposium 15/16 Oktober 1981* (Cologne, Berlin, Bonn, and Munich: Carl Heymanns Verlag, Schriften zur Rechtslage Deutschlands, vol. 5, 1983), p. 206.

84 Honoré M. Catudal Jr, *A Balance Sheet of the Quadripartite Agreement on Berlin – Evaluation and Documentation* (Berlin: Berlin Verlag, 1978), p. 121.

85 *Ibid.*, p. 109.

86 *Bundesgesetzblatt*, nr. 25, pt 2 (9 June 1973), p. 429, for Declaration of the two Germanies with reference to Berlin (West), 21 December 1972.

87 Gottfried Zieger, 'Die Perspektiven des Berlin-Abkommens', in Zieger (ed.), *Zehn Jahre Berlin-Abkommen*, pp. 253–4.

88 Gerhard Wettig, 'Die Bindungen West-Berlins als Verhandlungs – und Vertragsgegenstand der Vier Mächte 1970/71', *DA*, vol. 12, 3 (1979), p. 289.

89 *Zehn Jahre Deutschlandpolitik – Die Entwicklung der Beziehungen zwischen der Bundesrepublik Deutschland und der Deutschen Demokratischen Republik, 1969–1979 – Bericht und Dokumentation* (Bonn: Bundesministerium für innerdeutsche Beziehungen, 1980), p. 257, for Article 6 of the Protocol, 14 March 1974.

90 Jens Hacker, 'Die aussenpolitische Resonanz des Berlin-Abkommens', in Zieger (ed.), *Zehn Jahre Berlin-Abkommen*, pp. 243–4.

91 See *Zehn Jahre Deutschlandpolitik*, p. 242, for reference to the ruling of the West German Constitutional Court of 31 July 1973 on the legal status of Berlin in connection with Article 23 of the Basic Law.

92 *Collection of the Agreements concluded by the European Communities*, vol. 6,

1976 (Luxembourg: Office for Official Publications of the European Communities, 1979), ACP–EEC Convention of Lomé I, 30 January 1976, Council
Regulations (EEC) no. 199/76 of 30 January 1976 on ACP–EEC Convention
signed at Lomé, 28 February 1975, p. 1217, Annex XXIV, 'Declaration by
the representative of the Government of the Federal Republic of Germany
concerning the application to Berlin of the ACP–EEC Convention of Lomé.'

93 *Collection of the Agreements concluded by the European Communities*, vol. 11,
1981, pt. 2 (1985), ACP–EEC Convention of Lomé, signed at Lomé, 31
October 1979, p. 2142, Annex XXXV, 'Declaration by the representative of
the Government of the Federal Republic of Germany concerning the
application to Berlin of the Convention.'

94 *Collection of the Agreements* . . ., vol. 6, p. 1217; and vol. 11, pt. 2, p. 2141.

95 Wiedemann, *Sp* (3 March 1980), p. 58.

96 *Ibid.*, p. 59.

97 *Keesing's*, pp. 27050 and 28047.

98 Winrich Kuhne and Bernard von Plate, 'Two Germanies in Africa', *Africa
Report*, vol. 25, 4 (1980), pp. 13–14. The agreement, on generous terms,
stipulated that West Berlin firms should be eligible for tenders – see, 'East
Germany: the African connection', *Africa Confidential*, Year 20, 3 (31
January 1979), p. 8.

99 See *Against Racism*, pp. 240–4, for the text of the Joint Communiqué on
Honecker's visit to Angola, 19 February 1979. Here, see p. 243; and,
pp. 258–64 for the text of the Joint Communiqué on Honecker's visit to
Mozambique, 24 February 1979. Here, see, p. 261.

100 *Keesing's*, p. 29423.

101 Henning von Löwis of Menar, 'Die DDR als Schrittmacher im Weltrevo-
lutionären Prozess – zur Honecker–Visite in Äthiopien und im Südjemen',
DA, vol. 13, 1 (1980), pp. 40–1, quoting *National Zeitung*, 14 November
1979.

102 See *Against Racism*, pp. 333–7, for the text of the Joint Communiqué on
Honecker's visit to Ethiopia, 15 November 1979. Here, see, p. 337.

103 *Sp* (3 March 1989), p. 61.

104 Günter Siemund, 'Der Zweite Hinauswurf – zur Ausweisung des BRD –
Botschafters aus Addis Abeba', *H*, Year 11, 6 (1978), p. 6.

105 *Keesing's*, p. 30017.

106 *Ibid.*, p. 28994.

107 *Ibid.*, p. 28636. Again, as in the Somali example, it appears that both
Germanies had simultaneously provided aid for the Ethiopian police for
several months.

108 *Deutscher Bundestag*, 8 Wahlperiode, Drucksache 8/3463, Bonn, 4
December 1979, p. 9, 'Antwort der Bundesregierung auf die Grosse
Anfrage der Abgeordneten . . . und der Fraktion der CDU/CSU – Zur
Sicherung von Freiheit, Stabilitat, Frieden und Entwicklung in Afrika.'

109 Wilhelm Bruns, 'Mehrheitsfähigkeit und Opportunität – Die beiden
deutschen Staaten in der 34. UNO–Generalversammlung', *DA*, vol. 13, 6
(1980), pp. 600–1.

110 *Dokumente*, 1979, vol. 27, pt 1 (1984), pp. 489–91.

111 Von Löwis of Menar, 'Die DDR als Schrittmacher', p. 41.
112 Klaus Willerding, 'Zur Afrikapolitik der DDR', *DAPK*, vol. 24, 8 (1979), p. 5.
113 Johannes Kuppe, 'Investitionen, die sich lohnten – zur Reise Honeckers nach Afrika', *DA*, vol. 12, 4 (1979), p. 347.
114 See *ND*, 19 February 1979, for the text of the Joint Declaration.
115 *Ibid.*, 16 February 1979.
116 *Ibid.*, 19 February 1979.
117 *Ibid.*, 1, 3 and 4 September 1979.
118 *Dokumente*, vol. 27, pt 1, pp. 478–81, for the text of the treaty, 19 February 1979.
119 Meissner, 'The GDR's position', pp. 371 and 381–2.
120 *Dokumente*, vol. 27, pt 1, 618–21, for the text of the Treaty of Friendship and Cooperation between the GDR and Mozambique, 24 February 1979.
121 See Sodaro, 'The GDR and the Third World', p. 120, for these points.
122 A point, noted by Kuppe, 'Investitionen, die sich lohnten', pp. 349–50. For the text of the banquet speeches see, *ND*, 19 February 1979.
123 *ND*, 26 February 1979.
124 See *Against Racism*, p. 242, for the text of the Joint Communiqué on Honecker's visit to Angola.
125 *Ibid.*, p. 224; and *ND*, 19 February 1979, for the banquet speeches.
126 *ND*, 19 February 1979.
127 *ND*, 23 November 1979.
128 See *ND*, 22 February 1979, for the text of the Joint Declaration.
129 Noted by Wokalek, 'Zur Afrikapolitik der DDR', p. 10.
130 *ND*, 22 February 1979.
131 *ACR*, vol. 12 (1979–80), B950.
132 See *ND*, 22 February 1979.
133 *Ibid.*
134 *Frankfurter Rundschau*, 24 February 1979.
135 *ND*, 5 September 1979.
136 *Against Racism*, p. 260, for the text of the Joint Communiqué on Honecker's visit to Mozambique. A number of economic accords were also signed.
137 *ND*, 24/25 February 1979.
138 *Against Racism*, p. 262.
139 *ACR*, vol. 11 (1978–9), B341; and, David L. Morison, 'Soviet and Chinese policies in Africa in 1978', *ibid.*, A74.
140 Noted by Wokalek, 'Zur Afrikapolitik der DDR', p. 17.
141 *ND*, 24/5 and 26 February 1979.
142 Kuppe, 'Investitionen, die sich lohnten', p. 352.
143 See *Against Racism*, p. 334, for the text of the Joint Communiqué on Honecker's visit to Ethiopia.
144 *Dokumente*, vol. 27, pt 1, pp. 506–9, for the text of the Treaty of Friendship and Cooperation between the GDR and Ethiopia, 15 November 1979.
145 Sodaro, 'The GDR and the Third World', p. 120, noted the exclusion of the self-determination clause.

146 *Ibid.*, p. 119.
147 *ND*, 13 November 1979.
148 *Against Racism*, p. 337.
149 *Ibid.*, p. 329, speech by Honecker, 13 November 1979.
150 *ND*, 15 November 1979.
151 *Against Racism*, pp. 332–3, statement by Honecker on the occasion of his visit to the Headquarters of the OAU in Addis Ababa, 14 November 1979.
152 *Deutscher Bundestag*, Drucksache 8/3463, p. 8.
153 *ACR*, vol. 11 (1978–9), B502.
154 For Touré's visit, see *ND*, 8 October 1979; and for the visits of Tisch and Sindermann, see *ND*, 21 May 1979 and, *ibid.*, 2 November 1979 respectively.

4 East German military/security involvement in Africa

1 *International Herald Tribune* (*IHT*), 24 July 1978.
2 *Dokumente*, vol. 21, pt. 1, p. 123.
3 *Against Racism*, p. 418. In a similar speech to the 26th CPSU Congress on 3 February 1981 Brezhnev reserved the right to provide 'fraternal assistance' if socialist-oriented states in the Third World were threatened by counter-revolution, see, *CDSP*, vol. 33, 8 (25 March 1981), p. 7.
4 Wolfgang Baatz, 'Zur Militarhilfe der BRD an afrikanische National-alstaaten', *AAL*, vol. 2, 6 (1974), p. 947.
5 *Ibid.*, p. 948.
6 Cervenka and Dederichs, *ACR*, vol. 11 (1978–9), A102.
7 Klaus-Ulrich Schloesser, 'Zur Rolle der Armee in national befreiten Staaten Asiens und Afrikas', *DAPK*, vol. 27, 10 (1982), pp. 73–4.
8 Willerding, 'Zur Afrikapolitik der DDR', p. 16.
9 Moreton, 'The East Europeans and the Cubans', p. 79.
10 Meissner, 'The GDR's Position', p. 376.
11 Thompson, *Ghana's Foreign Policy*, p. 402.
12 *Die Welt*, 11 June 1966.
13 *ACR*, vol. 2 (1969–70), B197–8.
14 Kupper *et al.*, *Die Tätigkeit der DDR in . . . arabische Staaten und Israel*, p. 104.
15 *ACR*, vol. 3 (1970–1), B163.
16 Ulrich Post and Frank Sandvoss, *Die Afrikapolitik der DDR* (Hamburg: Institut fur Afrika-kunde im verbund der Stiftung Deutsches Ubersee-Institut, Arbeiten aus dem Institut für Afrika-kunde, 43, 1982), p. 130.
17 *ACR*, vol. 6 (1973–4), B252.
18 *Der Tagesspiegel*, 23 February 1971.
19 *Africa Confidential*, vol. 20, 3 (31 January 1979), p. 8.
20 *SBZ Archiv*, no. 15 (1 August 1967), p. 225.
21 SIPRI, *The Arms Trade*, p. 667; and, *Sp*, Year 34, 10 (3 March 1980), p. 43.
22 Henning von Lowis of Menar, 'Militarisches und Paramilitarisches Engagement der DDR in der Dritten Welt', in Siegfried Baske and Gott-fried Zieger (eds.), *Die Dritte Welt und die beiden Staaten in Deutschland*

(Asperg, Stuttgart: Edition Meyn, Gesellschaft für Deutschlandforschung Jahrbuch, 1982, 1983), p. 130.
23 SIPRI, *The Arms Trade*, p. 637.
24 Von Löwis of Menar, 'Militarisches und Paramilitärisches Engagement', p. 129.
25 Thomas M. Forster, *The East German Army – The Second Power in the Warsaw Pact*, trans. Dereyck Viney (London: Allen and Unwin, 1980), p. 99 – referring to *Österreichische Militärisches Zeitschrift*, 2/1977, p. 150.
26 SIPRI, *Yearbook 1983: World Armaments and Disarmament* (New York and London: Taylor and Francis, 1983), p. 368.
27 'DDR-Militars knüpften freundschaftliche Kontakte – Horizont Gespräch mit Mitgliedern einer Militärdelegation der DDR nach ihrer Reise durch die Republik Irak und die Arabische Republik Agypten', *H*, Year 4, 47 (1971), pp. 3–4.
28 *National Zeitung*, 17 April 1971.
29 'DDR-Militärdelegation im befreundeten Algerien', *Volksarmee*, 14 June 1972.
30 Von Löwis of Menar, 'Militärisches und Paramilitärisches Engagement', p. 130. No details concerning the result of this 'secret visit' are given.
31 *ND*, 5 November 1972.
32 Lamm and Kupper, *DDR und Dritte Welt*, p. 147.
33 *Deutscher Bundestag*, Drucksache 8/3463, p. 12.
34 See Valenta and Butler, 'East German security policies in Africa', p. 152, who contend that a military agreement was concluded between the GDR and the MPLA in 1973.
35 Coker, 'Pact, pox or proxy', p. 577.
36 John A. Marcum, *Exile Politics and Guerrilla Warfare (1962–76)*, vol. 2 (Cambridge, Mass. and London: The MIT Press, 2nd edn, 1981), pp. 201, 221 and 229; and Jiri Valenta, 'Soviet decision-making on the intervention in Angola', in Albright (ed.), *Africa and International Communism*, p. 99.
37 Anon., 'Angola after independence; struggle for supremacy', *Conflict Studies*, no. 64 (London: Institute for the Study of Conflict, 1975), pp. 12–13.
38 W. Raymond Duncan, *The Soviet Union and Cuba – Interests and Influence* (New York, Philadelphia, Toronto, Hong Kong, Tokyo, Sydney and East-bourne: Praeger, Studies of Influence in International Relations, 1985), pp. 128–9.
39 See, respectively, Trond Gilberg, 'Eastern European military assistance to the Third World', in John F. Copper and Daniel S. Papp (eds.), *Communist Nations' Military Assistance* (Boulder, Colorado: Westview Press, 1983), p. 83; David E. Albright, 'The communist states and Southern Africa', in Gwendolen M. Carter and Patrick O'Meara (eds.), *International Politics in Southern Africa* (Bloomington: Indiana University Press, 1982), pp. 8–9; and 'The special comrade', *The Economist*, 9 August 1980, pp. 14–15.
40 Glass, 'East Germany in Black Africa', p. 311.
41 Bertil Dunér, *The Bear, the Cubs and the Eagle – Soviet Bloc Interventionism in the Third World and the US Response* (Aldershot, Hants., Brookfield, USA,

Hong Kong, Singapore, Sydney: Gower, Swedish Studies in International Relations, no. 22, The Swedish Institute of International Affairs, 1987), pp. 10–15.

42 *Ibid.*

43 *Ibid.*, p. 40.

44 *Ibid.*, p. 13.

45 *Ibid.*, pp. 12–14.

46 Coker, 'Pact, pox or proxy', pp. 579–80.

47 E.g., Robinson's tabulation of East German 'military forces' without advisers in Africa and the Middle East in May–June 1978 must be questioned. See, Table 7, and, William F. Robinson, 'Eastern Europe's presence in Black Africa', *Radio Free Europe*, RAD Background Report/142 Eastern Europe, 21 June 1979, p. 10.

48 Schloesser, 'Zur Rolle der Armee', p. 74.

49 Heinz Hoffmann, 'Die sozialistische Militarkoalition-zuverlassiger Schild des Sozialismus', E, Year 35, 5 (1980), p. 476.

50 'Bei Freunden im Süden und am Horn von Afrika – Interview mit Armeegeneral Heinz Hoffmann', H, Year 12, 28 (1979), p. 4.

51 *Deutscher Bundestag*, Drucksache 8/3463, p. 10.

52 Von Löwis of Menar, 'Militarisches und Paramilitarisches Engagement', p. 133.

53 Hans-Joachim Spanger, 'Militärpolitik und militarisches Engagement der DDR in der Dritten Welt', *DA*, vol. 18, 8 (1985), pp. 832–45.

54 *ARB*, vol. 15, 4 (1978), 4819; and vol. 15, 11 (1978), 5050–1.

55 *The Guardian*, 8 November 1978.

56 Zdenek Cervenka and Mario R. Dederichs, 'The two Germanies in Africa – Eastern advances and Western isolationism', *ACR*, vol. 12 (1979–80), A148.

57 *IHT*, 24 July 1978.

58 *ND*, 2 February 1979.

59 *Keesing's*, p. 28740.

60 *Die Welt*, 17 May 1978.

61 *NZZ*, 9 August 1979.

62 Halliday and Molyneux, *The Ethiopian Revolution*, pp. 253–4. As recently as 1975 Castro had referred to the Eritrean cause as a progressive one.

63 Crozier, 'The surrogate forces', p. 10.

64 Henning von Lowis of Menar, 'Das Afrikanische Erbe von Werner Lamberz – Ost-Berlins Athiopien-Abenteur', *DA*, vol. 11, 4 (1978), pp. 349–50.

65 *ND*, 18–19 and 22/3 October 1977.

66 For reference to Lamberz' role, see, 'Standhaft fur die Sache des Fortschritts – Interview mit Werner Lamberz uber seine Reise in afrikanische und arabische Länder', H, Year 11, 1 (1978), pp. 3–4.

67 *ND*, 6 December 1977.

68 *Ibid.*, 8 December 1977.

69 *Ibid.*, 12 December 1977.

70 *Dokumente*, vol. 26, pt 1, pp. 609–15, Joint Communiqué on the official friendship visit to the GDR of Ali Nasser Mohammed, 16 January 1978.

71 According to one source, although South Yemeni forces most probably clashed with the Eritreans near Massawa late in 1977, after victory in the Ogaden these troops were recalled in order not to offend the sensitivities of the EPLF–ELF who operated a bureau in Aden. See Bereket Hable Selassie, *Conflict and Intervention in the Horn of Africa* (New York and London: Monthly Review Press, 1980), p. 146.
72 *Dokumente*, vol. 26, pt 1, pp. 615–16. News of the visit of a military delegation from South Yemen to the GDR, 2 June 1978.
73 *Dokumente*, vol. 27, pt 1, pp. 618–21.
74 *ND*, 28 May 1979.
75 *ACR*, vol. 12 (1979–80), B738.
76 Henrik Bischof (ed.), *Entwicklungspolitik kommunistischer Länder – Trends und Analysen (EAKL)* (Bonn: Forschungsinstitut der Friedrich-Ebert-Stiftung), 1/1980, p. 91.
77 *ND*, 1 June 1979.
78 *Deutscher Bundestag*, Drucksache 8/3463, p. 12.
79 See *ACR*, vol. 9 (1976–7), C151–3, for the text of the Treaty of Friendship and Cooperation between the USSR and Angola, 8 October 1976 – see, Articles 7 and 10; *ACR*, vol. 10 (1977–8), C17–9, for the text of the Treaty of Friendship and Cooperation between the USSR and Mozambique, 31 March 1977, see, Articles 4 and 10; and *ACR*, vol. 11 (1978–9), C84–6, for the text of the Treaty of Friendship and Cooperation between the USSR and Ethiopia, 20 November 1978, see Articles 7 and 10.
80 Robin A. Remington, *The Warsaw Pact – Case Studies in Communist Conflict Resolution* (Cambridge, Mass. and London: The MIT Press, 1971), p. 14.
81 Andrzej Korbonski, 'The Warsaw Treaty after twenty-five years: an entangling alliance or an empty shell', in Robert W. Clawson and Lawrence S. Kaplan (eds.), *The Warsaw Pact: Political Purpose and Military Means* (Wilmington, Delaware: Scholarly Resources Inc., 1982), p. 11.
82 Frank Sandvoss, 'The German Democratic Republic's policies in Africa, 1983–1984–a balance sheet of losses and gains', *ACR*, vol. 17 (1984–5), A181.
83 *H*, Year 12, 28 (1979), p. 3.
84 Cervenka and Dederichs, 'The two Germanies in Africa', A105. For a brief reference to Petroff's arrival see *ND*, 1/2 May 1976.
85 *ARB*, vol. 13, 10 (1976), 4193.
86 *ND*, 20 June 1976.
87 'Angola – "Thwarting Intelligence"', *Africa Confidential*, vol. 20, 17 (22 August 1979), p. 8.
88 P. Chaigneau and R. Sola, 'North Korea as an African power: a threat to French interests', *Institute for Strategic Studies, University of Pretoria, Strategic Review (Strategic Review)* (December 1986), p. 10.
89 *Die Welt*, 31 January 1985.
90 *Ibid.*, 10 December 1983 and 22/3 June 1985.
91 *Africa Confidential*, vol. 20, 3 (31 January 1979), p. 8.
92 *NZZ*, 8 June 1984.
93 Ian Greig, 'East Germany's drive for influence in Africa', *Strategic Review* (June 1985), p. 23.

94 *EAKL*, 11/1980, p. 65; and *Keesing's*, p. 30614.
95 Henning von Löwis of Menar, 'Die DDR und Afrika', in Gernot Gutmann and Maria Haendcke-Hoppe (eds.), *Die Aussenbeziehungen der DDR* (Heidelberg: Edition Meyn, Gesellschaft fur Deutschlandforschung, Jahrbuch 1980, 1981), p. 225.
96 *FAZ*, 28 March 1987.
97 Cervenka and Dederichs, 'The two Germanies in Africa – Eastern advances', A160.
98 'Congo-Brazzaville: enigma with variations', *Africa Confidential*, vol. 18, 23 (18 November 1977), pp. 3–5.
99 *FAZ*, 17 May 1985, this account was prompted by the arrival in East Berlin of President Sassou-Nguesso, accompanied by the commander of the Congolese People's Militia, Michel Ngakala – see *ND*, 18/19 May, 1985.
100 For reference to Machel, see Cervenka and Dederichs, 'The two Germanies in Africa', A104–5; for reference to Mengistu, see von Löwis of Menar, 'Das Afrikanische Erbe', p. 350; for reference to dos Santos, see Chaigneau and Sola, 'North Korea as an African power', p. 10; and for reference to Ghaddafi, see Francis Fukuyama, 'Soviet strategy in the Third World', in Korbonski and Fukuyama (eds.), *The Soviet Union and the Third World*, p. 37, n. 33 – referring to *L'Express*, 4–10 November 1983, pp. 104–5.
101 Steven R. David, 'Third World interventions – review', *P of C*, vol. 33, 3 (1984), p. 68.
102 Crozier, 'The surrogate forces', p. 10.
103 *Keesing's*, p. 29340; and *Der Morgenpost*, 9 September 1978.
104 *Deutscher Bundestag*, Drucksache 8/3463, p. 10.
105 Cervenka and Dederichs, 'The two Germanies in Africa – Eastern advances', A156–7.
106 *Deutscher Bundestag*, Drucksache 8/3463, p. 10.
107 Cervenka and Dederichs, 'The two Germanies in Africa', A102. According to *ND*, 14 October 1977, on the 13 October 1977 Yhombi-Opango, accompanied by Hoffmann and Lamberz, visited the Technical NCO's College, NVA 'Erich Habersaath', in Prora on the island of Rugen.
108 Sandvoss, 'The German Democratic Republic's policies in Africa, 1983–1984', A184.
109 *Sp*, Year 34, 10 (3 March 1980), p. 45.
110 See *Die Welt*, 30 March 1983, for reference to the training of military officers from Zimbabwe; see *NZZ*, 10/11 June 1984 and *Sp*, Year 38, 12 (19 March 1984), p. 148, for details concerning ANC and SWAPO bases in the GDR. However, according to another report, there was no evidence of the GDR providing instruction outside Angola for SWAPO's military wing, the Namibian People's Liberation Army, see Henning von Löwis of Menar, 'Die Ausbildung von SWAPO–Kadern in der Deutschen Demokratischen Republik', *Namibia Information Office, Dokumentation Nr. 23* (Bonn: November 1983), p. 23.
111 *Der Tagesspiegel*, 8 February 1979.
112 Forster, *The East German Army*, p. 101.

113 For reference to the GDR–POLISARIO connection in Algeria, see *Der Morgenpost*, 15 May 1977, and *Der Bayern Kurier*, 17 June 1978. For various sources referring to a continued East German military presence in Algeria in the 1980s, see Table 7.

114 *FAZ*, 28 February 1978 and 21 August 1984.

115 Forster, *The Third World Army*, p. 101; and Cervenka and Dederichs, 'The two Germanies in Africa – Eastern advances', A156.

116 Coker, *NATO, the Warsaw Pact*, p. 198.

117 Henning von Löwis of Menar, 'Machtpolitik südlich des Sambesi – Sambia und Moçambique als Adressaten der DDR–Aussenpolitik', *DA*, vol. 13, 11 (1980), p. 1170, quoting, *Marches Tropicaux et Méditerranée* (Paris), 8 June 1979.

118 *The Sunday Times*, 25 June 1978.

119 *The Times*, 20 September 1985.

120 Post and Sandvoss, *Die Afrikapolitik der DDR*, p. 55; and, *Sp*, Year 34, 10 (3 March 1980), p. 45.

121 *Africa Confidential*, vol. 20, 3 (31 January 1979), p. 8.

122 International Institute for Strategic Studies, *The Military Balance, 1987* (London: IISS, 1987), p. 126.

123 Post and Sandvoss, *Die Afrikapolitik der DDR*, p. 133; and, *EAKL* 1/1981, p. 58.

124 *Deutscher Bundestag, Stenographische Berichte*, 8 Wahlperiode, 197 Sitzung, Bonn, 18 January 1980, p. 15725, speech by Roth.

125 Robinson, 'Eastern Europe's presence', p. 9; and, *Der Tagesspiegel*, 2 February 1978.

126 US Arms Control and Disarmament Agency (ACDA), *World Military Expenditures and Arms Transfers 1987*, ACDA Publication 128 (Washington DC: US Government Printing Office, 1988), pp. 127–8.

127 *Ibid.*, pp. 85–126.

128 *Deutscher Bundestag*, Drucksache 8/3463, p. 10.

129 'DDR–Kalaschnikows für die Dritte Welt', *Sp*, Year 30, 36 (30 August 1976), pp. 60–2.

130 Forster, *The East German Army*, p. 98, referring to *Österreichische Militärische Zeitschrift*, 2/1977, p. 150.

131 SIPRI, *Yearbook 1983*, pp. 367–8.

132 See Michael Brzoska, 'Arms transfer data sources', *Journal of Conflict Resolution*, vol. 26, 1 (1982), pp. 77–108.

133 Childs, *The GDR*, p. 304, referring to *Der Morgen*, 27/8 December 1980.

134 *Sp*, Year 30, 36 (30 August 1976), p. 63; Forster, *The East German Army*, p. 181; and Dale R. Herspring, 'Die Rolle der Streitkräfte in der Aussenpolitik der DDR', in Jacobsen *et al.* (eds.), *Drei Jahrzehnte Aussenpolitik*, p. 321.

135 Thomas H. Snitch, 'East European involvement in the world's arms market', in US ACDA *World Military Expenditures and Arms Transfers, 1972–82*, ACDA Publication 117 (Washington DC: US Government Printing Office, 1984), p. 121.

136 Zdenek Cervenka, 'The two Germanies and Africa during 1980 – rivals for influence', *ACR*, vol. 13 (1980–1), A148–9.

137 *H*, Year 12, 28 (1979), p. 3.

138 *ND*, 31 May 1979.

139 Horst Schötzki, 'In festen Kampfbündnis vereint – Begeisterte Aufnahme für Erich Honecker im Sozialistischen Äthiopien und in der Volksdemokratischen Republik Jemen', *H*, Year 12, 48 (1979), p. 3.

140 *ND*, 23 May 1979.

141 Robinson, 'Eastern Europe's presence', p. 7, for reference to the slogan.

142 See Post and Sandvoss, *Die Afrikapolitik der DDR*, p. 117, for reference to a 'solidarity gift' for the strengthening of the defence capacity of Mozambique received by the officiating Defence Minister of Mozambique, Guebuza, in East Berlin in October 1979; and see, von Löwis of Menar, 'Machtpolitik sudlich des Sambesi', p. 1170, for reference to Fleissner handing over a military gift in Maputo in March 1980.

143 *Keesing's*, p. 28423.

144 Robinson's 'Eastern Europe's presence', pp. 7–8.

145 *Newsweek*, 9 July 1979.

146 *Sp*, Year 34, 10 (3 March 1980), p. 47; and *ACR*, vol. 12 (1979–80), B971.

147 *Dokumente*, vol. 27, pt 2, *Zeittafel*, p. 1143.

148 *Sp*, Year 30, 36 (30 August 1976), p. 63.

149 *EAKL* 1/1980, p. 70.

150 *Keesing's*, p. 29838.

151 See 'Eine Reise der Waffen-bruderschaft – "Volksarmee" – Interview mit dem Stellvertreter des Chefs der Politischen Hauptverwaltung der Nationalen Volksarmee, Generalleutnant Ernst Hampf', *Volksarmee*, 26 May 1978, for an account of Hoffmann's tour in 1978. For details of the 1979 trip, see *H*, Year 12, 28 (1979), pp. 3–4.

152 See Edward J. Lawrence, 'Soviet arms transfers in the 1980s: declining influence in Sub-Saharan Africa', in Bruce E. Arlinghaus (ed.), *Arms for Africa – Military Assistance and Foreign Policy in the Developing World* (Lexington, Mass. and Toronto: D.C. Heath, 1983), pp. 47–8, for reference to the arms deal between the USSR and Zambia on 7 February 1980.

153 *Le Monde*, 2 May 1977; and, *The Times*, 3 May 1977.

154 *ND*, 2 May 1977.

155 *The Observer*, 21 May 1978.

156 Henning von Löwis of Menar, 'Solidaritat und Subversion – Die Rolle der DDR im sudlichen Afrika', *DA*, vol. 10, 6 (1977), pp. 645–6.

157 Robinson, 'Eastern Europe's presence', p. 9.

158 'Militärdelegation bei afrikanischen Freunden – Interview mit Armeegeneral Heinz Hoffmann', *H*, Year 11, 25 (1978), pp. 3–4.

159 Liebscher, 'Die Afrika-politik des BRD-Imperialismus', pp. 96–7.

160 *Deutscher Bundestag*, Drucksache 8/3463, p. 10.

5 East German economic relations with Africa

1 For further details, see appropriate years in *Statistisches Jahrbuch der Deutschen Demokratischen Republik (Statistisches Jahrbuch)* (Berlin [East]: Staatsverlag der DDR).

2 *Statistisches Jahrbuch*, Year 31 (1987), pp. 103–4.

3 Hans-Dieter Jacobsen, 'Strategie und Schwerpunkte der Aussenwirtschaftsbeziehungen', in Jacobsen *et al.* (eds.), *Drei Jahrzehnte Aussenpolitik*, p. 295.
4 *Dokumente*, vol. 15, pt 1, p. 105.
5 Jacobsen, 'Strategie und Schwerpunkte', p. 310.
6 See *Materialien zum Bericht zur Lage im geteilten Deutschland, 1987, Deutscher Bundestag*, 11 Wahlperiode, Drucksache 11/11, 18 February 1987 (Bonn), p. 958; and see Table 1.
7 See Table 1, and Hillebrand, *Das Afrika-Engagement der DDR*, pp. 131–4. Hillebrand does not satisfactorily answer the question why the GDR should have included trade turnover with Ethiopia, Mozambique and Angola under the category of 'socialist states' and not 'developing states'.
8 For instance, taking the figures for 1984, if one subtracts from the total trade turnover with 'developing states' the accumulated total of trade turnover with individual developing states listed for that year (excluding those developing states Hillebrand included under the categories of the CMEA and 'socialist states') then VM 1,074.3 million remains unaccounted for out of the total trade turnover of VM 8,243.2 million – my calculations from *Statistisches Jahrbuch*, Year 30, 1986 (1986), p. 241. This suggests that East German trade turnover with a number of other African and other Third World states was included under the category 'developing states', although no figures on individual trade turnover with these states were given.
9 For general discussions of these points, see Hillebrand, *Das Afrika-Engagement der DDR*, pp. 162–3; and Marie Lavigne, 'Consequence of economic developments in Eastern Europe for East–West and East–South relations', *Trade and Development – An UNCTAD Review*, no. 4 (Winter 1982), p. 139.
10 According to Bernard von Plate, 'Die Handelsbeziehungen der DDR mit den Entwicklungsländern and die neue Weltwirtschaftsordnung', *DA*, vol. 13, 8 (1980), p. 820, payments agreements were previously concluded in non-convertible currencies with the following Third World states: Ghana (19 October 1961), Sudan (6 October 1967), India (23 January 1969 and 12 September 1974), and Iran (25 September 1973).
11 Wolfgang Schoeller, '"Komparativer Nachteil" und "Wechselseitiger Nutzen" – zur Kooperation zwischen COMECON und Entwicklungsländern am Beispiel Mosambiks', *DA*, vol. 16, 12 (1983), pp. 1037–8.
12 See Table 2 for all other references in the text concerning 'official' East German data on trade with particular African states and certain oil exporting states.
13 Jonathan Steele, 'Soviet relations with Angola and Mozambique', in Robert Cassen (ed.), *Soviet Interests in the Third World* (London and Beverly Hills: Sage Publications, for the Royal Institute of International Affairs, 1985), p. 294.
14 Schoeller, 'Komparativer Nachteil', p. 1303.
15 *Mozambique Information Agency*, 22 August 1984.
16 Reime, *Die Tätigkeit der DDR . . . Schwarzafrika*, pp. 98 and 185–6.

17 *Ibid.*, pp. 185–6. Trade with Rhodesia was recorded in 1964 and 1965. South Africa received East German imports regularly between 1960 and 1968.
18 Post and Sandvoss, *Die Afrikapolitik der DDR*, pp. 64–6. The breakdown of trade between the GDR and South Africa in the 1970s was as follows (not including possible hidden East German imports of key South African raw materials) ($US thousands):

	1970	1974	1975	1976	1977
Imports from the GDR	1,046.0	3,242.0	1,438.0	3,106.0	1,969.0
Exports to the GDR				128.8	2.3

These figures also include possible trade with Namibia, Botswana, Lesotho and Swaziland – all members of the South African Customs Union. Note, no trade turnover between the GDR and the Union was recorded in UN statistics for the 1980s.
19 For details of these accusations, see Wilhelm Bruns, 'Mehr Konflikt als Kooperation – Die beiden deutschen Staaten auf der 31. UN – Generalversammlung', *DA*, vol. 10, 9 (1977), p. 971. For East German condemnation of the reports of commercial links between the GDR and Rhodesia see, *ND*, 17 February 1977.
20 Christopher Coker, 'Adventurism and pragmatism: the Soviet Union, COMECON and relations with African states', *International Affairs*, vol. 57, 4 (1981), pp. 618–33; and Colin Lawson, 'The Soviet Union and Eastern Europe in Southern Africa: is there a conflict of interest?', *International Affairs*, vol. 59, 1 (1982/3), pp. 32–40.
21 See Coker, 'Adventurism and pragmatism', and also by Coker: *NATO, The Warsaw Pact*; 'The Soviet Union and Eastern Europe: pattern of competition and collaboration in Southern Africa', in R. Craig Nation and Mark V. Kauppi (eds.), *The Soviet Impact in Africa* (Lexington, Mass., Toronto and London: Lexington Books, D.C. Heath, 1984), pp. 59–85; and *The Soviet Union, Eastern Europe and the New International Economic Order*, *The Washington Papers*, vol. 12, 111 (New York: Praeger, with the Center for Strategic and International Studies, Georgetown University, 1984).
22 *Dokumente*, vol. 12, pp. 564–8.
23 *Dokumente*, vol. 27, pt 1, p. 74.
24 Rolf Scharschmidt, 'DDR/Entwicklungslander – Traditionelle und neue Formen der wirtschaftlichen Zusammenarbeit', *H*, Year 17, 7 (1984), p. 23.
25 See *UNCTAD TD/B/1003/Add. 1*, 31 July 1984, p. 11, table 8, for the first two figures quoted. The 1985 figure is from *International Trade 1985–1986 – General Agreement on Tariffs and Trade* (Geneva: GATT, 1986), p. 107.
26 Haendcke-Hoppe, 'Die DDR-Aussenwirtschaft', p. 53, from official West German sources.
27 See *Proceedings of the United Nations Conference on Trade and Development*, 4th Session, 5–31 May 1976, Nairobi, vol. 1, Report and Annexes (New York: United Nations, 1977), pp. 130–1, UNCTAD TD/195.

28 *H*, Year 17, 7 (1984), p. 23. Note that the 1984 figure was considerably higher than that given by the *Report by the UNCTAD Secretariat, UNCTAD VI, TD/280,* 6 June 1983, p. 2, where it was alleged that the percentage of total CMEA imports from the developing states in these product categories only amounted to 20 per cent at most.
29 Willerding, 'Die DDR und die national befreiten Staaten', p. 695.
30 Günther Barthel, 'Die OPEC in der Kapitalistischen Welterdolwirtschaft', *DAPK*, vol. 20, 7 (1980), pp. 87–90.
31 Asmus, 'The East German search', p. 5.
32 'Wirtschaftsbeziehungen der DDR zu Entwicklungsländern – keine neuen Trends in Hilfe und Handel', *Deutsches Institut für Wirtschaftsforschung – Wochenbericht (DIW – Wochenbericht),* vol. 52, 51–2 (20 December 1985), p. 584, n. 24.
33 *ND*, 18 October 1982.
34 *Ibid.*, 15 October 1982.
35 Johannes Kuppe, 'Zum Staatsbesuch Honeckers in Mexico', *DA*, vol. 14, 10 (1981), pp. 1022–6.
36 *ND*, 26 April 1975.
37 See Dieter Hollmann, 'Gemeinsamen im antiimperialistischen Kampf – Zum Offiziellen Freundschaftsbesuch Muammar el Ghaddafis', *H*, Year 11, 28 (1978), p. 3; and *ND*, 19 February 1979.
38 Christopher Coker, 'Eastern Europe and the Middle East: the forgotten dimension of Soviet policy', in Cassen (ed.), *Soviet Interests*, p. 54.
39 *EAKL* 1/1980, p. 11.
40 *ND*, 19 December 1984.
41 *Dokumente*, vol. 27, pt 2, Zeittafel, p. 1149, for reference to the visit by Petroleum Minister Augusto Morais on 2 March 1979. His successor, Pedro Van-Dunen, visited the GDR in June 1981 and June 1983. See, *ND*, 17 June 1981 and 30 June 1983.
42 Asmus, 'The East German search', p. 4.
43 Lawson, 'The Soviet Union and Eastern Europe in Southern Africa', p. 86, n. 16.
44 'Weiterer Ausbau der Beziehungen DDR–Nigeria – Horizont Gespräch mit Horst Sölle, Minister für Aussenhandel der DDR', *H*, Year 7, 46 (1974), p. 21.
45 *ND*, 1 December 1980.
46 Frank Sandvoss, 'The German Democratic Republic's policies in Africa, 1982–1983, balancing aid with trade', *ACR*, vol. 16 (1983–4), A220.
47 *ND*, 27 July 1983.
48 See Liebscher, 'Die Afrika-Politik des BRD-Imperialismus', p. 92; and a comment by Wilhelm Bruns, 'Zeitschriftenschau – Aussenpolitik', *DA*, vol. 11, 7 (1978), p. 704.
49 Wolfgang Seiffert, 'Ist die DDR ein Modell?', *DA*, vol. 20, 5 (1987), p. 472.
50 Daniel Franklin and Edwina Moreton, 'Inside Comecon – A Survey', *The Economist*, 20 April 1985, p. 13.
51 *Materialien zum Bericht . . . 1987*, p. 14. The figure of 6.6 million is computed from East German and CMEA statistics, whilst the second figure of almost 14 million is derived from additional sources in the data banks of

the Deutsches Institut für Wirtschaftsforschung. The second figure may also be estimated by deducting the total East German oil consumption quoted in the text from the official East German total of GDR oil imports given in Table 9.

52 *Ibid.*, p. 418. In 1984 alone East German oil imports from the USSR totalled 17.1 million tonnes, of which approximately only 9.6 million tonnes were consumed at most.

53 This point is suggested in, Barthlomiej Kaminski and Robert W. Janes, 'Economic rationale for Eastern Europe's Third World policy', *P of C*, vol. 37, 2 (1988), p. 18.

54 'Der Primärenenergieverbrauch in der DDR und seine Struktur', *DIW – Wochenbericht*, vol. 52, 51–2 (20 December 1985), p. 578.

55 Alan H. Smith, 'Soviet trade relations with the Third World', in Cassen (ed.), *Soviet Interests*, p. 149.

56 Irwin L. Collier, 'Intensification in the GDR: a postscript', *Studies in Comparative Communism*, vol. 20, 1 (1987), p. 71.

57 *Statistisches Jahrbuch*, Year 27, 1983 (1983), p. 247.

58 *Materialien zum Bericht . . . 1987*, p. 409.

59 See Wolfgang Stinglwagner, 'Genügend Energie für die Zukunft? Effizienz und Strukturmerkmale des Energieeinsatzes in der DDR', *DA*, vol. 16, 3 (1981), p. 265, for a calculation of these figures from various GDR Statistical Yearbooks.

60 Coker, *NATO, the Warsaw Pact*, p. 176.

61 See *ibid.*, pp. 175–6, 187 and 199, for these points and other interesting observations on East German mining operations in Mozambique.

62 Hillebrand, *Das Afrika-Engagement der DDR*, p. 156.

63 *Dokumente*, vol. 27, pt 1, pp. 677–80, for the text of the Agreement, 21 February 1979.

64 *EAKL* 11/1980, p. 111.

65 Coker, *The Soviet Union, Eastern Europe and the New International Economic Order*, pp. 33–5.

66 *Trends in Trade and Economic Co-operation Among Countries having Different Economic and Social Systems*, study prepared by Michael Kaser, UNCTAD/ST/TSC/9, 5 November 1987; pp. 18–19; and *ND*, 23 April 1986.

67 Gertraud Liebscher and Thomas Friedländer, 'Positionen und Aktivitäten des BRD-Neokolonialismus zu Beginn der achtziger Jahre', *AAL*, vol. 10, 6 (1982), pp. 985–94.

68 *Proceedings of the United Nations*, 4th Session, vol. 1, UNCTAD TD/195, pp. 130–1.

69 *Dokumente*, vol. 12, pp. 553–8, Basic Declaration of the Government of the GDR to the UNCTAD session, April 1964; and also pp. 558–64, Declaration of the government of the GDR to the UNCTAD session on the principles and advantages of long-term agreements between the GDR and the developing states, April 1964.

70 *Ibid.*, pp. 554–5, Basic Declaration; and see Table 1.

71 *Dokumente*, vol. 16, pt 1, pp. 516–21, Memorandum of the Government of the GDR to the UNCTAD II session on Point 9 of the Agenda, 'Trends and

problems of World Trade and development', 10 February 1968; and *Dokumente*, 1972, vol. 20, pt 2 (1975), pp. 1081–3, Declaration of the Government of the GDR to the UNCTAD III session, 5 April 1972 – DT/155.

72 *Dokumente*, 1976, vol. 24, pt 2 (1980), pp. 1083–90.

73 *Against Racism*, p. 280.

74 Heinz Schulz and Georg Weber, 'Zur 11. UN Sondertagung – Demokratische Umgestaltung der internationalen Wirtschaftsbeziehungen – ein dringendes Gebot unserer Zeit', *H*, Year 13, 33 (1980), pp. 22 and 24.

75 See, e.g., *ND*, 16/17 June 1984, for the text of the CMEA Declaration at the Moscow Summit Meeting on 'The Maintenance of Peace and International Economic Cooperation' (12–14 June 1984).

76 *Proceedings of the United Nations Conference on Trade and Development*, 6th Session, 6 June–2 July 1983, Belgrade, vol. 1, Report and Annexes (New York: United Nations, 1984), pp. 151–2, 'Assistance given by the German Democratic Republic to developing countries and liberation movements in 1982', Conference Doc. TD/304. For further details see chapter 6.

77 See Roger E. Kanet, 'East European states', in Thomas H. Henriksen (ed.), *Communist Powers and Sub-Saharan Africa* (Stanford: Hoover Institution Press, 1981), pp. 37–8, for these figures and percentages taken from UN Statistical Yearbooks. Between 1975 and 1977 East German aid commitments to non-communist developing states increased to $479 million.

78 *OECD 1985 Report – Twenty-Five Years of Development Cooperation – A Review* (Paris: Organisation for Economic Cooperation and Development, November 1985), p. 93. According to these statistics the GDR offered $98 million in aid in 1975–6. Discrepancies with previously quoted UN figures result, in part, from OECD estimates in 1983 prices and exchange rates, although precise details of East German development aid are difficult to acquire and assess accurately.

79 *Deutscher Bundestag*, Drucksache 8/3463, p. 6.

80 *OECD 1985 Report*, p. 93. These percentages of GNP were modified according to OECD figures released most recently. See Table 10. Note also that the percentage of West German GNP allocated to ODA has declined somewhat since 1983.

81 See Bernard von Plate, 'Die DDR und die Entwicklungsländer', *DDR-Report*, vol. 15, 2 (1982), p. 74, referring to US CIA figures.

82 *Against Racism*, p. 416.

83 According to Zdenek Cervenka, 'The two Germanies in Africa: increase of Bonn's aid and GDR military assistance', *ACR*, vol. 14 (1981–2), A196, obligations to support the Polish economy compelled the GDR to restructure economic activities in Africa where donations were reduced to 'symbolic acts of solidarity'.

84 See *Dokumente*, vol. 24, pt 2, p. 1089, speech by Sölle at the UNCTAD IV session, 10 May 1976; and *H*, Year 13, 33 (1980), p. 22.

85 Joseph Dolezal, 'Entwicklung, Ziele, Methoden und Instrumente der DDR – Aussenpolitik in der Dritten Welt', in Baske and Zieger (eds.), *Die Dritte Welt und die beiden Staaten*, p. 35.

86 Siegfried Büttner, 'DDR – Hilfe für Entwicklungsländer', *E*, Year 35, 10 (1980), p. 1081.

87 Hans-Joachim Spanger, 'DDR legt erstmals offizielle Zahlen über ihre Entwicklungshilfe vor', *DA*, vol. 16, 7 (1980), p. 681.

88 Coker, *The Soviet Union, Eastern Europe and the New International Economic Order*, pp. 77–9.

89 *OECD 1985 Report*, p. 118.

90 Karia Hahn and Eleanore Jacob, 'Charakter und Hauptformen der Wirtschaftsbeziehungen DDR-Entwicklungsländer', *AAL*, vol. 14, 1 (1986), pp. 5–14.

91 This list is by no means a comprehensive one. Details of credit commitments may be obtained from such sources as *ND*, *ACR*, and *EAKL*.

92 Gerhard Scharschmidt and Wolfgang Spröte, 'DDR an der Seite der Entwicklungsländer im Kampf um demokratische Umgestaltung der internationalen Wirtschaftsbeziehungen', *IPW-Berichte*, vol. 13, 9 (1984), pp. 16–22.

93 *Statistisches Jahrbuch*, Year 31, p. 247.

94 *ND*, 11 September 1984.

95 *Ibid.*, 23 August 1984.

96 *Ibid.*, 14 September 1984, Honecker was in Ethiopia on the occasion of the tenth anniversary of the Ethiopian Revolution. For further details, see chapter 6.

97 Cervenka and Dederichs, 'The two Germanies in Africa – Eastern advances', A158; and *NZZ*, 9 October 1980.

98 See Patrick Gutman, 'Tripartite industrial cooperation and Third countries', pp. 337–64, and Carl H. Macmillan, 'Comments on Part V – new forms of East–West–South cooperation', pp. 365–8, in Christopher T. Saunders (ed.), *East–West–South: Economic Interactions between Three Worlds* (London and Basingstoke: Macmillan, 1981).

99 *Proceedings of the United Nations*, 4th Session, vol. 1, UNCTAD TD/195, pp. 130–1; and *Proceedings of the United Nations*, 6th Session, vol. 1, Annex: 'Trade Relations among Countries having Different Economic and Social Systems and all Trade Flows Resulting Therefrom', pp. 31–2.

100 E.g., see, *Proceedings of the United Nations*, 4th Session, vol. 1, 'Joint Statement by the Socialist Countries', TD/211, p. 158; and, *Dokumente*, vol. 26, pt 2, p. 1029, Declaration by the delegation of socialist states on point 58(a) on the agenda of the 33rd session of the UN General Assembly, 17 October 1978.

101 Gutman, 'Tripartite industrial cooperation', p. 361.

102 This list is by no means comprehensive. See, *ibid.*, pp. 362–4, and, *EAKL* (various years).

103 Gutman, 'Tripartite industrial cooperation', p. 337.

104 Paul Friedländer, 'Intersystemare Kooperation in Entwicklungsländern – eine neue Strategische Linie des Neokolonialismus', *DAPK*, vol. 15, 4 (1970), pp. 589–90.

105 Sibylle Busch, 'Drittlandlandkooperation: Ost–West–Zusammenarbeit in dritten Ländern', *Osteuropa Wirtschaft*, vol. 28, 1 (1983), pp. 6 and 17.

106 For reference to the April 1975 agreement, see *The Economist*, 26 April 1975, pp. 111–12.
107 Siegfried Wenger, 'Wirtschaftszusammenarbeit der RGW-Länder mit den Entwicklungsländern', *DAPK*, vol. 21, 4 (1976), p. 547.
108 *Against Racism*, p. 280.
109 Noted by Paul Freiberg, Jürgen Nitz and Gerhard Scharschmidt, 'Zum Charakter der dreiseitigen Wirtschaftskooperation', *IPW-Berichte*, vol. 8, 2 (1979), p. 19.
110 Gerhard Scharschmidt, 'Stellung und Perspektiven der Ost–West-Zusammenarbeit auf Drittmarkten aus der Sicht der DDR', *IPW-Berichte*, vol. 13, 7 (1984), pp. 7–14.
111 Jürgen Nitz, 'GDR–FRG economic relations: determinants, trends and problems', in F. Stephen Larrabee (ed.), *The Two German States and European Security* (Basingstoke and London: Macmillan, in association with the Institute for East–West Security Studies, 1989), p. 303.
112 Lothar Kruss, Christine Fiedler, and Paul Freiberg, 'Wirtschaftliche Ost–West-Zusammenarbeit auf Drittmarkten', *IPW-Berichte*, vol. 13, 7 (1984), p. 28.
113 H, Year 17, 7 (1984), p. 23.
114 Rolf Hofmeier, 'West Germany and Africa – Between charity and self-interest', *ACR*, vol. 17 (1984–5), A201. Compare with the GDR's trade turnover with developing states in Table 1.

6 The GDR in Africa in the 1980s

1 Honecker, *Report . . . X Congress of the SED*, p. 38.
2 Bernard von Plate, 'Die DDR und Gesellschaftspolitische Entwicklungsmöglichkeiten in der Dritten Welt', in Baske and Zieger (eds.), *Die Dritte Welt und die Beiden Staaten*, pp. 94–9.
3 'Fruchtbarer Erfahrungsaustausch SED–COPWE – Interview mit Horst Dohlus, Mitglied des Politbüros und Sekretar des ZK der SED', H, Year 14, 52 (1981), p. 3.
4 *ND*, 10 September 1984.
5 *ND*, 5 December 1985.
6 Christopher Coker, 'The Soviet Union's year in Africa – the Gorbachev factor', *ACR*, vol. 18 (1985–6), A272–3.
7 *ND*, 18/19 February 1984.
8 *Ibid.*, 17/18 March 1984.
9 For reference to König's visits to Luanda and Maputo respectively, see *ND*, 17 April and 19 April 1984. For reference to the FRELIMO raid, see, *FAZ*, 26 March 1984.
10 *FAZ*, 22 April 1985.
11 *ARB*, vol. 19, 3 (1982), 6402.
12 For a general background discussion, see Keith Somerville, 'The Soviet Union and Zimbabwe: the liberation struggle and after', in Nation and Kauppi (eds.), *The Soviet Impact*, p. 197.
13 *ND*, 8 February 1977.

14 According to a private interview with Herr Horst Brasch in East Berlin, 3 April 1987 (referred to previously), the GDR preferred links with Nkomo rather than Mugabe on account of the former's trade unionist credentials. The importance of Soviet–Chinese rivalry was downplayed.
15 Coker, *NATO, the Warsaw Pact*, p. 194.
16 Post and Sandvoss, *Die Afrikapolitik der DDR*, p. 26.
17 *Die Welt*, 30 May and 2 June 1983.
18 Dunér, *The Bear, the Cubs*, p. 11.
19 David Martin and Phyllis Johnson, *The Struggle for Zimbabwe – The Chimurenga War* (London and Boston: Faber and Faber, 1981), p. 266.
20 Cervenka, 'The two Germanies in Africa during 1980', A151.
21 The USSR established diplomatic relations with Zimbabwe on 18 February 1981. Only Romania and Yugoslavia, in Eastern Europe, had established diplomatic relations with Zimbabwe before the GDR.
22 *ND*, 25 May 1983.
23 *Keesing's*, p. 32776.
24 Coker, 'The Soviet Union's Year in Africa', A274.
25 *ACR*, vol. 18 (1985–6), B929.
26 Rudi Bartlitz, 'Simbabwe – Vereinigung im Interesse der Nation', *H*, Year 21, 2 (1988), p. 11.
27 *ND*, 27 April 1988.
28 *Ibid.*, 28 April 1988.
29 Keith Somerville, 'China and Africa – maintaining a low profile', *ACR*, vol. 18 (1985–6), A200.
30 *ND*, 30/1 August 1986.
31 *Against Racism*, p. 420.
32 *ND*, 23/4 February 1985.
33 Horst Schötzki, 'Apartheid in Vergangenheit und Gegenwart – Südafrikas Rassisten in Wachsender Bedrängnis', *H*, Year 18, 9 (1985), p. 8.
34 Liebscher and Friedländer, 'Positionen und Aktivitaten des BRD-Neokolonialismus', p. 993.
35 *ND*, 25 August 1980.
36 *Frankfurter Rundschau*, 26 August 1980; and *Der Tagesspiegel*, 27 August 1980.
37 Ammer, 'Zu den Beziehungen DDR–Libyen', pp. 1–2.
38 For the texts of the treaties with the relevant articles, see *Dokumente*, 1980, vol. 28, pt 1 (1984), pp. 209–11, for Kampuchea. Article 8, p. 211; *ibid.*, pp. 275–9 for Cuba. Here, see Article 8, p. 278; *Dokumente*, 1982, vol. 30, (1985), pp. 130–1, for Laos. Here, see Article 8, p. 131; and, *ND*, 2/3 June 1984 for North Korea. See Article 9. For the text of the treaty with Afghanistan, see *Dokumente*, vol. 30, pp. 254–6.
39 The SADCC was formally inaugurated in April 1980. It is composed of a number of southern African states seeking through enhanced regional cooperation to become less economically dependent on South Africa.
40 Kenneth W. Grundy, 'South Africa in the political economy of Southern Africa', in Carter and O'Meara (eds.), *International Politics in Southern Africa*, pp. 165–6.
41 *Keesing's*, p. 30700.

42 Christopher Stevens, 'The EEC and Africa in 1982 – clearing the decks for Lomé III', *ACR*, vol. 15 (1982–3), A118.
43 *ACR*, vol. 15 (1982–3), B604.
44 Norman Macqueen, 'Mozambique's widening foreign policy', *The World Today*, vol. 40, 1 (1980), p. 26.
45 *Bundesgesetzblatt*, nr 39, pt 2 (16 November 1982), p. 964.
46 *The Guardian*, 1 May 1985.
47 *ACR*, vol. 16 (1983–4), B609.
48 Sandvoss, 'The German Democratic Republic's policies in Africa, 1983–1984', A182.
49 Nicos Zafiris, 'The People's Republic of Mozambique: pragmatic socialism', in Peter Wiles (ed.), *The New Communist Third World – An Essay in Political Economy* (London and Canberra: Croom Helm, 1982), p. 158.
50 Zaki Laidi, 'Room for Black Africa in the World Socialist System', *The Journal of Communist Studies*, vol. 1, 1 (1985), p. 64.
51 Lawson, 'The Soviet Union and Eastern Europe in Southern Africa', p. 37.
52 From a private interview with Herr Brasch cited above (n. 14). Herr Brasch stated that Vietnam's admission to the CMEA was exceptional after the Vietnamese economy had been devastated as a consequence of war with the US.
53 Renate Wünsche, 'Zur Bedeutung des internationalen Faktors für die Entwicklung der Befreiten Staaten in Asien, Afrika und Lateinamerika', *AAL*, vol. 11, 5 (1983), p. 845.
54 *ND*, 18 April 1986. The Libyan delegation was unable to attend on account of the US bombing of Tripoli.
55 *ND*, 6/7 October 1984.
56 *ND*, 18/19 September 1982.
57 *ND*, 4/5 October 1986.
58 *ND*, 18/19 May 1985.
59 Coker, *The Soviet Union, Eastern Europe and the New International Economic Order*, pp. 51–2.
60 *ND*, 29 November 1980.
61 Coker, 'The Soviet Union's year in Africa', A274.
62 *ND*, 7/8 February 1987.
63 *ND*, 27 February and 29 May 1987.
64 *ND*, 21 April 1987.
65 Winrow, 'East German foreign policy', pp. 69–71.
66 *ND*, 20 December 1984.
67 *ND*, 20 December 1984.
68 *ND*, 8 May and 3 December 1986.
69 *ND*, 6 July 1987.
70 Honecker, *Bericht . . . XI Parteitag der SED*, p. 18.
71 *Keesing's*, p. 31253.
72 Galia Golan, 'Gorbachev's Middle East strategy', *Foreign Affairs*, vol. 66, 1 (1987), p. 49.
73 *ND*, 29 November 1983.
74 *ND*, 19 June 1986.

75 *ND*, 26 September 1986.
76 *ND*, 22/3 December 1984.
77 *Die Welt*, 15/16 September 1984.
78 For Honecker's trip to Ethiopia in September 1984, see *ND*, 13 and 14 September 1984. For Mengistu's visit to the GDR in April 1986 and his meeting with Honecker, see, *ND*, 13 April 1986.
79 *Proceedings of the United Nations*, 6th Session, vol. 1, pp. 151–2, 'Assistance given by the German Democratic Republic . . .', TD/304.
80 E.g., for the equivalent statistics for 1986, see, *ND*, 19/20 March 1988.
81 *ND*, 4 March 1983.
82 *Berliner Zeitung*, 17 August 1984.
83 *ND*, 5 and 7/8 February 1987.
84 *ND*, 19 September 1983.
85 *ND*, 22 September 1986.
86 *ND*, 23 April 1987.
87 Eberhard Fröhlich, 'Aspekte der Gewerkschaftsbewegung Afrikas', *H*, Year 20, 8 (1987), p. 10.
88 Noted by Alvin Z. Rubinstein, 'A Third World policy waits for Gorbachev', *Orbis*, vol. 30, 2 (1986), pp. 358–9.
89 Noted by Francis Fukuyama, 'Patterns of Soviet Third World policy', *P of C*, vol. 36, 5 (1987), p. 7.
90 Melvin A. Goodman, 'The Soviet Union and the Third World: the military dimension', in Korbonski and Fukuyama (eds.) *The Soviet Union and the Third World*, p. 61.
91 Fukuyama, 'Patterns of Soviet Third World policy', p. 7.
92 Honecker, *Report . . .X Congress of the SED*, p. 39; and, Honecker, *Bericht . . . XI Parteitag der SED*, p. 20.
93 Honecker, *Bericht . . . XI Parteitag der SED*, pp. 17–19.
94 See Wolfgang Gabelein and Andrej Reder, 'Die Entwicklungsländer in den Kämpfen unserer Zeit', *AAL*, vol. 14, 6 (1986), pp. 949–60. For the equivalent Soviet views, see Elizabeth Kridl Valkenier, 'Revolutionary change in the Third World – recent Soviet assessments', *World Politics*, vol. 38, 3 (1986), pp. 415–22.
95 Klaus Hutschenreuter and Albin Kress, 'Afrika – 25 Jahre nach der historischen Wende', *H*, Year 18, 10 (1985), pp. 8–9.
96 Honecker, *Bericht . . . XI Parteitag der SED*, p. 19.
97 *ND*, 23/4 August 1980.
98 Axel Reschke, 'DDR/Sambia – Erste Schritte der Kooperation', *H*, Year 14, 24 (1981), p. 23.
99 *ACR*, vol. 18 (1985–6), B900.
100 Dieter Volk, 'Moçambique – Lage analysiert', *H*, Year 21, 4 (1988); and Gerhard Wendorf, 'Angola – Programm zur ökonomischen Gesundung', *H*, Year 21, 3 (1988), p. 19. The latter article reported favourably on Angola's efforts to secure admission to the International Monetary Fund and the World Bank. Mozambique is already a member of these organisations.
101 *ND*, 23 October 1986.

102 Helmut Faulwetter, 'Entwicklungsländer organisierien wirtschaftliche Zusammenarbeit', *H*, Year 19, 3 (1986), p. 27; and Thomas Friedländer, 'Kolonialismus, Neokolonialismus und der Weg Afrikas in eine friedliche Zukunft', *IPW-Berichte*, vol. 14, 7 (1985), pp. 38–40.

103 See *DA*, vol. 21, 1 (1988), pp. 86–91 for text of the SED–SPD Joint Declaration.

104 Joachim Raabe, 'Dialog zu Problemen der Entwicklungsländer', *H*, Year 19, 12 (1987), p. 10.

105 Spanger and Brock, *Die beiden deutschen Staaten in der Dritten Welt*, pp. 119–20.

106 Helmut Zapf, 'Das antiimperialistische Potential der national befreiten Länder – methodologische und bündnisstrategische Aspekte aus der Sicht des Wissenschaftlichen Kommunismus', *AAL*, vol. 14, 3 (1986), pp. 386–94.

107 Gabelein and Reder, 'Die Entwicklungsländer in den Kämpfen unserer Zeit', pp. 949–60.

108 Mark N. Katz, 'Anti-Soviet insurgencies: growing trend or passing phase?', *Orbis*, vol. 30, 2 (1986), pp. 368–70; and, Coker, 'Pact, pox or proxy', p. 88.

109 Helmut Mardek, 'Das Ringen um die politische Lösung regionaler Konflikte – wesentlicher Beitrag zu Frieden und Sicherheit', *AAL*, vol. 16, 2 (1988), pp. 197–207.

110 *ND*, 21 June 1985.

111 *ND*, 23 December 1988.

112 Helga Witte, 'Südwestliches Afrika – Bemerkenswert Fortschritt', *H*, Year 21, 10 (1988), p. 20.

113 *ND*, 23 and 29 December 1988.

114 *ND*, 25 May 1989.

115 See J. E. Spence, 'A deal for southern Africa', *The World Today*, vol. 45, 5 (1989), pp. 81–2; and by the same author, *The Soviet Union, the Third World and Southern Africa* (Bloomfontein: The South African Institute of International Affairs, Bradlow Series, no. 5, 1988), pp. 27–8.

116 *Financial Times*, 27 and 28 April 1989.

117 'Regionale Konflikte – Der Stand ihrer Regelung', *H*, Year 21, 12 (1988), pp. 16–17.

118 *ND*, 20 December 1984.

119 *ND*, 14 July 1988.

120 *ND*, 17 May 1989.

121 *ND*, 18 May 1989.

122 *ND*, 27 June 1989.

123 *The Independent*, 13 March 1989.

124 *IHT*, 14 July 1989.

7 Conclusion

1 *ND*, 9 September 1987.

2 Ulla Plener, 'Dokumentation – Zu den Bewegungen der Solidarität und dem Kampf der Völker Afrikas, Asiens und Lateinamerikas in den 80er Jahren', *IPW-Berichte*, vol. 17, 7 (1988), pp. 58–61.

3 Croan, 'The Germanies at 30(1)', pp. 153–4.
4 Coker, 'East Germany and Southern Africa', *Journal of Social and Political Studies*, vol. 5, 3 (1980), pp. 236–7.
5 This line of argument was offered by Herr Brasch in a private interview referred to previously.
6 Childs, *The GDR*, p. 291.
7 Radu (ed.), *Eastern Europe and the Third World*, is the only recent publication in English with articles discussing individually the policies of East European states in the Third World. However, even this publication has no analysis of Bulgaria's relations with the Third World.
8 Dunér, *The Bear, the Cubs*, pp. 185–6.

Select bibliography

Abbreviations

AAL   Asien, Afrika, Lateinamerika
ACR   Africa Contemporary Record
DA   Deutschland Archiv
DAPK   Deutsche Aussenpolitik
E   Einheit
P of C   Problems of Communism
FAZ   Frankfurter Allgemeine Zeitung

Africa Confidential.
Africa Research Bulletin.
Against Racism, Apartheid and Colonialism – Documents published by the GDR,
   1977–1982 (Dresden: Verlag zeit im Bild, 1983).
Albright, David E. (ed.). *Africa and International Communism* (London and
   Basingstoke: Macmillan, 1980).
Ammer, Thomas. 'Zu den Beziehungen DDR–Angola', Paper of the *Gesamt-
   deutsches Institut-Bundesanstalt für Gesamtdeutsche Aufgaben*, Bonn, 22
   March 1979.
   'Zu den Beziehungen DDR–Libyen', Paper of the *Gesamtdeutsches Institut*,
   Bonn, 6 September 1983.
Asmus, Ronald. 'The East German search for oil', *Radio Free Europe Research*,
   RAD Background Report/187 GDR (25 July 1980).
Auswärtiges Amt der Bundesrepublik Deutschland (ed.). *Die Auswärtige
   Politik der Bundesrepublik Deutschland* (Cologne: Verlag Wissenschaft und
   Politik, 1972).
Baatz, Wolfgang. 'Zur Militärhilfe der BRD an afrikanische Nationalstaaten',
   AAL, vol. 2, 6 (1974), pp. 947–58.
Baerwald, Siegfried. 'Die Länder Asiens und Afrikas einig im Kampf um den
   Frieden', *E*, Year 10, 5 (1955), pp. 493–7.
Baske, Siegfried and Zieger, Gottfried (eds.). *Die Dritte Welt und die beiden
   Staaten in Deutschland* (Asperg, Stuttgart: Edition Meyn, Gesellschaft für
   Deutschlandforschung Jahrbuch, 1982, 1983).

266

Bericht der Bundesregierung und Materialien zur Lage der Nation, 1971 (Bonn: Bundesministerium für innerdeutsche Beziehungen).

Bischof, Henrik (ed.). *Entwicklungspolitik Kommunistischer Länder – Trends und Analysen* (Bonn: Forschungsinstitut der Friedrich-Ebert-Stiftung).

Blaustein, Albert P. and Flanz, Gisbert H. (eds.). *Constitutions of the Countries of the World*, Binder 6 (Dobbs Ferry, New York: Oceana Publications, 1987).

Brzezinski, Zbigniew. *The Soviet Bloc – Unity and Conflict* (Cambridge, Mass.: Harvard University Press, 2nd edn, 1971).

Bulletin des Presse- und Informationsamtes der Bunderegierung (Bonn).

Busch, Sibylle. 'Drittlandlandkooperation: Ost–West-Zusammenarbeit in dritten Ländern', *Osteuropa Wirtschaft*, vol. 28, 1 (1983), pp. 1–21.

Büttner, Siegfried. 'DDR-Hilfe fur Entwicklungsländer', *E*, Year 35, 10 (1980), pp. 1081–2.

Carter, Gwendolen M. and O'Meara, Patrick (eds.). *International Politics in Southern Africa* (Bloomington: Indiana University Press, 1982).

Cassen, Robert (ed.). *Soviet Interests in the Third World* (London and Beverly Hills: Sage Publications for the Royal Institute for International Affairs, 1985).

Cervenka, Zdenek. 'The two Germanies and Africa during 1980 – Rivals for influence', *ACR*, vol. 13 (1980–1), A140–52.

'The two Germanies in Africa: increase of Bonn's aid and GDR military assistance', *ACR*, vol. 14 (1981–2), A188–200.

Cervenka, Zdenek and Dederichs, Mario R. 'The two Germanies and Africa', *ACR*, vol. 11 (1978–9), A92–108.

'The two Germanies and Africa – Eastern advances and Western isolationism', *ACR*, vol. 12 (1979–80), A146–61.

Chaigneau, P. and Sola, R. 'North Korea as an African power: a threat to French interests', *Institute for Strategic Studies, University of Pretoria, Strategic Review* (December 1986), pp. 1–19.

Childs, David. *The GDR: Moscow's German Ally* (London: Allen and Unwin, 1983).

Coker, Christopher. *The Soviet Union, Eastern Europe and the New International Economic Order*, The Washington Papers, vol. 12, 111 (New York: Praeger, with the Center for Strategic and International Studies, Georgetown University, 1984).

NATO, the Warsaw Pact and Africa (London and Basingstoke: Macmillan, 1985).

'East Germany and Southern Africa', *Journal of Social and Political Studies*, vol. 5, 3 (1980), pp. 231–44.

'Adventurism and pragmatism: the Soviet Union, COMECON and relations with African states', *International Affairs*, vol. 57, 4 (1981), pp. 618–33.

'The Soviet Union's Year in Africa – the Gorbachev Factor', *ACR*, vol. 18 (1985–6), A267–84.

'Pact, pox or proxy: Eastern Europe's security relationship with Southern Africa', *Soviet Studies*, vol. 40, 4 (1988), pp. 573–84.

'The Soviet Union and Eastern Europe: patterns of competition and collaboration in Southern Africa', in Nation and Kauppi (eds.) (1984), pp. 59–85.

'Eastern Europe and the Middle East: the forgotten dimension of Soviet policy', in Cassen (ed.) (1985), pp. 46–67.

Collection of the Agreements Concluded by the European Communities, vols. 6 and 11 (Luxembourg: Office for Official Publications of the European Communities, 1979 and 1985).

Croan, Melvin. East Germany: The Soviet Connection, The Washington Papers, vol. 4, 36 (Beverly Hills and London: Sage Publications for the Center of Strategic and International Studies, Georgetown University, Washington DC, 1976).

'The Germanies at 30(1), "New country, old nationality"', Foreign Policy, no. 37 (1979–80), pp. 142–60.

'A New Afrika Korps?', The Washington Quarterly, no. 4 (Winter 1980), pp. 21–37.

Crozier, Brian. 'The surrogate forces of the Soviet Union', Conflict Studies, no. 92 (1978).

Dawisha, Adeed and Dawisha, Karen (eds.). The Soviet Union in the Middle East: policies and perspectives (London: Heinemann, for the Royal Institute of International Affairs, 1982).

Dawisha, Karen and Hanson, Philip (eds.). Soviet–East European Dilemmas: Coercion, Competition and Consent (London: Heinemann, for the Royal Institute of International Affairs, 1981).

Der Spiegel.

Deutscher Bundestag, Stenographische Berichte (Bonn).

Deutscher Bundestag, 8 Wahlperiode, Drucksache 8/3463, 4 December 1979 (Bonn).

Doeker, Günther, Jens A. Bruckner and Ralph Freiberg (eds.). The Federal Republic of Germany and the German Democratic Republic in International Relations, vols. 1 and 3 (Dobbs Ferry, New York and Alphen aan den Rijn: Oceana Publications and Sijthoff and Noordhoff, 1979).

Dokumente zur Aussenpolitik der Deutschen Demokratischen Republik, vols. 11–30 (Berlin [East]: Staatsverlag der DDR, 1965–1985).

Dokumente zur Aussenpolitik der Regierung der Deutschen Demokratischen Republik, vols. 1–10 (Berlin [East]: Rütten and Loening, 1954–63).

Dolezal, Joseph. 'Entwicklung, Ziele, Methoden und Instrumente der DDR-Aussenpolitik in der Dritten Welt', in Baske and Zieger (eds.) (1983), pp. 29–61.

Dummer, Egon and Langer, Emil. 'Grundtendenzen der nationalen Befreiungsbewegung', E, Year 35, 1 (1980), pp. 9–16.

Dunér, Bertil. The Bear, the Cubs and the Eagle – Soviet Bloc Interventionism in the Third World and the US Response (Aldershot, Hants., Brookfield, USA, Hong Kong, Singapore, and Sydney: Gower, for the Swedish Institute of International Affairs, Swedish Studies in International Relations no. 22, 1987).

'Proxy intervention in civil wars', Journal of Peace Research, vol. 18, 4 (1981), pp. 353–61.

End, Heinrich. Zweimal deutsche Aussenpolitik – Internationale Dimension des innerdeutschen Konflikts, 1949–1972 (Cologne: Verlag Wissenschaft und Politik, 1973).

Florin, Peter. *Deutscher Aussenpolitik, zur Aussenpolitik der souveränen sozialistischen DDR* (Berlin [East]: Dietz Verlag, 1967).

Forster, Thomas M. *The East German Army – The Second Power in the Warsaw Pact*, trans. by Derecyk Viney (London: Allen and Unwin, 1980).

Freiberg, Paul, Jürgen Nitz and Gerhard Scharschmidt. 'Zum Charakter der dreiseitigen Wirtschaftskooperation', *IPW-Berichte*, vol. 8, 2 (1979), pp. 17–28.

Friedländer, Paul. 'Intersystemare Kooperation in Entwicklungsländern – eine neue Strategische Linie des Neokolonialismus', *DAPK*, vol. 15, 4 (1970), pp. 588–97.

Friedländer, Thomas. 'Kolonialismus, Neokolonialismus und der Weg Afrikas in eine friedliche Zukunft', *IPW-Berichte*, vol. 14, 7 (1985), pp. 38–40.

Fukuyama, Francis. 'Patterns of Soviet Third World policy', *P of C*, vol. 36, 5 (1987), pp. 1–13.

Gabelein, Wolfgang and Andrej Reder. 'Die Entwicklungsländer in den Kämpfen unserer Zeit', *AAL*, vol. 14, 6 (1986), pp. 949–60.

Glass, George. 'East Germany in Black Africa: a new special role?', *The World Today*, vol. 36, 8 (1980), pp. 305–12.

Greig, Ian. 'East Germany's drive for influence in Africa', *Institute for Strategic Studies, University of Pretoria, Strategic Review* (June 1985), pp. 19–26.

Grewe, Wilhelm G. *Deutsche Aussenpolitik der Nachkriegszeit* (Stuttgart: Deutsche Verlags-anstalt, 1960).

Gutman, Patrick. 'Tripartite industrial cooperation and third countries', in Saunders (ed.) (1981), pp. 337–64.

Gutmann, Gernot and Haendcke-Hoppe, Maria (eds.). *Die Aussenbeziehungen der DDR* (Heidelberg: Edition Meyn, Gesellschaft fur Deutschlandforschung Jahrbuch 1980, 1981).

Haendcke-Hoppe, Maria. 'Die DDR-Aussenwirtschaft am Beginn des Fünfjahrplanperiode 1986–1990', *DA*, vol. 20, 1 (1987), pp. 49–55.

Hahn, Karia and Eleonore, Jacob. 'Charakter und Hauptformen der Wirtschaftsbeziehungen DDR-Entwicklungslander', *AAL*, vol. 14, 1 (1986), pp. 5–14.

Halliday, Fred and Maxine Molyneux. *The Ethiopian Revolution* (London: Verso editions and NLB, 1981).

Heikal, Mohamed. *Nasser – The Cairo Documents* (London: The New English Library, 1972).

Hillebrand, Ernst. *Das Afrıka-Engagement der DDR* (Frankfurt, Bern, New York and Paris: Verlag Peter Lang, Münchner Studien zur internationalen Entwicklung, vol. 5, 1987).

Hoffmann, Heinz. 'Die sozialistische Militärkoalition – zuverlässiger Schild des Sozialismus', *E*, Year 35, 5 (1980), pp. 474–81.

Holsti, K. J. *International Politics – A Framework for Analysıs* (Englewood Cliffs, New Jersey: Prentice-Hall International, 4th edn, 1983).

Honecker, Erich. *Bericht des Zentralkomitees der Sozialistischen Einheitspartei Deutschlands an der IX Parteitag der SED* (Berlin [East]: Dietz Verlag, 1976).
Report of the Central Committee of the Socialist Unity Party of Germany to the X Congress of the SED (Dresden: Verlag Zeit im Bild, 1981).

Bericht des Zentralkomitees der Sozialistischen Einheitspartei Deutschlands an der XI Parteitag der SED (Berlin [East]: Dietz Verlag, 1986).

Horizont.

Hosmer, Stephen T. and Thomas W. Wolfe. *Soviet Policy and Practice toward Third World Conflicts* (Lexington, Mass. and Toronto: Lexington Books, D.C. Heath, 1983).

Hottinger, Arnold. 'Die Hintergründe der Einladung Ulbrichts nach Kairo', *Europa Archiv*, vol. 19, 20 (1965), pp. 107–14.

Jacobsen, Hans Adolph, Gert Leptin, Ulrich Scheuner and Eberhard Schulz (eds.). *Drei Jahrzehnte Aussenpolitik der DDR* (Munich and Vienna: R. Oldenbourg Verlag, 1979).

Jacobsen, Hans-Dieter. 'Strategie und Schwerpunkte der Aussenwirtschafts-beziehungen', in Jacobsen *et al.* (eds.) (1979), pp. 293–311.

Joswiakowski, Gerhard. '"Portugiesisch" – Guinea im Kampf gegen Salazar und NATO', *DAPK*, vol. 7, 6 (1962), pp. 703–5.

Keesing's Contemporary Archives.

Klein, Peter, Herbert Krüger, Joachim Krüger, Karl Seidel and Johannes Zelt. *Geschichte der Aussenpolitik der Deutschen Demokratischen Republik – Abriss* (Berlin [East]: Dietz Verlag, 1968).

Korbonski, Andrzej. 'Eastern Europe and the Third World; or "limited regret strategy" revisited', in Korbonski and Fukuyama (eds.) (1987), pp. 94–122.

Korbonski, Andrzej and Francis Fukuyama (eds.). *The Soviet Union and the Third World – The Last Three Decades* (Ithaca and London: Cornell University Press, from the RAND-UCLA Center for the Study of Soviet International Behaviour, 1987).

Kruss, Lothar, Christine Fiedler and Paul Freiberg. 'Wirtschaftliche Ost–West-Zusammenarbeit auf Drittmärkten', *IPW-Berichte*, vol. 13, 7 (1984), pp. 27–31.

Kuhne, Winrich and Bernard von Plate. 'Two Germanies in Africa', *Africa Report*, vol. 25, 4 (1980), pp. 11–15.

Kuppe, Johannes. 'Investitionen, die sich lohnten – Zur Reise Honeckers nach Afrika', *DA*, vol. 12, 4 (1979), pp. 347–52.

Kupper, Siegfried in cooperation with Alparslan Yenal and Roswitha Zastrow. *Die Tätigkeit der DDR in den nichtkommunistischen Ländern – VI – arabische Staaten und Israel* (Bonn: Forschungsinstitut der Deutchen Gesellschaft für Auswärtige Politik, 1971).

Lamm, Hans Siegfried and Siegfried Kupper. *DDR und Dritte Welt* (Munich and Vienna: R. Oldenbourg Verlag, 1976).

Lawson, Colin. 'The Soviet Union and Eastern Europe in Southern Africa: is there a conflict of interest?', *International Affairs*, vol. 59, 1 (1982/3), pp. 32–40.

Le Monde.

Liebscher, Gertraud. 'Die Afrika-Politik des BRD-Imperialismus', *DAPK*, vol. 23, 5 (1978), pp. 89–102.

Liebscher, Gertraud and Thomas Friedländer. 'Positionen und Aktivitäten des BRD-Neokolonialismus zu Beginn der Achtziger Jahre', *AAL*, vol. 10, 6 (1982), pp. 985–94.

Löwenthal, Richard and Boris Meissner (eds.). *Der Sowjetblock zwischen Vormachtkontrolle und Autonomie* (Cologne: Markus Verlag, 1984).

Ludwig, Harald. 'Die "DDR" in Afrika (I) – Der Einfluss der SBZ auf die unabhängigen afrikanischen Lander', *SBZ Archiv*, no. 6 (1965), pp. 83–6.

'Die "DDR" in Afrika (II) – Die Aktivität in den arabischen Ländern', *SBZ Archiv*, no. 22 (1965), pp. 351–6.

Mampel, Siegfried and Karl C. Thalheim (eds.). *Die DDR – Partner oder Satellit der Sowjetunion?* (Munich: Politica Verlag, Gesellschaft für Deutschlandforschung Jahrbuch 1979, 1980).

Mardek, Helmut. 'Das Ringen um die politische Losung regionaler Konflikte – wesentlicher Beitrag zu Frieden und Sicherheit', *AAL*, vol. 16, 2 (1988), pp. 197–207.

Marsh, William W. 'East Germany and Africa', *Africa Report*, vol. 14, 3–4 (1969), pp. 59–64.

Materialien zum Bericht zur Lage im geteilten Deutschland, 1987. Deutscher Bundestag, 11 Wahlperiode, Drucksache 11/11, 18 February 1987 (Bonn).

Matthies, Volker. 'Die Staatenwelt zwischen Sahara und Sambesi', in Schwarz (ed.) (1975), pp. 325–31.

McAdams, A. James. *East Germany and Détente – Building Authority after the Wall* (Cambridge: Cambridge University Press, 1985).

'The new logic in Soviet–GDR relations', *P of C*, vol. 37, 5 (1988), pp. 47–60.

McCauley, Martin. *Marxism–Leninism in the German Democratic Republic – The Socialist Unity Party (SED)* (London and Basingstoke: Macmillan, 1979).

Meissner, Boris. 'Die völkerrechtichen Beziehungen zwischen der DDR und der Sowjetunion auf dem Hintergrund der Bündnisverträge', in Mampel and Thalheim (eds.) (1980), pp. 143–62.

'The GDR's position in the Soviet alliance system', *Aussenpolitik* (English edition), vol. 35, 4 (1984), pp. 369–89.

Moreton, N. Edwina. 'The Impact of Détente on Relations Between the Member States of the Warsaw Pact: Efforts to Resolve the German Problem and Their Implications for East Germany's Role in Eastern Europe. 1967–1972' (University of Glasgow: unpub. Ph.D. thesis, 1976).

'Foreign Policy Perspectives in Eastern Europe', in Dawisha and Hanson (eds.) (1981), pp. 172–94.

'The East Europeans and the Cubans in the Middle East: Surrogates or Allies?', in Dawisha and Dawisha (eds.) (1982), pp. 62–84.

(ed.). *Germany between East and West* (Cambridge: Cambridge University Press, in association with the Royal Institute of International Affairs, 1987).

Müller, Kurt. *The Foreign Aid Programs of the Soviet Bloc and Communist China*, trans. Richard H. Weber and Michael Roloff (New York: Walker, 1967).

Nation, R. Craig and Mark V. Kauppi (eds.). *The Soviet Impact in Africa* (Lexington, Mass.: Lexington Books, D.C. Heath, 1984).

Neues Deutschland.

Niblock, Timothy C. *Aid and Foreign Policy in Tanzania. 1961–68* (University of Sussex: unpub. D.Phil. thesis, 1971).

Nimschowski, Helmut. 'Probleme der Einheitsfront der antiimperialistischdemokratischen Kräfte in Staaten mit sozialistischer Orientierung', *AAL*, vol. 5, 4 (1977), pp. 535–45.

Nitz, Jürgen. 'GDR–FRG economic relations: determinants, trends and problems', in F. Stephen Larrabee (ed.), *The Two German States and European Security* (Basingstoke and London: Macmillan in association with The Institute for East–West Security Studies, 1989), pp. 293–307.

OECD 1985 Report – Twenty-Five Years of Development Cooperation – A Review (Paris: Organisation for Economic Cooperation and Development, 1985).

Oldenburg, Fred. 'Die Autonomie des Musterknaben – zum politischen Verhältnis DDR–UdSSR', in Löwenthal and Meissner (eds.) (1984), pp. 153–97.

'East German foreign and security interests', in Moreton (ed.) (1987), pp. 108–22.

Piazza, Hans. 'Die Grundlegung der Bündnispolitik der SED mit den Völkern Asiens, Afrikas und Lateinamerikas (1946 bis 1949)', *AAL*, vol. 4, 3 (1976), pp. 333–42.

Plener, Ulla. 'Dokumentation – Zu den Bewegungen der Solidarität mit dem Kampf der Völker Afrikas, Asiens und Lateinamerikas in den 80er Jahren', *IPW-Berichte*, vol. 17, 7 (1988), pp. 58–61.

Post, Ulrich and Frank Sandvoss. *Die Afrikapolitik der DDR* (Hamburg: Institut für Afrika-Kunde im verbund der Stiftung Deutsches Übersee-Institut, Arbeiten aus dem Institut für Afrika-Kunde, 43, 1982).

Pötschke, Günter. 'Die Belgrader konferenz nichtpaktgebundener Staaten – ein Sieg der Kräfte des Friedens', *E*, Year 16, 10 (1961), pp. 1151–61.

Proceedings of the United Nations Conference on Trade and Development, 4th Session, 5–31 May 1976, Nairobi, vol. 1, Report and Annexes (New York: United Nations, 1977).

Proceedings of the United Nations Conference on Trade and Development, 6th Session, 6 June–2 July 1983, Belgrade, vol. 1, Report and Annexes (New York: United Nations, 1984).

Radde, Jürgen. *Die aussenpolitische Führungselite der DDR – Veränderungen der sozialen Struktur aussenpolitischer Führungsgruppen* (Cologne: Verlag Wissenschaft und Politik, 1976).

Radu, Michael (ed.). *Eastern Europe and the Third World – East vs. South* (New York: Praeger, 1981).

Reime, Sibyl. *Die Tätigkeit der DDR in den nichtkommunistischen Ländern – VIII – Schwarzafrika* (Bonn: Forschungsinstitut der Deutchen Gesellschaft für Auswärtige Politik, 1972).

Robinson, William F. 'Eastern Europe's presence in Black Africa', *Radio Free Europe*, RAD Background Report/142 Eastern Europe, 21 June 1979.

Rosenau, James N. 'Pre-theories and theories of foreign policy', in R. Barry Farrell (ed.) *Approaches to Comparative and International Politics* (Evanston: Northwestern University Press, 1966), pp. 27–92.

Sandvoss, Frank. 'The German Democratic Republic's policies in Africa, 1982–1983, balancing aid with trade', *ACR*, vol. 16 (1983–4), A217–24.

'The German Democratic Republic's policies in Africa, 1983–1984 – a balance sheet of losses and gains', *ACR*, vol. 17 (1984–5), A179–85.

Saunders, Christopher T. (ed.). *East–West–South: Economic Interactions between Three Worlds* (London and Basingstoke: Macmillan, 1981).

Scharschmidt, Gerhard. 'Stellung und Perspektiven der Ost–West–Zusammenarbeit auf Drittmärkten aus der Sicht der DDR', *IPW-Berichte*, vol. 13, 7 (1984), pp. 7–14.

Scharschmidt, Gerhard and Wolfgang Spröte. 'DDR an der Seite der Entwicklungsländer im Kampf um demokratische Umgestaltung der Internationalen Wirtschaftsbeziehungen', *IPW-Berichte*, vol. 13, 9 (1984), pp. 16–22.

Schatten, Fritz. 'Zur Afrikapolitik des deutschen Kommunismus – Grundlagen, Absichten, Schwerpunkte', *Der Ostblock und die Entwicklungsländer*, no. 19 (1965), pp. 15–27.

Schleicher, Ilona. 'Internationalistische Entwicklung der FRELIMO und ihre Beziehungen zur SED', *DAPK*, vol. 24, 7 (1979), pp. 62–76.

Schloesser, Klaus-Ulrich. 'Zur Rolle der Armee in national befreiten Staaten Asiens und Afrikas', *DAPK*, vol. 27, 10 (1982), pp. 64–75.

Schoeller, Wolfgang. '"Komparativer Nachteil" und "wechselseitiger Nutzen" – zur Kooperation zwischen COMECON und Entwicklungsländern am Beispiel Mosambiks', *DA*, vol. 16, 12 (1983), pp. 1303–11.

Schuster, Rudolph. 'Die "Hallstein-Doktrin" – ihre rechtliche und politische Bedeutung und die Grenzen ihrer Wirksamkeit', *Europa Archiv*, vol. 17, 18 (1963), pp. 675–90.

Schwarz, Hans-Peter (ed.). *Handbuch der deutschen Aussenpolitik* (Munich and Zurich: R. Piper Verlag, 1975).

Sieber, Günter. 'Bruder haben sie in aller Welt!', *E*, Year 43, 11–12 (1988), pp. 1036–41.

Snitch, Thomas H. 'East European involvement in the world's arms market', in US ACDA (1984), pp. 117–21.

Sodaro, Michael. 'The GDR and the Third World: supplicant and surrogate', in Radu (ed.) (1981), pp. 106–41.

Sodaro, Michael J. and Sharon L. Wolchik (eds.). *Foreign and Domestic Policy in Eastern Europe in the 1980s – Trends and Prospects* (London and Basingstoke: Macmillan, 1983).

Spanger, Hans-Joachim. 'DDR legt erstmals offizielle Zahlen über ihre Entwicklungshilfe vor', *DA*, vol. 16, 7 (1980), pp. 681–3.

'Die beiden deutschen Staaten in der Dritten Welt I', *DA*, vol. 17, 1 (1984), pp. 30–50.

'Militärpolitik und Militarisches Engagement der DDR in der Dritten Welt', *DA*, vol. 18, 8 (1985), pp. 832–45.

Spanger, Hans-Joachim and Lothar Brock. *Die beiden deutschen Staaten in der Dritten Welt – Die Entwicklungspolitik der DDR – eine Herausforderung fur die Bundesrepublik Deutschland?* (Westdeutscher Verlag, Opladen, 1987).

Starrels, John M. *East Germany – Marxist Mission in Africa* (Washington DC: The Heritage Foundation, 1981).

Statistisches Jahrbuch der Deutschen Demokratischen Republik, vols. 10–32 (Berlin [East]: Staatsverlag der DDR, 1966–1988).

Stockholm International Peace Research Institute. *The Arms Trade with the Third World* (Uppsala: Almqvist and Wiksells, 1971).

SIPRI. *Yearbook 1983: World Armaments and Disarmament* (New York and London: Taylor and Francis, 1983).

Suhrke, Astri. 'Gratuity or tyranny: the Korean alliances', *World Politics*, vol. 25, 4 (1973), pp. 508–32.

Thompson, W. Scott. *Ghana's Foreign Policy, 1957–1966 – Diplomacy, Ideology and the New State* (Princeton: Princeton University Press, 1969).

US Arms Control and Disarmament Agency. *World Military Expenditures and Arms Transfers 1972–1982*, ACDA Publication 117 (Washington DC: US Government Printing Office, 1984).

US ACDA *World Military Expenditures and Arms Transfers 1987*, ACDA Publication 128 (Washington DC: US Government Printing Office, 1988).

Volksarmee.

Valenta, Jiri and Shannon Butler. 'East German security policies in Africa', in Radu (ed.) (1981), pp. 142–68.

Von Löwis of Menar, Henning. 'Das Engagement der DDR im Portugiesischen Afrika', *DA*, vol. 10, 1 (1977), pp. 33–42.

'Solidarität und Subversion – Die Rolle der DDR im südichen Afrika', *DA*, vol. 10, 6 (1977), pp. 643–8.

'Das politische und militärische Engagement der Deutschen Demokratischen Republik in Schwarzafrika – Ein Überblick von 1953 bis 1978', *Beiträge zur Konfliktforschung*, vol. 8, 1 (1978), pp. 5–54.

'Das Afrikanische Erbe von Werner Lamberz – Ost-Berlins Äthiopien-Abenteur', *DA*, vol. 11, 3 (1978), pp. 348–51.

'SED-Journalismus als Exportartikel – Die journalistische Entwicklungshilfe der DDR', *DA*, vol. 12, 10 (1979), pp. 1016–8.

'Die DDR als Schrittmacher im Weltrevolutionaren Prozess – Zur Honecker-Visite in Äthiopien und im Südjemen', *DA*, vol. 13, 1 (1980), pp. 40–9.

'Machtpolitik südlich des Sambesi – Sambia und Moçambique als Adressaten der DDR-Aussenpolitik', *DA*, vol. 13, 11 (1980), pp. 1161–71.

'Die DDR und Afrika', in Gutmann and Haendcke-Hoppe (eds.) (1981), pp. 221–30.

'Militärisches und Paramilitärisches Engagement der DDR in der Dritten Welt', in Baske and Zieger (eds.) (1983), pp. 125–40.

Von Plate, Bernard. 'Aspekte der SED-Parteibeziehungen in Afrika und der arabischen Region', *DA*, vol. 12, 2 (1980), pp. 132–49.

'Die Handelsbeziehungen der DDR mit den Entwicklungsländern und die neue Weltwirtschaftsordnung', *DA*, vol. 13, 8 (1980), pp. 819–33.

'Der Nahe und Mittlere Osten sowie der Maghreb', in Jacobsen *et al.* (eds.) (1979), pp. 673–98.

'Die DDR und Gesellschaftspolitische Entwicklungsmöglichkeiten in der Dritten Welt', in Baske and Zieger (eds.) (1983), pp. 93–108.

Wenger, Siegfried. 'Wirtschaftszusammenarbeit der RGW-Länder mit den Entwicklungsländern', *DAPK*, vol. 21, 4 (1976), pp. 531–52.

Willerding, Klaus. 'Die DDR und die national befreiten Staaten Asiens und Afrikas', *AAL*, vol. 2, 5 (1974), pp. 687–700.

'An der Seite der Kàmpfer gegen Imperialismus und Kolonialismus; für nationale Befreiung und sozialen Fortschrift', *AAL*, vol. 4, 6 (1976), pp. 837–51.

'Zur Afrikapolitik der DDR', *DAPK*, vol. 24, 8 (1979), pp. 5–19.

Winrow, Gareth M. 'East German foreign policy and the Arab–Israeli problem', *Journal of Economics and Administrative Studies* (Istanbul), vol. 2, 1 (1988), pp. 57–78.

Wokalek. 'Zur Afrikapolitik der DDR', Paper of *Gesamtdeutsches Institut – Bundesanstalt für Gesamtdeutsche Aufgaben*, Bonn, 19 March 1979.

Wünsche, Renate. 'Zur Bedeutung des internationalen Faktors für die Entwicklung der Befreiten Staaten in Asien, Afrika und Lateinamerika', *AAL*, vol. 11, 5 (1983), pp. 839–45.

Zapf, Helmut. 'Das antiimperialistische Potential der national befreiten Länder – methodologische und bündnisstrategische Aspekte aus der Sicht des Wissenschaftlichen Kommunismus', *AAL*, vol. 14, 3 (1986), pp. 386–94.

Zeitlin, Arnold. 'Hegelian re-entry – The Germans are back in Africa', *Africa Report*, vol. 12, 2 (1967), pp. 37–45.

Zenker, Jurgen. 'Zusammenarbeit der SED mit revolutionär-demokratischen Parteien in Afrika und Asien', *DAPK*, vol. 22, 10 (1977), pp. 93–106.

Zieger, Gottfried (ed.). *Zehn Jahre Berlin-Abkommen 1971–1981 – Versuch einer Bilanz, Symposium 15/16 Oktober 1981* (Cologne, Berlin, Bonn and Munich: Carl Heymanns Verlag, Schriften zur Rechtslage Deutschlands, vol. 5, 1983).

Zimmerman, William. 'International regional systems and the politics of system boundaries', *International Organisation*, vol. 26, 1 (1972), pp. 18–36.

Index

Adamshin, Anatoli, 216
Adenauer, Konrad, 8, 26, 37, 38, 217
Adoula, Cyrille, 61
Adressendiplomatie, 48, 201
affiliate, definition of, 9–10
Afghanistan, 178, 197; invasion of, 29,
  138, 187
African National Congress (ANC), 78–9,
  191. *See also* GDR and ANC, USSR and
  ANC
African Party of Independence for
  Guinea and Cape Verde (PAIGC), 60;
  and China, 83. *See also* FRG and
  Guinea-Bissau, GDR and
  Guinea-Bissau, Socialist Unity Party of
  Germany, USSR and Guinea-Bissau
Afro-Asian People's Solidarity
  Organisation, 53
Afro-Asian Solidarity Committee (GDR),
  60
Albania, 17
Albright, David, 1
Algeria, 80, 103, 104; and China, 53; and
  Cuba, 132, 133; and Czechoslovakia, 182
Ali, Robaya, 137
Alleinvertretungsanspruch, 18, 19, 35, 38,
  71, 217
Allgemeiner Deutscher Nachrichtendienst
  (ADN), 49, 81; agreements with
  African news agencies, 49, 89
Alves, Nito, 140
Alvor Accord, 131
Amin, Idi, 141, 148
Angola, 96, 97, 187, 190; and China, 101,
  116, 119–20; and CMEA, 159; and
  Cuba, 6–7, 132, 133, 134, 211, 242n27;
  and *Land* Berlin Clause, 111, 186, 197,
  198–9, 200; and South Africa, 190–1,
  211, 213, 214
Angola–Namibia Accords, 211, 213, 214,
  225

Antar, Lt. Col., 137
Arab Front of Steadfastness, 103, 115
Arab Socialist Union (ASU), Egypt, 51,
  102
Arab Socialist Union (ASU), Libya, 102
Arafat, Yasser, 203
Argentina, 211
Aswan Dam, 41, 54
Austria, 32
Axen, Hermann, 94, 103, 114, 116, 117,
  193, 215

Babu, Abdul Rahman Mohammed, 64
Bandung Conference, 36, 38, 53
Bangladesh, recognition of GDR, 72
Barré, Said, 98, 100, 105, 192
Basic Law, 11–12, 18, 20, 218
Basic Treaty, 23, 72, 85, 108, 117, 192, 218
Beil, Gerhard, 161
Belgium, 30
Ben Bella, Ahmed, 52, 53, 68
Bendjedid, Chadli, 120, 203
Benti, Teferi, 90
Berlin, 11, 17, 20, 106–8, and
  Quadripartite Agreement, 22–4, 106–7,
  111, 112, 197
Berlin Agreement, 107
Berlin Wall, 16, 61, 67, 196–7
Bismarck, Otto von, 196
Bokassa, Jean-Bedel, 77, 81, 83, 176
Botha, P. W., 191, 213, 214
Botsio, Kojo, 46, 56
Boutrous-Ghali, Boutros, 204
Brandt, Willy, 20, 22, 24, 72, 74–5, 80
Brasch, Horst, 238n86
Brazil, 185, 211
Brentano, Heinrich von, 38, 39, 62
Brezhnev, Leonid, 72, 204, 207, 247n3
Brezhnev, Doctrine, 138–9
Britain, 9, 17
Brutents, Karen, 210

277

Brzezinski, Zbigniew, 2, 11
Bucharest Formula, 25, 165
Bulgaria, 17, 224; and Africa, 223;
    development aid, 176, 179–80, 182;
    trade with developing states, 44,
    161

Cabora Bassa Dam, 98
Cabral, Amilcar, 60, 79
Cabral, Luiz, 91, 110, 140, 190
Cambodia Formula, 74–5, 76
Cameroon, 34
Cameroons, see Cameroon
Castro, Fidel, 7, 9, 52, 249n62
Central African Republic (CAR): and
    France, 77
Chile: and FRG, 75; recognition of GDR,
    72
China, 17; and Africa, 53, 64, 79, 82–3,
    101, 116, 119–20, 195. See also GDR and
    China
Chingunji, Tito, 140
Chipenda, Daniel, 131
Chirac, Jacques, 130
Chissano, Joaquim, 92, 213
Christian Democratic Union (CDU), 50
clientelism, 3
Coker, Christopher, 4, 6, 8–9, 134, 160,
    172, 193, 221
Cominform, 15, 35
Commission for Organising the Party of
    the Working People of Ethiopia
    (COPWE), 190
Communist Party of the Soviet Union
    (CPSU), 20th Congress, 51, 52; 21st
    Congress, 51; 24th Congress, 129; 26th
    Congress, 24, 207, 247n3; 27th
    Congress, 207–8
Congo Conference, 196
Congo PR, 81; and China, 82; and Cuba,
    132, 133
constitution of GDR, 1949, 18; 1974, 2,
    22, 24, 25
Conté, Seydou, 62, 63, 64
Convention People's Party (CPP), 51
Costa, Manuel Pinto da, 79, 91, 92
Council of Mutual Economic Assistance
    (CMEA), 17, 25, 26, 27, 160, 173,
    199–200; and Comprehensive
    Programme, 22, 160; and NIEO, 174,
    185; and OPEC, 161, 170; and SADCC,
    202
Croan, Melvin, 3, 4, 27, 221
Crozier, Brian, 7
Cuba, 52; and Africa, 6–7, 131–4, 212,
    225; and FRG, 18, 39; and USSR, 6–7,
    9, 207. See also GDR and Cuba

Czechoslovakia, 17, 25, 26, 224, 233n82;
    and Africa, 223; arms exports, 36, 145,
    223; development aid, 176, 179–80,
    182; invasion of, 19, 74, 78, 81, 82;
    military training, 129; trade with
    developing states, 44, 161

Democratic Farmer's Party of Germany
    (DBD), 50
Denton, Jeremiah, 7
Department of Information and Security
    of Angola (DISA), 140
Dickel, Friedrich, 124
Dohlus, Horst, 95–6, 190
Dordan, Werner, 97
Dunér, Bertil, 8, 9, 132, 225

Ebert, Friedrich, 94
Egypt, 72, 74, 80, 235n27; and China, 53;
    and Czechoslovakia, 36, 78, 180; and
    Yugoslavia, 68
Eichorn, Ewald, 140
End, Heinrich, 43, 75
Erhard, Ludwig, 68
Eritrean Liberation Front (ELF), 136,
    250n71
Eritrean Liberation Front–Revolutionary
    Council (ELF-RC), 100
Eritrean People's Liberation Front
    (EPLF), 100, 216, 250n71
Ethiopia, 98, 100, 187; and China, 53,
    118; and Cuba, 6–7, 131, 132, 133, 136,
    180; and Czechoslovakia, 78, 147; and
    Kenya, 118; and Land Berlin Clause,
    111–12; and Yugoslavia, 147
Ethiopian Workers' Party (WPE), 190, 205
Etzdorf, Hasso von, 63
Eurafrica Project, 59
European Development Fund (EDF), 59,
    186
European Economic Community (EEC),
    59, 197–8, 200; and Lomé I
    Convention, 109, 111, 112; and Lomé II
    Convention, 109, 111, 198; and Lomé
    III Convention, 197–8, 199

Farouk, King, 34
Federal Republic of Germany (FRG) and
    Algeria, 55, 75; economic aid, 55;
    trade, 169
FRG and Angola, 60, 97, 111; Land Berlin
    Clause, 111, 197, 198–9
FRG and Cameroon, 34
FRG and CAR, 75, 77; economic aid, 77
FRG and Cuba, see Cuba
FRG development aid, 43, 51, 93, 176–7,
    178, 179

FRG and Egypt, 38, 40–1, 53–4, 67–70, 75; economic aid, 41, 54, 68, 69–70, 75, 76; trade, 169

FRG and Ethiopia, 112, 200, economic aid, 112, 182–3, 185, and *Land* Berlin Clause, 112, 200; security assistance, 112, 245n107

FRG and France, 59

FRG and Gambia: trade, 159

FRG and GDR, *see* GDR and FRG in Europe, GDR and FRG in Africa

FRG and Ghana, 56; economic aid, 56

FRG and Guinea, 56, 62–4, 75, 81, 104–5, 112; economic aid, 56, 62; military aid, 122; trade, 238n93

FRG and Guinea-Bissau, 110; and PAIGC, 60; and *Land* Berlin Clause, 110

FRG and Israel, 33, 37, 53–4, 67, 68, 69

FRG and Libya, 70; trade, 169

FRG and Morocco, 70, 103–4

FRG and Mozambique, 98, 111, and *Land* Berlin Clause, 111, 197–8, 199–200; and FRELIMO, 60–1

FRG and Namibia, 106

FRG and Nigeria, 83; trade, 169

FRG and Portugal, 60, 61, 98

FRG and Rhodesia, *see* FRG and Zimbabwe

FRG and Saõ Tomé and Príncipe, and *Land* Berlin Clause, 111, 197, 199

FRG and Somalia, 105, economic aid, 112; security assistance, 105, 122, 125, 243n70

FRG and South Africa, 60

FRG and Sudan, 75; economic aid, 75, 184, 185

FRG and Tanganyika, 65

FRG and Tanzania, 34–5, 65–7; economic aid, 66; military training, 66

FRG and Togo, 34

FRG and trade with Africa, 43, 186

FRG and Tunisia, 70

FRG and USSR, 17, 18, 20, 37–8, 107–8

FRG and Zaire (Congo-Leopoldville), 60

FRG and Zanzibar, 64–7

FRG and Zimbabwe, 193, 194

Finland, 108

Fischer, Oskar, 93, 114, 201, 204, 214–15; trips to Africa, 94–6, 99, 102, 168, 200, 204

Fleissner, Werner, 138

France, 17; and Africa, 52, 54, 56, 59, 77, arms exports, 145–6

Frank-Falin Formula, 107–9, 110

Free German Trade Union Federation (FDGB), 49, 207; and Africa, 49

Free German Youth (FDJ), 49; training African youth, 49–50; Friendship Brigades in Africa, 50, 100, 104, 192, 206

Fritsch, Gunther, 64, 65

Gambia, 110

Gaulle, Charles de, 55

Geburtsfehlertheorie, 72, 74

General Agreement on Tariffs and Trade (GATT), 156

General People's Congress, 103

German Democratic Republic (GDR) and ANC, 78–9, 90, 101, 117, 191, 206, 211, 214, military training, 142, 143; visits by Tambo, 90, 91–2, 201 *See also* GDR arms exports

GDR–Africa Society, 50

GDR and Algeria, 41, 49, 50, 55, 70, 89, 94–6, 103, 120, 126–7, 203, 235n31, diplomatic recognition, 73, 80, economic aid, 76, 180, 182, and liberation war, 55; military aid, 132, 133, 142–3, party agreements, 89, 189; and POLISARIO, 104, 143; trade, 57–8, 168, visits by Fischer, 95, 96; visits by Hoffmann, 94, 130 *See also* GDR arms exports, Honecker, oil

GDR and Angola, 89, 94–6, 97, 126–7, 134, 206, 211–12, diplomatic recognition, 73, 97; economic aid, 97, 116, 180, 210; and ideological development, 88, 189, 208–9; and *Land* Berlin Clause, 200, and Lusaka Agreement, 191; military aid, 97, 122, 132, 133, 135–6, 142, 143, party agreements, 89, 97, 98, 189, 190, and MPLA, 61, 78–9, 97, 125, 130–1, 138, security assistance, 97, 140, 141, trade turnover, 58, 156, 158, 168, 172, Treaty of Friendship and Cooperation, 113, 114, 115–16, 130, 175, 197; visit by Fischer, 95; visit by Hoffmann, 94, 149, 150–1, visit by Neto, 90, 91, 97; visit by dos Santos, 92. *See also* GDR arms exports, Honecker, oil, Socialist Unity Party of Germany

GDR–Arab Society, 50

GDR arms exports, 145, 146–8, and ANC, 101, 147, 148; and Algeria, 143, and Angola, 147; and Egypt, 125; and Ethiopia, 146, 147; and FRELIMO, 125; and Libya, 148; and Mozambique, 146, 147; and Nigeria, 129; and MPLA, 125; and SWAPO, 101, 147, 148; and Tanzania, 146, 148; and Zambia, 147; and ZAPU, 101, 147–8

GDR and Benin (Dahomey), 49, 50, 61,
88, 127; diplomatic recognition, 73;
trade, 153, 156; visit by Fischer, 95
GDR and Botswana: diplomatic
recognition, 73
GDR and Burkina Faso: diplomatic
recognition, 73
GDR and Burundi: diplomatic
recognition, 73; trade, 153, 156
GDR and Cameroon, 50; diplomatic
recognition, 73; economic aid, 182;
trade, 153, 156
GDR and Cape Verde Islands, 91, 96–7,
127; diplomatic recognition, 73;
economic aid, 180; military aid, 138;
party agreements, 89; trade, 153, 157
GDR and CAR: diplomatic recognition,
73, 75, 77; economic aid, 77;
resumption of relations, 73, 77;
suspension of relations, 73, 75, 77
GDR and Chad, 89; diplomatic
recognition, 73
GDR and China, 53, 64, 79, 101, 156, 195;
and African condemnation of invasion
of Vietnam, 116, 117, 118, 119–20,
192–3
GDR and Comores: diplomatic
recognition, 73
GDR and Congo PR, 89, 94–5, 126–7,
129, 130, 141, 202, 206; diplomatic
recognition, 73; economic aid, 180;
military aid, 130, 132, 133, 141, 142;
party agreements, 89, 189; trade, 57–8,
visit by Fischer, 95; visit by Hoffmann,
94, 130, 149; visit by Sassou-Nguesso,
92, 202, 251n99; visits by
Yhombi-Opango, 91, 130, 141, 142,
251n107
GDR and Cuba, 115, 131–2, 156, 178,
197, 225; diplomatic recognition, 18,
39, 40
GDR development aid, 43, 51, 76–7, 93,
175–81, 185–6, 205–6, 236n37; and
tripartite ventures, 181–4, 185
GDR and Djibouti: diplomatic
recognition, 73; visit by Fischer, 96
GDR and Egypt, 36–7, 38, 40–1, 42, 46,
49, 51, 53–5, 67–70, 84, 89, 94, 96, 126,
204–5; and Arab–Israeli War, 1967, 80,
and Berlin Wall, 61, 102; and
ideological development, 211;
diplomatic recognition, 73, 75, 80;
economic aid, 54, 68, 69, 70, 76, 180;
military training, 84, 125, 130; party
agreement, 89, 102, security assistance,
125; trade, 33–4, 36, 43, 47, 56, 57–8,
154, 159, 168, 172, 180, 204, 211; visits

by Fischer, 94, 96, 102, 204; visit by
Grotewohl, 54–5; visit by Hoffmann,
129–30. See also GDR arms exports, oil,
Socialist Unity Party of Germany,
Ulbricht
GDR and Equatorial Guinea: diplomatic
recognition, 73; security assistance, 141
GDR and Ethiopia, 37, 46, 89, 94–6,
99–100, 137, 190, 206, 211–12, 215; and
Berlin Wall, 61; diplomatic recognition,
73; economic aid, 118, 180–1, 182–3,
185; and Ethiopian liberation
movements, 100, 118, 136, 212, 215;
and ideological development, 189,
208–9; and Land Berlin Clause, 200;
military aid, 122, 131, 132, 133, 136,
138, 143–4; party agreements, 89, 189,
204; security assistance, 100, 140, 141,
142, 245n107; trade, 57–8, 156, 159,
172; Treaty of Friendship and
Cooperation, 114, 118, 197; visit by
Fischer, 94, 99; visit by Hoffman, 95,
138, 147, 149; visits by Mengistu, 91–2,
99–100, 204, 215. See also GDR arms
exports, Honecker, Socialist Unity
Party of Germany
GDR and FRG in Africa: cooperation,
182–3, 184, 185, 210, 220; East German
criticisms, 35, 78, 80, 103–4, 105–6, 112,
122, 151, 169, 173–4, 196, 210; East
German praise, 220–1; rivalry, 42–3,
50, 56, 59–61, 62–71, 104–13, 195–200;
West German criticisms, 81, 122–3
GDR and FRG in Europe; cooperation,
22–3, 26, 28, 29–31, 85, 220; rivalry,
14–15, 18–19, 20, 24, 106–8
GDR and France, 30
GDR and Gabon, 50, 61; diplomatic
recognition, 73
GDR and Gambia: diplomatic
recognition, 73; trade, 159
GDR and Ghana, 41, 42, 46, 50, 56, 89,
142, 235n31, diplomatic recognition,
73; economic aid, 180, and ideological
development, 102; and Kruger Affair,
56, 59, 124–5; party agreement, 51;
trade, 56, 57–8, 172, 254n10. See also
Socialist Unity Party of Germany
GDR and Guinea, 40, 41, 42, 49, 50–1,
89, 126–7, 235n31; and Berlin Wall, 61;
diplomatic recognition, 18, 40, 42,
62–4, 73, 81; economic aid, 76, military
aid, 132, 133, 149, party agreement, 89;
trade, 56, 57–8, 153, 172, 238n93; visit
by Hoffmann, 94, 149; visit by Touré,
91, 120. See also Socialist Unity Party of
Germany

GDR and Guinea-Bissau, 88, 89, 91, 94, 96–7, 127, 206; and PAIGC, 60, 78–9, 97; diplomatic recognition, 73; and *Land* Berlin Clause, 110–11; military aid, 133; party agreements, 89, 189; security assistance, 140, 190; trade, 153, 155
GDR and Ivory Coast, 90, 119; diplomatic recognition, 73, 201
GDR and Kenya, 61; diplomatic recognition, 73; visit by Fischer, 94
GDR and Lesotho: diplomatic recognition, 73, 201–2; visit by Jonathan, 92, 200, 201
GDR and Liberia, 50; diplomatic recognition, 73; trade, 153, 156
GDR and Libya, 41, 89, 94–6, 103, 115, 127, 196–7, 203–4, 208, 262n54; diplomatic recognition, 73; economic aid, 103, 115, 182; military aid, 133, 134, 142, 144, 203–4; party agreement, 89; security assistance, 140, 141, 203–4; trade, 57–8, 156, 159, 167–8; visit by Ghaddafi, 91, 103, 115, 167, 196. *See also* GDR arms exports, Honecker, oil, Socialist Unity Party of Germany
GDR and Madagascar, 89; diplomatic recognition, 73; economic aid, 180, party agreement, 89; trade, 153, 155; visit by Fischer, 94
GDR and Malawi, 90, 119, 201
GDR and Mali, 41, 42, 49, 50, 56, 78, 126, 191–2, 235n31; and Berlin Wall, 61, diplomatic recognition, 73; economic aid, 76; and ideological development, 102; military aid, 133; party agreement, 89
GDR and Mauritania: diplomatic recognition, 73; trade, 159
GDR and Mauritius: diplomatic recognition, 73
GDR and Morocco, 41, 49, 103–4, 214; diplomatic recognition, 73; resumption of diplomatic relations, 73, 104, suspension of diplomatic relations, 73; 104; trade, 57–8, 172, visit by Fischer, 96
GDR and Mozambique, 89, 94–6, 98, 101, 127, 134, 206, 211–12, and CMEA, 199–200; diplomatic recognition, 73, 98; economic aid, 98, 117, 158, 171–2, 180, 210; and ideological development, 189, 208–9; and FRELIMO, 60–1, 78–9, 98, 125, 132; military aid, 98, 122, 132, 133, 137–8, 142, 143, and Nkomati Accord, 191; party agreements, 89, 98, 117, 189; security assistance, 98, 140,

141; trade, 58, 156–7, 158–9, 171–2; Treaty of Friendship and Cooperation, 113, 114, 115–16, 117, 137, 147, 175, 197; visit by Chissano, 92, 213–14; visit by Fischer, 94; visit by Hoffmann, 95, 143, 149; visits by Machel, 90, 91–2, 98, 206 *See also* GDR arms exports, Honecker, Socialist Unity Party of Germany
GDR and Namibia, 211, 213; and SWAPO, 78–9, 90, 116, 132, 142, 143, 206, 211, visits by Nujoma, 91–2, 201. *See also* GDR arms exports
GDR and Niger, 94; diplomatic recognition, 73
GDR and Nigeria, 49, 50, 83, 94, 127; diplomatic recognition, 73; economic aid, 180; military aid, 125, 129, 133, 134, 149, trade, 57–8, 168–9, 172; visit by Fischer, 95, 168; visit by Hoffmann, 94, 149. *See also* GDR arms exports
GDR and OAU, 119, 215
GDR and POLISARIO, 104, 143, 214–15
GDR and Rhodesia, *see* GDR and Zimbabwe
GDR and Rwanda: diplomatic recognition, 73
GDR and SADR, 214
GDR and São Tomé and Príncipe, 89, 94, 96–7, 116, 126–7, 200, 206; diplomatic recognition, 73; and MLSTP, 97; party agreements, 89, 189; trade, 157; visit by Pinto da Costa, 79, 91–2
GDR and Senegal, 50; diplomatic recognition, 73
GDR and Seychelles: diplomatic recognition, 73
GDR and Sierra Leone: diplomatic recognition, 73; trade, 153, 157
GDR and Somalia, 89, 94, 100, 126, 192; diplomatic recognition, 73; party agreement, 89, 100; security assistance, 105, 125. *See also* Socialist Unity Party of Germany
GDR and South Africa, 52, 90, 191, 201, 213; trade, 60, 159, 255n18
GDR and Sudan, 41, 55, 70, 83–4, 103, 126, 141–2, 235n31; diplomatic recognition, 72, 73, 75, 80; economic aid, 76, 84, 184, 185; security assistance, 84, 124, trade, 37, 57–8, 254n10
GDR and Swaziland, 90, 119, 201
GDR and Tanzania, 40, 42, 49, 50, 65–7, 78, 82, 126–7; diplomatic recognition, 73; economic aid, 76; military assistance, 132, 133, trade, 57–8, 157; visit by Fischer, 94. *See also* GDR arms exports

GDR and Togo, 50; diplomatic
recognition, 73; trade, 153, 157
GDR trade with Africa, 43, 56, 57–8,
152–9, 171–2, 184–5, 221. *See also* oil
GDR trade with developing states, 44,
152–5, 160–61, 154, 172–3, 174–5, 221.
See also oil
GDR and Tunisia, 41, 89, 95, 127;
diplomatic recognition, 73; economic
aid, 76, 182; party agreement, 189;
trade, 57–8, 172; visit by Fischer, 96;
visit by Hoffmann, 94, 149. *See also* oil
GDR and Uganda: diplomatic
recognition, 73; party agreement, 189;
security assistance, 141; trade, 153, 157
GDR and UN, 18–19, 77–8, 93, 102, 106,
120, 187, 214–15
GDR and USSR in Africa, 47, 52–3, 71,
81–2, 86, 103–4, 131–4, 188–9, 219, 226
GDR and USSR in Europe, 16–17, 18, 19,
20–2, 29, 30–2, 37, 224; and Berlin,
106–7; preferential economic
treatment, 17, 19, 21, 26–9, 86, 170–1,
188, 220; support for invasion of
Czechoslovakia, 19, 78; Treaty of
Friendship, 17, 20, 37; Treaties of
Friendship, Mutual Assistance and
Cooperation, 2, 17, 19, 22. *See also* oil
GDR and Zaire (Congo Leopoldville), 60,
61, 134, 150–1; diplomatic recognition,
73; resumption of diplomatic relations,
73, 150; suspension of diplomatic
relations, 73, 150; trade, 153, 157
GDR and Zambia, 41, 83, 89, 93, 94–6,
117, 124, 127; diplomatic recognition,
73; economic aid, 117, 172, 180, 209;
military aid, 133, 143; party
agreements, 89, 101, 117; trade, 57–8,
153, 157, 172; visit by Fischer, 95; visit
by Hoffmann, 95, 147, 149; visit by
Kaunda, 92, 117, 149, 196, 209. *See also*
GDR arms exports, Honecker, Socialist
Unity Party of Germany
GDR and Zanzibar, 64–7, 82, 192–4;
closure of GDR embassy, 40, 66–7;
diplomatic recognition, 18, 40, 64, 73;
economic aid, 64, 65, 82; military
training, 64, 125; security assistance,
125
GDR and Zimbabwe, 52, 90, 192–4, 206;
diplomatic recognition, 73, 193;
military aid, 142; party agreements,
189, 194; trade, 58, 60, 157, 159–60, 172,
193; visit by Fischer, 95; visit by
Mugabe, 92, 193–4; visits by Nkomo,
90, 91–2, 192; and ZANU, 101, 117,
148, 192–3; and ZAPU, 78–9, 90, 117,

132, 143, 192, 193. *See also* GDR arms
exports, Socialist Unity Party of
Germany
German East Africa, 34
German Journalist Union (VDJ), 48–9,
206; agreements with African
journalists' unions, 49, 89
German Trade Union Federation, 49
Ghaddafi, Muammar, 91, 103, 115, 140,
141, 167, 196–7, 203
Ghana, 72; and China, 53; and invasion
of Czechoslovakia, 78
Ghiorgis, Dawit Wolde, 112
Gizenga, Antoine, 61
glasnost, 31
Goethe Institute, 50
Gomoa, Shaarawi Mohamed, 125
Gorbachev, Mikhail, 15, 31, 187–8, 189,
195, 224, 225; and New Political
Thinking, 188, 189, 207–8, 210–12, 224,
226, 227
Gotting, Gerald, 50, 61
Greece, 30
Grewe, Wilhelm, 39, 40, 41, 69, 71
Gromyko, Andrei, 80
Grotewohl, Otto, 35, 54, 55, 56
Grüneberg, Gerhard, 94, 102
Guebuza, Armando Emilio, 38
Guinea, 72; and China, 53, 82; and Cuba,
132, 133, 134; and France, 56
Guinea-Bissau, 190; and Cuba, 133; and
Land Berlin Clause, 110–11

Hager, Kurt, 31
Hallstein, Walter, 39
Hallstein Doctrine, 11, 18, 19, 39–40, 42,
46–7, 71, 78, 153; and Egypt, 42, 54, 69,
71; and Guinea, 42, 64; and *Land* Berlin
Clause, 109–10; modification of, 72,
74–6; and Tanzania, 42, 67, 71; and
Zanzibar, 42, 64
Hartmann, Horst, 142
Heikal, Mohamed, 67, 68, 70
Helsinki Final Act, 23, 85, 117, 118
Herder Institute, 50, 206
Hillebrand, Ernst, 156, 172
Hoffmann, Heinz, 93, 124, 129, 135,
136–7, 139, 251n107; trips to Africa,
94–5, 129–30, 138, 143, 147, 149, 150–1
Holsti, K. J., 9
Honecker, Erich, 21–3, 24, 27, 88, 99,
103, 124, 136, 137, 140, 191, 204, 215,
225, 230n37, 241n6; and 7th SED
Congress, 22; and 8th SED Congress,
79; and 9th SED Congress, 87–8, 90,
101; and 10th SED Congress, 29, 189,
208; and 11th SED Congress, 173, 203,

208–9, 211; against export of counter-revolution, 122, 212; and Chissano, 214; and Gorbachev, 31, 224; and Jonathan, 201; and Mugabe, 193–4; significance of 1979 African tours, 113–14, 219; speech in East Berlin October 1980, 177, 196; and tripartite ventures, 183; visit to Algeria, 95, 168, 200, 203; visit to Angola, 95, 111, 114, 115–16, 119–20, 148; visit to China, 195; visits to Ethiopia, 95, 112, 118–19, 147, 181, 200, 204; visit to FRG, 30, 220; visit to France, 30; visit to India, 86; visit to Kuwait, 167; visit to Libya, 95, 114–15, 167; visit to Mexico, 167; visit to Mozambique, 95, 111, 114, 117, 193; visit to North Korea, 86; visit to Philippines, 86; visit to Syria, 167, visit to Vietnam, 86; visit to Zambia, 95, 114, 116–17, 172, 193

Hosmer, Stephen, 7
Hungary, 17, 26, 32, 223, 224; and Africa, 223; military training, 129; trade with developing states, 44, 160, 154

Ibrahim, Hassan, 70
India, 38, 86, 211, 254n10; recognition of GDR, 72
Indonesia, 211
International Confederation of Free Trade Unions (ICFTU), 49
International Institute for Strategic Studies, 144
International Monetary Fund, 210
International Union of Students (IUS), 48, 49
Iran, 57–8, 167, 254n10. See also oil
Iraq, 57–8, 70, 142, 152–3, 166, 254n10; and FRG, 74; recognition of GDR, 72, 74, 80–1; and USSR, 80. See also oil
Ismail, Abdel Fattah, 137
Israel, 52, 54, 80, 102. See also FRG and Israel
Italy, 30

Jalloud, Abdul Salam, 167
Jonathan, Leabua, 92, 200, 201

Kamoni, Simba, 202
Kampuchea (Cambodia), 115, 156, 178, 197; and FRG, 74; recognition of GDR, 72, 74
Kapwepwe, Simon, 83
Karume, Abeid, 64, 65, 66, 82
Kaufmann, Erich, 38

Kaunda, Kenneth, 83, 92, 93, 96, 116, 117, 196, 209
Keita, Modibo, 52, 56
Kenya: and invasion of Czechoslovakia, 78
Kenyatta, Jomo, 61
Kessler, Heinz, 124
Khrushchev, Nikita, 36, 51, 52, 181
Kiesewetter, Wolfgang, 61, 66, 83
Kiesinger, Kurt, 72, 74
Kleiber, Gunther, 95–6, 204
Kodjo, Edem, 119
Kohl, Helmut, 30
Kohl, Michael, 112
Konig, Gerd, 191
Korbonski, Andrzej, 7
Krenz, Egon, 124
Krolikowski, Werner, 94–6, 190
Kruger, Kurt, 59, 125
Kurella, Alfred, 50
Kuwait, 57–8, 70, 167. See also oil

Lamberz, Werner, 90, 93, 136, 137, 190, 251n107; trips to Africa, 94, 98, 99, 100, 101, 103, 135, 137, 140, 192
Land Berlin Clause, 108–12, 113, 120, 186, 197–200, 218
Lankes, Christian, 112
Laos, 155, 178, 197
Lawson, Colin, 159, 173
League for People's Friendship, 50
Lebanon, 37
legitimacy, definition of, 12–13
Leipzig trade fair, 48, 157
Lekhanya, General-Major, 202
Liberation Front of Mozambique (FRELIMO), 60, 101; and China, 83; and Cuba, 132; and USSR, 78–9, 83, 132. See also FRG and Mozambique, GDR and Mozambique, Socialist Unity Party of Germany
Liberia, 37
Libya, 37, 103, 104; and Bulgaria, 204, and Cuba, 133; and Czechoslovakia, 204; and Romania, 204
Liebknecht, Karl, 31
Liebscher, Gertraud, 105
Lubke, Heinrich, 34
Lumumba, Patrice, 53
Lusaka Agreement, 190, 191, 211
Luxemburg, Rosa, 31

McCormick, Gordon, 8
Machel, Samora, 79, 91–2, 98, 101, 117, 141, 193, 199, 206
Madagascar: and Cuba, 133
Maldive Islands: recognition of GDR, 72

Maleuda, Günther, 203
Mali: and China, 53; and invasion of
  Czechoslovakia, 78
Mandela, Nelson, 201
Manila Declaration, 166, 174, 175, 181
Mao Zedong, 82
Mariam, Wolde, 138
Marrese, Michael, 26–7
Matern, Hermann, 51
Mbumba, Nathaniel, 150
Medienpolitik, 89–90
Mengistu, Haile Mariam, 91–2, 99–100,
  112, 118, 136, 137, 141, 147, 204, 215
Mexico, 57–8, 167, 211. *See also* oil
Mielke, Erich, 124
Mittag, Günter, 94–5, 114
Mitterrand, François, 30
Mobutu, Joseph, 134, 150, 151
Mohammed, Ali Nasser, 137
Mongolia, 17, 115, 156, 178
Morais, Augusto, 256n41
Moreton, Edwina, 2, 3, 4, 6, 8, 18, 123
Morocco: and China, 53; and Cuba,
  134
Movement for the Liberation of São
  Tomé and Príncipe (MLSTP), 79. *See
  also* GDR and São Tomé and
  Príncipe
Mozambique, 96, 187, 190; and ANC,
  191; and Angola, 101; and Britain, 212;
  and China, 101, 117; and CMEA, 159,
  199–200; and Cuba, 132, 133; and *Land
  Berlin* Clause, 111, 186, 197–8, 199–200;
  and Portugal, 212; and South Africa,
  190–1, 211, 213
Mubarak, Hosni, 204
Mufti, Ibrahim el, 55
Mugabe, Robert, 92, 101, 117, 192, 193,
  194
Müller, Gerhard, 203
Munangagwa, Emmerson, 194
Museveni, Yoweri, 141
Mwananshika, Luke John, 202–3

Namibia, 34, 35
Nascimento, Lopo di, 97
Nasser, Gamel Abdel, 34, 36, 52, 53–5,
  67–70, 80, 84
National Congolese Liberation Front
  (FLNC), 150, 151
National Democracy, 51–2, 88
National Liberation Front (FLN), 55
National Liberation Front of Angola
  (FLNA), 116, 140; and China, 116
National People's Army (NVA), 121, 123,
  221; and Africa, 123, 125, 129, 132,
  134–9

National Union for the Total
  Independence of Angola (UNITA), 79,
  135, 140, 190, 191, 211, 212, 213; and
  China, 79, 116
Naumann, Konrad, 94–5
Netherlands, 30
Neto, Agostinho, 79, 91, 97, 116, 131,
  140, 191
Neumann, Alfred, 94, 106
New International Economic Order
  (NIEO), 113, 154, 165, 173–8 *passim*,
  185, 209
Ngakala, Michel, 251n99
Nguema, Francisco Macias, 141
Nigeria, 83; and invasion of
  Czechoslovakia, 78
Nimeiry, Jaafar, 80, 83–4
Nkomati Accord, 190–1, 211
Nkomo, Joshua, 91, 101, 117, 147–8, 192,
  193, 194
Nkrumah, Kwame, 46, 51, 52, 56, 88,
  125, 141
Nohr, Klaus, 62, 63
Non-Aligned Movement: Belgrade
  conference, 46; Cairo conference, 46,
  69
North Atlantic Treaty Organisation
  (NATO), 5, 15, 60, 115, 187
North Korea, 17, 86, 115, 156, 178, 197;
  and Africa, 100
Nujoma, Sam, 91–2, 101, 116, 148, 201
Nyerere, Julius, 35, 65, 66, 67, 82, 101,
  192

oil: from Algeria, 162–3, 165, 168, 169;
  from Angola, 166, 168, 170; from
  Egypt, 154, 162, 165, 166, 168; from
  FRG, 165; from Iran, 162–3, 165, 166,
  167; from Iraq, 152–3, 162–3, 165, 166;
  from Kuwait, 162, 165, 167; from
  Libya, 159, 163, 165, 166, 167–8, 169;
  from Mexico, 166, 167; from Nigeria,
  168–9; from Syria, 162–3, 166, 167;
  from Tunisia, 162, 165; from USSR, 25,
  26–7, 28–9, 160, 161, 162–3, 166, 169;
  from Venezuela, 162, 165; oil
  reexports, 170–1, 221
*Orbital Transport und Raketen
  Aktiengesellschaft*, 151
Organisation for Economic Cooperation
  and Development (OECD), 170, 171,
  176, 178, 179, 180
Organisation for Petroleum Exporting
  Countries (OPEC), 25, 158, 161, 166,
  169–70, 171
Organisation of African Unity (OAU),
  102, 119, 125, 214, 215

Ott, Harry, 210

Palestine Liberation Organisation (PLO),
 101, 103, 104, 203, 241n16
Pan-Africanist Congress of South Africa
 (PAC), 79; and China, 79
Parti Démocratique de Guine, 51
Pereira, Aristides, 91
perestroika, 31
Petroff, Andre, 140
Philippines, 86
Pieck, Wilhelm, 62, 63
Pisani, Edgard, 198
Poland, 17, 20, 24, 25, 27, 32, 177, 224,
 233n82; and Africa, 223; arms exports,
 145; military training, 129; trade with
 developing states, 44, 161
Popular Front for the Liberation of
 Saguia el Hamra and Rio do Oro
 (POLISARIO), 104. See also GDR and
 POLISARIO
Popular Movement for the Liberation of
 Angola (MPLA), 61, 116; and Cuba,
 131. See also GDR and Angola, Socialist
 Unity Party of Germany, USSR and
 Angola
Popular Movement for the Liberation of
 Angola, Party of Workers (MPLA–PT),
 97, 190. See also Socialist Unity Party of
 Germany
Portugal and Africa, 60, 61, 96, 98, 116,
 212
Potsdam Treaty, 38
Provisional Military Administrative
 Council (PMAC), 99, 112
proxy, definition of, 7–9

Radio Berlin International, 47
Rau, Heinrich, 36, 38
Renamo, 190, 191, 211, 212, 213–14
Revolutionary Committee of
 Mozambique (COREMO), 79; and
 China, 79
Revolutionary Democracy, 52, 88
Roberto, Holden, 140
Romania, 17, 19, 72, 74, 224; and Africa,
 223; trade with developing states, 44,
 155, 161; and tripartite ventures, 182
Rosenau, James, 2, 3
Roth, Kurt, 110
Rundfunkpropaganda, 47, 48

Sabri, Ali, 125
Sadat, Anwar as-, 3, 84, 102, 103, 125,
 204
Saharan Arab Democratic Republic
 (SADR), 214

Salazar, Antonio de Oliveira, 60–1
Salek, Ould, 214–15
Santos, Eduardo dos, 92, 141, 191
São Tomé and Príncipe; and Land Berlin
 Clause, 110, 111, 197, 199, 200
Sassou-Nguesso, Denis, 92, 141, 149,
 202, 251n99
Saudi Arabia, 70
Schalk, Alex, 144
Scheel, Walter, 75
Scheel Doctrine, 75–6, 78
Schloesser, Klaus-Ulrich, 123, 135
Schmidt, Helmut, 30, 122–3
Scholz, Ernst, 50, 55, 61
Schröder, Gerhard, 56
Schulze, Rudolph, 50
Schweitzer, Albert, 50
Selassie, Haile, 37, 235n19
Senegal: and invasion of Czechoslovakia,
 78
Shaba uprisings, 134, 150–1
Shelepin, Alexandr, 67
Shimuyarira, Nathan, 194
Sieber, Gunther, 194
Sierra Leone: and Cuba, 133
Simango, Uria T., 60–1
Sindermann, Horst, 94–6, 102, 120
Smith, Ian, 60, 159
socialist orientation, 88
Socialist Unity Party of Germany (SED),
 12, 15, 21, 22, 48, 76, 90, 106, 122, 129,
 160, 210; 7th Congress, 22, 79, 154; 8th
 Congress, 79; 9th Congress, 87–8, 90,
 101; 10th Congress, 189, 208; 11th
 Congress, 173, 200–1, 203, 205, 208–9,
 211; and PAIGC, 79; agreements with
 African parties, 50–1, 89, 189; and ASU
 (Egypt), 102; and ASU (Libya), 102;
 and CCP, 51; and WPE, 205; formation
 of, 15; and General People's Congress,
 103; and legitimacy, 13, 14, 16, 21, 23,
 27, 218, 221–2; and FRELIMO, 89, 98,
 117, 190; and military/security
 establishment, 123–4; and Parti
 Démocratique de Guinee, 51, and
 MPLA, 89, 97; and MPLA–PT, 190;
 Programme, 1946, 35; and Somali
 Revolutionary Socialist Party, 100;
 Statute, 1976, 22; and UNIP, 101, 117;
 and ZANU, 193, 194
Sodaro, Michael, 4, 7
Sölle, Horst, 168, 175, 183
Somalia, 81; and China, 53, 82; and
 Cuba, 100, 192; and North Korea,
 100
Somali Revolutionary Socialist Party,
 100

South Africa, 37, 190; and Cuba, 214; and
    Czechoslovakia, 37, 78
Southern African Development
    Coordination Council (SADCC), 197–8,
    201, 202
South Korea, 185
South West Africa, see Namibia
South West African People's
    Organisation (SWAPO), 78–9, 251n10;
    and Cuba, 132. See also GDR and
    Namibia, USSR and Namibia
South Yemen, 75, 103, 114, 118, 136–7,
    156, 250n71; recognition of GDR, 72, 75
Soviet zone of occupation, 2, 11, 15, 35
Spain, 103
Sri Lanka (Ceylon), 67, 75; recognition of
    GDR, 72
Stalin Josef, 3, 15, 22, 35, 36
Starrels, John, 7
Stockholm International Peace Research
    Institute (SIPRI), 129, 139, 145, 146
Stollmeyer, Captain, 125
Stoph, Willi, 76, 94–5, 100, 114, 124, 137,
    138, 173, 201–2
Sudan; and China, 53; and invasion of
    Czechoslovakia, 78; and Libya, 141
Suez Canal, 33, 52, 53–4
Suhrke, Astri, 9, 22
surrogate, definition of, 7–8
Syria, 37, 57–8, 70, 75, 80, 103, 166, 167,
    235n27; recognition of GDR, 72, 75. See
    also oil

Taiwan, 53
Tambo, Oliver, 79, 91–2, 101, 117, 201
Tanzam railway, 82, 101, 195
Tanzania, 64–5; and Bulgaria, 148; and
    China, 82, 101; and Cuba, 132, 133;
    and invasion of Czechoslovakia, 78;
    and ZANU, 192
Thalmann, Ernst, 35
Tisch, Harry, 95–6, 115, 120
Tito, Josef Broz, 68, 74
Togo, 34
Tonha, Commandante, 128
Touré, Sekou, 52, 62–4, 81, 91
Tunisia: and China, 53; and invasion of
    Czechoslovakia, 78
two camp doctrine, 35–6

Uganda: and Cuba, 133; and invasion of
    Czechoslovakia, 78
Ulbricht, Walter, 15–16, 19–22, 54, 56, 61,
    64, 76, 80, 154; visit to Egypt, 41, 67–9,
    113
Union of Soviet Socialist Republics
    (USSR) and ANC, 78–9, 187, 214

USSR and Algeria, 52, 55, 80; arms
    exports, 144; economic aid, 55, 81;
    military aid, 81, 132, 133
USSR and Angola, 119, 190, 207, 242n27;
    arms exports, 144; military aid, 132,
    133, 138; and MPLA, 78–9, 130–1;
    trade, 157
USSR arms exports to developing states,
    132, 144, 145, 148
USSR and Benin: arms exports, 144
USSR and Burundi: arms exports, 144
USSR and Cape Verde Islands: arms
    exports, 144
USSR and CAR: economic aid, 77
USSR and China, 19, 46, 53, 64, 79, 81–2,
    138, 148, 195
USSR and Congo PR, 190, 202; arms
    exports, 144; economic aid, 81; military
    aid, 81, 132, 133, 190
USSR and Cuba, see Cuba and USSR
USSR development aid, 178, 179–80
USSR and Egypt, 33, 52, 53, 54–5, 80,
    102, 204, 211; arms exports, 36, 80, 102;
    economic aid, 67–8, 69, 71, 81; military
    aid, 67–8, 125; security assistance, 125
USSR and Equatorial Guinea: economic
    aid, 81; military aid, 81
USSR and Ethiopia, 119, 190, 207,
    215–16; arms exports, 145; military aid,
    131, 132, 133, 136, 138, 215
USSR and FRG, see FRG and USSR
USSR and GDR, see GDR and USSR in
    Africa, GDR and USSR in Europe
USSR and Ghana, 52, 71
USSR and Guinea, 52, 71; arms exports,
    145; economic aid, 81; military aid, 81,
    132, 133
USSR and Guinea-Bissau; and PAIGC,
    78–9, 83; arms exports, 145; military
    aid, 133; security assistance, 140, 190
USSR and Libya, 197, 203–4; arms
    exports, 145; military aid, 133, 134
USSR and Madagascar: arms exports, 145
USSR and Mali, 52, 71; arms exports,
    145; military aid, 133
USSR and Morocco, 103, 214
USSR and Mozambique, 119, 190–1, 199,
    207; arms exports, 145; economic aid,
    171–2; military aid, 132, 133, 138, 190–1
USSR and Namibia, 132; and SWAPO,
    78–9, 132, 187
USSR and Nigeria: military aid, 134
USSR and SADR, 214
USSR and São Tomé and Príncipe: arms
    exports, 145
USSR and Somalia, 98, 100, 192;
    economic aid, 81; military aid, 81

USSR and South Africa, 37, 211, 214
USSR and Sudan, 83, 141–2; military aid,
  37
USSR and Tanzania, 65; arms exports,
  145; economic aid, 82; military aid, 82,
  132, 133
USSR trade with developing states, 44,
  155, 161
USSR and Zaire (Congo-Leopoldville),
  53, 61
USSR and Zambia: arms exports, 149
USSR and Zanzibar, 64, 71; military aid,
  64
USSR and Zimbabwe, 193, 194, 261n21;
  trade, 194; and ZANU, 193; and
  ZAPU, 78–9, 132, 148, 192, 193
United National Independence Party
  (UNIP), 100, 101, 117
United Nations Conference on Trade and
  Development (UNCTAD), 154, 173,
  181–2; 1st session, 159–60, 174–5; 2nd
  session, 174–5; 3rd session, 174–5; 4th
  session, 175; 5th session, 175, 183; 6th
  session, 175–6, 205–6
United Political Organisation National
  Front, 137
United Progressive Party, 83
United States, 6, 17, 144, 188, 194, 214
US Arms Control and Disarmament
  Agency (ACDA), 144–5, 146, 148
Ustinov, Vyachislav, 214

Van-Dunen, Pedro, 256n41
Vanous, Jan, 26–7, 170
Vieira, Joao Bernardo, 190
Vietnam, 17, 86, 115, 156, 178, 197, 199;
  invasion by China, 101, 116, 117, 118,
  138, 192–3

Warsaw Treaty Organisation (WTO),
  17–18, 19, 114, 123, 129, 145, 150, 221;
  and Brezhnev Doctrine, 138; Political
  Consultative Meeting, 1978, 129, 143
Weber, Max, 11
Wechmar, Rüdiger von, 113

Weiss, Gerhard, 68
Western Contact Group, 106
Wilhelm, Kaiser, 111
Willerding, Klaus, 88, 123
Winkler, Heinrich, 129, 130
Winzer, Otto, 74, 80, 106, 122
Wischnewski, Jurgen, 112
Wolf, Kurt, 235n17
Wolfe, Thomas, 7
World Federation of Democratic Youth
  (WFDY), 48, 49
World Federation of Trade Unions
  (WFTU), 48, 49, 207

Yemen, 70, 80
Yhombi-Opango, Joachim, 91, 130, 141,
  142, 251n107
Yugoslavia, 15, 68; and FRG, 18, 39, 54,
  74; recognition of GDR, 18, 39, 40, 46,
  54; and tripartite ventures, 182

Zaire (Congo-Leopoldville), 53, 60, 72;
  and invasion of Czechoslovakia, 78
Zambia: and China, 82, 116; and Cuba,
  133; and invasion of Czechoslovakia,
  78; and US, 209
Zanzibar, 64–5, 72; and China, 64, 82
Zhao Ziyang, 195
Zhdanov, Andrei, 35
Zhou Enlai, 53, 195
Zimbabwe. and Britain, 194; and
  Czechoslovakia, 193–4; and Hungary,
  193–4; and Romania, 261n21; and
  Yugoslavia, 261n21
Zimbabwe African National Union
  (ZANU), 79, 192; and China, 79, 82,
  101, 192, 193; and Cuba, 192. See also
  GDR and Zimbabwe, Socialist Unity
  Party of Germany, USSR and
  Zimbabwe
Zimbabwe African People's Union
  (ZAPU), 78–9, 194; and Cuba, 132, 193.
  See also GDR and Zimbabwe, USSR
  and Zimbabwe
Zimmerman, William. 12

Soviet and East European Studies

63 PAUL G. LEWIS
Political authority and party secretaries in Poland 1975–1986

62 BENJAMIN PINKUS
The Jews of the Soviet Union
The history of a national minority

61 FRANCESCO BENVENUTI
The Bolsheviks and the Red Army, 1918–1922

60 HIROAKI KUROMIYA
Stalin's industrial revolution
Politics and workers, 1928–1932

59 LEWIS SIEGELBAUM
Stakhanovism and the politics of productivity in the USSR, 1935–1941

58 JOZEF M. VAN BRABANT
Adjustment, structural change and economic efficiency
Aspects of monetary cooperation in Eastern Europe

57 ILIANA ZLOCH-CHRISTY
Debt problems of Eastern Europe

56 SUSAN BRIDGER
Women in the Soviet countryside
Women's roles in rural development in the Soviet Union

55 ALLEN LYNCH
The Soviet study of international relations

54 DAVID GRANICK
Job rights in the Soviet Union: their consequences

53 ANITA PRAŻMOWSKA
Britain, Poland and the Eastern Front, 1939

52 ELLEN JONES AND FRED GRUPP
Modernization, value change and fertility in the Soviet Union

51 CATHERINE ANDREYEV
Vlasov and the Russian liberation movement
Soviet reality and émigré theories

50 STEPHEN WHITE
The origins of détente
The Genoa Conference and Soviet–Western relations 1921–1922

49 JAMES MCADAMS
East Germany and détente
Building authority after the Wall

48 S. G. WHEATCROFT AND R. W. DAVIES (EDS.)
Materials for a balance of the Soviet national economy 1928–1930

47 SYLVANA MALLE
The economic organization of war communism, 1918–1921

46 DAVID S. MASON
Public opinion and political change in Poland, 1980–1982

45 MARK HARRISON
Soviet planning in peace and war 1938–1945

44 NIGEL SWAIN
Collective farms which work?

43 J. ARCH GETTY
Origins of the great purges
The Soviet Communist Party reconsidered, 1933–1938

42 TADEUSZ SWIETOCHOWSKI
Russian Azerbaijan 1905–1920
The shaping of national identity in a muslim community

41 RAY TARAS
Ideology in a socialist state
Poland 1956–1983

50 SAUL ESTRIN
Self-management: economic theory and Yugoslav practice

39 S. A. SMITH
Red Petrograd
Revolution in the factories 1917–1918

38 DAVID A. DYKER
The process of investment in the Soviet Union

36 JEAN WOODALL
The socialist corporation and technocratic power
The Polish United Workers Party, industrial organisation and workforce control 1958–1980

35 WILLIAM J. CONYNGHAM
The modernization of Soviet industrial management

34 ANGELA STENT
From embargo to Ostpolitik
The political economy of West German–Soviet relations 1955–1980

32 BLAIR A. RUBLE
Soviet trade unions
Their development in the 1970s

31 R. F. LESLIE (ED.)
The history of Poland since 1863

30 JOZEF M. VAN BRABANT
Socialist economic integration
Aspects of contemporary economic problems in Eastern Europe

28 STELLA ALEXANDER
Church and state in Yugoslavia since 1945

27 SHEILA FITZPATRICK
Education and social mobility in the Soviet Union 1921–1934

23 PAUL VYSNÝ
Neo-slavism and the Czechs 1898–1914

22 JAMES RIORDAN
Sport in Soviet society
Development of sport and physical education in Russia and the USSR

14 RUDOLF BIĆANIĆ
Economic policy in socialist Yugoslavia

The following series titles are now out of print:

1 ANDREA BOLTHO
Foreign trade criteria in socialist economies

2 SHEILA FITZPATRICK
The commissariat of enlightenment
Soviet organization of education and the arts under Lunacharsky, October 1917–1921

3 DONALD J. MALE
Russian peasant organisation before collectivisation
A study of commune and gathering 1925–1930

4 P. WILES (ED.)
The prediction of communist economic performance

5 VLADIMIR V. KUSIN
The intellectual origins of the Prague Spring
The development of reformist ideas in Czechoslovakia 1956–1967

6 GALIA GOLAN
The Czechoslovak reform movement

7 NAUN JASNY
Soviet economists of the twenties
Names to be remembered

8 ASHA L. DATAR
India's economic relations with the USSR and Eastern Europe, 1953–1969

9 T. M. PODOLSKI
Socialist banking and monetary control
The experience of Poland

10 SHMUEL GALAI
The liberation movement in Russia

11 GALIA GOLAN
Reform rule in Czechoslovkia
The Dubcek era 1968–1969

12 GEOFFREY A. HOSKING
The Russian constitutional experiment
Government and Duma 1907–1914

13 RICHARD B. DAY
Leon Trotsky and the politics of economic isolation

15 JAN M. CIECHANOWSKI
The Warsaw rising of 1944

16 EDWARD A. HEWITT
Foreign trade prices in the Council for Mutual Economic Assistance

17 ALICE TEICHOVA
An economic background to Munich
International business and Czechoslovakia 1918–1938

18 DANIEL F. CALHOUN
The united front: the TUC and the Russians 1923–1928

19 GALIA GOLAN
Yom Kippur and after
The Soviet Union and the Middle East crisis

20 MAUREEN PERRIE
The agrarian policy of the Russian Socialist-Revolutionary Party
From its origins through the revolution of 1905–1907

21 GABRIEL GORODETSKY
The precarious truce: Anglo-Soviet relations 1924–1927

24 GREGORY WALKER
Soviet book publishing policy

25 FELICITY ANN O'DELL
Socialisation through children's literature
The Soviet example

26 T. H. RIGBY
Lenin's government: Sovnarkom 1917–1922

29 MARTIN CAVE
Computers and economic planning
The Soviet experience

33 MARTIN MYANT
Socialism and democracy in Czechoslovakia 1944–1948

37 ISRAEL GETZLER
Kronstadt 1917–1921
The fate of a Soviet democracy

Lightning Source UK Ltd.
Milton Keynes UK
UKHW010259111218
333800UK00001B/292/P

9 780521 122597